D0163579

BK

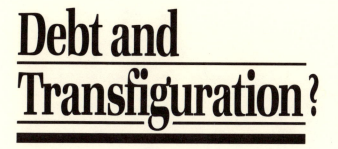

Debt and Transfiguration?

Debt and Transfiguration?

Prospects for Latin America's Economic Revival

David Felix

EDITOR

M. E. Sharpe, Inc.
Armonk, New York
London, England

Available in the United Kingdom and Europe from M. E. Sharpe, Publishers, 3
Henrietta Street, London WC2E 8LU.

Library of Congress Cataloging-in-Publication Data

Debt and transfiguration? : prospects for Latin America's economic revival /
    edited by David Felix.
        p. cm.
        Papers of a conference.
        ISBN 0-87332-646-6
        1. Debts, External—Latin America—Congresses. 2. Latin America—
Economic conditions——1982-   —Congresses. 3. Latin America—
Economic Policy—Congresses.   I. Felix, David, 1921–
HJ8514.5.D447   1990
336.3′435′098—dc20   89-29811
                                                                        CIP

Printed in the United States of America.

                                ∞

BB   10   9   8   7   6   5   4   3   2   1

Contents

Figures

Tables

Preface

The publication of this collection of papers could not be more timely. The Latin American debt crisis and its relation to the economic future of the region has seized the attention of economists, bankers, and policy-makers since it first erupted in 1982. The Jerome Levy Economics Institute of Bard College is particularly pleased to join forces with the National Autonomous University of Mexico and Washington University in St. Louis in co-sponsoring a conference on this topic of paramount importance for public policy. The conference, held at the Institute on October 13–15, 1988, brought together a distinguished roster of participants whose thoughtful and provocative contributions can be read in the pages of this volume.

The aim of the Jerome Levy Economics Institute is to promote open debate on the economic problems that concern governments and policy-makers in the United States, in other industrialized nations, and in countries with developing economies. The conference, of which this volume is the fitting outcome, could not have been a more convincing tribute to the Institute's seriousness of purpose: "To pursue knowledge of economics that will enable nations to enlarge personal freedom, promote justice, and maintain stable economies with full employment and rising standards of living."

It would be inappropriate of me to preempt what the editor and the authors of these papers have to say on the financing of Latin American growth, but perhaps I can be allowed to echo one of the general themes common in most, if not all, of the papers. The resolution of the debt problem and the rescue of the region do not depend on the application of a simple theoretical model but on an honest comprehensive appraisal of the basic needs of the debtor countries and the guarantees required by the creditor financial institutions, both of which must be framed in an environment of political and economic stability.

Dimitri Papadimitriou
Executive Director
Jerome Levy Economics Institute
Bard College, Annandale-on-Hudson

Introduction

The extensive interconnections of Latin America's ongoing debt crisis force analysts out of their normal domains of expertise. One becomes a generalist *malgré lui*, pronouncing on the power factors behind the economic trends, the economic factors behind the political trends, the sharing of moral responsibility for the debt crisis and its resolution, etc. Or, one organizes a multidisciplinary conference to share the task of generalizing.

This volume is the end product of such a conference. The invited papers were to focus on aspects of the debt crisis that fell mainly within their authors' disciplinary domains. The chosen aspects spanned much of the gamut of ramifications, with the individual country studies selected to highlight heterogeneities as well as similarities between major debtor countries. The forward looking title of the conference, "Financing Latin American Growth in the 1990s," sought to impart commonality to the time frames shaping the various papers. Finally, the ideological and disciplinary diversity of the participants would, it was hoped, challenge and deflate pomposities masquerading as warranted generalizations.

How well did it come off? As an organizer of the conference and co-author of a paper, it would be unseemly for me to grade the results. I will, however, summarize the central points of each paper and then assess how the areas of agreement and dispute relate to the Brady Initiative. The assessment is conjectural, since the Initiative came on the scene after most of the papers had their final revision.

A Summary of the Papers and Discussion

The Part I papers assess the creditor debt containment strategy of the 1980s prior to the Brady Initiative. They document statistically the ineffective restructuring of the debtor economies, their oppressively large outward resource transfers, inequitable burden sharing between socioeconomic classes, etc. But they also push beyond this familiar indictment. The Felix-Caskey paper emphasizes less publicized "political economy" aspects, such as that the overstretching of the fiscal capacity of the debtor governments derived in large part from their generous bailouts of over-leveraged private firms and from chronic capital flight. By the mid-1980s, Argentina, Mexico, and Venezuela had each a stock of private foreign assets about equal to its public foreign debt, with the public debt substantially augmented by the government's *ex post facto* assumption of legal responsibility for foreign debts of private firms.

The López-Ruiz paper argues for a more inward-directed restructuring that would ease the adjustment burden by reemploying the industrial capacity and labor idled during the 1980s under the export-oriented policies that the creditors have urged on the debtor governments. The López-Ruiz alternative would also change the fiscal expenditure mix so as to reverse the deteriorating levels of social welfare and the human capital and infrastructural decay associated with the current restructuring strategy. Both papers use simulation modeling to estimate external financial requirements for revived growth in the 1990s. A conclusion of each paper is that reconciling growth with full debt servicing would require, even through an inward strategy, flows of foreign financing that are probably unattainable from normal commercial channels.

In their comments, Bartell and Van Ryckeghem expand on some of the themes of the two papers and weave sceptical obligatos around others. Bartell doubts that rising political tensions in the debtor countries will soon force either open defaulting from the debtors or comprehensive debt writedowns from the creditors. Rather, he expects the untidy *ad hoc* responses to threatened breakdowns to continue: i.e., more disguised partial defaults and piecemeal writedowns. Van Ryckeghem questions the feasibility of the López-Ruiz strategy of combining maximum use of existing capacity with channeling investment and new capacity in more market efficient directions: "... such a strategy is wishful thinking and contrary to any country's experience of the last decades."

Political questions are the focus of the Part II papers. Karen Remmer rejects on three counts the thesis that the hardships associated with the debt crisis are eroding popular support for democracy in the Latin American debtors. One is that in Latin America, "widespread support for democracy neither guarantees the installation of competitive rule nor its survival in the face of concerted elite or foreign resistance." Secondly, since the debt crises reflect economic policy failures of the military regimes of the 1970s, the chastened military is now much less eager to take on management of the debt crisis. "From this perspective, the debt crisis may be seen as an obstacle to the breakdown of democracy rather than a provocation." Finally, she contends that democratic regimes in Latin America have done no worse than military ones in managing austerity programs.

In his comments, Barry Ames accepts the first two points but qualifies his support of the third. Democratic regimes in Latin America may manage austerity programs no worse than autocratic regimes but are less likely to introduce them for fear of losing elections.

Barbara Stallings asks why Latin American debtors have not opted for unilateral moratoria or formed a united front of debtors to improve their bargaining power vis-à-vis the creditor cartel? She points out that in past debt crises Latin American debtors had often been able to invoke moratoria unilaterally that shifted the debt service burden forward for protracted periods and usually resumed debt servicing after negotiated writedowns of the debt. In the present crisis, however, most debtor governments have chosen not to default unilaterally thus far, despite the havoc that the efforts to keep up debt payments have been wreaking on their societies. Neither have they been able to organize a "debtors cartel" to confront their creditors.

Rejecting explanations that stress internal power relations in the debtor countries, she emphasizes instead international power imbalances: " . . . the industrial country governments, multilateral agencies, and private banks have formed a united front" that leaves "little leeway for debtors to rebel, unless they want to cut themselves off entirely from international credit" and access to the large United States goods markets. Key institutional mechanisms, such as the IMF and World Bank, were lacking for implementing "carrot and stick" strategies in the earlier debt crises. She sees some hope for the debtors, however, in the expanding financial clout of Japan, which has been pushing the United States to accept concerted debt writedowns. (For example, the Miyasawa debt relief proposal, which the United States rebuffed in 1988, has resurfaced in 1989 as the Brady Initiative.)

Jeffry Frieden finds Stallings's explanation of the wimpishness of Latin American debtor governments incomplete. To fill out the story, it is necessary to bring in "domestic distributional conflicts." The business elites in the debtor countries, he contends, have preferred maintaining cordial relations with the creditor countries and with international financial markets to achieving debt relief by confrontational tactics, such as debtor cartels and unilateral defaulting. The power of the business elites to shape debtor strategies has differed, however, between countries: this explains why some debtors, e.g., Brazil and Peru, have been somewhat more willing to test aggressive tactics than others, e.g., Chile and Mexico. The variance in business power may also explain the failure of efforts to form a debtor cartel. "The problem may not have been that the debtors faced an n-person Prisoners' Dilemma" (Stallings's view), but rather that debtor preference functions differed.

The country studies of Part III vary in focus. Eliana Cardoso's comparison of Argentina and Brazil begins with an historic analysis of debt cycles in the two countries and concludes with a solution to the current debt crisis based on "interest recycling." Creditor banks would agree to take most of their interest receipts in the debtor's currency for an extended period—perhaps a decade—if the debtor government agreed to implement various fiscal-monetary reforms. The creditor banks could use their local currency receipts to acquire government debt and private assets of the debtor country. Cardoso illustrates the scheme with a mathematical model that incorporates wage and domestic savings rates as conditioning variables. In his comments on the proposal, Miguel Molina contends that interest recycling alone would not enable the debtors to achieve "adequate" economic growth. The creditor countries would also have to write off part of the debt and furnish new medium-term loans to the debtors.

Ffrench-Davis analyzes the somewhat exceptional Chilean experience. In 1982–83 the Chilean economy was toppled from its pedestal as Latin America's free market success story by its pandemic banking crisis and collapse of output and employment, the worst among the Latin American debtors. By 1988, Chile had been put back on the pedestal as role model by the World Bank and other advocates of free market restructuring strategies. Ffrench-Davis documents Chile's recovery, but points out that Chile's free market strategy was responsible also for the unusual depth of the earlier collapse. He also assigns some credit for Chile's rebound to the World Bank, the IMF, and the Inter-American Development Bank, all of whom augmented their lending to Chile lavishly after 1982, just as the commercial banks were striving to reduce their Chilean exposure (a point documented in Table 1.8 of the Felix-Caskey paper). He acknowledges, however, that Chile's skillful use of debt-equity and debt-debt swaps contributed to the recovery by substantially lowering the 1980s burden of debt servicing. The dark side is that the debt-equity swaps and negotiated debt servicing delays have created a large payment bubble for the early 1990s. His simulation modeling leads him to conclude that this, plus a drop of copper prices to more "normal" levels, will reopen the growth vs. debt servicing dilemma for Chile. His special concern is that the reopening will hit the first post-Pinochet parliamentary regime full blast.

Sebastian Edwards's comments provide additional detail on Chile's debt swap programs. The gains from the debt-debt swaps under Chapter XVIII, he believes, have been substantial; those from the debt-equity swaps under Chapter XIX are problematic. Overall, however, he is more sanguine about the robustness of Chile's economic recovery than is Ffrench-Davis.

Clemente Ruiz's paper on Mexico focuses on the abrupt turnabout in the role of the Mexican state after 1982. Through most of the postwar era, low taxes on profits and wealth and public investment in human and capital infrastructures, financed in part by foreign borrowing, had promoted private accumulation. This ceased with the debt crisis. Since 1982, the Mexican state has been devoting its monetary-fiscal efforts to extracting and transferring domestic resource surpluses to service the foreign debt. Moreover, it has generated the surpluses by drastic curtailment of outlays for human and physical infrastructure development rather than through tax increases. With government props removed, private investment has also fallen, along with employment, output per capita, and social welfare. Ruiz believes that it has been the autocratic power of the PRI (Partido Revolucionario Institucional) that has allowed the government to persist in these policies. The inference is that the PRI's loss of popular support, manifested in the 1988 presidential election, will force the new government to move toward more equitable and growth-oriented policies.

Sylvia Maxfield disputes Ruiz's political analysis. Even during the heyday of the PRI's political dominance, the business sector was able to abort efforts at tax reform or other egalitarian policy turns by threatening capital flight. That power has even been strengthened by the debt crisis, hence the rise of multiparty democracy in Mexico is not likely to greatly enlarge the prospects for Ruiz's preferred policies.

The Part IV papers explore the implications for the Latin American debtors of trends in the international financial environment. Pier Carlo Padoan argues that solving the "North-South Debt Crisis" requires a cooperative solution (in game theory language) of the "North-North" debt problem by Japan and the United States, i.e., of the rapidly rising United States indebtedness to other major trading powers, most notably to Japan. This is because the United States is no longer the prepotent hegemon of the world trade and financial system, able to supply it with two essential "public goods" for its stability: steady growth of aggregate demand and lender-of-last-resort liquidity. In the 1980s the United States was still able to supply the first, but at the cost of transforming itself into the world's leading debtor, which along with eroding its lender-of-last-resort powers is now undermining its capacity to stabilize world aggregate demand. In what has become a multi-polar world economy, supplying both "public goods" now requires the United States to coordinate with other major capitalist powers, notably with Japan, which must be willing to finance more United States debt over the medium-term and assume more of the aggregate demand stabilizing role over the longer term. Absent this cooperation, the "North-South" debt crisis, which thus far has been kept from pushing the international system into full crisis and debt deflation by the meliorating effect of expanding United States aggregate demand, could yet set off a global crisis.

Padoan's analysis is premised on Hyman Minsky's financial instability hypothesis as internationalized by Charles Kindleberger. The hypothesis holds that capitalist economies with long-term financial relations are inherently unstable, absent the two "public goods." Gary Hufbauer in his comments rejects the hypothesis and, therefore, the need for either an economic hegemon or intergovernmental collaboration as stabilizers. Markets, if allowed to function freely, could solve both the North-North and North-South debt problems by exchange rate and interest rate adjustments.

Richard Feinberg analyzes a perverse development in the flow of funds between the multilateral financial institutions and Latin America. Since 1987, interest and amortization payments from Latin America to the IMF, World Bank, and IDB have exceeded their new loan disbursements to the region. Feinberg is cognizant that this negative resource transfer, which he projects to continue into the 1990s, is a normal consequence of cumulative borrowing at interest. The timing of the crossover, however, he finds most unfortunate, since it coincides with the increasing reluctance of commercial banks to participate in new concerted loan packages. He proposes, therefore, various ways for the multilateral agencies to reverse their own negative net flows by stretching out amortization and accelerating disbursements.

To Francisco Báez, the negative resource transfers uncovered by Feinberg are merely part of a "systemic defunding" of Latin America, which serves as an instrument for the creditors to force their preferred restructuring policies on the Latin American debtors. If the multilateral agencies are to play a positive role in easing Latin America's travail, they will have to work to change creditor perceptions about how the Latin Americans should organize their societies and abandon the use of tight credit rationing to force their policy perceptions on the debtors.

Donald Lessard analyzes substitute modes of private foreign financing to replace the vanishing flows of general obligation loans that had been the mainstay of commercial bank lending before the debt crisis. His array of substitutes makes up what creditor publicists have dubbed the "Menu of Options Approach." Lessard appraises each option from the perspective of risk and benefit sharing, and suggests ways of circumventing obstacles to their use.

To Claudio Pardo, Lessard's analysis is too micro. Chile, for example, has had greater access to the options since 1985 than other Latin American debtors because its macroeconomic policies have made the options more attractive. Moreover, converting general obligation bank debt into other forms of private claims is insufficient to get Latin America out of its debt crisis, given the size of the debt overhang. Even in Chile's case, writedown of the general obligation bank debt through private sector buybacks, exploiting the large discounts on Chilean debt in the secondary market, has been more important than claim conversions in reducing general obligation bank debt. For Latin American debtors with more chaotic macroeconomies, debt forgiveness will need to be of even greater relative importance.

The presentations of Part V, mainly by *distinguidos* from the worlds of politics and finance, address many of the issues raised in the preceding academic papers with a different authority: fewer citations and tables and more *ex cathedra* pronouncements. The range of disagreement is, however, comparable.

Senator Daniel Patrick Moynihan's presentation is a colorful *j'accuse*, party flags flying, of the Reagan administration for having brought on the decline of United States global economic hegemony through fiscal mismanagement. Lord Lever directs his accusations at the creditor banks and governments for having allowed the lending boom of the 1970s to get out of hand. Since the geopolitical responsibilities of the creditor countries now require them to reverse the negative resource transfers afflicting debtor governments, Lever proposes intergovernmental loans, guarantees of new private bank loans, and concerted writedowns of old debt. Hans Angermueller, on the other hand, defends the behavior of the creditor banks and rejects as counterproductive proposals that would force creditor banks to absorb concerted debt writedowns. In the first place, such proposals, Angermueller contends, hit the panic button needlessly, since many of the debtors are making substantial progress in restructuring their economies. Negative resource flows may persist a while longer, but that's to be expected after such prolonged borrowing sprees. Secondly, the temporary relief that truncating the transfers at the expense of the creditor banks might bring would be more than offset by long-term losses to the debtors from delayed reaccess to international financial markets.

Rudiger Dornbusch sees most of the debtor economies deteriorating rather than restructuring, headed toward hyperinflation and political upheaval rather than economic recovery and normal debt servicing capacity. Nor are the creditor banks poised to resume lending to Latin America; they want out and are pressing debtor governments to expand debt-swap facilities in order to facilitate the withdrawal. Debt swapping, however, overloads the already deficit-ridden fiscal budgets of the debtors, fueling faster inflation. Accordingly, he favors proposals that keep the banks locked in. The Rotberg proposal[1] does this, though it is flawed because it calls for overall policy supervision by the World Bank, an institution with a proven record of failure in such efforts. His preference is, therefore, to lock in the banks through interest recycling on a case-by-case basis, with Mexico his choice for test case.

Carlos Tello deplores that the burden of adjusting to the debt crisis has fallen disproportionately on the debtor countries and within these countries on the poorer classes. He proposes a final go at negotiations with the creditors that would focus on financing the renewal of economic growth via new loans and debt reductions. If no agreement is reached within six months, he would have the debtors declare unilateral moratoria, preferably in concert.

Part V concludes with a summary of the question and answer session on the above presentations and those by Paul Volcker, former Chairman of the Board of Governors of the United States Federal Reserve System, and Eugene Rotberg. Neither the Volcker nor the Rotberg talks were available for inclusion in this volume.

Implications for the Brady Initiative

Books and articles on the evolving Latin American debt crisis tend to have short shelf lives, victimized by unexpected twists in the world economy and in debtor-creditor relations. The papers and comments herein have so far, however, passed one durability test. Virtually none gives a passing grade to the Baker Plan, recognizing that its new financing quotas were inadequate for the task and that the commercial banks were, in any event, not meeting their quota. They have not, therefore, been caught short by the death of the Baker Plan, but perhaps only by the speed with which the incoming Bush administration interred it.

Its replacement, the Brady Initiative, is still evolving at this writing. Its main initial features, as announced on March 10, 1989 by Secretary of the Treasury Nicholas Brady, are the following:

1. The Initiative aims at facilitating the reduction of commercial bank debt rather than the promoting of new bank loans, which had been the aim of the now defunct Baker Plan.

2. The options (such as surveyed in the Lessard paper herein) are to be reinforced and the distribution of costs and benefits tilted toward the debtors so as to bring about a significant reduction of their debt overhang. (A 20 percent writedown of commercial bank debts is the tentative target suggested by Treasury sources.)

3. Reinforcement would come in two ways:

a. The commercial banks would agree to suspend for three years the sharing and negative pledge clauses in the existing loan contracts. This would improve the bargaining power of the debtors by allowing them to strike deals with individual banks and to play banks off against one another.

b. The IMF and World Bank, with some added Japanese funding, would guarantee the reduced payments to the commercial banks. They would also grant "policy-based loans" to the debtors to fund cash buybacks of commercial debt.

4. To be eligible for the reinforcements, debtors would have to pursue market-based restructuring under the supervision of the IMF/World Bank. Restructuring should include market inducements to promote a return of flight capital.

Writing down the commercial debt by sweetening the Menu of Options gets mixed reviews in this volume. The Ffrench-Davis paper and Dornbusch's panel comments are negative. In their view, using reserves and new loans to repurchase debt would be a misuse of scarce hard currency at the prevailing market discounts. Others, e.g., Felix-Caskey and López-Ruiz, indicate that writing off 20 percent of the commercial bank debt, which is now not much more than half of the Latin American debt, would do little to reduce the negative resource transfer that's the main impediment to economic revival. Still other papers, however, e.g., Lessard's and Angermueller's, are sanguine on the benefits of expanding use of the Menu of Options to reduce debt.

Repatriating flight capital through market inducements, presumably by higher real interest rates, "realistic" exchange rates, stable price levels, and low taxes on property income, is another feature that gets mixed reviews. Lessard and Angermueller imply that the inducements would work, while Dornbusch and Felix-Caskey contend that a gridlock now exists in which the adverse repercussions on inflation and real aggregate demand in the debtor economies from such market inducements may encourage even more capital flight. They diverge, however, in their approaches to breaking the gridlock. Dornbusch would have the creditor banks jumpstart economic revival of the debtor economies by agreeing to take interest payments in the debtor's currency. The Felix-Caskey suggestion has the debtor government initiating the jumpstart by engineering a compulsory conversion of flight capital into domestic government debt, with creditor banks and governments helping out by feeding information on foreign asset ownership to the debtor government.

These approaches and that of the Brady Initiative face somewhat different but overlapping sets of political obstacles which are touched on, unfortunately too sketchily, in this volume. Interest recycling requires the creditor government to have the domestic political clout to overcome bank resistance, while the Brady Initiative requires similar clout to get the banks to agree to waive the negative pledge and sharing clauses for three years. The evidence on this is discouraging. The United States Treasury has recently eliminated the waiver proposal from the Initiative. "I think it was a mistake," Treasury Under-Secretary David Mulford explained.[2] Since this guts the effort to improve the power of the debtors in option bargaining with their creditor banks, one must assume that by "mistake" Mulford meant a political power miscalculation.

The compulsory repatriation of flight capital would avoid prolonged payment suspension and debt writedowns, but would have to overcome the same political obstacles that appear to have doomed the Brady waiver proposal and would probably doom interest recycling. Forced repatriation might make Latin American paper bankable again but would chill the hot money flows on which the international banks have been feasting and which most creditor governments still seem to accept as efficient market behavior. On the debtor side, governments would have to risk the hostility of the same business elites who have deterred them from engaging in unilateral defaulting, since these elites own most of the flight capital.

The expectation of the Brady Initiative that Japan will participate appears, however, to be better grounded, according to the Padoan and Stallings papers. Padoan's game theory analysis builds a logical case for Japanese participation, while Stallings cites evidence that the Japanese Ministry of Finance had been thinking along lines resembling the Brady Initiative. The degree of support from Japan and Europe will presumably become clearer after the July 1989 meeting of the G7 countries.

The Brady Initiative maintains the requirement of the earlier creditor strategies that the eligibility of the debtor country for the putative benefits be conditioned on its adopting and implementing market-based restructuring of the economy. Many of the papers and comments dispute the political viability of market-based restructuring, given the overhang of foreign debt and the negative resource transfers. Few seem to challenge the belief, however, that with adequate alleviation of the current debt overhang, market-based restructuring is the appropriate strategy. The lack of challenge may in some cases have been merely tactical; the specialist authors were not asked explicitly and most chose not to confront the question in their papers. The chief exceptions are the López-Ruiz paper, Ruiz's solo paper on Mexico, and some of the recorded comments by his compatriots which do dispute the strategy.

The challenge is on two grounds. In the short term, market-liberalization intensifies the adjustment burden by needlessly underutilizing existing industrial plant and labor of the semi-industrialized Latin American countries. In the longer term, it perpetuates the highly inequitable growth pattern that has made Latin America such a crisis-ridden, politically unstable region. A "growth with equity" strategy would, on the other hand, broaden the welfare benefits and promote social peace. It would require, however, deviations from the market-based strategy, including more inward oriented economic policies.

The dissenting view thus connects the issue of how to recover from the debt crisis with long-standing debates about Latin American development. Most of the participants probably accept the relevance of the connection, but a three-day conference on the first proved grossly inadequate for considered debate on the connection with the second. The characteristic riposte to the dissenters was to identify their growth-with-equity strategy, as Van Ryckeghem does in his critique of the López-Ruiz paper, with the oft-failed Latin American populist strategy of combining price, wage, and exchange controls with fiscal deficits to fuel a rapid expansion of aggregate demand. Considering Alan García's debacle in Peru, this critique of populism has obvious merit. Yet it leaves unanswered the question whether the market-based approach, with its emphasis on liberalizing financial markets, shrinking the public sector, and relying on private investment as the prime engine of economic growth, is compatible in the Latin American institutional context with introducing a reasonable modicum of distributional equity. If not, is market-based restructuring not destined to reinforce rather than dampen the economic and political instability of the region? For example, with capital controls precluded by financial market liberalization, the main financial instrument available to the debtor governments for deterring capital flight has been selling treasury bills in the open market. The liquidity and risk premia required by local capital for holding these bills rather than dollar assets have been enormous: 20–40 percent annualized real rates of return on Mexican CETES of 3–4 week maturity and similar returns on even shorter maturities in Argentina and Mexico. How many physical investment projects can compete for private funds with these financial assets?

Granted that eliminating the debt overhang would reduce the exorbitant liquidity and risk premia, would not a large residue remain? That is, since the liberated home markets will continue to be thin and less liquid, will not the governments have to contend with a permanent tilt of the financial playing field toward the thick, highly liquid financial markets of the politically stable money center countries?

In the pre–World War II decades, intermittent natural resource bonanzas drew in funds, while sluggish communication impeded outflows. During the Great Depression and World War II, the financial playing field tilt was temporarily reversed. The capital flight was from the disturbed money centers to Latin America, and in those special circumstances the populist economic strategy did quite well. After the war, private capital was drawn in for a time by the technological and marketing rents and low risks associated with import substituting industrialization, the *bête noire* of market liberalizing ideologues. With that strategy ruled out, what will offset the tilt in this age of instant communications? Resource bonanzas are hardly enough for the much more densely populated, urbanized Latin American countries of the 1990s. Latin America's industrialists are not capable of innovating technological rents on a significant scale in open markets. That leaves low taxes on capital and wage repression as the main instruments for raising expected yields on physical assets to match the high premia on domestic financial assets that is required to prevent capital flight. The market-based strategy seems thus to deprive Latin America of the means to broaden human capital formation through social expenditures, and the will to reduce income concentration through tax reform.

If so, market-based restructuring may be no more viable a recipe for stable growth, political democracy, and political stability than is economic populism. Is Latin America condemned then to oscillate between trying to square the circle, populist style, and market liberalization with vicious repression, Chilean style—an eternal García-Pinochet cycle? Whether this could be so gets little attention in this volume. The dissenters discuss the negative transfer of resources from the debtors without once mentioning capital flight; pro-Chile commentators praise Chile's economic recovery without discussing whether intensification of economic inequities and political repression are essential ingredients of the recipe.

This suggests the theme for a follow-up conference: "Growth with Equity: How Can Latin America Break Out of the García-Pinochet Cycle?" The conference should also have sessions on extra-regional linkages, notably with the Hegemon of the North, since, as the Part II papers emphasize, the hegemony of the United States penetrates deep into Latin America's domestic policy making space.

I conclude with acknowledgements and thanks to two groups of people whose contributions to the conference and to this volume should not go unrecorded. The chairpersons who ably kept the sessions on track and contributed importantly to the discussion were: Professors Irma Adelman of the University of California, Steven Fazzari and Hyman Minsky of Washington University, John Sheahan of Williams College, and Mr. David Levy and Dr. Dimitri Papadimitriou of the Jerome Levy Economics Institute. Co-editing the papers was my wife, Gretchen, whose eagle-eyed meticulousness compensated for my natural sloppiness. Finally, special thanks are due from Gretchen and me to Mr. Arbi Ben Abdallah, doctoral candidate in Economics at Washington University and hacker extraordinaire. He patiently brought us through many crises in this (our first) venture in editing by computer.

David Felix
Washington University, St. Louis

Notes

1. The proposal by Eugene Rotberg, Vice-Chairman of Merrill-Lynch, is for the commercial banks along with the World Bank to supply new loans that enable eligible debtors to meet their interest payments, with amortization to be put off twenty years. To be eligible, debtors would have to implement restructuring policies devised and supervised by a World Bank affiliate created for the occasion. The affiliate would also guarantee payment of the principal and a floor interest rate on the new loans.

Mr. Rotberg presented his proposal at the conference, but chose not to include the presentation in this volume. (See *The Economist*, 14 May 1988, for a more extensive summary.)

2. Quoted in Peter Truell and Matt Moffett, "The Brady Plan for Third World Debt Gets off to a Bad Start in Latin America," *The Wall Street Journal*, 10 May 1989.

PART I

THE CRISIS, RECOVERY STRATEGIES, AND PROSPECTS FOR LATIN AMERICAN DEBTORS

1

The Road to Default:
An Assessment of Debt Crisis
Management in Latin America

David Felix and John P. Caskey

The creditor strategy for containing Latin America's debt crisis is breaking down. Concerted lending packages under that strategy have defused threatened defaults long enough to allow creditor banks to lower their over-exposure in Latin America, but the associated adjustment policies required of the debtor countries have failed to achieve the twin goals of restoring normal debt servicing and reviving economic growth within a politically viable time frame. Now politics is in the saddle, debt writedown is in the air, and relevant questions are: will the writedowns come through concerted concessions by creditor banks and governments or from unilateral actions by the debtors, how large must they be, and how will the costs of the writedowns be distributed? But while such questions may be answerable mainly in the political arena, the related question of why the economic adjustment efforts are not succeeding is more a matter for economic analysis.

That analysis is the main purpose of this paper. The first part appraises the crisis management and restructuring efforts of the main Latin American debtor countries in the 1980s. Next, simulation modeling explores the external financing needed for sustained economic recovery through the 1990s under different growth strategies and world conditions, the debt servicing that this would entail, and the maximum consumption growth compatible with the increased investment and debt servicing required for the different rates and patterns of growth. Finally, the main findings of the two lines of analysis are used to illuminate the economic basis for the rising political pressures in the debtor countries to default on debt servicing.

David Felix is Professor (Emeritus) of Economics, Washington University in St. Louis. John P. Caskey is Assistant Professor of Economics, Swarthmore College.

Efforts to Mobilize Resources for Debt Servicing and for Economic Recovery: A Critical Evaluation

Mobilizing resources for economic growth competes with resource mobilization for foreign debt servicing. The first tries to direct resources to physical and human capital formation, the second to foreign creditors. Mobilizing for either objective also faces an external constraint. On economic growth it is the capacity to import, since higher production flows generally require higher import flows that have to be financed. Similarly, debt servicing must solve the "transfer problem"; the mobilized domestic resources must be transformed into trade surpluses large enough when valued in convertible foreign exchange to service the foreign debt.

Our review of these efforts by the Latin American debtors is in two sections. The first part briefly summarizes material made familiar by frequent repetition in the copious literature on the debt crisis. The second brings out less-publicized financial, ideological, and power factors that have shaped the restructuring efforts of the Latin American debtors and that now affect the choice of alternative policies.

Debt, Resource Transfers, and Growth Trends since 1980

Salient data are reported in Tables 1.1 through 1.6. The focus is primarily on the six most indebted Latin American countries, who collectively owed 86 percent of Latin America's foreign debt in 1982.

Table 1.1 shows the following evolution of the external debt since the crisis broke open that year:

After the virtual cessation of voluntary bank lending in 1982 the debt has kept rising—by 26 percent for all Latin America and 16 percent for the six major debtors through 1986.

Private lenders—chiefly commercial banks—remain the dominant claimants. Their share of total claims on the region has fallen only moderately, and absolute exposure at the end of 1986 was up from 1982.

The exposure has also undergone two qualitative changes. The banks are now locked into longer maturity loans, and the debtor governments have guaranteed, *ex post*, most of the foreign debt of their private sectors. The first change is indicated by the dramatic decline of short-term debt after 1982, most of which has been consolidated in longer maturity bank loans, along with much of the medium-term bank debt. The second is indicated by the sizeable increase in the publicly guaranteed share of total debt, which rose for all Latin America from 53.7 percent in 1982 to 79.5 percent in 1986.

Table 1.2 records external consequences of the restructuring policies required of the debtors. Curtailment of foreign lending after 1982 forced a drastic reversal of the external flow of resources. During 1980–82, the net resource flows were

Table 1.1

The Changing Size and Distribution of External Debt by Source and Liability, 1982 and 1986: Latin America and Its Major Debtor Countries

	Argentina	Brazil	Chile	Mexico	Peru	Venezuela	Latin America
1982							
Total external debt (millions of U.S. dollars)	43,734	91,576	17,348	86,111	12,285	31,933	332,029
% publicly guaranteed[a]	36.4	55.7	30.5	60.2	61.9	38.3	53.7
% from private lenders[b]	92.0	85.4	91.3	87.2	69.0	99.1	73.1
% short-term, excluding IMF credits	37.9	19.1	19.2	30.4	24.6	46.0	27.5
1986							
Total external debt	48,988	110,675	20,741	101,722	15,383	33,891	399,424
% publicly guaranteed[a]	93.5	78.6	80.1	77.7	79.2	72.2	79.5
% from private lenders[b]	81.7	75.7	75.1	82.0	57.2	97.7	66.3
% short-term, excluding IMF credits	6.4	8.1	7.1	6.5	14.3	4.3	7.8

Source: World Bank, *World Debt Tables, 1987–88.*

[a] Includes IMF credits.

[b] Short- and long-term loans. For lack of a breakdown, all unidentified short-term debt in the source tables is assumed to be owed to private lenders. This means that the private lending share of 1982 is probably moderately overestimated, but that of 1986 only negligibly so.

6

Table 1.2

Debt Service and Net Resource Transfers—Major Latin American Debtors, 1980–86

	Argentina	Brazil	Chile	Mexico	Peru	Venezuela
Net resource transfer[a] as % of GNP						
1980–82	-1.1	1.9	10.9	2.5	0.0	15.1
1983–84	-11.0	-7.0	-4.3	-18.0	-3.8	-22.6
1985–86	-9.3	-8.3	-6.5	-10.3	-11.2[b]	-12.6
Foreign debt divided by GNP						
1980–82	0.65	0.33	0.58	0.40	0.47	0.48
1983–84	0.70	0.52	1.08	0.65	0.66	0.66
1985–86	0.73	0.45	1.42	0.71	0.74	0.72
Foreign debt divided by exports of goods and services						
1980–82	3.31	3.30	2.70	2.67	2.48	1.40
1983–84	4.67	3.76	3.96	3.11	3.24	2.03
1985–86	5.02	4.01	4.16	3.77	3.99	2.59
Balance goods and nonfactor service trade divided by interest on foreign debt[c]						
1980–82	-1.09	0.81	-1.28	-0.66	-0.79	1.77
1983–85	0.67	0.73	0.14	1.22	0.23	1.88
1986	0.49	0.64	0.08	0.33	-16.0	0.83

Sources: World Bank, *World Debt Tables 1987–88*; Inter-American Development Bank, *Economic and Social Progress in Latin America,* Annual Reports, various years.

[a] Net resource transfer is the algebraic sum of the balance on capital account minus the balance of trade and nonfactor services minus net dividend and interest flows, all valued in current year U.S. dollars. These sums are divided by the GNP of each country, also valued current year U.S. dollars. Negative numbers are outflows.

[b] 1985 only.

[c] Interest is all interest owed on the foreign debt.

Table 1.3

Price and Quantity Effects on the Domestic Generation and International Transfer of Resource Surpluses for Debt Services, 1980–86

	1982	1983	1984	1985	1986
Exports of goods and nonfactor services (1980–81 = 100)					
Argentina					
Quantity trend	106.3	114.5	113.7	128.0	119.0
Value trend (U.S.$)	84.8	84.9	86.1	89.8	79.6
Brazil					
Quantity trend	99.6	113.8	138.9	147.9	125.7
Value trend (U.S.$)	93.5	97.5	120.3	118.5	100.8
Chile					
Quantity trend	99.8	100.4	107.3	114.6	125.9
Value trend (U.S.$)	86.5	81.3	81.0	78.5	88.4
Mexico					
Quantity trend	128.5	145.9	154.2	148.0	166.8
Value trend (U.S.$)	100.5	103.9	117.9	108.0	86.3
Peru					
Quantity trend	104.6	93.7	102.3	98.7	94.7
Value trend (U.S.$)	92.5	84.9	87.8	86.7	75.0
Venezuela					
Quantity trend	95.3	97.2	97.7	99.0	107.1
Value trend (U.S.$)	86.1	74.2	81.2	72.3	46.4
Imports of goods and nonfactor services (1980–81 = 100)					
Argentina					
Quantity trend	54.7	52.1	55.3	47.3	55.6
Value trend (U.S.$)	74.7	75.2	76.4	69.4	73.9
Brazil					
Quantity trend	87.8	72.5	70.3	70.4	87.2
Value trend (U.S.$)	105.9	83.3	80.8	79.2	80.5
Chile					
Quantity trend	68.3	58.0	67.5	60.1	65.9
Value trend (U.S.$)	80.4	64.3	74.1	64.4	68.4
Mexico					
Quantity trend	67.2	44.5	52.4	59.4	50.9
Value trend (U.S.$)	88.0	60.5	73.7	76.0	65.7
Peru					
Quantity trend	109.7	77.2	63.2	52.0	61.9
Value trend (U.S.$)	106.5	88.1	77.8	70.3	81.3
Venezuela					
Quantity trend	113.3	58.3	62.0	62.8	67.1
Value trend (U.S.$)	127.7	68.3	72.3	73.6	66.7

Sources: World Bank, *World Debt Tables*, individual country tables; Inter-American Development Bank, *Economic and Social Progress of Latin America, 1988 Report*, Appendix Tables B–4, B–5, D–3, D–4.

still inward; new loans financed sizeable import surpluses as well as the interest bills on accumulated debts.[1] The minor exceptions, Peru and Argentina, had prior financial crises that had discouraged further commercial bank lending—Peru in 1977 and Argentina toward the end of 1980. After 1982, the discouragement enveloped the others and forced all to generate trade surpluses for servicing their foreign debt. The severity of the turnaround from resource inflow to outflow is indicated in Table 1.2.[2] Despite the turnaround, the debt burden intensified. Table 1.2 also shows that the debt/GNP and debt/export ratios have risen sharply since 1982 in all six countries.

All the countries moved from deficit to surplus on trade in goods and services in the first three years of the debt crisis. Table 1.2 shows that only Mexico and Venezuela generated surpluses which fully covered the interest on their foreign debt. Moreover, in 1986 surpluses deteriorated so that all six countries were Ponzi financing,[3] a reversal that no doubt contributed to the hardening of the commercial banks' stance against further ''involuntary'' lending and to the present crisis of the creditors' crisis containment strategy.

Deteriorating terms of trade, which largely negated the contribution of rising export and falling import volume, contributed to the failure to solve the ''transfer problem.'' Export volume rose during 1980–86 for all the countries in Table 1.3 except Peru, but the dollar value fell rather substantially for all except Brazil. Concurrently, the dollar value of imports declined less than import volume in four of the six countries.

The share of GDP mobilized for debt servicing rose in all six countries after 1981, but as Table 1.4 shows, the main reason was the decline of the import share. Import/GDP ratios fell drastically in all six countries, whereas export/GDP ratios rose proportionately less in four of the countries and not at all in the other two. The ratios, moreover, give a somewhat inflated picture of resource mobilization, since the denominator, real GDP, fell for all except Brazil during this period (see Table 1.6).

Table 1.5 highlights another disturbing trend: despite the formal commitment of the debtors to ALADI's objective of regional trade integration, intra-regional trade after the onset of the debt crisis declined relatively more in volume and value than did total trade, just when import substitution on a regional scale might have brought some mutual relief to the dollar-short debtor countries. Intra-regional trade in manufactures, the focal point of Latin America's prolonged efforts to promote regional import substitution, declined the most. The policy views of the creditors have been antipathetic to trade diversion via regional trade preferences, at least between less-developed countries, and the debtor governments seem to have complied by gutting ALADI's integration efforts while professing adherence to its goals.[4]

Another dark side of the restructuring effort, sagging output and investment, is illuminated in Table 1.6. GDP growth declined in all four countries after 1980, turning negative in three of them. The higher coefficients of variation imply that greater output instability has accompanied the deterioration of GDP

Table 1.4

**Exports and Imports of Goods and Nonfactor Services
as Percent of GDP, 1970–87**
(constant price measurement)

	1970–79	1980–81	1982–83	1984–85	1986–87
Argentina					
Exports	9.9	12.1	14.3	15.5	14.2
Imports	9.1	18.0	10.3	9.7	10.7
Brazil					
Exports	7.8	10.0	10.9	13.5	10.9
Imports	13.2	10.6	8.7	7.0	8.0
Chile					
Exports	15.7	22.1	25.1	25.9	27.7
Imports	23.6	31.9	22.9	21.6	22.0
Mexico					
Exports	9.8	10.9	12.3	16.2	16.6
Imports	9.1	13.5	7.5	7.2	6.8
Peru					
Exports	22.5	23.3	24.0	25.6	20.8
Imports	22.7	25.1	24.3	15.2	14.7
Venezuela					
Exports	41.1	27.2	26.9	28.3	29.9
Imports	22.7	25.8	22.4	17.0	17.0

Source: Inter-American Development Bank, *Economic and Social Progress in Latin America, 1988 Report*, Statistical Appendix B.

growth. Also, the annual volume of investment in 1986–87 was below 1980 in all four countries and even below 1970 in two of the four. Since investment affects aggregate demand as well as restructuring, the reduced investment volume suggests that the falling Import/GDP ratios of Table 1.5 were due more to sagging aggregate demand than to import substituting restructuring.[5]

Finally, Table 1.6 shows that inflation accelerated in all but Chile after 1980. The Chilean exception is deceptive. Chile's inflation had declined from a three-digit to virtually a single-digit rate by 1981 but rebounded in the ensuing financial crisis. The acceleration in the debtor countries, according to a recent OECD study, ''was anything but accidental. It was the direct consequence of the

10

Table 1.5

Total and Intra-Regional Trade of the Latin American Association for Integration (ALADI), 1980–86
(1980–81 = 100)

	1982	1983	1984	1985	1986
Total trade of member countries					
Total exports					
Volume	110.1	120.4	130.0	133.8	128.0
Dollar value	98.5	100.2	111.6	108.7	85.0
Total imports					
Volume	80.2	61.4	64.2	65.0	70.3
Dollar value	81.5	58.6	61.6	61.0	57.9
Commodity terms of trade	87.9	87.7	90.9	86.4	81.2
Intra-regional trade of ALADI					
Intra-regional imports					
Volume	91.8	71.3	79.6	69.2	81.5
Dollar value	93.5	67.7	75.7	65.8	67.4
Intra-regional manufactured imports					
Volume	74.4	59.5	68.0	63.7	n.a.
Dollar value	78.9	56.6	64.6	60.6	n.a.

Source: ALADI, *Síntesis ALADI*, Enero 1988, Cuadros 1, 2, 3.
Note: The members of ALADI are Bolivia, Colombia, Ecuador, Paraguay, Uruguay, plus the six major debtor countries.

Table 1.6

Trends in GDP Growth, Investment, and Inflation, 1970–87

Annual GDP growth rate (in percent)	1970–80	1981–86
Argentina		
Trend[a]	0.6	−1.2
Mean	0.8	−2.3
Coefficient of variation	381.2	−206.1
Brazil		
Trend[a]	5.4	1.7
Mean	5.8	0.6
Coefficient of variation	52.7	758.4
Chile		
Trend[a]	−0.3	−1.1
Mean	1.0	−0.8
Coefficient of variation	681.5	−842.5
Mexico		
Trend[a]	3.0	−2.4
Mean	3.3	−1.3
Coefficient of variation	61.8	−337.4

Annual inflation rate (CPI) (in percent)	1970–80	1981–87
Argentina		
Trend[a]	83.0	143.8
Mean	137.1	304.8
Coefficient of variation	84.5	76.1
Brazil		
Trend[a]	28.8	100.6
Mean	36.2	163.5
Coefficient of variation	53.3	758.4
Chile		
Trend[a]	90.2	20.1
Mean	158.1	21.0
Coefficient of variation	113.5	29.2
Mexico		
Trend[a]	15.9	58.2
Mean	16.8	75.7
Coefficient of variation	45.8	41.6

Annual gross investment in constant prices (1970 = 100)	1980	1986–87
Argentina	143.7	71.8
Brazil	244.0	205.9
Chile	131.3	96.3
Mexico	228.5	138.1

Source: I.D.B., *Economic and Social Progress in Latin America*, Annual Reports, Appendix Tables.

[a]coefficient of log regression.

fact that the public budget had taken over the servicing of the foreign currency liabilities and was consequently overstretched.''[6] This oversimplifies matters; overstretching also reflects rescuing the private sector from domestic over-indebtedness, as is shown in the following section.

On the Political Economy of Restructuring

The preceding material provides an incomplete perspective on the failure of restructuring. This section focuses on more shadowy features of the restructuring that are essential for understanding the failure, such as the socializing of private foreign liabilities, the capital flight phenomenon, the concurrent internal financial crises in the debtor countries and their monetary-fiscal consequences, and the unequal distribution of the burden of restructuring.

Socializing Private Foreign Liabilities

The OECD quotation on fiscal overstretching that concluded the preceding section refers delicately to a power play that has shaped debt crisis management: the enforced socialization by the debtor governments of their private sectors' foreign liabilities. The pressure to socialize came from the creditors, against weak resistance from the debtor governments. The rise in the publicly guaranteed share of foreign debt shown in Table 1.1 reflects this.

Especially dramatic was the surge of Argentina's publicly guaranteed share from 36.4 percent to 93.5 percent and Chile's from 30.5 percent to 80.0 percent. The devotion of the two countries' governments during the easy borrowing years to free market principles had included leaving enforcement of private loan contracts solely to the market and bankruptcy law. The creditor banks were more pragmatic. When the debt crisis broke they eschewed using bankruptcy courts to effect debt-equity swaps with delinquent private debtors, and insisted instead that the debtor governments assume responsibility for servicing the private debt, or else no debt rescheduling. With devotional trumpets silenced by the obdurate pragmatism of the creditors, the Chilean and Argentine governments gave in. Thus, one of the political economy consequences of the crisis has been an important alteration of property rights: the socialization of private foreign debt, most notably by the free market regimes of the Southern Cone.

Capital Flight

Foreign debt crises are a recurring Latin American phenomenon, but the capital flight associated with the present crisis is of unprecedented volume and persistence. This is one reason why the crisis is of unprecedented severity and duration. Table 1.7 presents estimates of private foreign assets of debtor countries for benchmark years and their ratios to foreign debt. Capital flight is measured as the

Table 1.7

Cumulated Foreign Debts and Foreign Assets of Six Major Latin American Debtor Countries at End of 1977, 1981, 1985
(millions of U.S. dollars)

	Foreign debt	Accumulated net private capital over-flow since 1970	Estimated value of private foreign assets	Private capital outflow÷ foreign debts	Private foreign assets÷ foreign debts
Argentina					
1977	11,429	2,801	3,161	0.25	0.28
1981	35,657	20,509	23,126	0.58	0.65
1985	48,335	26,129	42,372	0.54	0.88
Brazil					
1977	41,337	5,918	4,378	0.14	0.11
1981	79,979	12,148	12,750	0.15	0.16
1985	106,731	18,983	24,362	0.18	0.23
Chile					
1977	5,869	185	259	0.03	0.06
1981	15,704	1,185	000	0.08	0.00
1985	20,421	−1,801	000	−0.09	0.00
Mexico					
1977	31,170	11,901	12,033	0.38	0.39
1981	78,309	32,426	39,488	0.41	0.50
1985	97,135	59,435	88,529	0.61	0.91
Peru					
1977	9,117	1,881	2,363 (2,286)	0.21	0.26 (0.25)
1981	10,284	617	6,579 (1,910)	0.06	0.64 (0.19)
1985	13,638	477	2,712 (2,712)	0.03	0.20 (0.20)
Venezuela					
1977	10,727	6,218	4,486	0.58	0.42
1981	31,927	26,190	25,681	0.82	0.80
1985	32,079	40,710	52,275	1.27	1.63

Sources: World Bank, *World Debt Tables, 1987–88*, U.S. Federal Reserve Bulletin; Central de Reserva de Perú, *Memorias Anuales*.

Note: Numbers in parentheses are exclusive of domestic dollar deposits.

residual after algebraically subtracting the annual balance on current account and change in official reserves from the annual net increment to disbursed debt plus foreign direct investment. The method relies on officially recorded trade values, and hence cannot capture clandestine movements via over-invoicing of imports and under-invoicing of exports.[7] The cumulated value of foreign assets is derived by assuming that annual capital outflows, less returned dividends and interest, are put in foreign assets yielding on average the interest rate on ten-year United States treasury bonds.

The diversity as regarding capital flight supports the creditor's case by case approach to crisis management. In particular, with the foreign assets of Argentina, Mexico, and Venezuela about equal to their respective foreign debts, the debt servicing problem for these three countries is not excessive indebtedness but failure to mobilize foreign assets to service the debt. Were these countries to use the foreign assets of their nationals to collateralize or the income from the assets to service the foreign debt, 46 percent of Latin America's overall debt and 51 percent of its privately held debt could be released from intensive care, making handling of the region's remaining debt problem much more tractable. A swap of foreign assets for domestic debt by avoiding a writedown of the foreign debt would, moreover, regain normal access to foreign capital markets for the swapping country far sooner than is likely under the current crisis management strategy.

Compulsory asset swapping extends the precedent of socializing the foreign liabilities of the wealthy classes of the three debtor countries to include their foreign assets. There are also historic precedents for compensated nationalization of such assets to relieve major national crises. Britain and France used compulsory mobilization of foreign assets of their nationals to help finance import surpluses during World Wars I and II; the asset owners were compensated with domestic securities. Capitalism survived. Mexico in 1982 and Peru in 1985 abrogated dollar withdrawal rights on time deposits, thus imposing foreign for domestic asset swaps on the largely middle class depositors.[8] An effective asset mobilization in the Latin American ambience would probably require creditor banks and governments to help identify enough asset ownership to make the penalty for noncompliance a credible threat to owners of the assets. The debtor government could induce collaboration by setting a low limit on the percent of export earnings it would devote to debt servicing. Combining this with asset mobilization should make the partial moratorium less conflictive.[9]

Socializing the foreign assets of the Latin American wealthy rather than merely their liabilities remains, however, out of bounds. Mainstream analyses of the debt crisis limit themselves to circular solutions of the capital flight problem. Debtor countries should try to induce the return of capital by halting inflation, getting their exchange rates in equilibrium, and resuming economic growth. Since capital flight has been a major obstacle to achieving these *sine qua non*, the inducement advice solves a prisoners' dilemma gridlock by denying its exis-

Table 1.8

Major Debtor Country's Share of New Loans to Latin America, 1983–86, Divided by Its Share of Latin America's External Debt, 1982

| | Source of new loans, 1983–86: official sources | | | | | | |
| | Official sources | | | | | | |
Country	IMF	IBRD	IDB	All multilateral	Bilateral	All official	Private sources
Argentina	1.56	0.40	1.98	0.99	0.85	0.95	0.82
Brazil	1.07	1.47	0.29	0.95	1.17	1.02	1.04
Chile	1.90	2.27	3.42	2.46	-0.08	1.65	0.18
Mexico	1.11	0.87	0.12	0.75	0.37	0.63	1.46
Peru	0.16	0.40	1.35	0.58	1.16	0.76	0.27
Venezuela	0.0	-0.08	0.74	0.19	-0.07	0.12	0.64
Six major debtors	1.05	0.95	0.79	0.75	0.66	0.82	1.05

Source: World Bank, World Debt Tables, 1987–88.

Notes: The first five columns relate to loans from foreign governments and multilateral banks. The sixth column relates to loans from foreign private banks.

tence. The ideological constraints on policy in today's crisis are, evidently, much tighter than in the bad old days of laissez faire.

Chile, however, is held up to the other debtors as evidence that adequate inducements can break the vicious circle. Table 1.7 shows Chile with negligible capital flight.[10] But Chile is also a less attractive outlier in Table 1.2; its debt/GNP ratio had the most rapid rise of all between 1982 and 1986, to double the ratio of the other five, and its debt/export ratio also rose more than the others. And as is also shown in Table 1.2, Chile has relied far more than the others on Ponzi financing: its 1983–86 trade surplus financed merely one-eighth of the interest bill.

Who financed the rest? Not private lenders. According to Table 1.8, Chile's share of new private lending to Latin America in 1983–86 was only one-fifth of its share of the Latin American foreign debt. Nor was any of the interest bill financed by bilateral government loans; the Reagan administration's desire to do so was hemmed in by the human rights issue, and other creditor governments didn't take up the slack. The multilateral institutions did. Table 1.8 shows that Chile's share of IMF credits to all Latin America in 1983–86 was almost double its share of Latin American debt; its share of World Bank loans to the region in that period was more than double its debt share, while its share of new IDB lending was almost three and a half times its share of the region's debt. It appears that the Reagan administration used the pliant multilateral banks to circumvent congressional barriers against giving Chile preferential assistance.

The preferential treatment was apparently less to carry General Pinochet through a bad patch[11] than to rescue the Chilean free market model, which in 1982–83 had exploded into the worst financial blowup experienced by any of the debtors.[12] The Reagan administration viewed the debt crisis as an opportunity to force something like the Chilean free market model on the other debtors. As a high-ranking United States State Department official put it in a recent address to ECLAC:

> A narrow focus on the debt burden alone too often has obscured and distracted attention from the underlying and more important issue—how to put our economies on a path of noninflationary growth which is sustainable over the long term. . . . The hard experience of the 1980s has prompted most countries in our hemisphere to take steps toward a consensus that economic growth requires a fundamental shift away from the statist approach. It is this emerging consensus which I believe will set the policy framework for the Americas in the 1990s. . . . The role of the government needs to be carefully limited and defined to provide a clear and level playing field for business activity. Privatization of state-owned enterprises is . . . an increasingly important means to achieve this end. . . . The massive capital flight experienced by Latin American countries in the last decade . . . will be reversed only if the owners of capital believe that the rules have changed for the long haul. Likewise, foreign investment will follow adoption of sound economic policies.[13]

To reinforce the evangelism, the Reagan administration adhered to a crisis containment strategy that rewards true believers and keeps backsliders among the debtors on a short leash. This allows the domestic monetary and fiscal pressures of the debt burden to push them along the road to privatization and free marketing.

Internal Financial Crises in the Debtor Economies

The 1982 foreign debt crisis ended a borrowing boom that left the private sectors badly overleveraged in domestic as well as foreign currency denominated debt. Foreign borrowing had facilitated the leveraging, but added stimulus came from the deregulated Latin American financial environment of the latter 1970s. The high real interest rates and spreads that followed the lifting of "financial repression" augmented pressures and opportunities for speculative gaming with borrowed funds. And as in all financial bubbles, lenders, bemused by booming asset values, eagerly collaborated and wound up with unmanageable accumulations of delinquent loans when the music stopped. It may not be possible to disentangle fully the domestic from the foreign roots of the ensuing financial blowups, but two pieces of evidence highlight the importance of the domestic ones.

One is Colombia's 1982 financial crisis, when excessive bad loans instigated a wave of *financiera* and bank failures so pervasive the government felt impelled to assume the bad loan portfolios on subsidized terms to halt the panic. By 1986, over 70 percent of the assets of the financial sector were held by the government. A distinctive feature of this crisis is that it had virtually no foreign debt component. Colombia had deregulated domestic financial operations in the 1970s, but kept tight restrictions on private foreign borrowing. The excessive leveraging and loose lending that brought on the crisis was in domestic currency. The salvaging consequences were less distinctive. According to a recent analysis of the Colombian experience, the inflation rate was pushed up and the generous subsidization intensified income concentration.[14] The other piece of evidence is in Table 1.9, which shows that Argentina and Chile, the two countries that had most liberalized their domestic financial sectors, also had the highest run-up of private domestic debt in the years preceding 1982.[15]

The point is that when foreign banks cut off voluntary lending in 1982, the insolvency threat to the private sectors from excessive foreign liabilities of the debtor countries was magnified by excessive accumulation of domestic currency debt. Left to the market and bankruptcy law, "the magnitude and pervasiveness of private internal indebtedness and its close linkages to the national financial systems . . . would have required a massive transfer of property rights. Such a transfer was impossible to carry out due to the important political and social costs it would have involved."[16] In any event, none of the debtor governments were willing to try. Resource mobilization for foreign debt servicing has thus been constrained by the competing goal of restoring

Table 1.9

Internal Debt of Private Sector as Percent of GDP, 1975–85

	Argentina	Brazil	Chile	Mexico	Peru	Venezuela
1975	8	25	5	5	10	19
1976	6	25	5	5	9	24
1981	26	14	39	14	9	26
1982	22	14	60	13	11	28
1983	18	12	57	10	10	30
1984	—	10	53	8	9	28
1985	—	—	52	9	8	30

Source: Carlos Massad y Roberto Zahler, "Otto Ángulo de la Crisis Latinoamericana: La Deuda Interna," *Revista de la CEPAL* (Santiago de Chile) 32: (Agosto 1987), Cuadro 1.
Note: Internal debt of the private sector is defined here as credit of the financial system to the private sector, end of first half of each year.

solvency and capital value to over-indebted firms and banks—at least to the major ones.

Monetary-Fiscal Management of the Dual Debt Crises

The instruments for stanching the internal financial crises have included government takeovers of bad loans and excessive liabilities of private banks and firms on subsidized terms, interest rate subsidies, exchange rate subsidies in taking over private foreign liabilities, wage controls, tax relief, and the "inflation tax." These were used in differing proportions. The decline after 1981 of the Argentine private debt ratio shown in Table 1.9 was engineered mainly through the "inflation tax." This effort culminated in July 1982, when in the midst of a three-digit inflation rate the central bank rediscounted assets of the Argentine banking system equal to its deposit liabilities and concurrently froze the deposit interest rate.[17] The transfer from depositors to debtors was around 8 percent of GDP.[18] The sharp rise of the Chilean debt ratio after 1981 reflects, on the other hand, an extensive official takeover of bad loans and foreign liabilities of private banks with no restriction on deposit interest rates. Delinquent loans of Chilean banks in 1982 had reached three times their capital and reserves.[19] The transfers from government to private banks and firms that year are estimated at 7 billion United States dollars, about 27 percent of 1982 GDP and over twenty times the annual outlay on unemployment relief.[20]

Part of the fiscal overstretching is captured in Tables 1.10 and 1.11. Conventionally measured fiscal deficits—i.e., total fiscal expenditure less receipts from taxes and government services—rose as a percent of GDP in all six countries

Table 1.10

Fiscal Deficits and Tax Revenues as Percent of GDP

	1980–81	1982–83	1984–85	1986–87
Fiscal deficits as a percentage of GDP				
Argentina	–4.0	–8.9	–5.9	–5.6
Brazil	–2.2	–4.0	–8.8	n.a.
Chile	+3.3[c]	–3.1	–2.4	–0.5[b]
Mexico	–4.5	–9.8	–7.6	–14.0
Peru	–3.1	–5.2	–3.1	–4.4
Venezuela	–1.1	–1.4	–2.4	–0.6
Tax revenue as a percentage of GDP				
Argentina				
All taxes	9.2	7.2	7.3	10.7
Direct taxes[a]	1.9	0.9	0.8	2.6
Brazil				
All taxes	17.9	19.2	15.8	n.a.
Direct taxes[a]	8.0	8.7	7.0	n.a.
Chile				
All taxes	21.7	19.1	20.2	20.1[b]
Direct taxes[a]	3.7	3.1	2.2	2.0
Mexico				
All taxes	14.4	15.6	15.9	13.2
Direct taxes[a]	5.3	4.2	3.9	3.3
Peru				
All taxes	14.4	11.4	11.7	9.7
Direct taxes[a]	4.5	2.9	2.4	2.7
Venezuela				
All taxes	20.9	18.2	20.2	17.4
Direct taxes[a]	15.8	11.8	12.5	8.2

Source: Inter-American Development Bank, *Economic and Social Progress Report, 1988*, Appendix Tables C–1, C–4, C–7, C–8.

[a] Income and property taxes.

[b] 1986 only.

[c] Surplus.

after 1981 (Table 1.10). This correlates with rising shares of fiscal outlays on interest payments (Table 1.11), mainly the local currency counterpart of foreign debt servicing by the central government. Curbing deficits by increasing tax revenue was ineffective. Income and property taxes declined absolutely and as a share of GDP in all six countries after 1981 (Table 1.10), presumably as part of the bailout of the over-indebted private sector. Indirect taxes rose as a share of GDP in four of the six countries, insufficiently, except in Argentina, to prevent the overall tax/GDP ratio from tending downward. Cutting nonfinancial budget outlays has been more vigorous. Table 1.11 shows declining investment expenditure shares in four of the six countries. Government outlays on human capital, e.g., on education and health, have followed a similar pattern. And, of course, real public sector salaries have been cut drastically.

The cuts in nonfinancial outlays have pushed the primary fiscal budget—the overall budget less interest payments and transfers—into surplus in many of the debtor countries. For example, Mexico's primary budget has been in the black since 1983, averaging 3.6 percent of GDP, whereas its overall fiscal deficit has averaged 8.8 percent and continues to rise.[21] The contrast became a bone of contention in negotiations with the IMF. Rising overall deficits implied excess aggregate demand to the IMF, requiring further cuts of nonfinancial outlays. Governments contended, on the other hand, that this would further increase the primary surplus and depress real aggregate demand, output, and employment. Recently the IMF accepted the relevance of a compromise concept, the operational budget, i.e., the primary budget plus price deflated fiscal interest payments. The rationale is that with nominal interest rates liberated (more or less) under IMF pressure, and thus free to move with inflation, nominal interest payments and the real value of the fiscal debt will change in opposite but mutually offsetting proportions under inflation. Adding deflated interest payments to the primary budget, therefore, adequately measures the impact of fiscal operations on real aggregate demand.

A non-negative operational deficit is now judged essential for heterodox stabilization plans like the Austral and Cruzado to succeed. The idea is that if the operational budget is balanced, eliminating "inertial" inflation by freezing commodity and factor prices will also balance the fiscal budget. If, however, the operational budget is in deficit, an overall budget deficit persists at zero inflation, and its financing upsets the delicate expectational equilibrium and revives inflationary spiraling. The Austral and Cruzado plans failed, according to this view, because they were undertaken with operational budgets in deficit. Mexico's current effort at heterodox stabilization, El Pacto de Solidaridad Económica, would appear to have better prospects, the operational budget having been in surplus since 1983, at an average 0.4 percent of GDP. Unfortunately, this is not true of Mexico's *adjusted* operational budget, which has been in deficit at an average 3.8 percent of GDP since 1983.[22]

Adjustments are required because the Mexican government has been financing some of its domestic operations at negative real interest rates, in effect shifting part of the deficit to the central bank. Such shifting has been sufficiently

Table 1.11

Interest Payments and Government Investment as a Percent of Fiscal Expenditures, 1970–87

	1970	1980	1982	1983	1984	1985	1986	1987
Interest payments as percent of fiscal expenditures								
Argentina[a]	3.2	0.3	1.2	0.4	5.9	19.2	12.8	10.6
Brazil[b]	4.5	7.2	13.0	13.7	24.0	28.7	n.a.	n.a.
Chile[c]	2.5	2.7	1.4	3.5	3.9	5.8	4.9	n.a.
Mexico[b]	9.4	9.8	33.4	35.3	35.8	36.7	46.7	56.7
Peru[b]	5.2	18.4	18.3	23.2	23.5	25.2	15.0	11.7
Venezuela[b]	1.6	5.9	7.3	8.5	11.7	11.1	11.4	15.8
Government investment as percent of total fiscal expenditures								
Argentina[a]	6.7	15.9	16.1	12.0	10.6	5.6	n.a.	n.a.
Brazil[b]	9.9	5.9	6.0	5.1	3.3	1.5	n.a.	n.a.
Chile[c]	17.5	8.4	5.6	6.8	7.4	9.2	9.6	n.a.
Mexico[b]	12.2	12.1	8.4	5.2	5.5	5.8	3.4	3.1
Peru[b]	13.2	15.3	17.7	14.8	16.5	14.0	14.6	8.2
Venezuela[b]	12.9	6.1	7.5	6.2	4.6	3.4	9.2	9.4

Source: Inter-American Development Bank, 1988 Economic and Social Progress Report, Appendix Tables C–17, C–20.
[a] National Administration.
[b] Central Government.
[c] General Government.

widespread in Latin America for IMF and central bank economists to offer yet another deficit concept, the quasi-fiscal deficit. This is the accounting loss to the central bank when interest payments on its liabilities exceed the income from its assets. Quasi-fiscal deficits, generated mainly by financial rescue operations, have been sizable according to preliminary estimates. They averaged 2 percent of GDP in Argentina during 1984–87 as compared to 4.4 percent for fiscal deficits proper.[23] In Uruguay, they averaged 4.7 percent of GDP during 1982–86 compared to 4.9 percent for the fiscal deficit[24] and have probably been quite high in Chile. The estimates are, however, experimental, since the measurement conventions are still under discussion.[25]

One unsettled matter is whether to record income from nonperforming loans and other dubious assets taken over by the central bank on a cash or accrual basis. The matter is important, as the nonbank debtors seem to be treating the emergency interest subsidies and payment extensions as permanent entitlements. "Perhaps the principal negative aspect of these types of measures is that they did not provide incentives for the domestic debtors to carry out their financial commitments: they expected instead to obtain renewal of these facilities."[26] This may explain why the quasi-fiscal deficits of Argentina and Uruguay have declined less than the fiscal deficits from the peak crisis years.

Distributional Consequences in the Debtor Economies

The scope and generosity of the bailouts of insolvent firms and banks has imposed a disproportionate share of the resource mobilization burden on wage and salary earners, pensioners, and holders of domestic currency deposits. Table 1.12 supports the widespread impression that income concentration worsened in many of the debtor countries during the 1980s. The table shows that although consumption per head declined less than GDP per head after the crisis broke, the minimum wage—a rough proxy for blue collar wages—fell much more than did consumption per head in four of the six countries. These data feed the political component of our case that defaults or debt writedowns have become virtually unavoidable. But before summarizing the case we must first explore further another of its key components, the external financing barriers to economic recovery.

Foreign Lending Requirements for Economic Revival

The Baker Plan, a 1985 mid-course correction to the creditor strategy, sought to augment the flow of concerted lending so as to enable the debtor economies to grow while servicing the debt. A reaction to rising political pressure in the depressed debtor economies for moratoria and other unilateral modes of debt relief, the Plan was a partial success politically—it held back for a time the threat of unilateral default. But having failed to advance its economic goal, the threats are again on the rise. Did the plan fail because the concerted lending was too

Table 1.12

Real GDP, Consumption per Capita and the Real Minimum Wage, 1980–87 (1980 = 100)

	1981	1982	1983	1984	1985	1986	1987
Argentina							
GDP per capita	92.0	85.7	87.1	87.9	82.6	85.9	86.2
Consumption per capita	100.0	84.4	85.4	89.3	82.3	87.3	87.9
Minimum wage	97.8	103.6	152.9	167.5	113.1	113.1	101.6
Brazil							
GDP per capita	96.0	94.5	89.3	92.0	97.3	102.8	103.5
Consumption per capita	96.8	97.6	91.3	91.9	95.8	107.0	105.9
Minimum wage	98.7	99.2	87.9	81.3	83.9	82.0	59.4
Chile							
GDP per capita	103.9	87.7	85.6	89.5	90.1	93.7	97.4
Consumption per capita	106.8	93.8	89.5	89.1	86.7	88.5	90.4
Minimum wage	99.2	97.2	78.3	66.9	63.4	61.3	61.6
Mexico							
GDP per capita	104.8	101.0	92.9	93.8	94.0	88.2	87.5
Consumption per capita	105.1	103.9	94.3	95.6	96.1	91.9	88.5
Minimum wage	100.7	90.8	73.5	68.2	67.0	61.2	57.3
Peru							
GDP per capita	100.5	98.8	84.8	86.5	86.5	91.5	95.1
Consumption per capita	99.7	96.8	90.4	88.9	87.9	100.6	103.8
Minimum wage	84.4	78.3	79.8	62.3	54.7	56.4	60.6
Venezuela							
GDP per capita	96.7	94.6	86.8	83.4	82.3	85.6	84.7
Consumption per capita	100.2	97.7	87.2	81.1	79.9	82.7	79.1
Minimum wage	86.8	80.1	75.1	66.7	91.4	109.7	n.a.

Sources: Inter-American Development Bank, *Economic and Social Progress in Latin America*, 1986 Report, Table II–4, Appendix Table 4; 1988 Report, Tables II–5, A–1, B–3, and Country Statistical Profiles.

niggardly, or because the goal, debt servicing with economic growth, is unattainable?

In this part of the paper, simulation modeling is used to show that the goal is probably unattainable. Were the external financial requirements for a substantial revival of economic growth to be provided, it is unlikely that the debtors could service the resulting debt. Were the requisite financing reduced by scaling down the growth rate, per capita consumption would not recover enough to quell the political pressures for unilateral defaulting. Through actions by the debtors or concessions from the creditors, debt reduction is in the air.

Our conclusion is based on projections of external financing requirements of Argentina, Brazil, Chile, and Mexico over the next decade under a variety of scenarios. Specifically, we project the external financing required to support 1 and 2 percent real GDP per capita growth rates from 1989 to 2000 under different sets of assumptions about external economic conditions and development strategies. The economic model guiding the exercise is the two-gap model used widely in the economic development literature, in which external financing is the dominant obstacle to reaching the targeted growth rate. The exercise thus assumes away other obstacles to sustained economic recovery, some of which were touched on in the preceding sections.

In building the model, we assume that if these four countries are to sustain a 2 percent per capita growth rate, the gross investment ratio (I/GDP) in each of the countries must return to its 1970s average, and that this would be readily attained if the required import financing were available. Required investment is less for the 1 percent per capita growth rate target.

Required imports are estimated for each country from import elasticities obtained by linearly regressing imports on investment over 1970–86. Export elasticities are obtained by regressing export growth on United States growth rates in the case of Mexico and on OECD growth rates in the case of the other three countries. Since the resulting import and export elasticities seemed too far above unity to be sustainable over the long run, they have been modestly dampened over the period to generate asymptotic growth paths for the export/GDP and import/GDP ratios that conform to the growth-structure relations found by Chenery and colleagues.[27]

We also slowed the rebound of the investment ratios to their 1970s levels to allow for the increased use of idled capacity. The rationale for the specific adjustments, data sources, and comparability of the key parameters with those of other studies, are discussed in detail in an appendix to this paper available on request from the authors.

External financial requirements in the model also depend on the values of exogenous parameters, such as OECD growth rates, the commodity terms of trade, and the real interest rate on the foreign debt. Alternative estimates were therefore made using four different sets of values of the exogenous parameters. These are summarized as follows:

Parameters	Base case	Higher interest case	Pessimistic case	Optimistic case
OECD (U.S.) Annual Growth	2.25%	2.25%	1.75%	2.75%
Annual Terms of Trade Change	1.00%	1.00%	−1.00%	2.00%
Real LIBOR rate	3.50%	4.50%	3.50%	3.50%

A fifth set of estimates combine the base case parameter values with a shift by the debtor country to a more inward oriented strategy. This is crudely proxied by a 20 percent downward shift of the import elasticities and a 10 percent downward shift of the export elasticities.

Table 1.13 presents the required net new external financing in constant dollars under the five scenarios for the two target growth rates. For conciseness, only numbers for the initial year, 1989, and the terminal year, 2000, are reported. The projections are reported in more detail in the above-cited appendix. As shown in Table 1.13, the initial injection of net new lending required to finance the 2 percent per capita growth rate is very large compared to the annual flows that have prevailed since 1982. Moreover, except for the optimistic and the inward oriented scenarios, the required inflows rise substantially over the decade. A 1 percent rise in interest rates relative to the base scenario increases required external financing by about 10 percent. The pessimistic scenario results in an explosive increase in required financing, while the optimistic case would even permit Brazil and Chile to begin repaying principal in the second half of the 1990s. The inward oriented scenario also substantially reduces required external financing relative to the base scenario.

Were the annual GDP per capita growth rate reduced to 1 percent, Part B of the table shows that required external financing would fall rapidly over the decade, except in the pessimistic scenario. All except Argentina could begin repaying principal in the second half of the decade were interest rates to rise even moderately relative to the base scenario. Mexico could begin repaying principal immediately.

The slower growth rate would, however, have a big impact on consumption. In the model, the GDP per capita growth rate determines required investment spending which in turn determines imports. External conditions determine exports, and consumption is a residual, fixed by available productive capacity. Reducing the GDP per capita growth rate from 2 to 1 percent does not reduce exports, but only the growth of investment, imports, and consumer goods capacity. For any given GDP growth rate, therefore, changes in external conditions have disproportionate effects on consumption spending. That is, the model implicitly assumes that to maintain the targeted growth rate the authorities are able

Table 1.13

Projected Annual Net New Lending Requirements
(millions of 1988 U.S. dollars)

	Argentina		Brazil		Chile		Mexico	
	1989	2000	1989	2000	1989	2000	1989	2000
Assuming 2% GDP per capita growth rate								
Base scenario	$5,225	$8,830	$6,265	$15,115	$1,125	$2,188	$2,403	$25,391
1% Rise in real interest rate	5,790	10,729	7,518	18,626	1,360	2,846	3,431	28,503
Pessimistic scenario	5,516	16,056	7,327	42,241	1,333	7,460	3,449	50,755
Optimistic scenario	5,027	2,710	5,532	(8,414)	981	(2,335)	1,686	3,848
Inward oriented scenario	4,809	6,274	5,178	4,723	910	284	1,317	8,424
Assuming 1% GDP per capita growth rate								
Base scenario	$4,229	$3,183	$3,088	$(7,690)	$1,026	$ (2,530)	$(1,477)	$(4,618)
1% Rise in real interest rate	4,794	4,736	4,341	(5,477)	1,261	(2,110)	(449)	(3,151)
Pessimistic scenario	4,520	10,532	4,150	20,015	1,235	2,888	(430)	21,660
Optimistic scenario	4,031	(3,065)	2,355	(31,832)	883	(7,206)	(2,193)	(27,129)
Inward oriented scenario	4,011	2,099	2,642	(11,717)	831	(3,094)	(1,793)	(12,241)

Note: Numbers in parentheses are repayments.

Table 1.14

Permitted Average Annual Increase in per Capita Consumption from 1989 through 2000

	Argentina	Brazil	Chile	Mexico
Assuming 2% GDP per capita growth rate				
Base scenario	1.5%	1.8%	2.0%	1.9%
1% Rise in real interest rate	1.5	1.8	2.0	1.9
Pessimistic scenario	2.0	2.2	3.2	2.7
Optimistic scenario	0.9	1.3	0.7	1.1
Inward oriented scenario	1.3	1.5	1.6	1.6
Assuming 1% GDP per capita growth rate				
Base scenario	0.2%	0.5%	−0.2%	0.3%
1% Rise in real interest rate	0.2	0.5	−0.2	0.3
Pessimistic scenario	0.9	1.1	1.3	1.3
Optimistic scenario	−0.5	0.0	−1.9	−0.6
Inward oriented scenario	0.1	0.4	−0.3	0.2

to squeeze consumption when export demand booms, and stimulate consumption when the demand slumps so as to maintain full capacity utilization. A Keynesian type model, with exogenously given marginal propensities to consume domestic and imported goods, would more realistically roduce swings in capacity utilization and destabilizing repercussions on imports and consumption. But that merely reinforces the implications of our supply-side model concerning the incompatibility of growth with debt servicing.

Table 1.14 gives the average annual increases in per capita consumption under the various scenarios, assuming a 2 percent per capita GDP growth rate. For all of the countries, the optimistic scenario has much slower consumption growth than the pessimistic scenario: if exports boom, consumption must grow slowly to maintain an overall 2 percent GDP growth rate. Since exports are determined by external demand alone, reducing the GDP growth rate does not reduce exports. Thus, as is also shown in Table 1.14, the 1 percent per capita growth rate yields significantly less consumption growth than the higher target; in some of the scenarios consumption actually falls over the next decade.

Since the growing political pressure for unilateral debt relief is related to the prolonged drop of per capita consumption in the 1980s, only scenarios with rising per capita consumption in the 1990s are likely to be politically viable. We assume this limits the viable set to scenarios that allow per capita consumption to grow by more than a half percent per annum during the decade. The set includes all the 2 percent GDP per capita growth rate scenarios plus the pessimistic scenario with 1 percent

Table 1.15

Projected Debt Burden Ratios
(ratios expressed as percentages)

	Argentina		Brazil		Chile		Mexico	
	1989	2000	1989	2000	1989	2000	1989	2000
Assuming 2% GDP per Capita Growth Rate								
Base scenario								
Debt/GDP	70.0	92.8	37.9	38.2	123.9	130.3	74.5	89.9
Interest/exports	40.9	42.0	25.6	20.0	24.1	18.9	22.8	20.4
Nonfinancial goods and services trade balance/interest	(—)	(—)	28.5	(—)	29.0	7.4	62.7	(—)
1% Rise in real interest rate								
Debt/GDP	71.3	103.5	38.6	43.1	126.3	147.6	75.3	98.4
Interest/exports	46.5	52.4	29.1	25.1	27.4	23.9	25.6	25.1
Nonfinancial goods and services trade balance/interest	(—)	(—)	25.1	(—)	25.5	5.9	55.9	(—)
Pessimistic scenario								
Debt/GDP	70.4	122.5	38.2	64.2	125.0	225.2	75.3	144.7
Interest/exports	42.1	76.0	26.3	45.3	24.8	43.5	23.4	45.3
Nonfinancial goods and services trade balance/interest	(—)	(—)	17.1	(—)	16.5	(—)	50.0	(—)
Optimistic scenario								
Debt/GDP	69.8	68.9	37.7	17.0	123.1	53.5	74.0	45.7
Interest/exports	40.1	26.1	25.0	8.3	23.6	7.7	22.3	9.1
Nonfinancial goods and services trade balance/interest	(—)	53.6	36.8	207.2	37.3	270.1	71.7	31.9
Inward oriented scenario								
Debt/GDP	69.5	80.6	37.5	27.3	122.0	89.9	73.8	53.4
Interest/exports	41.0	39.1	25.7	15.9	24.0	14.6	23.0	13.8
Nonfinancial goods and services trade balance/interest	(—)	6.4	40.5	45.9	41.3	77.4	76.5	(—)

Note: (—) indicates that the nonfinancial goods and services balance is negative.

Table 1.16

Projected Debt Burden Ratios (ratios expressed as percentages)

	Argentina		Brazil		Chile		Mexico	
	1989	2000	1989	2000	1989	2000	1989	2000
Assuming 1% GDP per capita growth rate								
Base scenario								
Debt/GDP	69.5	73.7	37.3	15.4	124.5	45.8	72.5	22.3
Interest/exports	40.9	31.0	25.6	8.7	24.1	7.8	22.8	5.7
Nonfinancial goods and services trade balance/interest	(—)	43.2	63.7	220.7	34.9	334.6	111.0	193.0
1% rise in real interest rate								
Debt/GDP	70.8	84.4	38.0	19.7	127.0	61.6	73.2	28.7
Interest/exports	46.5	39.5	29.1	12.0	27.4	11.0	25.6	7.9
Nonfinancial goods and services trade balance/interest	(—)	33.9	56.0	160.0	30.7	237.3	98.8	139.2
Pessimistic scenario								
Debt/GDP	69.8	107.5	37.6	45.0	125.7	154.8	73.2	85.5
Interest/exports	42.1	60.6	26.3	29.3	24.8	28.0	23.4	24.7
Nonfinancial goods and services trade balance/interest	(—)	(—)	52.1	(—)	22.6	(—)	98.3	(—)
Optimistic scenario								
Debt/GDP	69.2	46.4	37.0	-8.9	123.8	-43.1	72.0	-28.8
Interest/exports	40.1	17.2	25.0	-0.6	23.6	-1.3	22.3	-2.7
Nonfinancial goods and services trade balance/interest	1.7	176.7	72.0	n.a.	43.2	n.a.	119.7	n.a.
Inward oriented scenario								
Debt/GDP	69.2	67.4	37.1	10.3	122.7	27.6	72.3	3.7
Interest/exports	41.0	30.3	25.7	7.0	24.0	6.0	23.0	2.5
Nonfinancial goods and services trade balance/interest	2.2	59.1	68.5	348.6	45.8	496.7	114.8	812.0

Notes: (—) indicates that the nonfinancial goods and services balance is negative. In these cases, the countries have become creditors and are not making external debt interest payments.
n.a. indicates "not applicable."

GDP per capita growth. Is the external financing required to support the growth rates targeted by the scenarios of this relevant set likely to be forthcoming?

The debt burden indicators in Tables 1.15 and 1.16 imply a largely negative answer. With 2 percent growth, all the countries would in the base, higher interest, and pessimistic scenarios experience rising debt/GDP ratios, little or no decline in their interest/export ratios, and rapidly diminishing surpluses on goods and nonfinancial services relative to their rising interest bills. Only the optimistic scenario leads to an improvement in the ability to service the debt that could pursuade lenders to risk supplying the requisite external funding in all the countries. The inward oriented scenario also produces improvements in all three ratios, albeit at a more moderate pace, but financing may not be available for a different reason. It is hard to visualize Washington, which has been fervently pushing a market-liberalizing, export oriented strategy on the debtors, facilitating the requisite financing for a breakaway from that strategy, even if it showed promise. Finally, with a 1 percent rate of growth of GDP per capita, the debt servicing indicators move favorably in all but the pessimistic scenario. But only the pessimistic scenario allows consumption per capita to grow at the minimum acceptable rate.

Given this diversity of outcomes, judgment on whether lending on the required scale would be self-liquidating in time or would merely push the debtor countries deeper into unserviceable debt depends on one's assessment of the relative likelihood of the different outcomes. The external growth rates and the terms of trade improvement of the optimistic scenario are on the high side of the current range of forecasts. While the weak track record of such forecasts doesn't allow the optimistic scenario to be ruled out as too improbable, the stricture also applies to the pessimistic scenario, which is on the low side of current forecasts. Since the other scenarios are not encouraging, with the partial exception of the inward oriented one, the compatibility of economic growth and increasing consumption levels with debt servicing rests on a very fragile base. If the requisite loans are forthcoming, they are not likely to be repayable, and if they are not forthcoming, either standards of living remain depressed or servicing of the existing debt will have to give way.

The Political Economy of Defaulting: A Summary

Our analysis of the Latin American debt crisis has shown that from its inception, political choices have shaped the course of economic policies. Creditors have imposed on debtor governments the obligation of socializing *ex post* the foreign liabilities of their private sectors. Debtors and creditors have found it politic to play down the capital flight phenomenon: both its negative consequences for the debtor economies and the possibility of using the accumulating foreign assets to engineer a positive sum solution to the debt crisis. The debtor governments chose to burden their restructuring effort further with generous rescues of over-leveraged banks and firms, with fiscal-monetary costs falling disproportionately on

Table 1.17

Real Gross Investment per Worker, 1970, and 1980–87 (1980–81 = 100)

	1970	1982–84	1985	1986	1987
Argentina	87.4	60.7	42.0	49.0	56.3
Brazil	61.2	68.1	68.5	82.8	82.5
Chile	88.5	36.5	46.4	51.7	63.6
Mexico	63.6	62.7	61.0	47.0	47.6
Peru	54.8	69.2	42.5	52.7	52.3
Venezuela	104.0	72.7	59.0	61.1	60.2

Sources: Inter-American Development Bank, *Economic and Social Progress in Latin America*, 1986 Report Appendix Table 5: 1987 Report, Tables VII–1 and VII–3; 1988 Report, Table B–4.

wages, salaries, and public expenditures on the social and physical infrastructure.

Our conclusion that the current approaches to the debt crises will be abandoned in favor of debt reduction through default or concessionary writedown also derives from interweaving political with economic factors. It is easy to buttress the case that economically destructive trends have parallelled the restructuring efforts of the debtors. The sharp fall in the volume of investment shown in Table 1.6, and of investment per worker shown in Table 1.17, imply weak restructuring progress at best, if not retrogression, as does the drop in public investment shown in Table 1.11. The deep and prolonged cuts in education, health, and nutritional budgets, the prolonged depression of real wages and salaries, and the accelerating brain drain have surely been deleterious to human capital formation. Increasing dollarization of the working capital of larger firms, such as shown in Table 1.18, and the shift from cash and deposits to more inflation-shielded liquid assets, reflected in the continuing decline of M1 relative to higher order Ms, are evidence that the effectiveness of the inflation tax is eroding. Ongoing capital flight (a safety net for the rich) and the expanding black economy (a tax shelter for the small businessman and a safety net for the poor) are eroding the visible tax base.

It is harder, however, to show conclusively that destructive economic effects dominate the restructuring, since diehard supporters of the restructuring can always extend its required economic time frame and dub the adverse evidence transitional costs. What they cannot do is to keep extending the political time limits for showing results. The current resurgence of left-wing populism in the Latin American debtor countries is evidence that the political limits have been reached.

Our prediction of impending default or debt writedown comes down to the

Table 1.18

Private Foreign and Domestic Deposits, 1980–85
(year-end data in billions of U.S. dollars)

	1980–81	1982	1983	1984	1985
Argentina					
In domestic banks	27.4	7.9	8.2	7.6	7.0
In foreign banks	6.6	5.7	8.6	8.4	9.0
Foreign/domestic (%)	24.0	72.4	105.3	110.7	128.1
Brazil					
In domestic banks	41.0	45.5	33.0	36.0	23.5
In foreign banks	4.8	4.3	11.4	17.3	16.6
Foreign/domestic (%)	14.6	9.4	34.4	48.1	70.6
Mexico					
In domestic banks	59.6	30.9	34.8	42.9	34.6
In foreign banks	10.8	10.9	18.0	21.8	21.5
Foreign/domestic (%)	18.2	35.1	51.9	50.8	62.2
Venezuela					
In domestic banks	28.0	34.6	42.6	26.8	—
In foreign banks	17.2	12.9	17.1	19.1	22.2
Foreign/domestic (%)	61.2	37.4	40.1	71.2	—

Source: Helmut Reisen and Axel Van Trotsenburg, *Developing Country Debt: The Budgetary and Transfer Problem* (Paris: OECD Development Centre, 1988), Table 1.19.

Notes: Domestic deposits include demand, time, and savings deposits in domestic currency converted to dollars at year-end exchange rate. Foreign deposits are the gross liabilities of banks in the BIS reporting system to each of the above countries.

following blending of economic and political arguments. The economic case is that the restructuring policies of the debtor economies have not produced net positive results in the 1980s, and if continued on course there is small chance that they will restore economic growth, pre-crisis consumption levels, and normal debt servicing by the 1990s. Modest economic growth in the 1990s has a better chance to be compatible with debt servicing, but it would allow little or no recovery of consumption per capita from the depressed 1980s levels. Since the decline of consumption has been borne unequally, the wage dependent classes suffering more than the propertied classes, the resurgence of populism implies that it is no longer feasible politically to extend this unequal sharing of income and consumption losses. The business classes, the main domestic opposition to risking a break with international capital by defaulting, will therefore have to bear a larger share of the economic cost of decelerating inflation, restoring essential public sector services, and servicing the foreign debt. In this politically altered environment, debt servicing will appear less compelling to many business people, thus eroding the main political bastion against unilateral moratoria and other modes of defaulting.

An alternative is for the creditors to preempt default with concessionary debt writedowns. There appears to be growing interest in creditor circles in such action, but no consensus thus far. Moreover, even if agreement on the necessity for a writedown were reached, the political fight over the distribution of the costs is likely to be severe and drawn out. Whether we will see a negotiated compromise or unilateral action now depends on comparative political dynamics and on whether the creditors can reach consensus on sharing the costs of concessionary debt writedowns in time to overtake the rising political pressures in the debtor countries for unilateral action.

Notes

1. Net dividends are included with net interest in the resource flow calculations. This is because debt-equity swaps, the current enthusiasm, alter the time shape of the foreign exchange outflows related to the debt, but could well augment the cumulated volume. In any event, net dividend flows have been a small fraction of the 1980s net interest flows; their deletion would not reduce the flow ratios much.

2. Values of the annual ratios are in current year United States dollars. The declining trends of the real dollar exchange rates of the debtors in the 1980s thus lower the denominators. The rationale for incorporating exchange rate effects is that it gives a truer measure of changing resource costs of traded goods than do calculations using a fixed exchange rate. Indeed, those who believe chronically weak balance of payments of the debtors imply overvalued exchange rates should view the ratios of Table 1.2 as underestimates.

3. Ponzi financing is the new lending required by deficit units with cash flow shortfalls to pay interest on their existing debt. The colorful terminology, Hyman Minsky's, is conveniently succinct.

4. ALADI is the acronym for the Asociación Latinoamericana de Integración, a more modest successor to LAFTA, the Latin American Free Trade Association, which failed to meet its ambitious regional free trade targets.

5. The IMF type restructuring strategy calls for import liberalization in order to promote greater production efficiency. The short and intermediate term effect of such liberalization should be to raise the import/GDP ratio, unless offset by declining aggregate production.

6. Helmut Reisen and Axel Van Trotsenburg, *Developing Country Debt: The Budgetary and Transfer Problem* (Paris: Organization for Economic Co-operation and Development, Development Centre Study, 1988), p. 64.

7. Another possible source of underestimation is that the World Bank's 1985 debt data tend to be lower than those of the OECD/BIS: around 20 percent lower for Chile, 11 percent for Argentina and Peru, and 7 percent for Venezuela. At the time, the World Bank's data sources were debtor country reports, whereas the OECD/BIS based its estimates on reporting by creditor countries. The latter data are believed to be more comprehensive and reliable. Since 1985, the two agencies have been coordinating their estimates to reduce discrepancies.

8. For the size of Peruvian dollar deposits in 1981, subtract the number in parentheses from the number to its left in Table 1.7. These deposits carried an interest rate of LIBOR less 3 percent, whence the inference that it was the Peruvian middle classes rather than the wealthy who mainly exploited that facility for dollarizing their portfolios.

9. See David Felix, "Solving Latin America's Debt Crisis," *Challenge* (November/December 1985): 44–51, for more details on a proposal along these lines.

10. Table 1.7 underestimates Chile's capital flight. The evidence (in footnote 7) that Chile's foreign debt was understated by a larger percentage than the others—reducing the residual in the capital flight formula—is backed up by the fact that Chile set up a facility in 1985 for capital repatriation. Presumably, the authorities knew there was capital to be repatriated. However, there is no question that Chile's foreign asset/debt ratio is low.

11. As late as 1985, Pinochet support seems to have been an additional factor. Thus in February 1985, the then United States Assistant Secretary of State for Inter-American Affairs, Langhorne Motley, proclaimed on a visit to Chile that "the destiny of Chile is in very good hands . . . the democracies of the Western World owe a debt of gratitude for what the people of Chile did in 1973." *El Mercurio* (Santiago), 24 February 1985, as cited in NACLA, *Report on the Americas* XXII, no. 2: (March/April, 1988), p. 29.

Human rights critics of United States policy agree, however, that the United States has since distanced itself from Pinochet and would prefer to see him replaced by a less repressive regime—one, however, that continues the general lines of his neo-liberal economic strategy. Cf. ibid.

12. See David Felix, "Financial Blowups and Authoritarian Regimes in Latin America," in *Latin American Political Economy: Financial Crisis and Political Change*, ed. Jonathyn Hartlyn and Samuel A. Morley (Boulder, Colorado: Westview Press, 1986).

13. Address by Richard S. Williamson, Assistant Secretary for International Organization Affairs, to the Economic Commission for Latin America and the Caribbean, Rio de Janeiro, 26 April 1988, reprinted in *Policies for the Americas in the 1990s*, Current Policy, No. 1071 (Washington, D.C.: United States Department of State, Bureau of Public Affairs).

14. Mauricio Carrizosa and Antonio Urdinela, "El endeudamiento privada interna en Colombia, 1975–85," *Revista de la CEPAL* (Santiago de Chile) 32 (Agosto 1987): 27–53.

15. Uruguay, the other Southern Cone neo-liberal regime of that era, had a debt run-up similar to Argentina and Chile. See Carlos Massad and Roberto Zahler, "Otro ángulo de la crisis latinoamericana: la deuda interna," *Revista de la CEPAL* (Santiago de Chile) 32 (Agosto 1987): 11–25, Cuadro 1.

16. Massad and Zahler, op. cit., p. 13.

17. Julio A. Piekarz, "El déficit fiscal del Banco Central," paper presented to the Centro de Estudios Monetarios para América Latina (CEMLA), *Seminario: 'Efectos Monetarios de la Política Fiscal,'* Brasilia, Agosto 1987, p. 30.

18. Massad and Zahler, op. cit., p. 19.

19. Roberto Zahler, "Recent Southern Cone Liberalization Reforms and Stabilization Policies: The Chilean Case, 1974–82," *CEPAL Review*, 1984, p. 326.

20. J. Perez de Arce, "Diferencias entre recursos del Estado destinados a la banca y por combatir el desempleo," *Diario La Tercera: Informe Económico*, 2 (May 1983), cited in Zahler, op. cit., footnote 29.

21. Jesús Reyes Heroles, "Operaciones 'cuasi-fiscales' en un contexto de estabilización: un apunte sobre la experiencia de México en 1986–87," paper presented to CEMLA, *Seminario: 'Efectos Monetarios de la Política Fiscal,'* Brasilia, Agosto 1987, Cuadro 2.

22. Banco de México, *Informe Anual, 1987*, Cuadro 30.

23. Piekarz, op. cit., Appendix table.

24. D. Onandi and L. Viana, "El déficit parafiscal: un análisis de la experiencia Uruguayana," paper presented to CEMLA, *Seminario: 'Efectos Monetarios de la Política Fiscal,'* Brasilia, Agosto 1987, Cuadro 10.

25. So is the title of the deficits: quasi-fiscal or para-fiscal?

26. Massad and Zahler, op. cit., p. 23.

27. Hollis B. Chenery, *Structural Change and Development Policies* (New York: Oxford University Press, 1979).

COMMENTS

Ernest J. Bartell

The paper by Felix and Caskey is consistent with the theme of the conference in emphasizing the importance of economic growth in the Latin American debtor countries. Until recently this assumption has not been widely shared by the creditor banks, certainly not in the first three rounds of debt negotiations, which single-mindedly emphasized conditions and adjustments within debtor countries to meet foreign exchange requirements for debt service. It is heartening to observe finally an increasing awareness among some of the creditors of the importance of growth in the debtor countries, even if only to improve the possibilities for debt service.[1]

However, it is not clear that this salutary broadening of vision on the part of creditor banks extends to debt forgiveness, even if "debt writedown is in the air," as Felix and Caskey state. Creditor banks as a group are in better financial condition with respect to their Latin American debts than they were in the first years of the debt crisis, having been able to build up larger reserves for losses, write down the value of some debts, and dispose of debt on secondary markets. Consequently, they can afford to be more magnanimous in their approach to options for debt relief. However, relatively few support debt relief beyond what the markets afford, e.g., through debt-equity swaps, the option most generally favored by the banking community.[2] Allowing debtor countries wide latitude to buy up their own discounted debt on secondary markets, for example, is still considered a violation of the rules of the game by many.

Moreover, those that favor some form of nonmarket debt forgiveness do so by supporting schemes that would shift some of the burden of forgiveness to the public sectors of creditor countries through the intermediation of multilateral lending institutions empowered to purchase and convert the bad debts to more marketable instruments. This stance is, of course, consistent with the earlier insistence of the creditor banks that the governments in the debtor countries assume responsibility for

Ernest J. Bartell is Executive Director of the Helen Kellogg Institute for International Studies, University of Notre Dame.

foreign debts of the private sector. The required capital of the multilateral institutions for the newly proposed conversions would, of course, come from tax supported subscriptions by governments in creditor countries.

Growth in the debtor countries demands savings and foreign exchange, and the simulation scenarios developed by Felix and Caskey demonstrate the enormous capital requirements for growth of the major Latin American debtor countries. Lopez and Ruiz in their paper in this volume also call attention to the underutilization of existing productive capacity in the same countries, the potential for more favorable capital output ratios and certain welfare considerations, but do not deny a continuing capital constraint. The "inward oriented" scenario of Felix and Caskey also incorporates an allowance for idle capacity but still produces discouragingly high capital requirements.

The discouraging enormity of the practical policy implications in all but the most optimistic two-gap simulation scenarios is reinforced by preliminary data for 1988 that indicate an increase of 55 percent over 1987 in net external transfers for Latin America as a whole despite debt reschedulings, swaps, conversions, and painful internal adjustment programs of debtor countries. While net payments abroad of profits and interest increased by 10 percent during the year, the net inflow of capital dropped in 1988 by more than two-thirds to the lowest level in three years.[3]

Felix and Caskey seek to reinforce their analysis of the intractability of the resource transfer problem by referring to deteriorating terms of trade as an important contributing factor to rising debt-export ratios for the major debtor countries during the 1980–86 period. However, as adherents of inward looking development strategies learned long ago, the instability of data on terms of trade makes extrapolation for the sake of argument a chancy business. In fact, since 1986 external debt as a percentage of the value of exports has declined for all of Latin America and for the major debtor countries treated by Felix and Caskey. Of course, these favorable data are positively influenced by debt rescheduling and by an increased volume of industrial and nontraditional exports.

Nevertheless, it is important to note that the data have also been favorably influenced by the behavior of world prices of primary products, which are still mainstays of exports in the major debtor countries. In 1987 and especially in 1988, there happened to be substantial growth in the prices of major primary exports of the subject countries, e.g., in 1987–88 of copper (+65 percent), fish meal (+61 percent), soybeans (+43 percent), beef (+19 percent), and in 1988 of coffee (+20 percent), and grains (+22 percent).[4] The drop in oil prices, of course, hurt Venezuela and Mexico but presumably improved the terms of trade of the oil importing countries in the group. Overall, four of the six major debtor countries, excepting only Mexico and Brazil, have experienced some improvement in their terms of trade since 1986.[5]

Felix and Caskey seek to downplay the significance of Chile's low level of capital flight by citing Chile's less attractive debt/export and debt/GNP ratios through 1986.

The fact is, however, that the boom in both volume and prices of traditional and nontraditional primary products in Chile has fueled rapid growth in both GNP and exports, such that preliminary estimates for 1988 show the debt/export ratio to have fallen by 42 percent since 1986.[6] The cumulative improvement in Chile's overall terms of trade since 1986 has been more than 26 percent.[7] In addition, Chile had cumulative growth of GDP during 1987–88 of 12 percent accompanied by a decline of about 8 percent in its total disbursed external debt.[8] Such felicitous synchronicity is scarcely sufficient evidence, however, for complacency about future resource transfers. Nor is there much evidence to support optimistic long-term assumptions about the terms of trade for primary products as a further basis for complacency, given the fact that there is no uniformity in the behavior of terms of trade among the Latin American debtor countries.

The magnitude of the externally financed capital requirements for growth demonstrated by Felix and Caskey demands not simply a few debt relief instruments in financial markets, but rather the whole menu of financial instruments complemented by an integrated program of financial and fiscal policies and institutions, all driven by exceptional political will on the part of both creditor and debtor countries. Even then, it is worth noting that preoccupation with identifying capital sources to meet the challenges of growth may take priority over the largely ignored distributional issues that have emerged from the debt crisis and the adjustments to it.

Felix and Caskey rightly note that the distribution of income and wealth has worsened in the debtor countries during the years of debt-mandated internal economic adjustment. All four countries reviewed in these papers except Argentina have had some cumulative growth, albeit well below historic averages, since 1980. However, in 1988 only Chile had average real wages as high as they were in 1980. Moreover, urban real minimum wages in all four countries in 1988 are well below their 1980 levels, ranging from a high of 95.8 percent in Argentina to a low of 53.6 percent in Mexico.[9]

In addition, pressures for privatization of publicly-owned productive assets suggest further skewing of income and wealth distribution. Chile has been most persistent in its efforts to privatize, often at prices far below critics' estimates of market values. The 1970s round of privatizations produced some notorious financial fortunes (and in truth some subsequent financial busts). In Chile's current round of privatizations, which at the end of 1988 included over thirty enterprises, there is probably less subsidy built into the sale prices than before, although anecdotal evidence still points to some apparent bargain basement sales.[10] This time around, the distributional implications of privatization in Chile are not simply between the domestic rich and poor but between foreign and domestic asset holders, as some foreign investors are allowed to purchase shares in privatized enterprises, often at prices effectively discounted by the use of debt-equity swaps.

Felix and Caskey also note the worsening income distribution that has resulted from bailouts of private banks by Latin American central banks, from cuts in social policies that reduce investment in human capital, and from underemployment of skilled labor. The distributional implications of the bank bailouts in Chile, to which Felix and Caskey refer, also are not simply a source of potential conflict between rich and poor. Personal interviews with bankers in Chile in 1988 revealed the displeasure of the foreign banks operating there with the preferential interest rates on thirty-year loans offered by the central bank to favored domestic private banks during the bailout. According to their competitors, these domestic banks now enjoy a long-term competitive advantage in the cost of loanable funds as a result of the preferential bailout loans.

Additional distributional effects, as others have noted,[11] have accompanied the depreciation of local currencies that has been necessary to promote exports of debtor countries. The depreciation is typically accompanied either by inflation or by budget balancing efforts, both of which most likely penalize wage earners relative to other income recipients, since real wages must decline relative to the price of tradeables in order to maintain employment levels while boosting exports. The smaller the export sector, the greater must be the depreciation of local currency to generate a given quantity of foreign exchange, and therefore the greater the distributional distortions. These distortions are likely to penalize purchases of basic goods by low-income people, either through rises in import prices or through price increases of domestically produced goods induced by a shift of domestic resources to the production of externally traded goods.

Chile's unique record of growth in recent years has been fueled in part by the development of temperate zone export agriculture. Although employment is rising, wage rates in agriculture remain low while the price of agricultural land rises with the profitability of the export crops. This combination of effects is not likely to create incentives for increases in either domestic production or imports of commodities for basic needs. Mexico, even while expanding manufactured exports to offset the oil bust and privatizing a majority of state-owned firms along with reducing its budget deficit, is in even worse distributional shape. Real wages are slightly more than half their level at the beginning of the decade, while official unemployment holds at 20 percent with underemployment perhaps close to double that level.

The menu of policy options for managing Latin American external debts has grown with every suggestion of greater willingness of creditor banks to broaden debt negotiations to include objectives of growth and development. Most of these options include larger and more complex commitments by private creditor banks, the United States and other creditor country governments and the multilateral lending institutions which, like the private creditor banks, have become net resource transfer recipients from Latin America since 1987. As some of the funding of the options is shifted to creditor governments and their taxpayers, the ultimate incidence of the cost of these options becomes murkier. Consequently, it is increasingly important that attention be paid to the social effects of these efforts if economic equity is to be supported in the debtor countries. Since expectations for economic equity underlie much of the impetus for political change in Latin America and threaten the survival of fragile new democracies, the implications of debt relief proposals for political stability are obvious.

These issues of economic equity and political stability, as well as the usual search for sources of foreign exchange and capital, warrant the attention given by Felix and Caskey to the potential for debtor nations to bridge some or all of their foreign exchange gaps through mandatory socialization of the foreign assets held by their own nationals. They utilize a conventional approach to measurement of capital flight defined as a residual outflow in order to arrive at the familiar high estimates of Latin American capital flight.[12]

The relatively high totals from a measurement of capital flight, however, are likely to capture the residual foreign deposits by government-owned corporations and financial institutions in debtor countries as well as the private investments that are really the focus of the Felix and Caskey policy proposal to socialize foreign assets of private investors. Presumably, the foreign exchange from income earned on foreign assets of financial institutions and government-owned corporations is already available for debt service or other purposes. The capital itself is presumably a matter of record and could be made available domestically by administrative decree or legislation.

Some breakdowns of capital flight, however, further distinguish between foreign income-earning deposits by businesses and individuals, and that portion of private capital flight which does not yield investment income and therefore is not subject to the growth by compounding that helps to raise the estimates of current values of foreign private assets in the Felix and Caskey analysis. These estimates of foreign income earning deposits by private sectors in Argentina, Brazil, Chile, Mexico, Peru, and Venezuela (the subject countries of the Felix and Caskey study) are much smaller for the years 1977–84 and therefore much less promising as sources of capital repatriation than the Felix and Caskey cumulative totals.[13]

Moreover, the task of locating and identifying unregistered and non-income-earning assets could be more difficult than the authors imply. Unlike many of the foreign assets of Europeans during the world wars, many of these clandestinely transferred assets are, one suspects, deliberately concealed. This is true even of Chile, where capital flight has not recently been a serious problem, but where foreign "shell" corporations can be useful to Chilean citizens who wish to profit from the terms of debt-equity swaps available only to foreigners.

Finally, capital flight from the private sector is a way of life that has surmounted various attempts at regulation, such as the elaborate exchange controls that were common during the era of development based on import substitution and growth of domestic markets. As pressures for liberalization of markets continue to be a strong influence on development policy, the familiar opportunities for capital flight are not likely to diminish, e.g., overinvoicing of imports and underinvoicing of exports.[14]

Consequently, in the present climate favoring liberalization it is not difficult to understand the persistence of the argument that the most efficient strategies to socialize private assets held abroad are market instruments like debt-equity swaps made available to debtor country nationals with foreign assets, along with conventional market incentives like attractive positive real domestic interest rates (implying domestic price stability), undervalued (or less overvalued) domestic currencies, and stability of political regimes and economic policies. Chile's success in converting six billion dollars, 40 percent of its foreign private debt, through the use of swaps will continue to be touted to promote voluntary conversion strategies.[15]

On the other hand, the increased concentration of productive wealth and income that has resulted from economic liberalization in the debtor countries of Latin America may indicate greater potential mobilization of capital in the hands of those with the greatest experience and opportunities for capital flight. In the absence of clear empirical evidence, the debate is likely to continue on grounds that are at least partially ideological.

The simulation model used by Felix and Caskey to evaluate capital needs for growth appears to be appropriate and revealing. The targets established in the model are reasonable, while the welfare considerations, variation in capital-output ratios, and existence of idle capacity noted by López and Ruiz are useful additions to the analysis. The high sensitivity of the model to changes in OECD growth rates and to the terms of trade should warm the hearts of traditional dependency theorists. Nevertheless, the model is conservative in many respects, e.g., in its growth rate targets of 2 percent per capita and in its use of gross investment ratios of the 1970s.

Some of the assumptions of the simulation are admittedly too simple to capture fully the implications of the authors' prior analysis, especially in the area of political economy. For example, the constant income elasticities of export demand do not allow for the possibility of demand-dampening protectionist measures by governments of importing countries. Treating domestic consumption and savings as residuals not only introduces an optimistic bias to the authors' export driven projections, as they point out, but also appears not to allow for testing the possibility of directly influencing savings by market signals and government policies.

Capital flows, subject to so many political and market influences, are unlikely to maintain the constant relationship to world inflation rates that is assumed by the model. Nor is investment spending likely to remain a constant level of GDP during prolonged political instability. Moreover, the lack of attention in the simulation to internal financial policies of the debtor countries implies that these remain constant, while the prior analysis of Felix and Caskey stresses the importance of internal financial policy changes to both economic growth and capacity for debt service. Nevertheless, the implications of the resulting projections are not likely to be qualitatively weakened by quibbles such as these, since the biases in assumptions do not appear to coalesce strongly in any one direction.

The qualitative results of the projections support the conclusions by Felix and Caskey that the most likely scenarios are default or debt reduction schemes by creditors, given the "small chance" that restructuring policies of the debtor countries will succeed in generating growth, pre-crisis levels of consumption, and normal debt service into the 1990s. In fact, a cynic might argue that despite the rhetoric of creditors, the history of the debt crisis is very much a story of hard-line negotiating strategies by creditor banks, not simply to force debt payments but to buy the time necessary to improve their own balance sheets and operating statements sufficiently to permit the debt to be reduced or written off in orderly stages. Behind the imposition of restructuring policies on the debtors has been the more noble rhetorical assumption of an implicit virtuous circle: that improved creditworthiness will elicit new lending, which will elicit higher growth rates and therefore still greater creditworthiness.

However, the United Nations Association report cited earlier bluntly confirms the lack of willingness by major creditor banks to commit new money for growth-related investments, even as the creditworthiness of some debtor countries improves and despite Baker Plan appeals.[16] Many of the obstacles to new lending originate outside the debtor nations. The improved financial condition of creditor banks makes it easier for them not only to make new loans, but to reduce their exposure in Latin America by discounting Latin American paper on secondary markets in order to shift portfolios toward more promising loan opportunities. These opportunities may be enhanced in OECD countries by such events as the liberalization of banking in Britain, the post-1992 European common market, the growth of markets in the Pacific Basin, and increased access to Japanese financial markets. New banking regulations implemented jointly by the United States, Britain, and Japan for measuring risk weighted capital adequacy are more stringent than before and may require many banks to reduce the amount of relatively risky holdings. Similarly, new accounting rules for treatment of loan loss reserves may reduce measured capital adequacy below permissible levels at many United States banks, while new tax laws will limit the use of foreign tax credits generated by loans to developing countries after 1990.

Direct foreign investment has not rushed in to fill the gap left by the absence of new foreign loan capital in Latin America. At the end of 1986 the level of direct foreign investment in Latin America was less than one third the level of 1981, while net private portfolio investment was negative for the third successive year.[17] As a result, even Chile with its relative success in restoring its creditworthiness has failed to experience a dramatic increase in the inflow of foreign capital. While attracting enough capital through debt-equity swaps to reduce its foreign debt substantially in recent years, the total inflow of foreign capital in 1987 was still less than 30 percent of its level in 1981.[18]

Meanwhile, despite debt fatigue on the part of both sides, many creditors continue to suggest that the present strategies of debt renegotiation are still viable, given the fact that over 200 billion dollars of debt has been successfully renegotiated and that attempts by some debtors to establish unilateral defaults, e.g., Brazil and Peru, have been generally unsuccessful. Partly because some creditor banks are in better financial condition than they were at the outbreak of the debt crisis, there is more willingness to consider publicly the possibility of debt reduction schemes. However, even that possibility remains conditioned by the demands for enhancement in the form of guarantees and co-financing alternatives that would shift at least part of the burden to multilateral institutions and through them to the public sectors of creditor governments.

It is, therefore, easy to agree with Felix and Caskey that externally financed growth is unlikely to be a feasible solution for servicing the debt and restoring politically viable levels of internal economic performance. However, it is not clear that substantial debt repudiation, perhaps followed by comprehensive inward looking growth strategies, are likely to follow. Less dramatic, but as likely, is a series of incremental changes in renegotiation packages to include just enough debt reduction to respond at a minimally acceptable level to threats of political instability in debtor countries. Nor is it obvious that the election of populist leaders in major debtor countries that are increasingly integrated into international markets for goods and finance and dependent upon their own private sectors will result in sustained large scale defaults. Such behavior in the short run would not only antagonize business elites but could quickly reduce the deteriorated standards of living throughout the society still further. Already, multinational firms are delaying investment decisions and moving capital out of Brazil pending the outcome of presidential elections despite more recent bullish attitudes toward growth in Brazil than their domestic counterparts.

Nevertheless, in light of deteriorating standards of living in debtor countries and the improved financial condition of major creditor banks, even the implicit threat of default can influence subsequent rounds of renegotiation so as to include at least incremental use of the various options for debt reduction now on the menu, including possibilities for conversions and buybacks. Moreover, in recent months the U.S. government, concerned with the security of its own borders, twice has responded financially outside the normal IMF brokered debt negotiating process to the threat of political instability in Mexico. It did so by participating in the partially successful Morgan Guaranty debt-swap scheme as well as by making a bridge loan of several billion dollars to Mexico. It remains to be seen whether even sophisticated and creative schemes for muddling through will improve the prospects for growth and a better life for the great majority of Latin Americans in the foreseeable future.

Notes

1. See Institute of International Finance, Inc., memorandum, September 7, 1988 and The Economic Policy Council of the United Nations Association of the United States of America, *Third World Debt: A Reexamination of Long-term Management*, 1988. The need for growth is also recognized in the 1988 renegotiation package for Brazil.

2. While acknowledging a variety of acceptable "voluntary, market-oriented debt conversion schemes as an acceptable way to ease the debt problem," the Institute for International Finance makes no mention of debt forgiveness and decries "debt relief schemes which involve the involuntary participation of private creditors."

3. Economic Commission for Latin America and the Caribbean, *Preliminary Overview of the Latin American Economy 1988,* Table 15.

4. Ibid., Table 11.

5. Ibid., Table 10. Extrapolations from recent favorable data on terms of trade are equally risky, when in fact there is simply little consistency and uniformity in the behavior of terms of trade among the major debtor countries. With 1985 rather than 1986 as base year, for example, the terms of trade have improved for Chile and Brazil, worsened for Mexico and Argentina, and fluctuated for Peru and Venezuela. See Inter-American Development Bank, *Economic and Social Progress in Latin America 1988 Report,* Part Three, Country Summaries, Statistical Profiles.

6. Ibid., Table 18.

7. Ibid., Table 10.

8. Ibid., Tables 2, 16.

9. Ibid., Tables 2, 6, 7.

10. See *Hoy,* No. 593, 28 November 1988, p. 29

11. Rudiger Dornbusch, "World Economic Issues of Interest to Latin America," in *Development and External Debt in Latin America; Bases for a New Consensus,* ed. Richard E. Feinberg and Ricardo Ffrench-Davis (Notre Dame: University of Notre Dame Press, 1988), pp. 23–24.

12. Capital flight calculated as a residual outflow is typically higher than capital flight calculated by aggregation from balance of payments data. See John Williamson and Donald D. Lessard, "Capital Flight: The Problem and Policy Responses," *Institute for International Economic Policy Analyses in International Economics,* no. 23 (November 1987), p. 6 ff. For lower estimates of Latin American capital flight using different balance of payments techniques see also John T. Cuddington, "Capital Flight: Estimates, Issues and Explanations," *Princeton Studies in International Finance,* no. 58 (November 1986), Table 1.

13. Frank Z. Riely, Jr. with the assistance of Mary L. Williamson, "Third World Capital Flight: Who Gains, Who Loses," *ODC Policy Focus* (Washington: Overseas Development Council, September, 1986, No. 5), Table 1, p. 3.

14. Estimates of underinvoicing of exports as a percentage of total exports in the major exporting countries of Latin America show no tendency to diminish during the first four years of the 1980s. See Cuddington, loc. cit., Appendix B, p. 38.

15. The success of swaps in Chile has been used to promote similar strategies as far away as Nigeria. See *New York Times,* 14 February 1989, p. 44.

16. United Nations Association of the United States of America, op. cit., pp. 18 ff.

17. Inter-American Development Bank, op. cit., Tables D13, D14, p. 573.

18. Cf. IMF, *Balance of Payments Statistics,* 1988 Yearbook, Vol. 39, Part 1, pp. 15, 91, 139.

2

Growth and Welfare in Latin American Semi-Industrialized Economies in the 1990s

Julio López Gallardo and Clemente Ruiz Durán

After almost a decade of declining per capita income and consumption levels in most Latin American countries, the resumption of economic growth has become a political imperative. The policies undertaken so far and the prevailing international conditions, however, make it unlikely that this imperative will be met, or, if met, make it unlikely that the poorest strata of the population would benefit significantly from the economic revival.

The purpose of this paper is twofold. First, we compare the current restructuring strategy being applied in Argentina, Brazil, Chile, and Mexico with a more equitable alternative. Secondly, we examine the investment and foreign exchange requirements associated with the two strategies and the conditions for meeting them.

Contractive Adjustment

The current strategy for coping with the debt crisis, urged on the debtors by the IMF and its creditor country sponsors, might accurately be called contractive adjustment. In this strategy, the main emphasis is on an initial reduction of domestic demand and imports, accompanied by drastic changes in relative prices through market liberalization designed to promote greater efficiency and in particular to promote more exports.

The overall economic consequences for four Latin American debtor countries pursuing the strategy have been poor. As shown in Table 2.1, the annual growth of GDP per capita was negative during 1980–87 in all except Brazil and was far

Julio López Gallardo and Clemente Ruiz Durán are Professors of Economics of the División de Posgrado de Economía, National Autonomous University of Mexico (UNAM).

Table 2.1

GDP per Capita Growth Rates
(annual averages)

	1960–70	1970–80	1980–87
Argentina	2.9	0.9	−2.4
Brazil	3.1	6.1	0.6
Chile	2.3	0.9	−0.4
Mexico	3.6	3.5	−1.7

Source: CEPAL, *Panorama Económico de América Latina*, various issues.

below the average rates of the two preceding decades in all the countries.

The adjustment strategy was motivated by the transfer problem, which required generating and transferring large trade surpluses to service the debt. During 1982–87 these countries collectively transferred 4.4 percent of their GDP abroad (about 125 billion U.S. dollars). Thus, the adjustments were related to the need to avoid default rather than to promote employment, capital accumulation, growth, and improved living standards. Consumption fell, with the incidence hitting labor income disproportionately hard. The severe drop of investment reduced demand for and use of existing capacity as well as the full capacity growth potential of these countries.

There was individual country variance around the general trends. Table 2.2 shows that of the four countries, only Chile had a substantial decline in the consumption share of GDP during the 1980s. Gross investment declined sharply in all four countries after 1980, with Argentina's investment share falling the most. Table 2.3 shows that the absolute decline of gross capital formation has been especially dramatic in Brazil and Mexico, where capital formation had been rising at a fast clip during 1950–80.

Table 2.2 also records the mediocre results to date from the effort to open up the debtor economies. The export/GDP ratios of all four countries rose during 1980–87, but the share of traded goods (exports + imports) to GDP increased only in Mexico, declining in Argentina and Brazil. Thus, except for Mexico, the trade surplus, which rising debt servicing and diminished new loans forced on the four countries, was generated more by import cutbacks than by export expansion. Since import liberalization has been an essential feature of the IMF type restructuring, the import cutbacks were achieved primarily by "dis-absorption," i.e., by depressing aggregate demand and production.

In the case of Mexico, the decline in investment has encompassed virtually all sectors. Export expansion stimulated new investment by a few—mostly multinational—firms, but most of the export expansion was supplied from existing

47

Table 2.2

Demand Structure (percent of GDP)

	Argentina		Brazil		Chile		Mexico	
	1980	1987	1980	1987	1980	1987	1980	1987
Domestic Absorption	103.8	93.9	102.4	95.8	104.1	89.6	102.3	90.5
Consumption	81.1	81.0	79.9	79.2	83.1	73.9	75.1	74.6
Investment	22.7	12.9	22.5	16.6	21.0	15.7	27.2	15.9
External Balance	−3.8	6.1	−2.4	4.2	−4.1	10.4	−2.3	9.5
Exports	11.9	14.6	8.8	10.5	23.0	30.3	10.7	17.6
Imports	15.7	8.5	11.2	6.3	27.1	19.9	13.0	8.1
GDP	100.0	100.0	100.0	100.0	100.0	100.0	100.0	100.0

Source: CEPAL, *Notas Para el Estudio Económico de América Latina y el Caribe 1987.*

Table 2.3

Gross Capital Formation: Average Annual Growth Rates

	1950–59	1960–69	1970–79	1980–86
Argentina	6.3	4.8	3.3	– 7.2
Brazil	5.8	5.8	9.6	– 5.8
Chile	4.0	4.1	0.1	– 6.5
Mexico	7.4	9.2	8.3	– 6.7

Source: Computed from CEPAL, *Estudio Económico de América Latina*, various issues.

productive capacity. Higher export expansion does not seem to have stimulated a higher investment by the favored industries. For example, a cross-sectional regression study, done by one of the authors on pooled 1983–86 data, found no statistically significant association between export and investment rates in the Mexican industrial sector.[1]

Contractive adjustment has depressed the use of industrial capacity. Table 2.4 presents estimates of trends in capacity utilization before and after 1982. Full capacity in these estimates is measured by linearly regressing the peak output year of each quinquennium during 1960–85 on time. "Capacity utilization is the ratio of actual output to corresponding year points on the linear regression" (Christiano 1981). In the case of Argentina, we were able to compare our estimates with a capacity utilization series based on self-declaration by reporting Argentine firms. The levels differ but the movements are quite similar.[2]

However, the extent to which the ample excess capacity of the 1980s might accelerate economic recovery depends on the restructuring strategy. Import liberalization plus domestic demand contraction renders more of the idle capacity permanently unprofitable than would a more inward oriented recovery strategy that seeks to maximize the use of existing capacity.

Another constraint on the use of idle industrial capacity to accelerate recovery is the decapitalizing of the social and economic infrastructure under the contractive adjustment strategy. This is because, as the Felix-Caskey paper shows, contractive fiscal measures have depressed public investment and human capital-building outlays disproportionately. Reliable indices of infrastructure capacity and its utilization are devilishly difficult to devise. It seems reasonable, however, to conclude that capacity, if not its utilization rate, declines as the period of poor maintenance and minimal new investment in infrastructure is extended, and that the stock of human capital decays as high underemployment, malnutrition, and reduced educational outlays persist. Thus the longer the contractive fiscal mea-

Table 2.4

Average Capacity Industrial Utilization Ratios by Decades

	Argentina	Brazil	Chile	Mexico
1960–1970	0.821	0.786	0.791	0.809
1971–1981	0.935	0.975	0.955	0.905
1982–1987	0.633	0.876	0.867	0.872

Notes: Capacity output estimates were obtained by regressing the peak output years of each quinquennium during 1960–85 on time. These estimates were divided into actual industrial output for the corresponding years and averaged.

sures of the 1980s persist, the more likely is it that even were export expansion eventually to reverse the decline of aggregate demand, industrial recovery would be dampened by infrastructural bottlenecks.

In general, the protracted contractive strategy is, in our view, showing itself to be not only unviable economically and socially, but also politically. Therefore, the next section sketches a possible alternative to that strategy which is socially and politically more appealing and may be more economically feasible.

A Growth with Equity Strategy

This strategy is directed at generating sustained economic growth along with a more egalitarian income distribution. The strategy would attempt to reform and strengthen the prevailing mixed economy patterns in the debtor countries by:

(a) a rapid recovery of economic growth;

(b) a strong rate of job creation in order to restore and further improve the levels of living of the mass of the population; and

(c) surpluses in the trade balance to help service as much of the external debt as is compatible with the growth and welfare objectives.

Attaining these goals would require a considerable internal effort by the debtors. It would also need, as will be shown below, new and more equitable formulas of international cooperation to lessen the burden of the external debt.

As regards the internal effort, the strategy would seek to maximize the use of the substantial idle productive capacity and underutilized labor extant in the debtor countries. Concurrently, however, it would seek to tilt new investment toward producing for regional as well as extraregional markets. In particular, we believe that the semi-industrial Latin American economies have attained high enough levels of industrial sophistication in some of their production lines for

Table 2.5

**Financial Requirements for a 2 Percent Growth Rate
of per Capita Consumption under an Egalitarian Recovery Strategy**

	Annual GDP growth rate %	Gross investment coefficient %	Required External Finance Under: egalitarian strategy	no egalitarian reforms
			(millions of U.S. dollars per annum)	
Argentina	3.2	16.8	4,311	10,344
Brazil	3.9	20.0	5,525	11,812
Chile	3.2	19.8	606	3,692
Mexico	4.1	20.3	6,682	16,131

integrating regional markets through preferential arrangements to be feasible and mutually beneficial.[3]

Maximizing the use of existing capacity requires restricting competing imports as well as augmenting aggregate demand. Since this will also increase the profitability of expanding existing product lines, the attainment of the longer-run objective of tilting new investment toward production for regional and extraregional markets requires investment planning and selective controls and subsidies to offset the attraction to private firms of import substituting investment. Our alternative strategy would, therefore, replace the heavy reliance on market liberalization of the current restructuring strategy with a dirigisme whose purpose would be to promote import substitution in the short run through greater use of underemployed capacity and labor, and exporting through new investment in order to enhance dynamic efficiency over the longer run.

Were the strategy adopted, what would be its internal and external requirements for successful implementation? We explore this tentatively with a modified version of the Felix-Caskey simulation model using the same 1990s time frame. The exercise assumes that the external state of the world is as in the basic Felix-Caskey model, and that the external financing requirements of the four debtor countries cover debt servicing as well as import needs. However, the following modifications are made to the growth target and domestic parameters. The target is 2 percent annual growth of per capita consumption rather than GDP, and we assume that the domestic consumer demand pattern becomes less import and capital intensive via redistributive fiscal reforms and selective controls. Specifically, we assume that this reduces the capital/output and the import/GDP ratios by 10 percent.

The results of the exercise, reported in Table 2.5, show that an egalitarian strategy could reduce external financial requirements substantially, but that very sizeable net financial inflows would nevertheless still be needed. Even under an egalitarian strategy, sustained revival of economic growth plus debt servicing requires a turnaround of the transfer relationship from the large resource out-flows of the 1980s to large resource inflows in the 1990s. Our concluding section therefore assesses various alternatives for effecting the turnaround.

Financing Latin American Growth in the 1990s

Our discussion of financial alternatives focuses on cooperative solutions of the debt crisis. This is because we believe that facilitating the economic recovery of the over-indebted countries through debt writedowns and new lending benefits creditor as well as debtor countries and is thus a superior solution to the exiguous IMF conditionality approach imposed by the creditors during the 1980s.

From the debtor country perspective, more generous treatment by creditors is essential, since most face an even more difficult domestic situation now than at the beginning of the crisis. Unless further cooperation with their creditors results in adequate financing for the resumption of growth, they will feel forced to reduce debt service unilaterally and use their exports to support economic growth. However, we assume that although the feasible space has been reduced by the prolonged crisis, cooperative approaches to growth financing are still possible. We discuss them under two headings: multi-year lending and writedowns.

Multi-year Lending

This is the least promising of the options. It seems unlikely under present condi-tions that "voluntary lending" by commercial banks is poised to revive, as had been assumed in many early analyses of the debt crisis, such as Cline's (1983).

During the 1980s, the only lending by commercial banks has been "concerted lending." Banks increased their exposure to debtors if and only if the latter reached an agreement with the IMF on a contractive adjustment program. Addi-tional bank exposure in Latin America under concerted lending has in fact been very limited (BIS 1988). Since, according to our estimates in Table 2.5, the four countries would require $30 billion of new loans annually to achieve the goals of the growth plus equity strategy, $40 billion per annum assuming the same growth goal but with no redistributive reforms, the concerted lending approach appears grossly inadequate.

Its prospects are further dimmed by the increase in capitalization ratios that the central banks of the major creditor countries are requiring of their deposit banks (IMF 1988). To reach the higher ratios, many of the banks will have to constrain new lending over the next few years.

The restrictive effect will, however, vary between countries; e.g., European banks have been less highly leveraged than U.S. and Japanese banks. Moreover,

Table 2.6

Required Bank Exposure to Finance the Equitable Growth Strategy in Selected Latin American Countries

	Actual 1988 exposure share		Exposure in 2000 (billions of U.S. dollars)
	Share (percent)	Amount (billions of U.S. dollars)	
Overall exposure	100.0	190	380
United States	32.5	62	123
United Kingdom	12.5	24	48
Japan	12.5	24	48
Canada	7.1	13	27
France	8.6	16	33
Germany	7.6	14	29
Switzerland	2.8	5	11

Source: IBCA, Banking Ltd., and authors' estimates.
Note: The selected Latin American countries are Argentina, Brazil, Chile, and Mexico.

banks of countries running large current account surpluses in the 1980s have been more aggressively expanding their international lending and have, therefore, become less resistant to proposals for multi-year conditional lending to highly indebted LDCs. Under such proposals commercial banks agree to a multi-year schedule of new loans to debtor countries who have signed a multi-year restructuring agreement with the IMF. The rationale is that a more generous and assured flow of new loans from the commercial banks and the international organizations would enable the debtor governments to resist populist pressures and to stick with the austerity and market liberalizing measures of the IMF restructuring program.[4]

Nevertheless, the likelihood that the multi-year packages could suffice to finance a 2 percent per capita consumption growth under our equitable growth strategy seems minimal. Table 2.6 projects the required increase of commercial bank exposure in constant dollars in the four countries as of the year 2000. The projections assume that the banks' share of all lending and the creditor country shares of bank lending to the four debtor countries remain unchanged from 1988. Under these assumptions, the banks collectively would have to lend an average of 15.8 billion U.S. dollars per annum just to the four countries, thus doubling their exposure to these countries between 1988 and 2000. Moreover, the U.S. share of the foreign bank debt of the four countries, which in 1988 was greater than the combined share of the banks from more financially robust Germany, Japan, and Switzerland, could well decline, in which case the required exposure of non-U.S. banks would have to rise well above 108 percent. For example, were the U.S. share to fall to 25 percent, the combined exposure of German, Japanese, and Swiss banks would have to rise by 180 percent to compensate. For prudential and geopolitical reasons, the probability that they would do this must be close to zero.

Writedown Approaches

Proposals to writedown the principal and/or interest on the Latin American debt vary widely in scope and degree.[5] We assess first the "Menu Approach," in which creditor banks and financial markets largely determine the size and extent of the writedowns. We then assess the more comprehensive proposal for an International Debt Facility, in which the creditor governments initiate and largely determine the writedowns.

The Menu Approach

The Menu Approach is the covering label given to a variety of market-based writedown arrangements that have emerged in an *ad hoc* fashion since 1985, reflecting the gradual disintegration of concerted lending by the creditor bank syndicates. As confidence in the IMF's contractive adjustment strategy dwindled, the less heavily exposed banks in the syndicates began breaking rank. By liquidating their Latin American paper at discounted prices, they could free themselves from the commitment to participate in new rounds of concerted lending. This, plus "window dressing" loan swaps between the large banks remaining in the syndicates, supplied an informal market for Latin American bank paper.

Under debt-equity swaps, the most active of the Menu programs, the buyers are mainly multinational firms with ongoing operations or prospective investment plans in the debtor countries that require injections of local currency. For these firms, the benefits from the swaps are transparent. Buying the loan paper at a deep discount and reselling it to the debt holder—usually the central bank—for local currency at a smaller discount in effect gives the multinational firm a preferential exchange rate for acquiring local currency. The benefits to the debtor are more problematic. It depends, in the first place, on the resale price to the debtor country of the loan paper. If it is 80 to 90 percent of face value, for example, the debt writedown is small and the benefit in foreign exchange saving is mainly short term. In present value terms it could be negative, since the mean expected profit rate on direct investment is generally much higher than the interest rate on the debt. Secondly, there is the "additionality" question. Do the swaps with their preferential exchange rates substantially augment foreign investment, or do they mainly subsidize investments that would have been made without the swaps? If the latter, the debt-equity swaps reduce rather than augment the inflow of foreign exchange from direct investment.[6]

The evidence, to date, on both these crucial matters is too scattered to allow definitive conclusions. As of 1988, debt-equity swaps involving the four debtor countries totaled merely $7.1 billion, a small fraction of the increment to the foreign debt of these countries since 1985 when the swap programs began. Chile has been most active in encouraging these swaps, whereas the other three have at various times suspended their swap programs because of perceived adverse effects. Even in the case of Chile, there is doubt whether Chile has gained from the swaps (see the discussion in the Ffrench-Davis and Edwards papers in this volume).

Another Menu option is debt-debt swaps. There are many versions of this option. Some countries, e.g. Argentina, have offered long maturity "exit bonds" in exchange for bank paper to creditor banks seeking to reduce their Argentine exposure and avoid participating in further rounds of concerted lending. The bond-for-paper swaps provide beneficial debt writedowns to the debtor countries, but their benefits to the creditor banks as compared to direct unloading of their loan paper in the secondary market is more problematic. With exit bonds, the banks are exchanging assets of doubtful creditworthiness in which the debtor carries the interest rate risk for doubtful assets that also shift the interest risk to the bank. Thus far, most banks anxious to exit from Latin American lending have preferred unloading their paper in secondary markets to exchanging it for exit bonds; the volume to date of exit bonds is miniscule.

A variant on the debt-debt swap option is the exchange of bank paper for zero coupon dollar-denominated bonds. The Mexican government and Morgan Guaranty initiated this scheme in 1988, but with disappointing results. The initial goal had been to swap $10 to $20 billion of bank debt for twenty-year zero coupon U.S. Treasury bonds. A positive payoff to Mexico depended on whether the present value of the difference between the expected interest rate on the bank paper and the lower implicit interest rate on the zero coupon bonds over the life of the bonds would exceed the front end dollar cost to Mexico of purchasing the bonds. In this case, the creditor banks showed virtually no interest in the swaps. The swap price was not attractive enough to cover the risk premium the banks wanted for assuming the interest rate risk that would result from swapping adjustable interest rate assets for fixed interest ones. A more favorable swap rate, on the other hand, would have reduced and could even have abolished Mexico's gain from the swap. Only $2 billion was exchanged under the program, with the coauthor Morgan Guaranty taking a major share.

Another of the Menu options is buybacks, in which the debtors are allowed to repurchase their bank debt in the secondary market, the debt writedown equaling the prevailing market discount on the debt. Since buybacks are ruled out by the cross-default clause of debt contracts, waivers are needed from the creditor banks. Thus far, Bolivia has been granted such dispensation on its bank debt of around $1 billion. This is small in the larger scheme of things, but a major gain for Bolivia, whose paper has been selling for less than ten cents on the dollar. Chile has also been recently granted buyback rights by its creditor banks, but for only a small fraction of its debt.[7] Apart from the reluctance of the creditor banks to grant waivers, the benefits to debtors of the buyback option are self-limiting. The debtors must accumulate sizeable foreign exchange reserves in order to achieve a significant writedown of the debt. They must also buy carefully and surreptitiously in the secondary market in order not to drive up the price of the debt. And they must anticipate that buying back their existing debt at a discount can further discourage banks from granting new loans.

In all, the Menu Approach, with its reliance on market forces, is not likely to provide more than marginal relief for a debt crisis that requires far more dramatic alleviation. Such large scale alleviation unavoidably requires more direct intervention by the creditor governments.

An International Debt Facility

There are many versions of the debt facility approach.[8] Here we examine the proposal recently put forth by James Robinson, President of American Express.[9] His proposal would establish a new Institute of International Debt and Development, possibly affiliated with the IMF or the World Bank. The Institute would take over the commercial bank loans to debtor countries and reimburse the banks with Institute securities. The interest and principal of the new securities would be below the face value of the existing bank debt, the discounts of the latter being linked to the secondary market discount on each of the participating debtor countries' paper. The swaps would be compulsory on the commercial banks for all of their loans to eligible participating debtors. Eligibility would require the debtor country to pursue an IMF type adjustment program with market liberalization, privatization, and all that, and stay au courant on its servicing at reduced terms of the debt acquired by the Institute. The Institute's receipts from debt servicing would in turn service the Institute's own securities. Those securities would, moreover, carry a residual G7 countries' guarantee. Backsliding debtors would be punished by loss of concessionary terms on their bank debt. New commercial bank loans to performing debtors would be encouraged by making the new loans senior to the old commercial debt.

Would such a writedown and new lending arrangement suffice to allow the four debtor countries to service reduced old debt and acquire enough new debt to sustain a 2 percent per capita consumption growth rate through the 1990s? Table 2.7, which reports the results of a simulation exercise, shows that an average 39 percent writedown of the debt of the four countries would have to be matched by an accumulation of over $86 billion of new debt over the 1990s to attain the growth target. The increase in required new external funding assumes that the Institute's conditionality requirement rules out our more inward directed growth

Table 2.7

A Writedown Scenario

		Millions of U.S. dollars			
	Debt writedown (%)	1988 debt	Debt after writedown	Required new finance	2000 debt
Argentina	36.0	60,542	38,937	34,234	73,171
Brazil	41.0	127,319	75,517	8,392	83,909
Chile	24.0	22,293	16,900	110	17,009
Mexico	43.0	104,325	59,809	43,676	103,485
Total	39.0	314,479	191,163	86,412	277,574

with equity strategy, which, as Table 2.5 shows, would require less external funding. The exercise is merely illustrative, since we have no foreknowledge of the percentage writedowns that would actually apply were the Robinson proposal to be adopted.

In any event, obtaining the required new financing through voluntary bank lending could be highly problematic, without strong impetus and support by the creditor governments. Moreover, other external conditions are essential for reconciling revived economic growth with debt servicing in the debtor countries. As indicated by the Felix-Caskey simulations, creditor country growth rates must also remain high, and their markets must stay open to exports from the debtors. The additional conditions, of course, further reduce the prospects for reconciliation, but they also reinforce the security argument for allowing the Latin American debtors to choose the more inward oriented growth with equity strategy. The choice would not merely be welfare superior, but would also lower the extreme dependence of growth in the debtor economies on a fragile set of favorable external conditions, such as characterizes the market liberalizing export-led growth strategy now being urged on the debtors.

Notes

The authors thank Professors Caskey and Felix for comments and suggestions on the two earlier versions of this paper, Mr. Hector Chavez of CIDE, who computed the simulations, and the Conference participants for their stimulating comments.

1. Julio López, "Evolución reciente del sector manufacturero mexicano," CIDE, México, mimeo, 1988.

2. The Argentine series are taken from *Fundación Latinoamericana Newsletters*, various issues.

3. ECLA is currently conducting studies of the extent of economic complementarity among Latin American countries.

4. Officials of the German Commerzbank suggested an approach along these lines for Latin America to one of the authors of this paper.

5. Jeffrey Sachs, "Nuevos Enfoques para la Crisis de la Deuda Latinoamericana," *El Trimestre Económico*, LVI no. 221 (Enero–Marzo 1989): 107–61.

6. For more detailed discussion of the "additionality" question with reference to Chile, see the Ffrench-Davis and Edwards papers in this volume.

7. See the Ffrench-Davis and Edwards papers in this volume for details.

8. The magazine, *International Economy*, publishes a summary table of these proposals in each issue.

9. J. Robinson, "The Institute of International Debt and Development," New York, mimeo, February 1988.

References

BIS (1988). *International Banking and Financial Market Development*, Basle 1988.

Christiano, L. J. "A Survey of Measures of Capacity Utilization." *Staff Papers* 28 no. 1 (March 1981): 144–198.

Cline, R. W. *International Debt and the Stability of the World Economy*, Institute for International Economics, 1983. *Policy Analyses in International Economics* 4.

Federal Reserve Bank of New York. *Recent Trends in Commercial Bank Profitability. A Staff Study*.

International Monetary Fund. *Survey*. 1988 (various issues).

Latinfinance. A Euromoney Publication. No. 4, February 1989.

Sachs, Jeffrey "Nuevos Enfoques para la Crisis de la Deuda Latinoamericana." *El Trimestre Económico*, Mexico. LVI, 221, Enero–Marzo 1989.

Tobin, J. *Essays in Economics, Volume 1, Macroeconomics*. Cambridge, Mass.: The MIT Press, 1987.

COMMENTS

Willy Van Ryckeghem

The paper by Julio López and Clemente Ruiz contrasts two alternative scenarios of growth and indebtedness for a representative group of Latin American economies in the next decade. They rightly dismiss a continuation of the contractive adjustment which characterized the 1980s and offer instead a growth with equity scenario for the 1990s, based on a cooperative solution to the debt crisis.

The rather depressing outcome of the eighties is attributed by the authors to IMF-inspired policies which reduced imports and investment in order to effectuate the net transfer of resources required to service the debt. This attribution may be unfair since it confuses the outcome of the strategy with its intent, which was to increase exports and domestic savings, and thus allow the indebted countries to grow their way out of the crisis. It might have proven productive to engage in some comparative research into the reasons why this strategy did not, in general, produce the intended result, especially on the savings side. The authors note that of the four countries that were analyzed, only Chile had a substantial decline in the consumption share of GDP during the 1980s, but they do not seem to attach any particular significance to this factor. Indeed, throughout the paper Chile is treated as conforming to the Latin American norm in terms of its adjustment process: falling per capita income, falling investment, falling imports, etc. This is because the authors present their statistical information as decade averages and thus lose essential information about the period which followed the regionwide recession of 1982–83. A more careful examination of the characteristics of the recovery process, which started in 1984, and of the policies associated with it provides more clues to differences in economic performance of the different Latin American economies than an analysis of decade averages. It reveals, e.g., that of the four countries analyzed, Chile was the only one whose investment rate recovered significantly from its 1983 low. This, combined with the increasing savings ratio noted, allowed the country to diversify its economic structure and

Willy Van Ryckeghem is Chief, Country Studies Division, Inter-American Development Bank.

to produce a trade surplus which covered an increasing part of its external debt obligations. The Chilean experience serves as a useful exception to the general pattern of contractive adjustment which has characterized the Latin American experience of the post-1982 period.

It also serves as a basis of comparison for the growth with equity strategy which the authors propose for the 1990s, and with which it shares the goals of economic growth, of job creation, and of trade surpluses to help service the external debt. The radical difference between both strategies resides in the means used to reach the goals. In the growth with equity strategy, the authors propose using existing capacity by restricting competing imports and by augmenting aggregate demand. This is precisely the approach which was used with catastrophic results in Peru since 1985, where after two and a half years of demand stimulation, the economy hit its capacity constraints, rapidly exhausted its foreign exchange reserves, and slid into hyperinflation. To assume, as the authors do, that such a strategy can translate *simultaneously* into import substitution and a more efficient use of capital, is wishful thinking and contrary to any country's experience of the last decades.

The growth with equity exercise attempted in this paper represents, therefore, little more than a sensitivity analysis of the baseline results in the Felix-Caskey model. It indicates that a simultaneous reduction in ICOR and the import coefficient of 10 percent would reduce the average annual external financing requirements corresponding to a given target growth rate from 50 to 80 percent.[1] It would have been interesting to conduct the sensitivity analysis separately for the reduction in ICOR and of the import coefficient to determine which is more important, and whether there is an interactive effect between the two parameters. In any event, the results presented in the paper reflect a rather impressive sensitivity to marginal changes in parameter values.

An important simulation result not noted by the authors is that under their GDP growth assumption of slightly less than 4 percent per annum,[2] interest payments on the external debt by the year 2000 would approximately equal net external borrowing. In other words, they have unwittingly identified the growth path under which the net resource transfer between Latin America and the rest of the world would tend to become zero. Even if the net external borrowing requirements of Latin America by the end of the next decade seem intimidating, it is useful to bear in mind that they would be matched by equally high interest payments.

In the final section of the paper such a scenario of growth with voluntary lending is dismissed because of likely constraints on the capacity (and willingness) to lend of the commercial banks in the industrialized countries.

As an alternative, a partial writedown approach is therefore explored. The results show that an average 39 percent writedown of the debt of the four countries would have to be matched by an accumulation of new debt to attain the predetermined GDP growth target, so that by the year 2000 the accumulated debt would rise to 88 percent of the 1988 debt. In addition, an examination of the simulation results shows that under the writedown scenario, interest payments on the reduced debt would again approach net external borrowing by the year 2000.

This result should not be surprising: it confirms that what constrains growth is the net transfer of resources, not the level of net external borrowing.[3] For a given target growth rate of GDP, we will therefore always converge to an identical net transfer of resources, *ceteris paribus*, as a percentage of GDP. The implication for a country's debt negotiating stance is that debt reduction should not be an objective per se, but a means to reduce the net transfer of resources.[4] This is not to say that debt reduction is not the preferable alternative, but that it still requires net external borrowing at a sufficient level to offset the interest payments on the reduced debt.

If, after a substantial debt reduction, net external borrowing were to fall short of the interest payments on the reduced debt, the lowered GDP growth rate might eventually lead to a higher debt/GDP ratio than that which would result from mere capitalization of the interest payments on the full amount of the debt.

Notes

1. In fact, the simulations are not strictly comparable, since the Felix-Caskey results are based on a given target growth rate in GDP, whereas the López-Ruiz results assume a given growth rate in consumption.

2. Specifically, 3.2 percent growth is assumed for Argentina, 3.9 percent for Brazil, 3.2 percent for Chile, and 4.2 percent for Mexico.

3. This result is easily derived from the following simple variant of the Harrod-Domar model. If investment $I = vY$ and domestic savings $s = sY$, the equilibrium condition:

$I-S = M-X = D-rD$, allows one to derive as the equilibrium growth rate, $g = s/v - (1/v)(rD-D)(1/Y)$ where $rD-D$ represents the net resource transfer, defined as the difference between interest payments, rD, and net external borrowing, D.

4. This seems to be the debt strategy of the present Mexican government, which is pursuing a combination of debt reduction and of new lending, which would reduce the net resource transfer from 6 percent of GDP to 2 percent of GDP.

PART II

POLITICAL ASPECTS OF THE CRISIS

3

Debt or Democracy?
The Political Impact of the
Debt Crisis in Latin America

Karen L. Remmer

In his provocative 1985 speech to the U.N. General Assembly, President Alan García of Peru bluntly defined the choices confronting Latin America: "It is either debt or democracy."[1] The same concern has been expressed over and over again in discussions of the debt crisis. A recent study of democratic legitimacy in Latin America concludes that "The newly emerging democracies in Latin America have arrived on the scene . . . at the worst possible moment. Their ability to legitimize themselves is limited by the reality of the economic crisis that, in many cases, was responsible in the first place for the withdrawal of the military and their subsequent coming to power."[2] Politicians and policy makers have taken up the same theme. According to Representative Stephen Solarz of New York, for example, "unless this debt crisis can be resolved, these nascent democracies in Latin America will be in great jeopardy because of the inability of their governments to meet the aspirations and expectations of their people."[3] In a similar vein, Senator Bill Bradley of New Jersey has warned, "For a country to keep paying past its means ultimately leaves only default or political upheaval as options."[4] Fears have even been expressed for the future of Mexico, whose political stability has long stood out in comparison with the rest of Latin America.[5]

The history of the region offers ample basis for such concerns. The magnitude of the current crisis rivals that of the Great Depression, which provoked political unrest throughout Latin America. Only two countries came through the 1929–34 period without a regime breakdown or irregular change in the head of state.[6] Moreover, in many instances these political crises represented crucial political watersheds. The overthrow of President Hipólito Irigoyen in Argentina termi-

---

Karen L. Remmer is Professor of Political Science, University of New Mexico, and Associate Editor, *Latin American Research Review.*

nated the longest period of liberal democracy in the nation's history to date, establishing the basis for five decades of military intervention and political instability. The depression era experience of El Salvador proved no less formative. The political opening of the 1920s ended abruptly in 1932 with a peasant uprising,[7] brutal repression, and the creation of an alliance between the upper class and the military that was to last into the 1980s. In other cases the principal political legacy of the period was long-term dictatorship. The regimes of Batista in Cuba, Trujillo in the Dominican Republic, Ubico in Guatemala, and Vargas in Brazil all grew out of the events of the early 1930s. Chile was the only country in which the outbreak of economic crisis undermined authoritarianism and worked in favor of the consolidation of democratic institutions.

More recent political events further underline possible tensions between economic crisis and democratic stability. The breakdown of democracy in the most socioeconomically advanced countries of the region during the 1960s and the 1970s took place against a background of accelerating inflation, low growth, and acute balance-of-payments problems. The incapacity of elected governments to cope with these difficulties accentuated political conflicts, setting the stage for the establishment of alliances between the military and privileged social groups. The process culminated in the installation of highly repressive military regimes, the notorious BAs (bureaucratic-authoritarian regimes).[8] Even Chile and Uruguay, which ranked among the oldest democracies in the world in the early 1970s, succumbed to these trends.

The puzzle confronting regional observers in the late 1980s is the failure of the international debt crisis to provoke a similar pattern of regime instability and democratic breakdown. Notwithstanding the fears of academics, Latin American political leaders, and U.S. policy makers, not one Latin American democracy collapsed between 1982 and 1988 in response to the strains of the regional economic crisis. Indeed, far from undermining democracy in Latin America, the debt problem accelerated the continent-wide shift away from authoritarianism. That shift began prior to the outbreak of the Mexican financial crisis of August 1982 with transitions to liberal democracy in Ecuador, Peru, and Honduras and continued through the mid-1980s, leading to the breakdown of authoritarianism in Argentina, Bolivia, Brazil, Uruguay, Guatemala, and El Salvador. By late 1988, less than 10 percent of the region's population was living under military rule. Even in Central America, where the process of democratization was hesitant, incomplete, and primarily a product of external political pressures, elections and civilian governance became the norm rather than the exception.

These democratic achievements were partially offset by continuing authoritarian rule in other countries, but the inauguration of a process of regime transition in Chile during 1988 indicated that democratization was continuing in spite of the debt crisis. By the 1988 meeting of the Latin American Studies Association, political scientists had even begun talking seriously about prospects for democracy in Paraguay, a country with no prior history of competitive rule.[9] In short, not only have pessimistic predictions about the political effects of the debt crisis failed to materialize, but the political panorama of the region has continued to shift away from authoritarianism in favor of democracy. The democratization wave of the 1980s has proved to be the longest and deepest in the history of Latin America to date.

What explains the failure of Latin American democracies to succumb to the stresses provoked by the debt crisis? Why has the process of democratization continued and even gained momentum in the face of the region's crippling external financial obligations? Are Latin American democracies more resilient than in the past, or have the political costs of plummeting living standards yet to be fully felt? The answers to these questions are not only important to policy makers concerned with the debt crisis; they are central to the development of a better theoretical understanding of the relationship between economics and politics.

Theoretical Perspectives

The pervasive pessimism about the capacity of democratic regimes to weather the debt crisis has been largely unshaken by the actual course of political events in Latin America. The assumption on the part of many observers is that the new democratic regimes that emerged in the region between the late 1970s and the mid-1980s enjoyed a breathing space during which they could plausibly shift the blame for economic difficulties not only to exogenous forces but to their authoritarian predecessors. The transition to democracy itself has also been seen as a safety valve, which in a sense permitted "political goods" to compensate for declining per capita incomes.[10] With time, however, it is expected these advantages will wane, subjecting democracies to the full political costs of high unemployment, acute shortages of foreign exchange, low investment, and restricted growth. The sustainability of competitive rule under such conditions is regarded as extremely doubtful. For most observers, the problem is less a matter of the specific characteristics of the democracies in question, such as their age or party system structure, than of weaknesses that are inherent to democratic governance.

At the simplest level, the vulnerability of Latin American democracies to breakdown is ascribed to the impact of economic setbacks on popular support for democratic institutions. The operative assumption here is that the installation and collapse of democracy is primarily a function of public opinion at the mass level. When democracy enjoys widespread popular support, it survives; when it does not, it collapses. The notion is one that is deeply imbedded in the political science literature on democracy dating back at least as far as Seymour Martin Lipset's *Political Man*,[11] and it accounts for much of the apprehension that has been expressed about the future of Latin American democracy. A recent article analyzing the political stability of Costa Rican democracy in the face of economic decline represents a key example. Finding that support for democratic rule remained strong among the Costa Rican public despite a crisis of government effectiveness, the authors conclude: "Democratic political systems can remain stable when undergoing crises of effectiveness as long as they enter those crises with the legitimacy of the system firmly established."[12] The implications for new democracies confronting a financial crisis are obviously anything but positive.

A second perspective specifically links the vulnerability of Latin American democracy to questions of economic policy formation. Following a line of analysis developed in Thomas E. Skidmore's seminal article on economic stabilization,[13] Latin American democracies are regarded as singularly incapable of managing economic crises through the adoption of appropriate programs of stabilization and adjustment. The reason has to do with the basic nature of democracy, which supposedly creates an agonizing dilemma for elected leaders attempting to cope with intractable balance of payments difficulties. To retain access to international financial markets, such leaders must impose programs of economic adjustment and stabilization; but those programs run up against popular resistance and undercut the electoral support upon which leadership positions depend. Belt-tightening is never politically palatable, but its costs are seen as particularly high when it is imposed from the outside. As Joan M. Nelson has suggested,[14] the only alternative may be chaotic adjustment, with scarcities, inflation, and atrophied output, but voters do not necessarily evaluate the costs of adjustment programs against counterfactual outcomes, particularly when, as in the case of the current debt crisis, they are coupled with the visible exercise of power by foreign banks and lending agencies and the net transfer of resources out of the country. Under such conditions, democratic leaders may be plausibly portrayed as confronting a choice between certain political death or probable economic suicide. The calculus is seen as one that pushes democracies in the direction of populist temptation and economic disaster, making their collapse in the face of the debt crisis appear all but inevitable. In essence, economic rationality clashes with political acceptability. The recent demonstration of the so-called "Cárdenas effect," which refers to the rise of political leaders advocating radical solutions to the debt problem, is consistent with this line of analysis.

A third and partially overlapping perspective on Latin American democracy reinforces the scenario pointing toward political collapse. Democracy in the hemisphere is seen as a cyclical phenomenon, which rises and falls in response to "the underlying tension between the imperative to accumulate capital for economic development and the need to build legitimacy to sustain political stability."[15] Governments that emphasize the former fail to build a base of political support by meeting demands for increased consumption, while those that concentrate upon the problem of legitimacy flounder on the shoals of entrenched elite resistance, democratic stalemate, and economic failure. The result is a populist/antipopulist policy cycle that drives Latin American politics through alternating waves of democracy and authoritarianism.[16] From this perspective, the days of recently established democracies are also numbered. Not only is their stability threatened by long-standing problems of the region's political economy, but their room for maneuver is narrower than at any point in time over the last fifty years.

Taken together, these three perspectives on Latin American democracy leave little room for optimism regarding the capacity of the region to avoid a resurgence of authoritarianism. Indeed, the complementarity of the arguments concerning the fragility of democracy in the face of economic decline and the consistency with which they have been articulated over the course of more than two decades make the survival of democratic institutions in Latin America in the 1980s begin to look positively miraculous. The same is true of the relative moderation with which regional leaders outside of Peru have negotiated their debt problems. After six years the "honeymoon period" enjoyed by new regimes has presumably been exhausted, allowing the pressures on democratic leaders to have built up to the point of political collapse. That symptoms of this long-heralded collapse still remain elusive suggests that a number of assumptions about the relationship between politics and economics in Latin America warrant reexamination. Prevailing conceptions about democracy in the region fail to provide an adequate basis for understanding the actual course of political events since 1982, because they grossly exaggerate the tension between democracy and economic crisis.

Democracy and Mass Support

In the first place, while it is evident that massive economic difficulties limit the capacity of governments to curry and maintain a base of support, the rise and fall of Latin American democracy cannot be adequately understood in terms of mass opinion. Quite apart from the ambiguous nature of the causal arrows that may be drawn between political culture and forms of governance, the argument that the survival of democracy depends principally upon the political support of popular sector elements flies directly in the face of empirical evidence, not to mention almost all major theoretical advances in the analysis of Latin American authoritarianism. The emergence and breakdown of democracy in the region in recent decades has corresponded less to mass opinion than to the activities of propertied elites and their international allies. To link the installation of a repressive military regime in a country such as Chile, for example, to a lack of popular support for democracy is not merely to blame the victims of historical events for their occurrence; it is to support a line of analysis that is blatantly at odds with factual information about the involvement of the United States in the conspiracy to overthrow Chilean democracy, as well as with data on Chilean public opinion. In 1973 only 25 percent of the Chilean public supported a military coup,[17] and given the orientation of the country's largest political party, it may be supposed that the majority of those coup supporters were expressing their views about the

incumbents of the political system rather than support for military over democratic rule per se.

To attribute the perpetuation of military rule to the average Chilean's lack
of enthusiasm for democracy would be equally absurd. Opinion polls con-
ducted under authoritarian rule have consistently shown the overwhelming
majority of citizens favoring the restoration of democratic rule.[18] These attitudes are not irrelevant to the transition process, because they shape the
political calculus of military and opposition leaders. Mass attitudes may also
condition opportunities for the consolidation, as distinct from the installation,
of democratic rule. But the contrasts that emerged between authoritarian
Chile and democratic Argentina or Peru in the 1980s simply cannot be explained in terms of political culture, any more than political culture can
explain the dynamics of Chilean politics. Widespread support for democracy
neither guarantees the installation of competitive rule nor its survival in the
face of concerted elite or foreign resistance. The error is to suppose that
regimes that function on the basis of public opinion also rise and fall on that
basis. Electorates oust incumbents, not regimes.

Far more relevant to understanding the installation and collapse of Latin
American democracy is the attitude of the region's dominant power. The more
the United States has been involved in the hemisphere, pressuring for elections in
an attempt to rally local allies against the dangers of leftist movements, the
greater the probability of democracy. The Mexican, Cuban, and Nicaraguan
revolutions all generated intense external support for the observation of democratic formalities, even in political contexts as singularly unpromising as Nicaragua in the 1920s and Guatemala in the 1980s. The extent and duration of the
current wave of democracy in the region can only be understood on such a basis,
which is to say that the process of democratization has depended and will continue to depend, at least in part, on United States policy. To the extent that the
banner of anticommunism remains raised in defense of competitive institutions
rather than to support military takeovers, as in Guatemala in 1954, Brazil in
1964, or Chile in 1973, the outlook for Latin American democracy in the 1980s
and 1990s is far more positive than in the past.

Also of fundamental importance for the survival of democracy are the attitudes of business leaders and the military. Both played key roles in the collapse
of Latin American democracy in the past, and their support for democratic institutions in the present is critical for understanding the capacity of democracies to
withstand the debt crisis. Outside of countries confronting major guerrilla challenges, no Latin American military establishment is likely to seize power under
present conditions. Several are still recuperating from the institutional damage
resulting from recent episodes of authoritarian rule; none appears anxious to
assume responsibility for economic management in the face of current difficulties. The return to civilian rule in countries such as Uruguay and Brazil was
accelerated precisely to avoid such responsibility. From this perspective, the debt

crisis may be seen as an obstacle to the breakdown of democracy rather than as a provocation.

The same is true with respect to the attitude of business elites. Although the situation varies from country to country, economic crisis has strengthened the bargaining position of business, leading to the unusual spectacle of the Mexican government formally negotiating with non-PRI private-sector organizations, making major concessions to foreign firms, and denationalizing state enterprises. The same heightened emphasis upon the creation of a more favorable investment environment prevails throughout most of the region, limiting the possibilities of a relapse into authoritarianism. The most notable exceptions to this generalization are El Salvador and Peru—countries that are also facing major guerrilla challenges and whose democratic regimes are thus in a doubly vulnerable position.

Democracy and Economic Management

Pessimism about the capacity of democracies to manage economic crises is equally ill-founded. Democracies, particularly new ones, not only enjoy some advantages over authoritarian regimes in managing economic difficulties, but their proclivity for breakdown in the face of painful economic realities has been grossly exaggerated. The experience of Latin American countries that administered IMF-sponsored stabilization programs under both democratic and authoritarian regime auspices between 1954 and 1984 indicates that (a) democracies are just as likely as authoritarian regimes to introduce politically painful stabilization programs; (b) stabilization programs have not been associated with high rates of regime breakdown, nor have the political risks of stabilization programs proved any higher for democracy than authoritarianism; (c) democracies have implemented stabilization programs just as successfully, if not more successfully, than authoritarian regimes; and (d) regime change enhances the prospects for effective economic stabilization, particularly under democratic auspices.[19] Based on this evidence, the choice confronting Latin America cannot be described as one of debt or democracy. Democracy is as likely to contribute to the resolution of the ongoing economic crisis as authoritarianism. Indeed, since past experience suggests that new democratic governments are unusually successful in implementing austerity programs, debt and democracy in Latin America can plausibly be seen as complementary rather than contradictory.

Broader claims about the tension between successful economic management and democratic governance in Latin America, which supposedly explain the cyclical alternation of democracy and authoritarianism in the hemisphere, also fail to stand up to empirical evidence. For every military success story of the Brazilian variety, it is possible to cite one or more instances of economic incompetence and failure. The disastrous policy errors committed by Southern Cone military regimes immediately before the outbreak of the debt crisis represent cases in point. Evidence drawn from all cases of military rule since the mid-1950s that allow for comparisons with prior or successor competitive regimes is equally telling. Out of a total of twenty-one comparisons of economic growth rates, military regimes outperformed their nonauthoritarian predecessors or successors only eleven times. Ten of the comparisons favored democratic regimes. In other words, the odds that a military regime will accelerate economic growth more rapidly than a competitive one appear to be only fifty-fifty. The results are the same if military and democratic regimes are compared as a group, rather than on a country-by-country basis. There is no statistically significant evidence that military regimes outperform competitive regimes in Latin America either in accelerating economic growth or containing inflation.[20]

To be sure, regime breakdowns in the Latin American region have been linked with deteriorating economic conditions; but that linkage is not peculiar to the breakdown of democracy nor is its nature unambiguous. Economic difficulties cause political crises, but they also reflect and reinforce them. The acute economic crisis provoked by the death of Juan Perón in Argentina during the 1970s is a case in point.[21] Available evidence also suggests that economic crisis has been neither a necessary nor sufficient condition for regime breakdown in Latin America. Transitions from democracy to authoritarianism have occurred under relatively favorable sets of economic conditions, as in Ecuador in 1972. Likewise, severe economic difficulties have not necessarily produced political collapse.

In this connection it should be emphasized that not only has the debt crisis yet to bring down a democratic regime in Latin America; not one of the eleven regime transitions that have occurred in the region over the course of the past decade can be attributed principally to economic difficulties. Five of the transitions were completed before the onset of the crisis (Nicaragua, Honduras, Peru, Ecuador, and Bolivia). Another three were already under way (El Salvador, Uruguay, and Brazil), although economic setbacks hastened the process of transition in two of these. In the remaining cases external political pressures and events, rather than economic disequilibrium, provoked regime breakdown (Argentina, Guatemala, and Haiti). The key point is that economic crises are not automatically translated into political crises. Much depends upon perceptions of the problems in question and expectations regarding their resolution.

Democracy and the Accumulation/Legitimation Cycle

The notion that Latin American democracy represents a purely cyclical phenomenon driven by contradictions between economic and political rationality is no less problematic than the popular support or economic management approaches. The difficulty is that such a perspective implies that the democracies of today share the same fragilities as their predecessors. The assumption is misleading on two distinct grounds. First, the majority of democracies in Latin America in the past can only be described as oligarchical or exclusionary democracies.[22] Far

Table 3.1

Ideological Identification of Chileans (in percent)

	1958	1961	1964	1970	1973	1986
Right	31.4	23.8	17.4	26.6	21.9	16.6
Center	17.8	28.2	29.0	24.2	26.8	41.2
Left	24.5	26.5	32.0	26.0	42.9	14.2
No response	26.3	21.5	21.6	23.2	8.4	28.0
Total	100.0	100.0	100.0	100.0	100.0	100.0

Source: Carlos Huneeus, *Los chilenos y la política*, p. 163.

from incorporating the majority of citizens into the political process, they functioned on the basis of limited participation and often limited competition. The recent wave of democratization has given rise to a very different form of democratic rule. For the first time in history, the overwhelming majority of competitive regimes in the region are inclusionary democracies that allow for the participation of both women and illiterates and are based upon the vote of more than 30 percent of the population. Their strengths and weaknesses are correspondingly different from those of competitive regimes in the past. Whereas the latter fell victim to socioeconomic modernization which undermines the viability of oligarchical rule by promoting resistance from below, threats to inclusionary democracy are more likely to stem from socioeconomic inequality and resistance from above.

Latin American democracy in the 1980s is also characterized by a far greater degree of pragmatism and ideological moderation than in the past. Particularly in Argentina, Uruguay, and Chile, the recent experience of exclusionary military rule left a political imprint that is evident in the political dialogue of the left, patterns of electoral outcomes, and public opinion surveys. The shift in the alignment of political forces is particularly impressive in the case of Chile, which had the most ideologically polarized party system in the Southern Cone prior to 1973. As indicated by Table 3.1, military rule has considerably strengthened the political center. Although the authoritarian political context in which recent Chilean opinion surveys have been taken probably biases the data in favor of conservative responses, the tendency toward moderation is evident at both ends of the political spectrum. Electoral outcomes in Uruguay have evinced a similar tendency.[23]

Not all countries, however, experienced the same highly repressive and conservative form of militarism in the 1970s. The political dynamic is consequently rather different in a polity such as Peru, where the most recent episode of military rule was inclusionary and had anything but a sobering and moderating effect on political life. In direct contrast to the Southern Cone, the Peruvian left emerged from military rule in an invigorated condition, creating strong incentives for populist policies and an environment altogether less conducive to pragmatic politics. The more established democracies (Colombia, Costa Rica, the Dominican Republic, and Venezuela) also have not experienced the trauma of exclusionary military rule.

These variations in the recent political experience of Latin American democracies in themselves point to the limitations of a cyclical version of political events and suggest that the political evolution of the region will not conform uniformly to either a highly pessimistic or optimistic scenario. The picture is far more complex and differentiated and cannot be adequately discussed in terms of the dichotomy drawn between debt and democracy.

The Variable Impact of Economic Crisis

Three sets of factors have conditioned the political impact of the debt crisis in Latin America. These are the scope of the economic problems presented by the crisis, the international political context, and the political dynamic established by prior political events.

To begin with the first of these sets of factors, Latin American countries entered the crisis in rather different situations, and their capacity to adapt to it has varied with factors such as the nature of export production. From the beginning, countries such as Bolivia and Nicaragua confronted unusually severe problems, and, as suggested by Table 3.2, their capacity to service their debt remains limited. The magnitude of the economic difficulties that characterize individual countries today, however, also reflects the policy choices made by Latin American governments after 1982. While some were quick to respond to the crisis, others, especially the governments of large countries with stronger international bargaining positions, postponed making major adjustments. Mexico, which managed to compile a government deficit equivalent to more than 15 percent of GDP in both 1986 and 1987, is a case in point.[24] Another key example is Peru, whose current economic plight reflects the García government's decision to pursue expansionary policies while at the same time limiting service payments on the foreign debt.

Objective economic realities, however, merely provide a starting point for understanding the variable political impact of the debt crisis. In Central America its effects have been swamped by the regional political crisis, with its attendant high level of United States intervention. Particularly important in this regard are the massive infusions of United States aid that have insulated countries such as Costa Rica from feeling the full effects of their debt burdens. International position may also prove relevant for understanding the political effects of the crisis in

Table 3.2

Principal Debt Ratios, 1986

	Total debt/exports	Debt service/exports[a]	Total debt/GNP
Argentina	533.9	50.4	65.8
Bolivia	676.7	23.6	118.8
Brazil	437.5	33.2	41.0
Chile	394.5	30.8	138.8
Colombia	225.0	27.6	46.8
Costa Rica	310.2	26.3	118.7
Dominican Republic	232.1	20.6	66.4
Ecuador	342.1	32.3	83.5
El Salvador	166.4	18.0	43.7
Guatemala	215.6	23.3	35.7
Haiti	227.6	6.1	32.7
Honduras	278.2	18.5	84.0
Mexico	428.1	36.8	83.8
Nicaragua	2,576.9	13.0	236.3
Panama	77.9	7.6	99.9
Paraguay	190.5	19.2	53.8
Peru	450.4	14.4	62.4
Uruguay	236.8	20.9	63.4
Venezuela	312.2	28.5	70.8

Source: World Bank, *World Debt Tables*, 1987–88.
[a] Public and publicly guaranteed debt.

Mexico, not only because of United States sensitivity to its economic plight but also because of the safety valve presented by immigration to the United States.

Third, and most important outside of Central America, the political consequences of the economic crisis have varied with the political dynamic established by prior events and political choices. The growing shakiness of Mexico's one-party system, for example, is a product of a political dynamic that stretches back to the late 1960s, as is the division within the government over the management of the economy. Books with titles such as *Mexico in Crisis*[25] began appearing in the 1970s, rather than the 1980s. Not even the economics of the current situation can be understood adequately in terms of the debt problem, since they reflect policy choices made by the administrations of Echeverría and López Portillo between 1970 and 1982. The debt crisis unquestionably has narrowed the parameters within which Mexican policy makers must act and restricted their capacity to maintain support for a political infrastructure heavily dependent upon clientelism; but the growing opposition challenge to the system, the enhanced power of technocrats within the regime, and other similar features of the current situation were established well beforehand.

Indeed, as one looks around the region it is difficult to identify many major political trends, apart from the loss of support for incumbent governments, that can be attributed principally to the impact of the debt crisis. The guerrilla challenges confronting Peru, Guatemala, El Salvador, and Colombia may have been reinforced by the current economic crisis, but they can hardly be ascribed to it. Arguably, the greatest growth in violence has occurred in Colombia where the external debt situation looks comparatively comfortable by regional standards. Other forms of political instability also seem tenuously, if not inversely, related to the depth of the crisis. The only successful coup that has occurred since 1982 took place in Haiti, whose debt burden ranks among the lowest of the region.

Attributing other prominent political trends to the crisis is equally problematic, and not merely because of the inherently controversial nature of counterfactual lines of argument. The populist tendencies of Aprista leadership in Peru, the restiveness of the military in Guatemala, the hardening of the Nicaraguan revolution, the transition to democracy in Brazil, labor unrest in Bolivia, Panamanian nationalism, narco-trafficking in Colombia, Stroessner's hold on the Paraguayan presidency, or the fragility of Christian Democratic governance in El Salvador all predated the outbreak of the debt crisis. Not even the rising strength of the Chilean opposition movement can be attributed unequivocally to the burden of external debt. Obstacles to the perpetuation of the Pinochet regime through a plebiscite formula originated with the fixed exchange rate policy of the late 1970s and early 1980s which produced financial collapse, the breakdown of the ruling coalition, and the related mobilization of the opposition. As in other cases, the debt burden is politically significant chiefly because it reinforced this preexisting political dynamic and narrowed the parameters of political choice.

Looking beyond the more spectacular political developments in the region, however, the debt crisis does provide a basis for understanding two critical but largely unheralded changes. In most of the region, it has strengthened the hand of orthodox policy advisers—a trend that recently has become partially manifest even in the case of Peru.[26] The results have varied considerably, enhancing the level of conflict and policy stalemate in countries such as Mexico and Brazil, where politics revolve around patronage, but restoring the cohesion of government economic teams in others, such as Chile. As indicated above, this change has been coupled with increased business sector influence in much of the region. For inclusionary regimes, which are threatened chiefly by the opposition of privileged groups and conservative forces, these two sets of changes have proved politically stabilizing. A principle weakness of inclusionary rule in the region in the past has been the lack of communication and accommodation between the government and the private sector. Where the relationship remains hostile, as in El Salvador and Peru, the prospects for democratic survival look anything but bright.

Elsewhere the key question is the capacity of political leaders to retain the loyalty of business interests while challenging international economic rules. Contrary to cyclical interpretations of Latin American democracy, the problem is not that political feasibility and economic rationality are on a collision course. The reality is that after six years the incentives to play by existing rules have diminished significantly. The region's debt burden has not declined, the outflow of capital has yet to be reversed by new investment or lending, and protectionism in the United States and Western Europe has gained momentum. Under these conditions, the search for new solutions has become not merely politically but economically rational.

Lessons of the Debt Crisis

The principal lesson to be drawn from the experience of the past six years is the relative resilience to economic crises of established political institutions, processes, and political dynamics in Latin America. Contrary to the assumptions of most observers, the political face of the continent has not been transformed by the collapse of democraci: ˙ or growing political extremism since 1982. Serious economic instability simply has not been converted into political instability. The principle reason is that socioeconomic modernization and diversification have increased the organizational breadth, density, and complexity of political life since the 1930s, enhancing its relative autonomy and protecting it from feeling the full force of financial calamity. Hence, whereas nearly every government on the continent collapsed in the face of the Great Depression, the debt crisis does not represent a comparable political watershed. Incumbents have suffered, such as Raul Alfonsín, but not one regime change, nor any other significant shift in political dynamics, can be attributed principally to the region's financial plight. Presumably, the political fabric is not infinitely elastic or malleable; nevertheless, it has proved surprisingly durable, confounding political predictions and exposing major weaknesses in our understanding of the relationship between politics and economics.

Of particular significance is the failure of the debt crisis to reverse the wave of democratization that began in the region in 1979. Not only did all established democracies weather the six years of austerity and economic uncertainty that followed the crisis, but new democracies continued to emerge. These trends underline the limitations of theoretical perspectives that stress the incapacity of democratic institutions to withstand or manage economic crises. The dire predictions that have been drawn from such perspectives may be designed to enhance the vitality of Latin American democracy by altering the manner in which the debt crisis is managed, but they also reinforce dangerous myths that undermine democratic institutions and buttress authoritarianism. Rather than hinge arguments which favor some form of debt relief or policy change around democratic fragility or incompetence, the debt issue should be addressed squarely in terms of economic realities which include sharply restricted standards of living in Latin America and economic uncertainty for the hemisphere as a whole.

Notes

1. As quoted in Christine A. Bogdanowicz-Bindert, "World Debt: The United States Reconsiders," in Congressional Research Service, Library of Congress, *Economic Development in Latin America and the Debt Problem: Selected Essays Prepared for the Use of the Subcommittee on Economic Growth, Trade, and Taxes of the Joint Economic Committee, Congress of the United States* (Washington, D.C.: United States Government Printing Office, 29 October 1987), p. 47.

2. Mitchell A. Seligson and Edward N. Muller, "Democratic Stability and Economic Crisis: Costa Rica, 1978–1983," *International Studies Quarterly*, 31 (1987): 323. Similarly, Pedro-Pablo Kuczynski has warned: "While increasing political maturity has greatly reduced the odds of a return to military rule in Argentina and Brazil, past history may well repeat itself in some countries if the economic strains of recent years do not ease significantly." *Latin American Debt* (Baltimore: Johns Hopkins, 1988), p. 146. These concerns have been echoed in the press. See, in particular, "Third World Debt Won't Wait," *New York Times*, 1 Oct. 1988, p. 4. On the tension between democracy and economic austerity, see also Rosemary Thorp and Laurence Whitehead, "Introduction," in *Inflation and Stabilisation in Latin America* ed. Rosemary Thorp and Laurence Whitehead (New York: Holmes & Meier, 1979), pp. 11, 18; Robert R. Kaufman, "Democratic and Authoritarian Responses to the Debt Issue: Argentina, Brazil, and Mexico," *International Organization*, 39 (Summer 1985): 473–503; Riordan Roett, "The Foreign Debt Crisis and the Process of Re-democratization in Latin America," in *A Dance along the Precipice: The Political and Economic Dimensions of the International Debt Problem*, ed. William N. Eskridge, Jr. (Lexington: Lexington Books, 1985), pp. 207–230; Chris C. Carvounis, *The Foreign Debt/National Development Conflict: External Adjustment and Internal Disorder in the Developing Countries* (New York: Quorun Books, 1986) pp. 181–197; James M. Malloy, "The Politics of Transition in Latin America," in *Authoritarians and Democrats: Regime Transition in Latin America*, ed. James M. Malloy and Mitchell A. Seligson (Pittsburgh: University of Pittsburgh Press, 1987), p. 249; Benjamin Cohen, "High Finance, High Politics," in *Uncertain Future: Commercial Banks and the Third World*, ed. Richard E. Feinberg and Valeriana Kallab, *United States Third World Policy Perspectives*, No. 2 (New Brunswick: Transaction Books, 1984), p. 122; Albert Fishlow, "Four Feasible Ways to Ameliorate the Debt Burden," in *Latin America's Debt Crisis: Adjusting to the Past or Planning for the Future?* ed. Robert A. Pastor (Boulder: Lynne Rienner, 1987), p.111; Inter-American Dialogue, *The Americas in 1988: A Time for Choices* (Lanham, Md.: University Press of America, 1988), pp. 21–39; Rose J. Spalding, "The Political Implications of Austerity," in *Rekindling Development: Multinational Firms and World Debt*, ed. Lee A. Tavis (Notre Dame: University of Notre Dame Press, 1988), pp. 59–60.

3. U.S. Congress House Committee on Foreign Affairs, *Global Debt Crisis*, 99th Congress, 2d. session, June 18, July 30, 1986, p. 76. See also *New York Times*, 16 February 1984, I, p. 27.

4. *Global Debt Crisis*, p. 59. See also the prepared statement of Rep. Don Bonker, the Chairman of the House Subcommittee on International Political Economy and Trade (ibid., p. 57); Jimmy Carter and Howard Baker, "Latin America's Debt and United States Interests," in *Latin America's Debt Crisis*, ed. Pastor, p. 2.

5. In his 1986 prepared statement for the House Committee on Foreign Affairs, Bruce Bagley argued that Mexico was likely to remain politically stable, but that "the additional stresses generated by prolonged economic austerity over the 1980s could conceivably provoke a full-blown legitimacy crisis and open the way for progressive militarization of the Mexican political system." *Global Debt Crisis*, p. 138.

6. Those countries were Costa Rica, which suspended civil guarantees in early 1932 but managed to weather the crisis without resort to military rule, and Colombia, where there was a shift in party control but not of regime.

7. On the events of this period see Thomas P. Anderson, *Matanza: El Salvador's Communist Revolt of 1932* (Lincoln, Nebr.: University of Nebraska Press, 1971).

8. For overviews of these developments that emphasize the economic roots of authoritarianism, see *The New Authoritarianism in Latin America*, ed. David Collier (Princeton: Princeton University Press, 1979); Guillermo O'Donnell, *Modernization and Bureaucratic Authoritarianism: Studies in South American Politics* (Berkeley, Calif.: Institute of International Studies, University of California, 1973); idem, "Reflections on the Patterns of Change in the Bureaucratic-Authoritarian State," *Latin American Research Review*, 13 no. 1 (1978): 3–38.

9. See, in particular, Diego Abente, "Post-Stronismo and the Prospects for Democracy in Paraguay," paper presented at the XIV International Congress of the Latin American Studies Association, New Orleans, March, 1988.

10. Kuczynski, *Latin American Debt*, p. 147. See also Malloy, "The Politics of Transition," p. 255.

11. *Political Man: The Social Bases of Politics* (Garden City, N.Y.: Doubleday, 1959).

12. Seligson and Muller, "Democratic Stability and Economic Crisis," p. 322.

13. Thomas E. Skidmore, "The Politics of Economic Stabilization in Postwar Latin America," in *Authoritarianism and Corporatism in Latin America*, ed. James M. Malloy (Pittsburgh: University of Pittsburgh Press, 1977), pp. 14–190.

14. Joan M. Nelson, "The Politics of Stabilization," in *Adjustment Crisis in the Third World*, ed. Richard E. Feinberg and Valeriana Kallab (New Brunswick: Transaction Books, 1984), p. 99.

15. Malloy, "The Politics of Transition," p. 239.

16. For an explicit presentation of this interpretation, see ibid., pp. 239–241.

17. Carlos Huneeus, *Cambios en la opinion pública: una aproximación al estudio de la cultura política de Chile* (Santiago: Centro de Estudios de la Realidad Contemporánea, 1986), p. 66.

18. Centro de Estudios de la Realidad Contemporánea, *Informe preliminar sobre primera encuesta nacional* (Santiago: CERC, 1988), p. 9. Even the right-wing think tank, the Centro de Estudios Públicos, failed to uncover much support for authoritarianism. Its poll of December 1986–January 1987 showed that 67.3 percent of the Santiago sample preferred democracy over the continuation of authoritarian rule. *Estudio social y de opinión pública en la población de Santiago* (Santiago: CEP, 1987), p. 140. See also FLACSO, *Opinión pública y cultura política* (Santiago: FLACSO, 1987).

19. Karen L. Remmer, "The Politics of Economic Stabilization: IMF Standby Programs in Latin America, 1954–1984," *Comparative Politics* (October 1986): 1–24. It may be noted that these findings are consistent with other recent studies of IMF stabilization programs. See, in particular, Stephan Haggard, "The Politics of Adjustment: Lessons from the IMF's Extended Fund Facility," *The Politics of International Debt*, ed. Miles Kahler (Ithaca: Cornell University Press, 1986), pp. 157–186.

20. Karen L. Remmer, "Military Rule: State Institutions and Political Outcomes in Latin America," unpublished manuscript, pp. 93–94. See also idem, "Evaluating the Policy Impact of Military Regimes in Latin America," *Latin American Research Review*, XIII no. 2 (1978): 39–55.

21. See Guido Di Tella, *Perón-Perón, 1973–1976* (Buenos Aires: Sudamericana, 1983); Gary W. Wynia, *Argentina in the Postwar Era: Politics and Economic Policy Making in a Divided Society* (Albuquerque: University of New Mexico Press, 1978); Liliana De Riz, *Retorno y derrumbe: el último gobierno peronista* (Mexico City: Folios Ediciones, 1981).

22. See Karen L. Remmer, "Exclusionary Democracy," *Studies in Comparative International Development* XX (Winter 1985–86): 64–85.

23. Writing about the Uruguayan election of 1984, Juan Rial has commented: "The 1984 vote was a vote for moderation, pacification, and democracy. . . . Many of those who in 1973 had an extreme Left position supporting different types of radical actions now defended moderate positions. Many who had espoused an extreme Right view abandoned it for a centrist one. Very few dared to be marked by the stigma of defending the military regime." "Political Parties and Elections in the Process of Transition in Uruguay," in *Comparing New Democracies: Transition and Consolidation in Mediterranean Europe and the Southern Cone*, ed. Enrique A. Baloyra (Boulder: Westview Press, 1987), p. 258. See also Juan Rial, "The Uruguayan Elections of 1984: A Triumph of the Center," in *Elections and Democratization in Latin America*, ed. Paul W. Drake and Eduardo Silva (San Diego: University of California, 1986), pp. 245–271; Charles G. Gillespie, "Uruguay's Transition from Collegial Military-Technocratic Rule," in *Transitions from Authoritarian Rule: Latin America*, ed. Guillermo O'Donnell, Philippe C. Schmitter, and Laurence Whitehead (Baltimore: Johns Hopkins, 1986), pp. 173–195.

24. Inter-American Development Bank, *Economic and Social Progress in Latin America: 1987 Report* (Washington, D.C.: IADB, 1987), p. 342. "Mexico Moves to Sustain Drop in Inflation Rate," *Wall Street Journal*, 16 August 1988, p. 19.

25. Judith Adler Hellman (New York: Holmes & Meier, 1978).

26. The *Wall Street Journal* described Peru's mid-1988 policies as "the sharpest austerity measures ever applied in Peru" ("Peru's President Imposes Sharp Austerity to Combat Inflation and Reserve Drain," 8 Sept. 1988, p. 23).

COMMENTS

Barry Ames

Will the debt crisis be the undoing of Latin America's fragile democracies? Unless we advance the simplistic argument that the debt crisis is a sufficient condition for democratic instability, this is likely to be a difficult question to answer. We might begin by examining the historical record of Latin American democracies under economic stress, but straightforward comparison of the current crisis with earlier ones is not so easy. What qualified as a democracy before might not do so now; the welfare effects of earlier crises were felt by groups less active politically than those who must be made to suffer today; and in earlier crises the creditors were perhaps more forgiving than they are in the 1980s.

In spite of the difficulties of the question, Karen Remmer has provided a very clear analysis. Her answer, by and large, is convincing. She argues, correctly I think, that the debt crisis has so far provoked neither instability nor democratic breakdown; indeed, the crisis actually seems to have accelerated the shift away from authoritarian rule. She argues as well that the pessimism of most extant theoretical explanations of the crisis—institutional collapse linkage—is misplaced. Popular support for democratic institutions may wane under harsh economic conditions, but democracy depends less on mass support than on the support of business and military elites. What matters most in determining the chances of democratic survival, besides the attitudes of military and business elites, is the behavior of the United States. Finally, Remmer points out, democratic governments have difficulty imposing austerity programs, but (if the 1954–84 experience of IMF stabilization programs is a guide), so do authoritarian regimes.

If the question is simply whether democratic regimes survive or collapse, Remmer may even be understating her case. Much of the pessimism of extant theory stems from the Latin American experience during the Great Depression. Were the frequent overthrows of democratic regimes caused by the depression? In at least two cases that Remmer accepts as crisis-related, the historical record is

Barry Ames is Professor of Political Science at Washington University in St. Louis.

less clear. Brazilian historians place the origins of Vargas's 1930 revolt not in the Depression but in the violation of the political agreement between São Paulo and Minas Gerais by *paulista* president, Washington Luis. In Argentina, historians divide over the causes of the coup of 1930, with one faction arguing that the effects of the Depression on unemployment were not felt until after the coup. If, therefore, the crisis-collapse linkage has been overstated for the Depression, we have even less reason to expect its repetition in the current situation. Remmer's argument thus gains in force.

Still, I am not sure the question should be posed purely in terms of the survival of a given set of institutions. Granted that we should not expect the imminent demise of the fledgling democracies, does the crisis affect competitive and authoritarian regimes differently? Here, I think that Remmer's evidence supports a slightly less optimistic interpretation. One key to successful adjustment, in the view of the international financial institutions, is reduction of public sector deficits. Only one country in all of Latin America, Chile, has really satisfied the institutions' demands to control public sector deficits. Chile's fiscal deficit as a percentage of expenditures has declined steadily since 1984. Neither Brazil nor Argentina, on the other hand, have been able to do very much in terms of deficit control, and Costa Rica's deficit as a percentage of expenditures rebounded to almost 17 percent in 1986 after dropping in 1984 to 3.2 percent. Mexico is even more instructive: the Mexican government did implement a brutal austerity program, but the public sector deficit has proved remarkably resistant. After declining between 1983 and 1984 from 19 percent to 7.3 percent of GDP, the deficit grew to 8.7 percent in 1985 and (as Remmer points out) to over 15 percent in 1986 and 1987.

Let me be perfectly clear I am referring here to the ability of governments to impose austerity on themselves, not on their societies. Unfortunately the state is too often a parasite draining resources from civil society. Governments have been remarkably more willing and successful to impose austerity on the people than on the state apparatus itself.

What explains Chile's success, in comparison to its democratic neighbors, in imposing public sector austerity? Is it not reasonable to suggest that Pinochet had the advantage of being able (at least until the plebiscite) to stifle opposition and impose austerity? Remmer downplays the type of regime and offers instead three factors as mediators between the crisis and economic management: the scope of economic problems confronting the country, the international political context, and the political dynamic established by prior events and political choices. Mexico is an example of the first: "the governments of large countries with stronger international bargaining positions . . . postponed making major adjustments." But initially the semi-democratic (semi-authoritarian?) Mexican regime did impose a stringent austerity program; it was only with the legislative elections of 1985 that fiscal austerity broke down. Rising dissatisfaction with the regime has now combined with the personal popularity of Cuahtemoc Cárdenas to produce a serious opposition. Mexico has moved from a one-party regime to a dominant party regime, and it would be surprising if the Mexican government imposed stringent austerity in the next few years.

In Brazil, the government of José Sarney has been unable to put together any sort of coherent program to reduce the size of the state. His administration has been obsessed with its own popularity and dominated by the distribution of petty favors and projects, what Brazilians call *fisiologismo*. Insecure deputies, focusing on re-election and lacking minimal party discipline, reinforce clientelism. The World Bank would like to put more money into Brazil, but the Sarney administration simply cannot organize itself sufficiently to propose credible policies or projects. A more skilled politician than Sarney might have been able to avoid his constant jockeying for position, but his self-perception of weakness clearly drives his desire for policies that impose as few sacrifices as possible.

A cynic might argue that if the democratic administrations haven't fallen, it's only because they haven't tried to impose stringent public sector austerity. But why haven't they? Prof. Remmer has demonstrated persuasively that democratic and authoritarian governments were willing to apply IMF stabilization programs between 1954 and 1984. Why are they less willing today? As Prof. Remmer points out, most early Latin American democracies were oligarchical and exclusionary. They limited participation and competition. The new democracies are inclusionary, with women and illiterates granted the right to vote and with voting participation at more than 30 percent of the whole population. Threats to inclusionary democracies are more likely to stem from socioeconomic inequality and resistance from above. Since the rich seldom object to being too rich, the effect of greater inequality must be to stimulate discontent among the masses.

I am not suggesting that these more participatory democracies are more likely to collapse because of popular discontent if they impose public sector austerity, only that they are less likely to impose austerity in the first place. Those that do so are likely to be societies where public sector labor is politically marginalized—like Colombia in the late 1960s—or where a dominant party controls patronage and the channels of political mobility, as in the case of Mexico's PRI.

In Brazil, labor in general is not particularly active, and the poor have accepted sharp reductions in living standards. Still, the government has proved unable to impose self-discipline. President Sarney was part of the old military regime. His desire to ensure the adoption of presidentialism over parliamentarism in the new constitution and to guarantee himself a five-year term led to a massive pork-barrel effort, and his Northeast ties have produced new and costly capital projects in that region. In recent months, there have been signs of government self control. Perhaps 1,000 percent inflation gets any president's attention, and perhaps Sarney feels more secure politically with his mandate defined. At the same time, Brazil has three national elections in the next three years. Since elections are typically preceded by increases in expenditures—but not increases in revenues—and Latin American voters tend overwhelmingly to reject incumbents, the sudden conversion to public sector austerity of Sarney and the deputies will be sorely tested.

The problem with austerity programs is not that people who face declining living standards will decide to overthrow the regime. They won't. They might, however, vote against the incumbent administration, especially in fledgling democracies where party loyalties are quite weak. Unhappy voters will get lots of encouragement from political entrepreneurs hoping to capitalize on discontent. It takes very skilled politicians to manage such delicate situations. Many Brazilians, for example, think that because Tancredo Neves had more support and more skill than Sarney, things would have been different if Tancredo had lived to take office.

In sum, Prof. Remmer has shown persuasively that the fledgling democracies will not collapse under the weight of the debt crisis. But for better or for worse, they also seem unlikely to impose the medicine of austerity on the public sector. Too many factors—weak politicians, frequent elections, mobilized populations, and weak party loyalties—encourage the formation of large coalitions, the avoidance of policies that impose costs on anyone, and a focus on short-term survival by politicians. Austerity has been imposed on society, but not on the state.

4

Debtors Versus Creditors:
Power Relations and Policy
Response to the 1980s Crisis

Barbara Stallings

Policy response to the debt crisis of the 1980s can be analyzed in two different ways. One is to look at the reponses that Latin American governments have actually adopted and try to explain the variation among them. This approach provides a spectrum ranging from Chile under Pinochet to Peru under García. Chile has followed highly "orthodox" macroeconomic policies and maintained cordial relations with the banks and international financial institutions. Peru—until September 1988—followed self-defined "heterodox" domestic policies and has refused to make payments to the commercial banks or to deal with the International Monetary Fund. Nevertheless, the García government did not break completely with the international financial system and has continued to hold meetings with the banks and OECD governments and to solicit loans from the World Bank and Inter-American Development Bank. Between these extremes, there have been other responses, with Mexico nearer the Chilean stance, Brazil nearer to Peru, and other countries filling out the spectrum. Several authors have tried to account for these differences, focusing on different political and/or economic variables.[1]

An alternative approach, which is adopted in this paper, is broader. Its focus is the possible policy responses rather than the actual ones. While such an approach can be developed in abstract theoretical terms,[2] here we will follow an historical analysis, comparing previous policies with current ones. Rather than why Pinochet's policies have differed from García's, the question becomes why have all policies in the 1980s been so remarkably conservative? Why have there been no complete, long-term moratoria or even repudiations of debts? Why have all

Barbara Stallings is Professor of Political Science at the University of Wisconsin–Madison.

governments—including García's Peru, Castro's Cuba, and Sandinista Nicaragua—sought to maintain their links with the international financial system, even at the cost of large-scale capital export? This second approach differs from the first in terms of independent as well as dependent variables. While the causal analysis of actual variation among countries has tended to privilege domestic factors, the analysis of the broader spectrum of possible variation places the main emphasis on international variables.

The first section of the paper briefly sketches the previous major debt crises in Latin America and outlines the differences between the response to them and to the current crisis. It then suggests several hypotheses that might account for the differences. The second section examines the contributions of factors on the creditor side in explaining responses to the 1980s crisis. The third section focuses on debtor-based explanations for the 1980s. Finally, the concluding section considers changes in international power relations and their implications for the debt crisis.

Debt Crises of the Past

The Latin American region has witnessed widespread debt crises every fifty years or so since independence in the early nineteenth century. Various theories have been put forward to account for these cycles,[3] but the main point of interest here is the outcomes of the crises rather than their causes. The crises of the 1820s, 1870s, and 1930s all ended in long-term moratoria, with creditors and debtors sharing the negative consequences of the downturn. In the 1980s, by contrast, the general pattern has been for the debtor nations to shoulder most of the burden, accepting the costs of economic austerity and political instability rather than declaring a cessation of payments.

In the final period of the independence struggles in the early 1820s, most of the new Latin American governments floated bonds in the London capital market.[4] These bonds, managed by reputable merchant banks as well as fly-by-night commercial agents, provided funds to buy ammunition and pay the armies involved in the continuing battles with Spain. Between 1823 and 1825, according to one estimate, over £17.5 million was borrowed.[5] Additional issues were floated by companies that wanted to invest in mining and other activities in the newly independent countries. The lack of resources to service these loans soon became apparent, however, and by the late 1820s all Latin American borrowers had declared default except Brazil. The governments decided that their domestic expenditures, especially those relating to the military, had to take precedence over debt payments. Although British bondholders tried to convince their own government to intervene on their behalf, the Foreign Office generally refused. As a consequence, most of the moratoria lasted a quarter century or more, until the Latin American economies improved sufficiently to make payments possible. When payments were resumed, new bonds were issued to cover interest arrears, but the interest rate was typically cut in half.

A new wave of loans to Latin American governments began in the early 1860s.[6] Again in the form of bonds issued in the London market, and to a lesser extent in other European capitals, many of these loans went to finance development projects in the young nations. Railways were the largest absorbers of funds, with ports and other transportation-related projects also common. Military expenditures and refinancing were other major uses of foreign funds. Approximately £110 million was borrowed by Latin American governments between 1860 and 1875.[7] Absent government regulatory policy in England, foreign lending often took on scandalous characteristics featuring enormous discounts on the face value of bonds, as revealed in the parliamentary investigation of 1875. This extortionary treatment, however, was mainly reserved for the smaller countries, while the larger ones could borrow on more reasonable terms. Thus, it is not surprising that by the mid-1870s, most Latin American countries had again declared defaults, but the three wealthiest—Argentina, Brazil, and Chile—continued payments.

Resolution of this second round of defaults occurred more quickly than the earlier case; the typical moratorium lasted a decade. The British Foreign Office again refused to support the bondholders with military force, so the investors had to rely on the newly formed Corporation of Foreign Bondholders. Some agreements involved issuing new bonds to replace the old ones. An alternative featured the exchange of property for old loans. In the best known case, the Peruvian government gave the bondholders control of the country's railroads for sixty-six years, together with an annual payment of £80 thousand for thirty years. Although Peruvians of all political persuasions came to see the new Peruvian Corporation as a shameful example of domination by a foreign power, it was not a particularly good business deal for the bondholders since the railroads were not profitable nor was the annuity paid.[8]

The third widespread wave of Latin American borrowing in London began during the early years of the twentieth century;[9] after World War I, the New York bond market replaced its British competitor.[10] Loans during the 1920s were similar in character to the late nineteenth century in that they went mainly for infrastructure creation and secondarily for refinancing—although the latter use increased in significance as the decade wore on. The loans were also similar in that many banks used questionable techniques to gain clients. Dollar loans during the 1920s totaled $1.5 billion, less on an annual basis than Britain had provided prior to the war.[11] With the beginning of the Great Depression in 1930, loans to Latin America ceased abruptly and exposed the latent financial problems in the region. Negative net transfers occurred in 1929–30, and governments were forced to choose between domestic expenditure and debt service.

Moratoria were declared in rapid order, beginning with Bolivia in 1931. By 1932, all countries were in default except Haiti; Argentina maintained service on a portion of its debt. When the United States government declined to support its bondholders, United States investors formed the Foreign Bondholders Protective Council (similar to its British counterpart) which gradually helped arrange settlements. Nevertheless, the moratoria lasted a decade or even two. Three kinds of settlements were offered: (a) those few governments that had maintained at least partial debt service gradually eliminated their debt by amortization at par or close to it; (b) most countries that had suspended payments offered settlements with lower interest rates and longer maturities but no reduction in principal; and (c) Brazil and Mexico asked for reduction in interest rate and principal.[12]

The fourth widespread debt crisis followed the lending spree of 1970–82.[13] In this latest instance, commercial banks lent their own deposits to Latin American governments, often through large-scale syndicates. Over $200 billion was lent over the thirteen-year period.[14] Some of the loans went to finance productive activities while others financed consumption, and refinancing was again a key use of funds, especially by the late 1970s. When lending ceased after Mexico's near default in 1982, a new round of debt crises erupted, but the outcome thus far has been quite different from earlier cases. Rather than generalized moratoria, most countries have continued interest payments, and in some cases amortization, running huge trade surpluses in order to do so. Since the surpluses proved insufficient, the banks have provided "concerted" loans to enable interest payments to be maintained. Nonetheless, net resource transfers of nearly $30 billion per year (3.5 percent of GNP) have occurred since 1982.[15]

Two important characteristics thus distinguish the 1980s debt crisis from its predecessors: the greater burden on the Latin American nations as reflected in the large-scale net transfers from Latin America to the creditor nations, and the lack of flexibility for the debtors to decide when it was in their interest to service debt rather than give priority to domestic needs. Both have clearly had negative consequences for Latin America in economic and political terms, although a precise comparison with earlier periods is difficult due to lack of data.[16]

How can we account for these differences in response? A first hypothesis is that the preferences of political leaders in debtor countries may have shifted in the 1980s in comparison to earlier periods. That is, they may now be more responsive to international lenders and to domestic interests that want to maintain international ties. A proper test of this hypothesis would require an extensive historical analysis, but political characteristics would seem to argue against it. The presence today of mass politics, including unions and leftist parties, should put more constraints on leaders' inclinations to attend to the interests of creditors. Likewise, the greater relative influence of import substituting industrialists rather than raw materials exporters should give leaders less incentive to sacrifice domestic interests to international ones, even in the short term.[17]

Table 4.1

Weight of Foreign Debt Service during Debt Crises in Peru, 1826–1983

| Year | Debt service[a] | |
	Exports[b]	Fiscal revenue[c]
1826	20.8%	55.4%
1876	25.3	42.3
1931	15.6	23.0
1983	57.1	74.7

Source: Barbara Stallings, "Incumplimiento de pagos vs. refinanciación: crisis de la deuda externa peruana, 1826–1985," Revista Latinoamericana de Historia Económica y Social, Lima, No. 6 (1985).

[a] Interest and amortization on public-sector long-term debt.

[b] Export of goods.

[c] Current revenue of central government.

A second hypothesis is that the balance of costs and benefits for cooperation have changed because of different economic situations within the debtor countries. The debts might be lighter in the 1980s and so could be more easily serviced. I am unaware of any regionwide statistics on this issue, but I have calculated some figures for Peru which suggest that this argument lacks plausibility. As Table 4.1 shows, debt service as a share of either exports or government revenue was substantially higher in the 1980s than in the three earlier crises. Even taking into account the greater fall in export revenues in the 1930s compared to the 1980s, for example, the ratio of debt service to exports is much higher in the current period. Scattered evidence on ratios of debt service to exports or government revenues for other Latin American countries suggests that the Peruvian figures are not atypical.[18]

A third hypothesis, which seems to have more validity, is that international structural differences are the main explanation. Three interrelated factors are especially important. First, the type of lender and lending instrument have changed. In the nineteenth and early twentieth centuries, bond issues were the main source of foreign capital. These bond issues were sold by investment banks and purchased by wealthy individuals. Since the banks were usually out of the process as soon as the bonds were sold, and the individuals lacked organized clout (despite the formation of the bondholders' committees), little pressure could be brought to bear to avoid defaults. In the 1980s, by contrast, the lenders were the world's largest commercial banks. They themselves maintained a substantial portion of the loans in their own portfolios and thus stood to lose if defaults occurred. Furthermore, the relatively small number of large institutions made coordination much more feasible than in the past.

Second, by the 1980s, there was a network of international financial institutions with substantial power as well as experience in dealing with Third World debt problems. The International Monetary Fund (IMF) in particular had been delegated the power to pressure governments to follow macroeconomic policies that would allow for debt service even at the cost of domestic recession. The key to this power was the agreement among other lenders, public and private, that they would refrain from providing funds to debtor governments until an agreement had been negotiated with the IMF. Although the Kemmerer Missions in the 1920s and 1930s had similar functions with regard to recommending policies, they had no direct source of power to back their recommendations.[19]

Third, and partially as a consequence of the other two points, the international economy has become much more interdependent in the 1980s than in previous epochs. There is much more coordination among the advanced industrial countries than occurred in the past, and the United States as hegemonic power has taken a more active role vis-à-vis the crisis. The latter was necessary, of course, because the health of the largest financial institutions was jeopardized. In the nineteenth century, the British government generally refrained from interfering in debt renegotiations. Likewise, in the 1930s, one of the main problems was the declining ability of Britain to act and the refusal of the United States to do so. As will be discussed in the concluding section, the ability of the United States to continue to play a dominant role may be undermined as its economic power wanes.

This third hypothesis, focusing on the behavior of international lenders and the structure of the international political economy, will be examined further in the next section. Both the negative and positive powers of lenders will be discussed. The behavior of debtors cannot be entirely ignored, however, and it will be taken up in the third part of the paper.

Creditor-Based Explanations for 1980s Policy Responses

The 1980s debt crisis was triggered by the Mexican Finance Minister's announcement on August 13, 1982 that his country could not continue to service its debt on the originally contracted basis. Although the United States government and banks had previously refused to acknowledge the existence of serious problems in the international financial system, the Mexican announcement immediately changed their stance. Indeed, the strategy with respect to the debt crisis during the initial years was orchestrated almost completely from Washington and New York. Governments and banks from Europe and Japan agreed to let the United States take the lead for two main reasons. On the one hand, Latin America—the epicenter of the crisis—was in the United States "sphere of influence," and United States banks had the largest share of exposure. On the other hand, the United States' approach of maintaining debt service at any cost was initially accepted by political leaders in Japan and the main European countries because of the necessity for quick action to protect the international financial system.

The first step in August 1982 was a short-term rescue package for Mexico, put together by Paul Volcker at the Federal Reserve and Jacques de Larosiere at the IMF. It was followed by protracted negotiations with the IMF and private banks to reschedule loans, provide new money, and agree on a set of economic policies for Mexico. At the same time, however, the banks stopped lending to other Latin American countries in response to the Mexican problem, thus spreading the crisis to the rest of the region. By mid-1983, all major Latin American borrowers except Colombia were involved in reschedulings.

To deal with these mounting problems, the United States government devised a basic strategy that was patterned after the Mexican experience. The strategy had four main elements: rescheduling of payments, usually with a grace period; new money from the private banks; additional finance from the international institutions; and (the *quid pro quo*) policies on the part of debtor countries to cut budget deficits and produce trade surpluses. According to a recent authoritative publication,[20] there were several assumptions behind this strategy. First, it was assumed that debtor countries could not pay without new loans. Second, it was assumed that private banks could be persuaded to increase their exposure. Third, it was assumed that the world economic situation would improve rapidly. And fourth, it was assumed that IMF policies would restore debtors' economic health and that voluntary lending would therefore be resumed. Despite the dubious nature of most of the assumptions, the strategy was put into effect.

The reason for the strategy, which called for new loans that would enable interest payments to continue, arose from the requirements of United States banking regulations. These regulations specify that if interest payments are more than ninety days overdue, then the loans in question must be put on "non-accrual" basis, with interest recorded only when it is actually paid. Non-accrual obviously has the effect of lowering bank profits which, in turn, is quickly reflected in bank stock prices. The short time horizon of United States investors, compared to those in Japan and many European countries, compounds this problem. Beyond non-accrual status, United States regulators can classify a country's loans as "sub-standard," "value-impaired," or "loss" if payments are not being made regularly. Beginning with the value-impaired classification, specific reserves must be set aside—usually 10 percent in the first year and 15 percent thereafter—and the value of the loan written down by the equivalent amount.[21] Since the United States banks had very low reserves in 1982, a strategy that did not provide for prompt debt service would have caused chaos in the financial system.

Based on this strategy, three rounds of negotiations took place between 1982 and 1985. A similar process was followed in each round. The banks organized themselves into creditor committees, one for each debtor nation. The committees were composed of about a dozen large banks, which negotiated on behalf of the hundreds of creditor institutions. The Latin American creditor committees were dominated by United States banks. United States banks chaired the committees, and the majority of members were from the United States. In addition, there were generally three or four representatives from Europe, Canada, and Japan.

The unified front of creditors facing individual debtors clearly gave the dominant power position to the former. Some authors suggest that this power was explicitly used to keep the debtors separated by providing help to key countries any time that debtor unity threatened.[22] In any case, creditor power initially led to interest spreads and commissions that were substantially higher than those set for the original loans—so the banks were making money on the reschedulings. Although some softening of terms came about as it became clear that the countries could not pay, there was also an increasing reluctance on the part of the banks to provide new money, even though most of that "new money" was going to pay interest.[23]

By mid-1985, it was obvious that the debt crisis was still unresolved. Even those countries that were successful in running trade surpluses were mired in recession. Real per capita economic growth in Latin American countries was negative between 1981 and 1983 and stagnant in succeeding years. This stagnation was mainly the result of the very policies that permitted debt service to continue. The principal source of the trade surpluses was a lower volume of imports, which often brought a fall in production. Moreover, the combination of high debt service payments and low capital inflow led to large net transfers from Latin America to the creditor countries, and thus a decline in both investment and consumption.

The widespread call for policies to promote growth found a response in the new United States Treasury Secretary, James A. Baker III. At the annual meeting of the World Bank and IMF in Seoul in October 1985, he announced the so-called Baker Initiative, which was to provide $29 billion to fifteen heavily indebted countries over three years. The money was to come from the international financial institutions and the private banks; governments of the advanced industrial countries were not directly involved. In order to get access to these funds, debtor countries were to implement a set of policies to open their economies, promote exports, and cut back on government economic activities. Together, the measures were expected to restore growth in contrast to the previous policies that had centered on austerity.[24]

The Baker Initiative never received enthusiastic support. Critics charged that it was insufficient to deal with the problems at hand, and they pointed to the lack of a role for the governments of the advanced industrial countries as a major drawback. Its only apparent success was the Mexican negotiations of 1986, which provided new money and the most favorable terms since the debt crisis began, and also authorized contingency funds if Mexico's growth rate fell below a specified target. Nevertheless, the negotiations were fraught with discord, and only United States government muscle enabled them to be completed. In follow-up negotiations, several Latin American countries—especially Argentina and Venezuela—tried to match the Mexican terms. The banks resisted until the Brazilian government declared a moratorium on debt service in February 1987. To avoid the spread of moratoria, agreements were quickly concluded with Argentina and Venezuela on terms nearly as favorable as those granted to Mexico.

Although the basic strategy—as modified by the Baker Initiative and the "Menu Approach"—continued to be supported by the executive branch of the United States government, independent initiatives began to multiply. Congressional leaders, academics, and other policy analysts began to propose alternative debt strategies.[25] More important, the banks began to take steps in their own sphere. In May 1987, Citicorp announced that it would add $3 billion to its loan loss reserves, equivalent to 20 percent of its Third World loan exposure. Albeit reluctantly, other United States banks followed Citicorp's lead. The new reserves enabled the banks to take a still harder stand against the debtor countries, although Citicorp's president said that the bank would continue to participate in reschedulings. In December, Morgan Guaranty Trust teamed up with the Mexican government and the United States Treasury to try out a securitization scheme.

None of these initiatives—those of the government or its critics—has managed to resolve the debt crisis. What they have done, however, is to assure that the debtor countries stay in the negotiations and continue to pay interest over and above new loans, unlike previous debt crises. The creditors have used both carrot and stick to achieve these results. On the one hand, the industrial country governments, multilateral agencies, and private banks have formed a united front, leaving little leeway for debtors to rebel, unless they want to cut themselves off entirely from international credit. On the other hand, these same organizations have provided new loans to debtor governments. New loans, plus access to the large and growing United States market, have been the incentive for debtors to continue to pay. Neither this particular carrot nor the stick were feasible in the pre–World War II period; both depended on changes that have emerged in the international political economy.

Debtor-Based Explanations for 1980s Policy Responses

The counterpart of creditor unity has been divisions among debtors. A number of regional meetings of Latin American governments were held after the crisis began, and creditors initially feared the formation of a "debtor cartel" to declare a joint default or at least demand more favorable treatment. The perception of differing interests among the debtor countries themselves, together with success-ful creditor tactics to divide them, undermined the possibility of joint debtor action. Reinforcing this process has been the relative success or failure of differ-ent national policies to deal with the crisis. Governments that have followed creditor rules have been favorably treated and have done reasonably well. Those who have rebelled have been isolated and have encountered severe economic problems.

Table 4.2 shows a partial list of meetings held by some or all of the principal Latin American debtor countries between 1983 and 1989 to try to establish a common approach to negotiations.[26] One of the earliest gatherings was held in conjunction with the IDB annual meeting in March 1983. An advisor to the Ecuadorian Finance Minister supposedly was going to present a proposal for a one-year moratorium, rescheduling over six years, reduction of interest spreads to 1–1.5 percent over LIBOR, and new credits from the banks. Although with hindsight the proposal appears very moderate, it never emerged because of opposition from the large debtor countries. Thus the meeting ended with the first of many collective sighs of relief from creditors because a debt cartel had been averted. In January 1984 in Quito, a set of proposals was introduced at a Latin American Economic Conference hosted by President Osvaldo Hurtado. The proposals were prepared at Hurtado's request by the Latin American Economic System (SELA) and the U.N. Eco-nomic Commission for Latin America (CEPAL). The declaration signed in Quito called for coordination of debt strategy (rather than a joint strategy), focusing on longer repayment periods, no increased costs as a result of re-schedulings, no lowering of per capita incomes as a result of debt service, and a link between debt payments and exports. Greater Latin American inte-gration was also advocated.

Perhaps the best known of the debt meetings was the one that took place in Cartagena, Colombia, in June 1984. This was the forum of presidents and finance ministers of eleven major Latin American countries that resulted in the "Cartagena Consensus." At the level of general principles, this new group called for political dialogue with governments of creditor countries, shared responsibility in the search for solutions, and symmetrical adjustment in debtor and creditor nations. In more specific terms, the declaration advo-cated such items as reduction of international interest rates, some deferment of interest payments, lengthened grace periods, maintenance of payments within a country's "capacity for economic recovery," increased lending from multilateral agencies, and elimination of protectionism and terms of trade deterioration. It also called for a "mechanism for consultation and regional follow-up." While many had again thought a debtors' cartel might emerge from Cartagena, the views of major participants in anticipation of the meeting should have dispelled such beliefs. Argentina's Juan Sourrouille, for example, said:

Table 4.2

Meetings of Latin American Debtors, 1983–89

Date	Location	Type of Forum
1983		
March	Panama	IDB Annual Meeting
July	Caracas	Bolivar Bicentenary Celebration
September	Caracas	OAS Conference on International Finance
1984		
January	Quito	Special meeting called by Presidents of Ecuador/SELA/CEPAL
March	Punta del Este	IDB Annual Meeting
June	Cartagena	Meeting of Latin American Presidents and Finance Ministers
September	Mar del Plata	Cartagena Consensus countries
1985		
February	Santo Domingo	Cartagena Consensus countries
July	Lima	Cartagena Consensus countries
July/August	Havana	Trade unionists/'personalities'
December	Montevideo	Cartagena Consensus countries
1986		
February	Punta del Este	Cartagena Consensus countries
1987		
September	Washington	IMF/World Bank Annual Meeting
November	Acapulco	Presidents of Group of 8
1988		
October	Punta del Este	Presidents of Group of 8
1989		
February	Caracas	Presidents of Group of 8

Source: Compiled from *Latin American Weekly Report*, 1983–89.

Only those who don't understand the problem can speak of a debtors' cartel
... What is a debtors' cartel? Lumping all the debts together? Setting the same
interest rate for all? Agreeing on a common calendar for repayments? This is
impossible: the magnitude, composition, terms of the debts vary from one
country to another. The debtor countries are very different entities. It is possible to unify criteria and to consolidate a joint political approach to the problem, but renegotiations must be carried out by each country individually.[27]

The most radical of the debt meetings were the ones attended by very few
high-level government representatives: the two meetings in Havana in July–
August 1985. The first of the two was a gathering of trade union leaders, while
the second was of "personalities." Castro recommended suspension of debt
payments, but virtually no government representatives were supportive. Cuba
itself, of course, kept up on its debt payments. The meetings attended by government leaders were more cautious. The most important such gatherings were
those of the presidents of the Group of Eight, the largest Latin American debtor
countries. A first meeting was held in November 1987 in Acapulco. A new topic
in Acapulco, since it included the leaders of many new democracies, was the
negative effect that debt could be expected to have on democracy. A follow-up
meeting was held in October 1988, but the most significant gathering was at the
inauguration of Carlos Andres Pérez in February 1989. Not coincidentally, this
meeting occurred shortly after the new administration took office in Washington
and indicated that debt policy was under review. In Caracas, the presidents
approved a proposal that had been tried by some individual countries to exchange discounted debt for bonds. Pérez was assigned to discuss the proposal
with governments of the United States, Japan, and Europe.

Why has this process continually failed in terms of uniting debtor countries
despite the unity of the creditors? Or, as Guillermo O'Donnell asks, "Why don't
our governments do the obvious?"[28] O'Donnell's use of game theory techniques
provides some useful insights. Although he does not use the term, he basically
describes a prisoner's dilemma type situation in the face of lack of information
about other countries' intentions and lack of confidence in them. The success of
the cartel in reducing debt to manageable proportions is the reward if all cooperate, while stiff sanctions are the punishment if all others defect. Side payments
from creditors are the promised rewards for defectors. O'Donnell's practical
conclusion from the exercise is that countries would need extremely reliable
information and simultaneous decisions to make a cartel possible. Special problems would be introduced for democratic governments to operate under such
conditions.

Other observers have also viewed the debt negotiations in terms of bargaining
theory and discussed the reasons for the individualistic approach taken by Latin
American debtors. Richard Feinberg of the Overseas Development Council talks
of problems of timing, belief in "unique" situations, lack of leadership, and

identification with creditors.[29] Similarly, Laurence Whitehead of Oxford University stresses lack of leadership, the reluctance to surrender sovereignty over decisions, the need for an insurance scheme to share the risks of retaliation by creditors, and the requirement for planning.[30] Mike Faber, former director of the Institute for Development Studies, presents fourteen reasons that debtors have not united![31]

A recent contribution, which takes a similar approach but with a different conclusion, is that of Diana Tussie, who previously worked for the Argentine government.[32] Unlike the other authors, she claims the debtors have acted in joint fashion. Saying that explicit threats of default would have been self-defeating because of the high cost of carrying them out, Tussie suggests that the Latin Americans were following Schelling's brinkmanship strategy. "The key to this sort of deterrent is that one may or may not carry out the threat; the final decision is not altogether under the threatener's control. The threat does not take the form of 'I may or may not according to rational calculations or choice' but rather 'I may or may not and even I cannot be completely sure' " (p. 300). Tussie admits, however, that such a strategy (if indeed there was one) has failed to alter the fundamental balance of power between creditors and debtors.

While factors focusing on the negotiation process are surely part of an explanation for debtors' failure to act jointly, it is also important to look beyond the bargaining table. Countries that have maintained good relations with the banks and international financial institutions have been treated well, while those that have broken relations have been isolated. Nonetheless, the causal mechanisms are more complex—and thus more interesting—than a simple model of power manipulation would imply. The governments that have maintained friendly, or at least quasi-friendly, relations with the international financial actors have also had the capacity to enforce austerity programs. The latter, in turn, is partially linked to the type of political regime in place and the resulting political processes relating to the charged issue of debt payments.

Chile and Peru are the extreme cases in this spectrum, so it is useful to briefly review their experiences. Mexico and Brazil also share some of their characteristics. Chile suffered one of the worst crashes in Latin American history when GDP fell by 14 percent in 1982.[33] Although there has been exhaustive debate about the reasons for this crash, the rapid and uncontrolled buildup of debt was obviously a prime cause. The fundamental character of the government, with its emphasis on being part of the world economy, meant that the public sector debt had to be serviced. In addition, the government was forced by the banks to assume responsibility for the large debt of the private financial sector. Although the government was not pleased with having to nationalize the private debt, other economic relations with creditors went relatively smoothly. IMF agreements were signed with alacrity, and by mid-1985 (after several finance ministers and changes in policy direction), the country's macroeconomic relationships were brought into equilibrium. This equilibrium, of course, was achieved by supressing wages and cutting social services, but growth did resume. In addition to reducing consumption, the other key factor in the Chilean recovery was the foreign capital inflow. This money did not come from the banks but from the international financial institutions, especially the IMF, World Bank, and IDB.[34] These funds, in turn, enabled the country to continue its debt service. Despite its authoritarian political system, Chile's 5 percent annual growth rate, low inflation, and external balance have made the country stand out in comparison to the disastrous state of the economies in much of the rest of Latin America. International capital has clearly sought to build Chile as a showcase of economic and debt management.

Peru since 1985 has been the virtual opposite in many senses.[35] Alan García's best-known pronouncement when he became president was that Peru would limit debt payments to 10 percent of exports and refuse to deal with the IMF. This was accompanied by macroeconomic policies based on administered prices, large wage and consumption increases, and a growing government deficit. While the banks and multilaterals did not like these policies, the debt stance was seen as more serious—a direct challenge that had to be met. Unfortunately, for those who would have liked to see García's debt policy work and so serve as an example for other debtors, the government engaged in massive mismanagement. The economy was run at such high speed that reserves were quickly drained, despite the initial ploy of purchasing foreign exchange from drug dealers in the jungle region. Moreover, the government actually paid far more than 10 percent in debt service (the figures for 1985–87 were nearer 30 percent), and no strategy for increasing foreign exchange was put into place. The combination meant that the economy contracted by 10 percent in 1988, inflation approached 2,000 percent, and the "heterodox" economic program had to be abandoned. Interestingly, at the same time they have been isolating Peru, the IMF and World Bank have been extremely eager to get the country back "into the fold." Large loans have been offered if the country would modify its economic policies and limit the hostile tone of its relations with the banks and multilaterals. Although García has been on the verge of accepting on several occasions, he always thus far has pulled back at the last moment.

Brazil and Mexico are less extreme versions of the Peru/Chile cases. Political pressures for rapid growth, similar to those in Peru, faced the Sarney government in Brazil.[36] That growth, resulting from a heterodox anti-inflation package that was accompanied by rising consumption and large budget deficits, cut the trade surplus substantially and forced the government to use its reserves to continue debt service. By early 1987, the combination was no longer feasible, and a choice was required between austerity and a moratorium on debt service. A moratorium was initially selected because of domestic political pressures in the new democratic setting. Unlike the Peruvian case, however, the banks and international financial institutions succeeded in luring the Brazilian government back with a large financial package. Brazil was too important for the banks to write off, as they have Peru, and Brazil was too dependent on international finance to provide future funding for its ambitious development plans.

Other than Chile, Mexico has been the most orthodox of the major debtors and has maintained generally friendly relations with the banks and IMF.[37] Because of its proximity to the United States and the heavy Mexican exposure of United States banks, Mexico has gotten special treatment. The large bridge loan in 1982, the first multi-year rescheduling agreement in 1984, and the 1986 rescheduling (with its oil price and growth rate trigger clauses) are all examples. The *quid pro quo* of this special treatment was a heavy dose of austerity, carried out by the quasi-authoritarian government of the PRI, which resulted in severe recession during the decade. In addition, of course, the special treatment was specifically designed to keep Mexico out of any joint action with other Latin American countries, and it has been effective with respect to that goal. Nevertheless, a type of joint action has resulted from the other nations waiting to see what Mexico would obtain in each rescheduling round and then asking for similar concessions.

Unity on the part of the debtors, then, has proved elusive, even in the face of unity among the creditors. Given the latter—unlike the situation in earlier debt crises—the cost of divisions among debtors has been high. It has kept them paying out far more in interest payments, and amortization in a few cases, than they receive in new loans. The creditors have worked effectively to maintain this division, both through strategic concessions to cooperative debtors and the use of sanctions against those who refuse to play by the rules established in Washington and New York.

Possible Changes in the Debt-Negotiation Process

Given the argument that international factors are the main reason that the 1980s debt crisis differs from those of the past, it is logical to look to the international sphere as the source of possible changes. In particular, in this final section, we want to ask how the shifting balance of international economic power among advanced industrial countries will affect policies on Third World debt.

The key change underway among creditors centers on the unstable relationship between the United States and Japan.[38] Until fairly recently, Japan was the most faithful supporter of the United States debt strategy. Japanese banks raised no objections in the creditor committees, were generally the first to put up their share of "new money," and no Japanese bank has dropped out of the rescheduling process. Since United States banks sought and found ways to lower their Latin American exposure, Japanese banks now hold more Latin American debt than United States financial institutions.[39]

Japanese support for the United States strategy, which was arguably against their economic interest, can be explained by various factors. One was clearly United States pressure, exerted both by the United States Treasury/Federal Reserve on the Japanese Ministry of Finance (MOF) and by United States money-center banks on their Japanese counterparts. Another was the particular correlation of forces within Japan itself. The key actor was the Bank of Tokyo, the most internationally oriented of the Japanese banks. Bank of Tokyo had the largest Latin American exposure, was the main source of expertise on Latin America, and traditionally had a special relationship with the Ministry of Finance. By following its own interests, Bank of Tokyo allied itself with the United States strategy and, together with the MOF, brought the other Japanese banks along.

The erosion of these factors, which originally led Japan to support the United States, is now stimulating change. Bank of Tokyo's preeminence is declining, and Japan's increased economic power relative to the United States has lessened United States influence with the MOF. In addition, the weight of Japan's Latin American portfolio has fallen because of the rise of the value of the yen and the increased value of other Japanese bank assets, even as the Japanese share has risen. The United States' and others' pressure for Japan to take a larger role in world economic management also has begun to have an effect.

Are there possibilities that Japan's increased economic power will prove favorable to Latin American debtors? There are at least two ways in which this could come about. On the one hand, less unity among creditors could increase the power of the debtors. The creditor cartel could crumble, and the debtors could play one creditor off against another to improve their terms. This could be done on an individual basis; debtor unity would not necessarily be required. On the other hand, an increased role for Japan could come about within a close alliance with the United States, but the preferences of that alliance could change in favor of the debtors. Saying that creditors are in a dominant position does not automatically mean that their only goal is the short-term maximization of profits. Indeed, the Japanese have traditionally taken a much longer-run view than the United States, and they have been especially concerned to renew growth in Latin America.

Current developments suggest that there is a movement underway to provide more favorable treatment for debtors and that the second of the two mechanisms is at the heart of the process. Two Japanese initiatives have been taken that are relevant for Latin America; both are based on the premise that growth must be restored. The first is the recycling scheme, whereby $30 billion is to be lent, directly or indirectly, to the heavily indebted countries. It is expected that the scheme will be extended soon. The second and more important initiative is the Miyazawa Plan, put forward at the Toronto Summit and the World Bank/IMF Annual Meeting in Berlin, that would securitize part of the Latin American debt and provide long-term rescheduling for the rest. Although the United States government initially rebuffed the Japanese proposals, it has now adopted them and labeled them the Brady Plan. The Japanese seem pleased with this outcome.[40] Despite doubts on the part of European governments, the IMF and World Bank have been enlisted in the new debt reduction plan, either to provide some type of guarantee for new debt instruments to be issued and/or to provide additional funds. The Japanese will then provide parallel loans. While there are crucial flaws with the Brady Plan—especially its aim to limit debt reduction to 20 percent—it marks an important step away from the stance that has prevailed until now. As usual, Mexico will be the test case for the new program.

Although the major source of change will come from the creditors, there are processes underway in Latin America that should reinforce such changes. In many countries new political leaders are emerging who express a much harder line on the debt question than does the current leadership. A quick look around the Latin American landscape shows several examples. In both Mexico and Chile, the two debtors who have been most favorable to the creditor position, important shifts are underway. The decline of PRI strength in Mexico, and the popularity of an opposition candidate who took a forceful stance on the debt, presage new policies there. The victory of the opposition in the Chilean plebiscite prevented General Pinochet from obtaining another eight-year term, and a new debt policy is high on the opposition's economic platform. In both Argentina and Brazil, populist leaders (Menem and Brizola) stand good chances of coming to power in the upcoming elections, although the policies followed by former populist Carlos Andres Pérez in Venezuela suggest caution in policy predictions, even if they do win the presidencies.

In summary, forces seem to be moving in such a way that Latin American governments may finally get more favorable treatment in terms of servicing their foreign debts. Ironically, some of the proposals are moving back in the direction of policies followed with bond defaults. Three factors are at work. The first is a shift in creditor preferences, as Japan, which has always put a premium on economic growth, becomes a more significant international actor. Second, changing political realities in Latin America appear to have influenced the policy perspectives of the Bush administration, making it more willing to follow the Japanese lead. And the objective realities of debt crises are third. Despite the institutional changes in the lending process in the post–World War II period, the basic nature of debt crises has not changed. Debtors without resources cannot pay without tremendous costs to themselves and the rest of the world economy. Unfortunately, it has taken seven years of decline in Latin America for the new set of creditors to acknowledge and find a way to deal with this fact.

Notes

The author thanks Conference participants, especially Jeff Frieden and David Felix, for comments on an earlier draft of this paper. Peter Evans and Stephany Griffith-Jones also provided valuable suggestions.
    1. For political analyses, see Jeff Frieden, "Classes, Sectors, and Foreign Debt in Latin

America," *Comparative Politics* (October 1988); Robert Kaufman and Barbara Stallings, "Debt and Democracy in the 1980s: The Latin American Experience," in *Debt and Democracy in Latin America*, ed. Barbara Stallings and Robert Kaufman, (Boulder: Westview Press, 1989); and Joan Nelson, "Conclusions," in *Economic Crisis and Policy Choice: The Politics of Adjustment in Developing Countries*, ed. Joan Nelson (Princeton: Princeton University Press, forthcoming). An analysis that asks some similar questions from an economist's perspective is Daniel McFadden et al., "Is There Life After Debt? An Econometric Analysis of the Creditworthiness of Developing Countries," in *International Debt and the Developing Countries*, ed. Gordon W. Smith and John T. Cuddington (Washington, D.C.: The World Bank, 1985).

2. The economic literature on this broader topic has mainly been centered on the issue of the debtor's reputation or creditworthiness. See, for example, Jonathan Eaton and Mark Gersovitz, "Debt with Potential Repudiation," *Review of Economic Studies* 48 (April 1981); Jeffrey Sachs, "Theoretical Issues in International Borrowing," *Princeton Studies in International Finance* 54 (1984); and Daniel Cohen and Jeffrey Sachs, "Growth and External Debt under Risk of Debt Repudiation," *European Economic Review* 30 (June 1986). An alternative approach, based on the threat of sanctions, is described in Jeremy Bulow and Kenneth Rogoff, "A Constant Recontracting Model of Sovereign Debt," *Journal of Political Economy* 97, no. 1 (February 1989) and "Sovereign Debt: Is to Forgive to Forget?" *American Economic Review* (forthcoming). For more empirically based analyses, see Thomas Enders and Richard Mattione, *Latin America: The Crisis of Debt and Growth* (Washington, D.C.: Brookings Institution, 1984) and Anatole Kaletsky, *The Costs of Default* (New York: Priority Press, 1985).

3. See, for example, A. K. Cairncross, *Home and Foreign Investment, 1870–1913* (Cambridge: Cambridge University Press, 1953); Charles Kindleberger, *Manias, Panics, and Crashes* (New York: Basic Books, 1978); and Barbara Stallings, *Banker to the Third World: United States Portfolio Investment in Latin America, 1900–1986* (Berkeley: University of California Press, 1987).

4. For general discussion of the 1820s loans and crisis, see Leland Jenks, *The Migration of British Capital to 1875* (New York: Knopf, 1927); P. L. Cottrell, *British Overseas Investment in the Nineteenth Century* (London: Macmillan, 1975); and Carlos Marichal, *A Century of Debt Crises in Latin America* (Princeton: Princeton University Press, 1989), Ch. 1, 2.

5. Jenks, *Migration*, p. 47.

6. On the lending wave ending in the 1870s and the subsequent crisis, see Jenks, *Migration*; Cairncross, *Home and Foreign Investment*; Marichal, *Century of Debt Crises*, Ch. 3, 4; W. H. Wynne, *State Insolvency and Foreign Bondholders*, Vol. 2 (New Haven: Yale University Press, 1951); Matthew Simon, "The Pattern of New British Portfolio Investment, 1865–1914," in *The Export of Capital from Britain 1870–1914*, ed. A. R. Hall (London: Methuen, 1968); Michael Edelstein, *Overseas Investment in the Age of High Imperialism: The United Kingdom, 1850–1914* (New York: Columbia University Press, 1982).

7. Calculated from Jenks, *Migration*, Appendix C. See also the cautionary comments in D. C. M. Platt, "British Portfolio Investment before 1870: Some Doubts," *Economic History Review* 33 (1980).

8. For discussion of the Peruvian debt resolution, see Rory Miller, "The Making of the Grace Contract: British Bondholders and the Peruvian Government, 1885–90," *Journal of Latin American Studies* 8, no. 1 (1976): 96–100; and Heraclio Bonilla, *Gran Bretaña y el Perú*, Vol. 5 (Lima: IEP, 1977), pp. 17–32.

9. There was also a lending spurt in the 1880s, which was concentrated in the Rio de la Plata region and culminated in the Baring Crisis. See David Felix, "Alternative Outcomes

of the Latin American Debt Crisis: Lessons from the Past,'' *Latin American Research Review* 22 (1987) and Marichal, *Century of Debt Crises*, Ch. 5, 6.

10. On U.K. lending, see Cairncross, *Home and Foreign Investment*; Edelstein, *Overseas Investment*; Simon "Pattern of Portfolio Investment;'' and Herbert Feis, *Europe: The World's Banker, 1870–1914* (New Haven: Yale University Press, 1930). On United States lending and the 1930s crash, see *Sale of Foreign Bonds or Securities in the United States*, Hearings before Committee on Finance, United States Senate, 1932; Herbert Feis, *The Diplomacy of the Dollar: 1919–1932* (New York: Norton, 1932); Ilsa Mintz, *Deterioration of the Quality of Foreign Bonds Issued in the United States, 1920–1930* (New York: National Bureau of Economic Research, 1951); Joseph Tulchin, *The Aftermath of War* (New York: New York University Press, 1971); and Rosemary Thorp, ed., *Latin America in the 1930s* (London: Macmillan, 1984).

11. Calculated from Stallings, *Banker*, Appendix I.A; some other sources put the figure at nearer to $2 billion.

12. United Nations Economic Commission for Latin America, *External Financing in Latin America* (Santiago: UNECLA, 1965).

13. Studies of the 1970s loans and 1980s crisis continue to expand at an exponential rate. For a sample of the most interesting work, from different perspectives, see William R. Cline, *International Debt: Systemic Risk and Policy Response* (Washington, D.C.: Institute for International Economics, 1984); John H. Makin, *The Global Debt Crisis* (New York: Basic Books, 1984); Gordon W. Smith and John T. Cuddington, eds., *International Debt and the Developing Countries* (Washington, D.C.: The World Bank, 1985); Harold Lever and Christopher Huhne, *Debt and Danger: The World Financial Crisis* (New York: Atlantic Monthly Press, 1985); Carlos Massad, ed., "The Debt Problem: Acute and Chronic Aspects,'' special issue of *Journal of Development Planning* 16 (1985); Miles Kahler, ed., *The Politics of International Debt* (Ithaca: Cornell University Press, 1986); Richard E. Feinberg and Ricardo Ffrench-Davis, eds., *Development and External Debt in Latin America: Bases for a Consensus* (Notre Dame, Ind.: University of Notre Dame Press, 1988); and Jeffrey Sachs, ed., *Developing Country Debt and the World Economy* (Chicago: University of Chicago Press, 1989).

14. Calculated from World Debt Tables. These data provide a serious underestimate of lending since net rather than gross figures are used. Data previously cited for bonds are gross statistics.

15. United Nations Economic Commission for Latin America and the Caribbean, *Preliminary Overview of the Latin American Economy, 1988* (Santiago: ECLAC, 1989).

16. A similar point about costs and benefits is made by Marichal, *Century of Debt Crises*, p. 239; Albert Fishlow, "Lessons from the Past: Capital Markets during the 19th Century and the Interwar Period,'' *International Organization* 39, no. 3 (1985): 91; and Peter H. Lindert and Peter J. Morton, "How Sovereign Debt Has Worked,'' in *Developing Country Debt and the World Economy*, ed. Jeffrey Sachs, (Chicago: University of Chicago Press, 1989), pp. 229–30.

17. Jeff Frieden has made a similar point as a way of differentiating debtors in the current period (see Comment following this chapter). The point is a different one—to compare the typical situation now with that of the past.

18. See Marichal, *Century of Debt Crises*, passim; UNECLA, *External Financing*, p. 28.

19. On the Kemmerer missions, see Paul Drake, *Money Doctor in the Andes* (Durham: Duke University Press, 1989).

20. Martin Feldstein et al., *Restructuring Growth in the Debt-Laden Third World* (New York: Trilateral Commission, 1987). Feldstein and his colleagues interviewed a vast array of people involved in the debt issue in preparation of this Trilateral Commission report.

21. A useful summary of United States regulation and its development is Karin Lissikers, "Bank Regulation and International Debt," in *Uncertain Future: Commercial Banks and the Third World*, Richard Feinberg and Valeriana Kallab, eds. (New Brunswick: Transaction Books, 1984).

22. Diana Tussie, "The Coordination of the Latin American Debtors: Is There a Logic Behind the Story?" in *Managing World Debt*, Stephany Griffith-Jones, ed. (New York: St. Martins Press, 1988).

23. The major source of statistical information on the negotiations is the U.N. Economic Commission on Latin America. Among their reports, see especially *External Debt in Latin America* (Boulder: Lynne Riener Publishers, 1985), pp. 57–72 and "Recent Economic Developments in Latin America and the Caribbean," document prepared for 13th session of the Committee of High-Level Government Experts, New York, August 1987, pp. 41–48. The annual *Economic Study of Latin America* also contains a section on debt negotiations.

24. For various views on the Baker Initiative, see Christine Bogdanowicz-Bindert, "World Debt: The United States Reconsiders," *Foreign Affairs* (Winter 1985/86); Riordan Roett, "Beyond the Baker Initiative," *SAIS Review* (Summer/ Fall 1986); Patrick Conway, "The Baker Plan and International Indebtedness," *The World Economy* (June 1987); and Cheryl Payer, "The World Bank: A New Role in the Debt Crisis?" *Third World Quarterly* (April 1986). For a Latin American view of the Baker Initiative, see "El Plan Baker y la deuda latinoamericana," in *Una coexistencia difícil: América Latina y la política económica de Estados Unidos*, Miguel Rodríguez Mendoza, ed. (Caracas: Editorial Nueva Sociedad, 1987).

25. For a summary of the major proposals, see Fred Bergsten et al., *Bank Lending to Developing Countries: The Policy Alternatives* (Washington, D.C.: Institute for International Economics, 1985).

26. The following section is based on analyses in various issues of the *Latin American Weekly Report*, 1982–89.

27. *Latin American Weekly Report*, June 29, 1984.

28. Guillermo O'Donnell, "External Debt: Why Don't Our Governments Do the Obvious?" *CEPAL Review* 27 (December 1985).

29. Richard Feinberg, "Latin American Debt: Renegotiating the Adjustment Burden," in *Development and External Debt in Latin America: Bases for a Consensus*, Richard Feinberg and Ricardo Ffrench-Davis, eds. (Notre Dame, Ind.: University of Notre Dame Press, 1988).

30. Laurence Whitehead, "Latin American Debt: An International Bargaining Perspective," paper presented at annual conference of British International Studies Association, Aberystwyth, Wales, December 1987.

31. Mike Faber, "Conciliatory Debt Reduction: Why It Must Come and How It Could Come," unpublished ms., Institute for Development Studies, University of Sussex, 1989.

32. Tussie, "Coordination of Latin American Debtors."

33. For data, see David Felix and John Caskey, this volume.

34. For background on the Chilean economic situation in the 1980s, see José Pablo Arrellano et al., Country Study 10: *Chile* (Helsinki: WIDER, 1987). More detailed studies are found in the biennial *Colección Estudios CIEPLAN*. See also Ricardo Ffrench-Davis, this volume.

35. Background on the Peruvian economy is provided by Richard Webb, Country Study 8: *Peru* (Helsinki: WIDER, 1987). On García's debt policy, see Barbara Stallings "Autodestrucción de una iniciativa positiva: la política de la deuda peruana bajo Alan García" in *El APRA de la ideología a la praxis*, ed. Heraclio Bonilla and Paul Drake (Lima: Nuevo Mundo, 1989).

36. See Dionisio Carneiro, Country Study 11: *Brazil* (Helsinki: WIDER, 1987), for a background study on Brazil in the 1980s. On the 1987 moratorium, see Luiz Carlos Bresser Pereira, "Solving the Debt Crisis: Debt Relief and Adjustment," testimony before the United States House of Representatives, Committee on Banking, Finance, and Urban Affairs, January 4, 1989. See also Eliana Cardoso, this volume.

37. Background information on Mexico can be found in Jaime Ros and Nora Lustig, Country Study 7: *Mexico* (Helsinki: WIDER, 1987). On the debt negotiations, see Angel Gurría, "Debt Restructuring: Mexico as a Case Study," in Griffith-Jones, *Managing World Debt*. See also Clemente Ruiz Durán, this volume.

38. The following section relies heavily on the analysis in Barbara Stallings, "The Reluctant Giant: Japan and the Latin American Debt Crisis," in *Japan and the Third World*, ed. Susan J. Pharr, forthcoming.

39. *New York Times*, April 17, 1989.

40. Interviews with Japanese government officials.

COMMENTS

Jeffry A. Frieden

As usual, Barbara Stallings has presented a fascinating paper on an important topic, and has handled the issues very well indeed. Her paper asks why the debt crisis of the 1980s has turned out so poorly for the Latin American debtors, especially in comparison with the crisis of the 1930s. In what follows, I focus on one set of analytical issues that Stallings addresses, the relative importance of international and domestic factors in explaining the Latin American response to the debt crisis.

Stallings proposes that since virtually all Latin debtors have experienced poor bargaining results in their attempts to reduce the debt burden, there must be a common cause of these national results, and it must be international. Stalling's argument considers two options open to the Latin American debtors that would have improved their lot but which have not been chosen, then tries to explain why potentially superior choices went unmade. First, individual debtor nations might declare unilateral moratoria, one by one. This would certainly reduce the burden of debt service, and historically creditor retaliation has been less than fully effective. With a few exceptions, however, lasting unilaterial moratoria have not been declared. Second, the Latin Americans might form a unified debtors' cartel to confront the creditors' cartel. There is little doubt that debtor unity would increase debtor bargaining power and would result in superior bargaining outcomes for the debtors. Yet debtor unity has not materialized; the debtors have taken different bargaining positions and have often balked at coordinating their efforts.

These two observations are certainly accurate, but we are left with the question of why we observe such outcomes. Stallings ascribes both results to a conscious strategy of unified creditors. This is not a particularly controversial explanation of the first phenomenon; most would agree that to some degree unilateral debtor actions have been foreclosed by creditor solidarity in threaten-

Jeffry A. Frieden is Assistant Professor of Political Science, University of California, Los Angeles.

ing sanctions. Unlike in the 1930s, private creditors have united amongst themselves and with their home governments to issue credible threats of retaliation against errant debtor governments. Stallings's explanation of the second phenomenon, the difficulties of achieving debtor unity, is more problematic. She appears to believe that creditor strategies were themselves the cause of debtor disunity. But this is not the only interpretation of the event, and of the relationship between the two "stylized facts," the existence of a creditor cartel and the absence of a debtor cartel.

Indeed, I see little evidence in Stallings's paper or elsewhere that the principal reason for debtor disunity was purposeful dissent-sowing by creditors. Of course, creditors have attempted to keep national negotiations separate and sometimes play one debtor against another, but these attempts have not often succeeded. Indeed, individual debtors have generally had enough bargaining strength on their own to ensure that concessions granted to one debtor have been extended to other debtors.

In my view, the principal stumbling block to debtor unity, and even coordination, has been underlying differences of interest among the debtors. Despite the strong possibility that debtor unity would lead to more favorable results for the debtors, some debtors actually preferred the maintenance of cordial relations with creditors (even if this meant foregoing debt relief) to successfully concerted negotiated debt relief, which presumably would involve some confrontation with creditors. While this may at first glance seem implausible, I believe that it was in fact the case that some governments were more concerned than others about maintaining good relations with creditors and less concerned than others about obtaining debt relief. This might be a function of fears that joining a debtor cartel would endanger other international economic relations or foreign-policy goals, or it might be a function of the preferences of domestic groups whose desires were not identical to the "national interest" in securing a more favorable outcome to the debt negotiations.

In other words, the alternative to Stallings's hypothesis of creditor-induced debtor disunity is the possibility that differences among the debtors were due to domestic political and economic features of the debtors themselves. In the game-theory terms she uses, the problem may not have been that the debtors faced an n-person Prisoners' Dilemma, but rather that debtor preference functions differed. This focuses the analytical problem on explaining why there were such differences in national preferences. More explicitly, it raises the possibility that government policies toward debt negotiations may be related to domestic distributional conflicts.

A comparison with domestic politics of debt policy in the creditor countries is instructive. Among creditors, there is little disagreement over the goal of maximizing receipts of debt service. Of course, there is some opposition to creditor demands from within creditor nations: creditor-country exporters to troubled debtors may resent the impact of debtor reductions in imports, while import-competing sectors may worry that debtors' desperate quest for foreign exchange will lead them to flood creditor markets with their products. Moral or foreign policy considerations may also enter into the debate. But still, the range of disagreement is very narrow: whether out of concern over general financial stability, out of belief in the sanctity of international contracts, or out of simple national solidarity, creditor policy toward the debtor nations has not been particularly contentious within the creditor countries. Distributional considerations have rarely entered into creditor-country calculations of optimal policy preferences or bargaining strategies.

Among the debtors, however, the proper response to creditor demands has been extremely controversial. Debates in the typical debtor nation have revealed the most extreme positions, often associated with highly polarized socioeconomic and political interests. Those groups whose economic activities are closely associated with international trade and payments want cooperation with creditors and often oppose a hard-line bargaining stance in the belief that it will endanger their own position. Groups less tied to the foreign sector have less to lose by incurring creditor wrath and support more hostile policies. Thus, there is a wide range of distributional issues that impinge on the domestic political dynamic. And although the domestic political process in the Latin American debtors is affected by international economic developments, until now such international factors have not been powerful enough to override underlying domestic political differences.

A few more minor observations about Stallings's paper also suggest themselves, primarily the 1930s–1980s comparison. For one thing, it is not yet clear how different the levels of unilateral reduction in debt service will be. In the 1980s, creditor banks have not realized fully the original contracted terms of their loans, but the total yield to maturity on these loans is still to be determined. And the defaults of the 1930s were by no means complete. Indeed, Marilyn Skiles has found that Brazilian dollar bonds issued in 1927–28 and sold thirty years later, after many renegotiations in the 1930s and 1940s, earned an actual annual yield of 3.1 percent, only 0.1 percent below a thirty-year Treasury bond issued in 1927–28 and sold in 1957–58.[1] More generally, Peter Lindert and Peter Morton have calculated that Argentine and Brazilian bonds issued between 1915 and 1945 ended up earning substantially more than the comparable U.K. consol or U.S. Treasury bond rate—1.95 percent and 0.70 percent more annually, respectively.[2] It is not yet obvious that debtor behavior has been fundamentally different in the 1980s than it was in the 1930s.

Even if it were the case that debtors end up paying more on their debt in the 1980s than in the 1930s, it is not clear that the two experiences are structurally different. After all, the decision to reduce debt service payments and incur creditor wrath depends fundamentally on what debtors expect the returns on good behavior to be, and this in turn depends on the attractiveness of the international commercial and financial system. If well-behaved debtors expect international trade and payments to provide significant benefits in the near future, the opportunity cost of noncompliance is very high, whereas if even well-behaved debtors face dismal international economic prospects, noncompliance becomes more attractive.

These considerations are relevant, of course, because the international crisis of the 1930s was far more severe than that of the 1980s. Between 1929 and 1933, the developed countries' combined GDP dropped 16 percent, while import volumes dropped 22 percent. Between 1980 and 1987, in contrast, their combined GDP grew by 15 percent, and import volumes rose 35 percent. Thus, while from 1929 to 1933 Latin America's terms of trade dropped 31 percent, export volumes by 24 percent, and import volumes by 55 percent, in the 1980–87 period the region's terms of trade fell by 15 percent, export volumes rose by 35 percent, and import volumes dropped by only 15 percent.[3] While some of this is due to Latin American policies in the 1980s—the decision to maintain debt service required increased exports—still the external shocks of the Great Depression were far greater than those of the 1980s. In these circumstances, it might well be fully rational for debtor nations to maintain a higher level of compliance with debt obligations in the 1980s than in the 1930s.

Stallings's central points are both accurate and important, and my purpose here has been primarily to try to sharpen the analytical focus of our attention. The most striking characteristic of the current debt crisis, as Stallings says well, has been the poor Latin American bargaining position. Both as individual nations and as a region, the Latin debtors have done poorly in their dealings with the united creditors' front.

I believe, however, that the principal causes of debtor disunity have been domestic. Indeed, I would argue that domestic factors account for the relatively malleable bargaining stance taken by debtor nations when negotiating on their own, even in circumstances where a tougher stance was both possible and eminently reasonable.

In a sense, we might be able to resurrect the 1930s comparison to better understand the relationship between the domestic and international factors in the Latin Americans' policy toward their foreign debt. In the 1930s, the international economic crisis was so severe that it overrode most domestic differences among the Latin debtors. In fact, in most countries (but not Argentina, at least not until the 1940s) the crisis destroyed the economic, social, and political bases of the domestic groups that wanted to safeguard the nations' international economic ties, and brought more nationalistic groups to the fore. The international economic situation in the 1980s, however, has not been so dramatic as to uniformly weaken Latin American domestic groups that favor international economic integration; in some cases, the export possibilities provided by the U.S. trade deficit have strengthened internationalist groups that favor more cooperative relations with creditors.

International factors have played an important role in affecting the Latin American bargaining response to the debt crisis. However, these international factors have been mediated by domestic socioeconomic interests and political institutions. Inasmuch as domestic political and economic conditions within the various Latin American debtors continue to diverge, these differences will continue to determine the regional response to the debt crisis.

Notes

1. Marilyn Skiles, "Latin American International Loan Defaults in the 1930s: Lessons for the 1980s?" *Federal Reserve Bank of New York Research Paper* No. 8812, April 1988, p. 39. Of course, the final holder of the bond was seldom the original purchaser, but this is irrelevant to the considerations at hand.

2. Peter H. Lindert and Peter J. Morton, "How Sovereign Debt Has Worked," in *Developing Country Debt and Economic Performance. Vol. 1: The International Financial System*, ed. Jeffrey D. Sachs (Chicago: University of Chicago Press, 1989), p. 53.

3. Figures from Angus Maddison, *Two Crises: Latin America and Asia 1929–1938 and 1973–1983* (Paris: OECD, 1985), and from Inter-American Development Bank, *Economic and Social Progress in Latin America: Annual Report* (Washington: IADB), various issues.

PART III
COUNTRY STUDIES

5

Debt Cycles in Brazil and Argentina

Eliana A. Cardoso

Macroeconomic comparisons between Brazil and Argentina suggest a striking repetition of events. In both countries, exceptionally high inflation rates have plagued authoritarian as well as democratic regimes. Brazilian and Argentinian debt crises have upset world capital markets for more than a century. Policies of their populist administrations result in deficit finance, rising inflation, and growing external disequilibrium. Debt/export ratios unavoidably increase when domestic mismanagement coincides with a deterioration of the terms of trade. In these circumstances creditors inevitably suspend lending, bringing about a balance of payments crisis. Funding loans and moratoria follow. Some years later, international lending resumes, only to give place to yet another cycle.

We are interested in examining the common features of debt cycles and inflation processes in Brazil and Argentina, but we also emphasize important differences. This presentation is in seven parts. The first section starts with comparisons of a broad nature and discusses the relationships among external debt, budget deficits, and inflation, introducing a theme that will be further exploited in the following sections. The second part reports on the crisis of the 1890s, and the third briefly reviews the debt cycle of the 1930s. The next section examines the buildup of the recent crisis, and the fifth investigates the current state of the two economies. The sixth part shows how interest recycling in domestic currency might promote investment and development. The concluding section discusses the prospective scenarios for Brazil and Argentina in the 1990s.[1]

Some Broad Comparisons

Figure 5.1 compares real GDP per capita in Brazil and Argentina.[2] Two major facts are worth emphasizing. First, Brazil appears to be more dynamic than

Eliana A. Cardoso is Associate Professor of International Economic Relations, The Fletcher School of Law and Diplomacy, Tufts University.

Figure 5.1. **Real GDP per Capita**

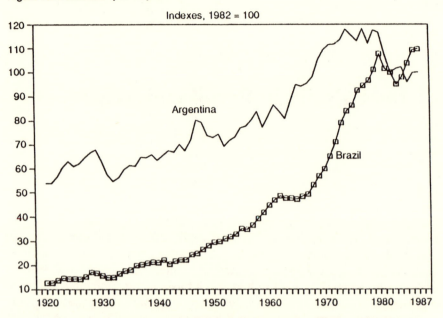

Indexes, 1982 = 100

Sources: Banco Central do Brasil, *Brasil Programa Económico*, Março, 1988; R. M. Zerkowski and M. A. Veloso, "Seis Décadas de Economía Brasileira Através do PIB," *Revista Brasileira de Economía*, 36 no. 3, 1982. R. Dornbusch and J. C. de Pablo, "Debt and Macroeconomic Instability in Argentina," *NBER*, mimeo, 1988.

Argentina to judge from its faster growth rates of real GDP per capita since the 1920s. Between 1920 and 1988, the average growth rate of GDP per capita in Brazil was 3.4 percent compared to 1 percent in Argentina.[3] Second, the Argentinian GDP figures show much greater instability than the Brazilian data. Between 1920 and 1988, the coefficient of variation of the growth rate of GDP per capita in Argentina was 4.5, while in Brazil it was 1.3.

The instability of the Argentinian economy is further illustrated by the extreme oscillations of its real exchange rate, shown in Figure 5.2. Table 5.1 shows the coefficient of variation of the real exchange rates in Brazil and Argentina. In Brazil, the real exchange rate becomes more stable after 1969, but in Argentina its volatility increases. Its extraordinary swings reflect economic policy mistakes. The outstanding episode is the appreciation of 1979–81, which was followed by the collapse of the peso. In Brazil, a pragmatic exchange rate policy has prevented any comparable episodes.

The period from 1945 to 1955 provides a good starting point for discussing differences in politics in the two countries.[4] Perón implemented a major redistribution of income from agrarian elites toward workers and small manufacturers. Vargas, who relied on a ruling coalition of military elites, coffee

Figure 5.2. **Argentina: Real Exchange Rate**

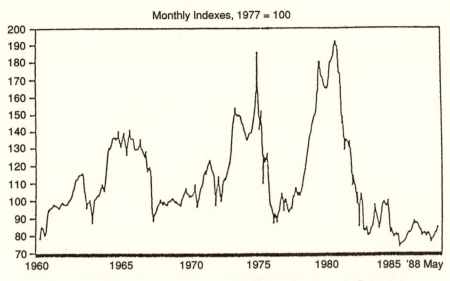

Monthly Indexes, 1977 = 100

Sources: IMF, *International Financial Statistics*; FIEL, *Indicadores de Coyuntura*.
Notes: The real exchange rate is defined as the ratio between domestic wholesale prices and U.S. wholesale prices, expressed in a common currency. An increase of the index represents a real appreciation.

Figure 5.3. **Brazil: Real Exchange Rate**

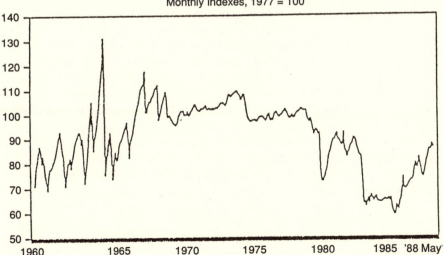

Monthly Indexes, 1977 = 100

Sources: IMF, *International Financial Statistics*; FGV, *Conjuntura Económica*.
Notes: The real exchange rate is defined as the ratio between domestic wholesale prices and U.S. wholesale prices, expressed in a common currency. An increase of the index represents a real appreciation.

Table 5.1

Real Exchange Rates: Coefficient of Variation of the Monthly Indexes, Argentina and Brazil, 1959.1–1988.3

	Argentina	Brazil
1959.1–1969.1	0.15	0.14
1969.1–1988.3	0.26	0.16

Sources: IFS, *International Financial Statistics*; FGV, *Conjuntura Económica*, and FIEL, *Indicadores de Coyuntura*.

Note: The real exchange rate was calculated as the ratio between domestic and U.S. wholesale prices, expressed in a common currency (1977 = 100).

exporters, and industrialists throughout the 1930s in Brazil, began to bid for the support of workers in the mid-1940s. But he did so within the framework of restrained militancy of organized labor and state control over union financing. With unions extensively supervised, Brazilian industrialists and exporters felt less threatened by populist mandates, and acquired a vested interest in the government subsidies and investment policies established during Vargas's era. During the decades to come, both countries were to operate under the legacy of their populist leaders.[5]

Perón's legacy was a polarized society, a decapitalized economy, endless political turmoil, and violence. Military intervention has since contributed to even more economic mismanagement and human rights abuses. Recurrent patterns of inflation and stabilization reflect a tense struggle between the interests of different groups, each with sufficient political resources to defend its share of national income. Labor leaders struggle with authorities over macro policies as fiercely as they bargain at the plant level. This is unavoidable, since wages are greatly affected by government interventions in the economy and by the implementation of successive anti-inflation stabilization programs. Each change of regime brings about major shifts in policy. Among industrialist and agro-exporting sectors, heightened uncertainty compresses time horizons and diverts resources from production to short-term speculative activities.

Brazilian society, with a weaker popular sector, entered the postwar era less bitterly divided. Continuing expansionist policies attenuated distributional conflicts, while relative bureaucratic stability blended the interests of business and bureaucracy. The political foundation of the Brazilian elitist structure of power was already consolidated by the time it encountered confrontation with the popular classes during Goulart's presidency. Goulart was ousted by the military in 1964.

O'Donnell's widely shared view of the creation of military regimes in Brazil

Figure 5.4. **Argentina: Monthly Inflation, January 1951–August 1988**

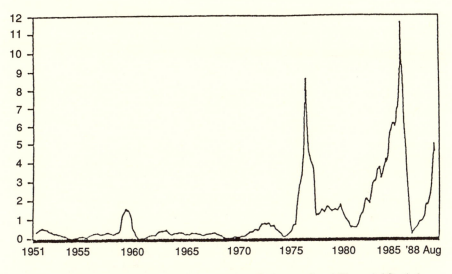

Sources: FIEL, *Indicadores de Coyuntura*; and IMF, *International Financial Statistics*.

Note: Monthly change of wholesale price index relative to same month of previous year (1 = 100 percent).

Figure 5.5. **Brazil: Monthly Inflation, January 1951–August 1988**

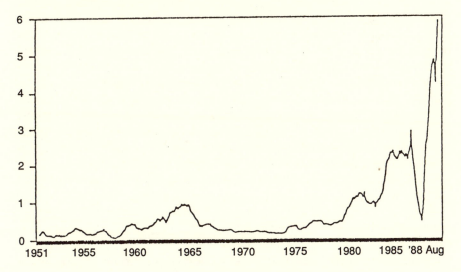

Sources: FGV, *Conjuntura Económica*; and IMF, *International Financial Statistics*.

Note: Monthly change of wholesale price index relative to same month of previous year (1 = 100 percent).

Table 5.2

**Inflation Rates: Average Annual Percent,
Argentina and Brazil, 1951.1—1988.3**

	Argentina	Brazil
1951.1—1959.12	31.8	18.3
1960.1—1969.12	23.6	45.9
1970.1—1979.12	134.1	28.9
1980.1—1988.3	278.8	154.0

Sources: FGV, *Conjuntura Económica*; and FIEL, *Indicadores de Coyuntura*.

in 1964 and Argentina in 1966 maintains that they were the political consequence of incomplete industrialization and class conflict in highly dependent
economies.[6] Since the 1940s, Argentina and Brazil had followed import substituting strategies. By the early 1960s, growth derived from the creation of consumer goods industries had been exhausted, and overvalued exchange rates
induced widening external imbalances. Authorities faced rising expectations of a
growing working class and tried to accommodate conflicts by using inflationary
finance. Eventually, policy makers decided that industrialization had to be broadened through the addition of basic industries in order to make growth possible
again. Their projects required external financing, and they realized that direct
investment would not be attracted to countries wracked by social conflicts and
political instability. The solution was bureaucratic authoritarianism. National security doctrine provided the ideological justification for military intervention by
claiming that the survival of free societies depended on putting an end to the
popular classes' resistance to authority.[7] In Argentina and Brazil, the new military governments announced a series of policies aimed at reducing the public
sector deficit, raising taxes, cutting import tariffs, establishing wage controls,
and allowing foreign investors easier access. Inflation fell, investment rose, and
protests of organized labor were succesfully repressed, at least for a while. Capital flows helped during the 1970s, but by the early 1980s inflation was higher
than ever before.

External Debt, Budget Deficits, and Inflation

Figures 5.4 and 5.5 depict the behavior of inflation rates in Brazil and Argentina.
The numbers in Table 5.2 show average inflation rates always above one digit
and increasing over the last decades.

The classical paradigm of sustained high inflation relies on budget deficits
financed by money creation. In Brazil, as in Argentina, the government directly

Table 5.3

Seigniorage and Inflation (percentage)

	Argentina		Brazil	
	ΔH/GDP	π	ΔH/GDP	π
1978	4.2	175.5	2.0	38.7
1979	3.2	159.5	3.3	52.7
1980	3.0	100.8	2.0	82.8
1981	2.5	104.5	2.0	105.6
1982	3.9	164.8	2.1	97.8
1983	5.5	343.8	2.0	142.1
1984	5.1	626.7	2.7	197.0
1985	4.3	672.1	2.7	226.9
1986	2.6	90.1	3.6	145.2

Source: IMF, *International Financial Statistics.*

Notes: Seigniorage, ΔH, is the increase in the money base, H, defined as line 14 in IMF, *IFS*, for Brazil and line 14a for Argentina. π is the annual inflation rate of consumer prices, line 64.

controls a substantial part of the economy, and the budget has been in substantial deficit. How much revenue does a government in Brazil and Argentina obtain from the printing of money? Table 5.3 shows seigniorage as a share of GDP. Table 5.3 also shows that there is no positive correlation between seigniorage as a share of GDP and the rate of inflation in Brazil and Argentina. This observation has led some economists to conclude that the budget is not the source of inflation in these countries.

The fact is that the money-goods model of monetarism is inappropriate to the Brazilian and Argentinian economies because it fails to account for changes in deficits not financed by money creation, and because it leaves aside other important sources of inflation. The Brazilian and Argentinian experiences have to be interpreted in light of the institutional reality of financial markets and external debt. In the early eighties, their highly indebted governments were deprived of foreign capital inflows but still needed to finance interest payments. The governments' answer to forced debt service has been, in part, an increase in taxes and a reduction in expenditures. But the response has also been to finance the purchase of foreign exchange not through taxes but by issuing debt or printing money. Observe that the inflationary impact of trade surpluses does not necessarily come from an increase in foreign reserves. If the trade surplus is used to pay interest on government debt and is not counterbalanced by an increase in taxes, it will increase money creation. It is no accident that Argentina and Brazil experienced extraordinary inflation in the aftermath of the debt shock in 1982.

Also observe that in order to produce the trade surpluses, the exchange rate is greatly depreciated. The inflationary consequences of a devaluation, through its impact on imported intermediate and final goods, are well understood. But devaluations also have an important impact on the domestic cost of servicing the external debt. The need to devalue in order to gain in competitiveness implies that debt service measured in domestic currency increases, and thus the budget deficit measured in that currency also increases. This, in turn, increases the required money creation and, hence, inflation. We return to the discussion of the recent acceleration of inflation in Brazil and Argentina in the last section. Now we turn to describe how Argentina and Brazil got into and out of previous debt crises.

In and Out of the 1890s Crisis[8]

Peters (1934) estimates the debt/GDP ratio in Argentina was 360 percent in 1890–91, when debt service difficulties developed. Argentina's failure to service her debt brought down Baring Brothers, the English banking house. Events leading up to the Baring crisis are described by Hyndman (1892) as follows:

> The history of the loans to the Argentine Republic, now that it has become history, is surprising, indeed. A country which had a national debt of £10,000,000 in 1875, contrived to raise it to £70,000,000 in 1889. . . . All the money markets were competing with one another for a share of these good things. London, Paris, Brussels, Berlin, each was ready to outbid the other for the privilege of taking up ventures and floating loans which, at any other time, would have been regarded as very doubtful security, when the nature of the country, the character of the population, and the instability of its political institutions were carefully considered.[9]

Rapid intervention by the Bank of England prevented a major collapse, and a funding loan for Argentina was arranged. Because Argentinian domestic policies remained deficient and the new loans were relatively small, the funding loan failed and a new settlement had to be reached in 1893. The so-called "Arreglo Romero" reduced Argentinian service obligations.

Contrary to common belief, the Baring crisis and external credit rationing were not decisive factors in the Brazilian experience of the 1890s. Fishlow (1988) observes that Brazil continued to contract external loans during 1893 and again in 1895–97. Transfers of resources from abroad were positive until the eve of the 1898 funding loan. The threat of Brazilian default in 1898 was brought about by continually falling coffee prices and domestic financial instability which expressed itself through budget deficits and money creation.

The Brazilian government's financial policies between 1889 and 1892 resulted in a proliferation of new banks. At the same time, new companies were started in every branch of commercial and industrial enterprise. As had just happened in Argentina, a boom was created. *The Economist* commented:

> As capital cannot be attracted, the printing presses are to be set to work, and new issues of inconvertible paper currency poured out. In that way temporary relief may be afforded, and fresh fuel will be heaped upon the fire of speculation. But what the ultimate result of this policy must be, we see in the case of Argentina, and it is time that all who have a stake in Brazil should be called upon to take note of the direction in which she is drifting.[10]

The Economist went further in its comparisons between Brazil and Argentina:

> Those interested in the stability of Brazilian finance are beginning to fear, and not without some cause, that the same policy of currency inflation that has brought the Argentine Republic to grief is being pursued by the Brazilian Government.[11]

Economic and political instability in Brazil were, in fact, on the rise. At the end of 1891, Marshal da Fonseca dissolved the Congress and proclaimed martial law throughout the country. The company mania subsided, and the first burst of wild speculation passed. For many bubble companies, the day of reckoning had come. Shares that once sold at a high premium now could not find buyers at less than half the paid-up capital. Banks ceased to pay interest on deposits. The process of liquidation was underway.

The milreis underwent rapid devaluation. Again the comparisons with Argentina are inevitable. Whether the peso depreciated because of the overissue of banknotes in Argentina or because of the sudden halt in new foreign lending is still debated in the literature. A monetarist position tends to attribute the depreciation to the new bank laws passed in Argentina in 1887, while Williams (1920) claims that cutoff of the capital flow produced the depreciation.[12] Similar questions arose in the case of Brazil. Fishlow (1988) argues that capital inflows did not affect the behavior of the Brazilian exchange rate in the 1890s, and Cardoso (1983) shows that the monetary expansion was not enough to explain the behavior of the exchange rate, which was clearly influenced by the price of coffee.

External confidence was shaken not only by the expansionary policies but also by the political instability. Despite mounting internal and external problems and the negative effects of the Baring crisis on the evaluation of Latin American creditworthiness, Brazil did not default and continued to have limited access to foreign loans. The milreis continued its decline until 1898, and matters went from bad to worse.

The hope that financial affairs in Brazil would improve with the coming to power of the new president, Dr. Campos Salles, soon gave way to the question of whether national bankruptcy could be avoided. The exchange rate had collapsed, adding very heavily to the cost of servicing the foreign debt. One current of opinion ascribed the impending default almost solely to the fall in coffee prices and called upon European financiers to come forward and save the credit of the country. *The Economist* argued the opposing view.

As it became evident that the financial position of the Brazilian government was desperate, rearrangement of the debt was organized in the form of a funding loan with conditions attached which required tight monetary policy. Despite its domestic unpopularity and resulting rebellion against it, Murtinho's contractionary policy, combined with large improvements in the trade balance (in part due to the emerging rubber boom), stabilized the exchange rate after 1903. The cost was economic recession. But soon thereafter, rising coffee prices and a favorable balance of payments would attract a new surge of foreign investment and renewed loans. Prosperity returned in the second half of the 1890s and would last for the next five years.

Argentinian recovery also came quickly. As a matter of fact, the forty-five years between 1870 and 1914 constitute the glorious period of Argentinian growth, notwithstanding the crisis of the early 1890s. Díaz-Alejandro (1970) estimated that GDP grew at an average annual rate of at least 5 percent during the half century preceding 1914. Street (1984) argues that growth was due to a complex combination of technological innovations and educational methods that were wholly novel. According to Street (1984), Sarmiento, who was president from 1868 to 1874, correctly identified the development needs of his country. He encouraged railway construction and free immigration, established a national system of popular education and created new institutes of scientific investigation. In the 1870s and 1880s, English breeds of sheep imported by immigrant ranchers from the British Isles began to replace the poor native flocks and made wool the major export product. This stage was followed by the upgrading of cattle, by the installation of cheap barbed wire fencing and steel windmills, and by the introduction of clover and alfafa. These increased the carrying capacity of the Argentine cattle ranges, permitting meat exports to take the lead. At the same time, the construction of railroads, port facilities, and packing houses utilizing European engineering techniques modernized the Litoral of the Rio de la Plata and the Pampa.

The key innovations at the end of the nineteenth century were the new methods of processing and shipping meat long distances under refrigeration. The discovery that beef could be chilled rather than frozen and shipped across the tropics to arrive in England in good condition opened up a vast new market. This stimulated the construction of packing houses with refrigeration and refrigerated steamships. By 1905, Argentina had displaced the United States as the chief exporter of fresh beef and mutton to the British market. The cereal phase of agricultural development, dominated by wheat production, followed. Development proceeded at fast rates, soon to give place to renewed balance of payments difficulties. In 1921, the sharp decline in commodity prices revived Argentinian debt service problems.

In and Out of the 1930s Crisis

By the mid-1920s, both Brazil and Argentina were borrowing extensively in international capital markets. For both countries, the 1928–33 period illustrates a standard debt crisis: an adverse terms of trade shock combined with cessation of capital flows.[13] Both countries suffered a dramatic fall of income, but both came out of it rapidly; in both countries, by 1938, the output level was well above the previous peak. There were, however, at least two important differences in adjusting to the debt crisis, as observed by Dornbusch and de Pablo (1988):

> Argentina's response to the debt crisis . . . differs from that of other Latin American countries, notably Brazil. The Brazilian decline in real income in 1929–32 averaged only 0.4 percent versus 4.8 percent for Argentina; Brazil's recovery in 1932–37 averaged 7.5 percent per year, versus 5.2 in Argentina. Active domestic industrialization policy via import substitution explains Brazil's superior performance because on the external side Brazil fared worse in the 1932–37 period. . . . But there is another important difference: Argentina faithfully sustained debt service throughout the period of adverse shock; Brazil, by contrast, entered a moratorium.

Brazil entered a moratorium and, shortly afterwards, negotiated a third funding loan. But in the next few years, regular debt service could not be maintained even with a restructuring. Service was suspended in 1931–32. Application of part of the reduced funds available for debt service to the market purchase of bonds, depreciated by the default, became common. In February 1934, a readjustment plan named after finance minister Osvaldo Aranha was put into effect. This was the first time that debt service terms were unilaterally reduced and some payments suspended. Starting in November 1937, there was a complete suspension of debt remittances. In late 1943, Brazil implemented a unilateral exchange offer to consolidate debt service.

In Argentina, by contrast, a conservative government protected the interests of the cattle industry by trading continued debt service for continuation of access to British markets. Internationalism was seen as the source of prosperity in the past, justifying the maintenance of the same posture during a period of economic crisis.

Although recovery was much faster in Brazil than in Argentina, in the 1940s Argentinians continued to be much richer than Brazilians. Buenos Aires was a splendid city in the 1930s and 1940s, with its broad boulevards, delightful parks, and attractive buildings. Today it does not look as good: its infrastructure is crumbling, the parks are dingy, and the streets are filthy. The deterioration of Buenos Aires reflects the decline of the Argentinian economy over the long run. The vigorous economic growth experienced from about 1870 to the beginning of World War I has given way to instability and stagnation since the mid-1970s.

Building Up to the 1980s Crisis

Argentina

When the Peronist regime was overthrown by the military coup in 1976, Argentina was on the verge of hyperinflation. The first priority of the new regime was to stabilize inflation. Martínez de Hoz quickly brought inflation down to 200 percent. A financial reform was implemented linking Argentina more effectively with world capital markets. Foreign exchange transactions were completely liberalized.

Because inflation failed to decline further after it had come down to the 150 percent range, policy makers opted for an "expectations managed approach."[14] Beginning in 1979 they pre-fixed the exchange depreciation rate with a "tablita," announcing gradually declining rates of depreciation. This policy was expected to lower inflation in three ways: by reducing the rate of import price inflation, by imposing discipline on price setters who would have to compete with cheaper imports, and by providing a benchmark to which inflation expectations could converge.

Inflation gradually fell below 100 percent, but since inflation continually exceeded depreciation, the real exchange rate appreciated. The overvaluation effects on trade and employment were slow to come. And in the meantime, relatively high domestic interest rates led to private sector borrowing abroad, and a massive inflow of capital resulted.

By 1980, the overvaluation had become so extreme that despite the government's assertion that the policy would continue, speculation led increasingly to capital flight. The Central Bank was forced to borrow massively to obtain the foreign exchange that would support the tablita. Private speculators, in turn, bought dollars and deposited them abroad.

The undoing of the overvaluation started with the change of presidents. General Viola's refusal to comment on the exchange rate policy months before taking office was a sign that devaluation was ahead. Capital flight became colossal, and Martínez de Hoz was forced to devalue.

Over the next few years, depreciation and inflation became rampant. Exchange controls were instituted again. The budget deficit increased with growing external interest payments. The deterioration of terms of trade and the Malvinas war amplified the devastation of the economy. The inflation rate was up to 600 percent by the time Alfonsín came to power in 1983.

Brazil

In contrast to Argentina, whose bloated debt had mainly facilitated a flight of capital overseas, Brazil put part of her debt to good use in productive investment. The first oil shock in 1973–74 caught Brazil at the peak of its economic "miracle": a GDP growth rate of 10 percent a year had prevailed since 1968, while inflation rates had been stable and relatively low. As the leading developing country importer of petroleum, and one whose industry and transport were centered on the car and truck industry, the blow was especially severe. To make matters even more delicate, a political transition was in its initial stages, for which continuing prosperity was regarded as a necessary condition. These circumstances predisposed Brazil to an adjustment strategy based upon high, although slower, rates of growth, and one in which there was more reliance upon government-stimulated import substitution investment than upon market-driven responses to changes in exchange rates or relative prices of petroleum. External debt played a central role in that strategy, financing investment and large current account deficits, thus postponing the negative real income effects of the shock.[15]

If there was demand for debt, there was also supply. Brazil was a favored and privileged participant in the Euro-currency market. It had started to borrow early, even before the oil shock, and its rapid growth and level of industrialization qualified the country as highly creditworthy.

The strategy succeeded in sustaining high rates of growth, but the debt/export ratio almost doubled. Brazil had thus become much more vulnerable to changes in the international economy as a result of its adjustment style. At the same time, there were signs of an accumulating domestic disequilibrium as the ambitious investment plan was followed. Government expenditure outran its finance, and monetary accommodation was increasingly necessary. The level of inflation had doubled from its pre–oil-shock level of 20 percent, and only a stop-and-go macro-policy and increasing direct controls prevented the situation from getting even more out of hand.

Even on the eve of the second oil shock, Brazil faced the need for a midterm modification of strategy. Such was the proposal of Mario Símonsen, the finance minister of the Figueiredo government installed in March 1979. But his approach, labeled "recessionist" by Brazilian critics, yielded to a more ambitious supply-side plan undertaken by Antonio Delfím Netto. Priority was given to credit expansion in order to finance investment in the agricultural and energy sectors. A maxi-devaluation of 30 percent, the first departure from the crawling peg implemented in 1968, would ease the foreign exchange constraint. Macroeconomic policy was supposed to contain inflation by reducing interest rates (a significant cost component) and by changing expectations through pre-announced internal monetary correction and exchange rate devaluation at 45 percent and 40 percent, respectively.

Delfím's strategy did not work. The balance of payments registered a record current account deficit in 1980. The inflation rate reached the three digit level, reflecting both excess demand and supply shocks like the increases of public sector prices, the effects of devaluation, and the consequences of a new wage law mandating a shorter adjustment lag. New finance was necessary, adding not only to the registered medium- and long-term debt, but increasingly to short-term liabilities.

In October 1980, a more orthodox package of fiscal and monetary restraint was fashioned. Banks then agreed to new loans in 1981 to meet immediate needs. But the financing, since it was increasingly allocated to debt service, did not leave a margin for real growth. Brazil reluctantly entered into a lengthy period of adjustment through recession that was to last until 1983, provoking a decrease in income greater than the fall in the 1930s.

In both Brazil and Argentina democracy had been restored by 1985, but the debt and inflation problems remained unchanged. Brazil's trade balance improved more rapidly than had been expected, due to the jump in exports in 1984. The new civilian government, free from the requirements of external creditors, soon opted for a more expansionist policy based upon increased internal demand. Gross domestic product grew more than 8 percent in 1985. Accelerating inflation, however, remained a concern and provoked popular discontent and political dissatisfaction. The response was the "Plano Cruzado," in the mold of the Austral Plan launched in Argentina in 1985.

Recent Developments

In June 1985 the annualized inflation rate in Argentina reached almost 6,000 percent. The situation was ripe for the Austral Plan, a program of stabilization, the key features of which were the use of wage-price controls and a fixed exchange rate. A similar program was introduced in Brazil in March 1986. Although fiscal consolidation was not achieved in either of the two cases, it was part of the initial program. The combination of fiscal correction and incomes policy have come to be known as "heterodox" programs, as opposed to conventional IMF packages that emphasize tight monetary policy and fiscal correction as the exclusive instruments of stabilization.[16]

Heterodoxy works, so long as fiscal consolidation takes place and the economy does not have to produce trade surpluses larger than those consistent with the improvement in the budget and reduced inflation rates. A consistent change in the budget and in the current account will provide for a new equilibrium at lower inflation rates.[17] The price freeze combined with remonetization will avoid the costly adjustment through cycles. But the program is doomed to failure if the fundamentals are not changed. A price freeze will reduce inflation temporarily, but once removed, inflation will rebound as the economy moves back to its previous equilibrium.

Brazil

Despite its initial success, the Cruzado Plan is now the most obvious example of the failure of heterodox programs to stop inflation. Motivated by strong popular support for the price freeze, controls were maintained far too long; the budget was allowed to deteriorate dramatically, and monetary policy was too loose. By the end of 1986 inflation exploded once more.

The disappearance in the last quarter of 1986 of the hitherto customary monthly trade surplus led to the declaration of a moratorium in February 1987. This was followed by a new stabilization plan and price controls. They did not last. In July 1988, inflation had reached the equivalent of an annual rate of 1,200 percent. The budget deficit had been increasing and, despite promises of stringency, projects of dubious worth (such as a railway from Brasilia to the home state of the president) were being undertaken. The government's attempt to cut its own wage bill failed, and Brazilian growth was predicted to be zero (at best) in 1988.

Brazil's social welfare indicators are strikingly low.[18] Infant mortality is 67 per thousand compared, for example, to 22 per thousand for Chile.[19] In the northeast of Brazil, it is higher than in much of Sub-Saharan Africa. In education, Brazil's profile is equally dramatic. Children in Brazil average fewer years in school than children in any other Latin American country except El Salvador and Nicaragua. Only 21 percent of Brazilian children attend secondary school compared to 90 percent in Korea. The reasons are not only a lack of social funds, but the fact that the existing funds are mistargeted away from the poorest sectors of society; they are badly managed by centralized government agencies, and their distribution is influenced by political interests, not to mention corruption.

The only front on which the current administration claims relative success has been the debt renegotiation of mid-1988. The renegotiation was a result of the growing trade surpluses. But even here, there seems to be turbulence ahead. In July 1988, the government was already devaluing the cruzado at approximately 1 percent per day. Nonetheless, exporters claimed that the exchange rate was getting overvalued, while the government was afraid that faster devaluation rates would stimulate inflation.

Today, the country has no effective government and the economic team has no plans. Some cosmetic changes proposed by Finance Minister Mailson da Nobrega, such as speeding up the collection of taxes, are far from representing a cure to Brazil's mounting problems.

Argentina

In Argentina, the Austral Plan combined a less stringent price freeze with more austerity and thus was more successful in achieving disinflation than the Cruzado Plan. But, as in the Brazilian case, without further dramatic cuts in the budget and as long as large trade surpluses have to be generated to service the external debt, sustained disinflation cannot be achieved.

By 1987, acceleration of inflation was once more the central feature of the economy. Along with it, real wages fell. Real government revenues declined as well, and as a result, the budget deficit increased. The economic recovery in 1986 and 1987 went hand in hand with a rapid increase in imports. At the same time, export revenues declined because of the persistent weakness of the international prices of agricultural goods and the lack of exportable surpluses. Despite the greater amount of external financing provided by multilateral agencies, external constraints continued to limit the growth prospect of the economy.

Although by mid-1988 Argentina's export prospects improved with the rise in grain and meat prices, the forecast trade surplus remained insufficient to cover debt service. The government has promised the IMF to cut the budget deficit to 3.9 percent of GDP in 1988 from 7.2 percent in 1987, but many economists believe the deficit is actually increasing. Per capita output is lower than fifteen years ago and the decline is bound to accelerate. With opinion polls predicting a Peronist victory in the general election set for May 1989, the current Radical government seems paralyzed by the fear that tough measures will bring electoral defeat.

A Case for Interest Recycling

The position of the public sectors in Brazil and Argentina today is badly compromised by the need to extract resources from the private sector for the service of the external debt. Between 1981 and 1986, Brazil and Argentina transferred abroad at least 2 percent of their GDP per year. In the absence of debt relief, they face the choice of paying interest and accepting stagflation, or suspending payments. Brazil tried a moratorium in 1987 without success. Argentina, having taken the austerity road, has done worse and was forced to cut investment while fighting inflation and social unrest.

This section shows how interest recycling in domestic currency can help to restore investment and development. A scheme that recycles a large part of the interest payments in the country does away with the need for trade surpluses and the resulting crowding out of investment. This would make it possible to have investment and growth, and yet provide creditors with debt service, albeit in investments that cannot be repatriated for the time being.

Recycling of interest could take place by adopting the following procedure. A small trade surplus (of perhaps 1 percent of GDP in the case of Brazil) would be used to service a minor part of the debt, such as trade credit and debts to governments and multilateral agencies. The major part of the debt service would be paid in local currency. Part of these payments must be automatically loaned to the government to finance investment, and the rest can be used to finance loans or acquisition of assets in the country. The only restriction on the disposal of these payments or the investments they generate would be that they could not be transferred abroad. In combination with a serious fiscal reform, this shift in debt servicing would restore normal growth and investment and, thereby, provide maximum assurance of an ultimate transfer of resources to the creditors.

Figure 5.6. **Interest Recycling with Flexible Real Wages**

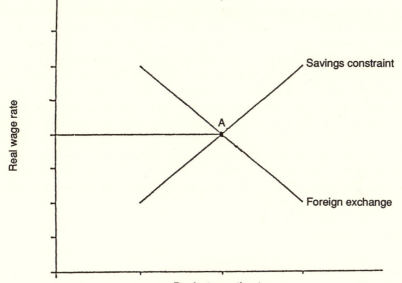

Figure 5.6 represents a model that can be used to evaluate the effects on growth rates that can be achieved through recycling. The results are formally derived in Appendix 1. In this section we use graphs to explain our results.

The model is summarized in two equations. The first one, depicted by the downward sloping schedule in Figure 5.6, represents the foreign exchange constraint. It defines an inverse relationship between the growth rate and the real wage: the larger the real wage, the less competitive a country is abroad and, given external credit rationing, the fewer imports it can afford for investment.

The upward sloping schedule denotes the savings constraint: given domestic savings and the budget deficit, the larger the noninterest current account that can be financed, the more the country can import, invest, and grow. As long as real wages are fully flexible, the exchange rate can be managed in such a way as to make the real wage consistent with point A in Figure 5.6, where the two constraints are binding.

Consider the case of a reduction of the budget deficit. The cut in the deficit releases resources for investment, shifting the schedule that represents the savings constraint to the right. If the government could further devalue the real exchange rate and reduce real wages, extra foreign resources to complement domestic savings would make greater potential growth possible. But consider the case where real wages are already too low and the economy faces real wage resistance. Under these circumstances, a reduction of the budget deficit would bring no benefits. Although it would increase domestic savings, no additional

Figure 5.7. **Interest Recycling with Real Wage Floor**

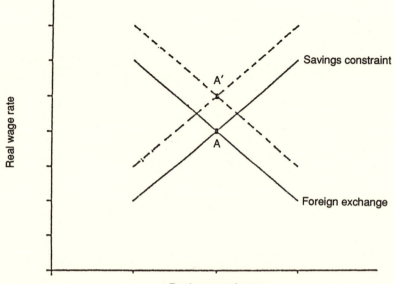

investment would take place since the economy cannot grow without imported goods. The economy would remain stuck at point A, with a real wage larger than the one prevailing at A'.[20]

Figure 5.7 shows the effect of interest recycling in the absence of budget correction. An economy in which both constraints are initially binding experiences no change in its growth rate if wages fully absorb the extra resources. But an economy where only the foreign exchange is initially binding, and where real wages are below the level consistent with interest recycling, will experience some increase in the growth rate. Table 5.4 summarizes the effects of interest recycling and budget consolidation in economies where both constraints are initially binding and where there is real wage resistance.

The case to concentrate on is the one where both budget consolidation and interest recycling take place simultaneously. This is represented in Figure 5.8. Point A represents an economy where both constraints are binding. Before this situation was reached, real devaluation in response to the debt crisis had brought real wages down. Now the economy faces real wage resistance. Real wages are low and the economy is stagnant. The government implements two measures.

First, a share of debt service is recycled in domestic currency. Recycling of interest amounting to 3 percent of GDP releases an equivalent amount for imports, and shifts the downward sloping schedule to the right. Note that the cur-

Table 5.4

Effects on Growth and Real Wages of Different Policies Where Both Constraints Are Initially Binding and There Is Resistance to Further Cuts in Real Wages

		Budget consolidation	
		Yes	No
Interest recycling	Yes	$\Delta\lambda>0$ $\Delta w\geq0$	$\Delta\lambda=0$ $\Delta w>0$
	No	$\Delta\lambda=0$ $\Delta w=0$	$\Delta\lambda=0$ $\Delta w=0$

Note: λ is the product growth rate and w is the real wage.

rent account remains unchanged. Assume that import requirement per unit of investment is 0.5. If the right policies were in place and domestic resources were available, the extra imports would be consistent with an increase in investment equal to 6 percent of GDP. Since the current account is unchanged, financing the extra 6 percent of investment requires an extra 6 percent in national savings. This calls for the second action: an increase in taxes and a cut in current expenditures that reduce the budget deficit by 6 percent. The economy would then be able to move to point A' where real wages are unchanged and potential growth is larger than before. The appendix gives the formula for calculating the positive impact on the growth rate. In an economy where the incremental capital/output ratio is 3, the import requirement per unit of investment goods is 0.5, and 3 percent of GDP is recycled, the annual growth rate can be increased by 2 percentage points.

As income grows reconstruction will take place. In ten years Argentina and Brazil should be able to start making transfers abroad without their severe current financial instability and social costs.

Concluding Remarks

Brazil and Argentina are among the most inflationary economies in Latin America. Along with Mexico, they have the largest economies (in terms of GDP) and the most advanced manufacturing sectors of the region. Postwar emphasis on import-substitution ran along similar lines in both countries. But, in contrast to Argentina, a part of the debt contracted during the 1970s was put to good use in Brazil and helped develop import substituting projects. While Argentina has been stagnant since 1975, Brazil has grown fast. And unlike Argentina, financial instability is a recent phenomenon in Brazil.

Figure 5.8. **Interest Recycling with Real Wage Floor and Deficit Reduction**

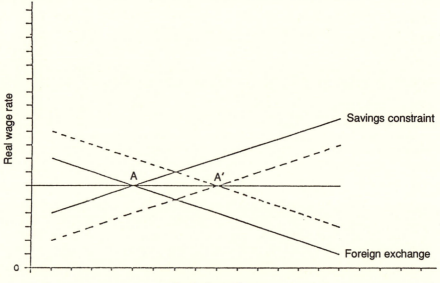

In the mid-1980s, Brazil caught the Argentine disease. In the middle of the most favorable external conditions—low oil prices, low interest rates, sharply increasing export prices—lack of political leadership is producing the most destructive economic policy Brazil has witnessed in this century. It does not take Peronist populism to break a country's productive structure. High and accelerating inflation, institutional instability, shortening policy horizons, and increasingly random and arbitrary policies of a government in search of revenue and favor can do the same.

Argentina and Brazil today illustrate economies striving to service the debt by generating trade surpluses, and thus face growing inflation despite their efforts to cut the budget. The situation gets easily complicated when one considers that people always find ways to avoid holding cash balances. The flight from money magnifies the inflation process. Inflation rates in Brazil today have become as high and as subject to sharp acceleration as in Argentina (see Figures 5.9 and 5.10). Inflation uncertainty implies short horizons for production decisions and concentration of assets on inflation hedging. The economic structure that results emphasizes finance at the expense of production. The next step is capital flight, a phenomenon that has been endemic in Argentina and that has increased in Brazil in the past few years.

While in the Argentinian case flight from money has traditionally meant capital flight into dollar deposits and cash, in Brazil it also created an ever more

Figure 5.9. **Brazilian Inflation**
(three-month moving average of monthly rate)

Percent

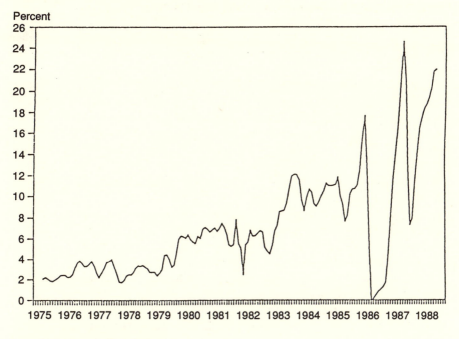

Figure 5.10. **Argentine Inflation**
(three-month moving average of monthly rate)

Percent

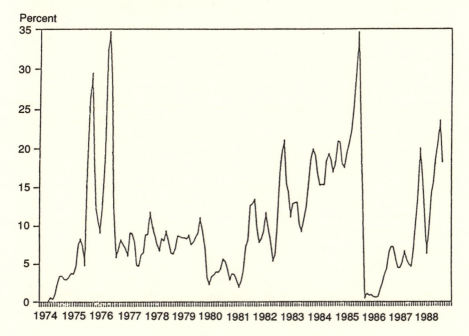

perfect domestic money market. The government has 35 billion U.S. dollars of domestic debt oustanding, and this debt has an effective maturity of one day. It is indexed and thus is, in principle, sheltered against the risk of inflation. But when the public loses confidence in the government's ability or willingness to pay full indexation, there will be flight from the overnights to real assets and to the dollar. Raising interest rates sky high would not increase confidence, because budget deficits would merely increase further and the debt would become un-sustainably large. The government would then be forced to pay its debts in cash, financing a flight into real assets and the dollar which would set off hyperinfla-tion.[21]

The other reason to fear inflation escalation comes from the economy's adap-tation to inflation, as buyers and sellers, borrowers and lenders, and the govern-ment and the taxpayers are engaged in a self-defeating rat race of shortening the lags on pricing and indexation, collection and payment. And the more successful they are in inventing new instruments and institutions, the more rapidly inflation escalates, causing the entire economy to center on the black market dollar. On the current course higher and higher inflation is likely.

Whether the Brazilian economy will experience the ultimate extreme of hyperinflation remains to be seen. At this point, there is still plenty of room for the government to manage inflation from month to month: it may well stretch out the time by freezes and squeezes, deals and mini-adjustments for a year or more as it has done twice already when inflation reached peak levels. But unless reconstruction is taken seriously, the economic scenario for Brazil in the 1990s is the Argentine scenario of an economy that grows at a very moder-ate rate with capital flight, emigration, frequent bouts of inflation and financial instability, low investment, and declining real wages. The economic pie will shrink and the infighting will become more fierce. Argentina has been trotting down this path, steadily sinking, steadily falling behind. Although she has had occasional growth, per capita consumption today is much lower than it was ten years ago. Brazil is nowhere near that point, but the risk of getting into the trap is far from negligible. This risk is larger when the government shows lack of realism—from the zero inflation target of the Cruzado Plan to the absurd renegotiation of external debt which is now one of the engines of money creation and inflation.

There are further reasons for apprehension. While everything is indexed, in-cluding wages, prices, interest rates, taxes, and accounting systems, there is a profound social impact for the lower classes whose subsistence is not protected. Escalation of conflicts in Brazil beyond their historical levels suggests that fudg-ing distribution issues through growth worked in the past but might not be possible in the future.

Argentina, which has traditionally had a better income distribution, now expe-riences growing poverty. Inflation might prove impossible to stop, and the exter-nal debt will remain a harrowing problem. There will be no payments on principal, and interest will be in jeopardy from time to time. Writedowns seem unavoidable.

This paper has argued that interest recycling offers a partial answer to those problems. It works by giving Brazil and Argentina some years to restore a normal macroeconomy before resuming resource transfers abroad.

Appendix 1
Interest Recycling

In this appendix the results stated in the text are derived formally, starting with national accounting. The variables are expressed in units of domestic goods. The budget deficit, BU, is:

$$(A.1) \qquad BU \equiv G + F - T$$

where

G = current expenditures except debt service
F = foreign debt service measured in domestic goods.
   aF is the fraction paid in dollars, while (1–a)F is paid in local currency.
T = taxes minus transfers, including interest payments on the domestic debt.

Gross Domestic Output, GDP, is:

$$(A.2) \qquad GDP \equiv C + GI + G + X - M$$

where

C = consumption of the private sector
GI = gross investment
X – M = non-interest current account.

Imports in units of domestic goods are $M = \phi/w$, where ϕ is the quantity of imported goods and w is the real exchange rate, expressed as the ratio between domestic and foreign prices measured in the same currency. Assuming that prices reflect wage costs, w is also a measure of relative wages at home and abroad.

Gross National Income, GNP, and Residents' Disposable Income, Y, are defined respectively as:

$$(A.3) \qquad GNP \equiv GDP - F$$

$$(A.4) \qquad Y \equiv GNP - T \equiv GDP - F - T = (c+s)[GDP - F - T]$$

where c and s are the marginal propensities to consume and save.

Combining the identities above we can write:

(A.5) $$s[GDP–F–T] – (G–T) – X + M + aF \equiv GI$$

Gross investment is:

(A.6) $$GI = I + (1–a)F = NI + DEP$$

where

I	=	gross investment by residents
(1–a)F	=	gross investment from interest recycling
DEP	=	depreciation
NI	=	net investment

We also observe that:

(A.7) $$GI/GDP – (NI/GDP) + (DEP/GDP) = k\lambda + h$$

where

k	=	incremental capital/output ratio
λ	=	growth rate of GDP
h	=	share of capital depreciation in output

Assuming that $GI = \min\{\beta(w)\phi, \theta(w)R\}$ where R = domestic resources. We can write the import requirements for investment as:

(A.8) $$M/GDP = m(w)GI/GDP = m(w)[k\lambda + h]$$

where $m(w) – 1/[w\beta(w)]$ is the required imports per unit of investment.

We divide (A.5) by GDP and substitute (A.7) and (A.8) in it to obtain:

(A.9) $$\lambda = \{1/k[1–m(w)]\}\{s(1–f–t)–(g–t)–[1–m(w)]h–x(w)+af\}$$

Assuming that the share of exports in output are inversely related to the real exchange rate, w, and that the marginal propensity to import is positively related to it, we draw equation (A.9) as the positively sloped schedule in Figure 5.6. The slope of the schedule representing the savings constraint is given by:

(A.10) $$d\lambda/dw = \{1/k[1–m(w)]\}v$$

where

$$v \equiv (x/w)\{q_x + [(m/x)(k\lambda + 1)qm]\}$$

q_x = the absolute value of the elasticity of the share of exports in output in relation to the real exchange rate.

q_m = the elasticity of the demand for imported inputs in relation to the real exchange rate.

The foreign exchange constraint is expressed as:

$$(A.11) \qquad \lambda = [1/km(x)][x(w)-af-m(w)h]$$

and is represented by the downward sloping schedule in Figure 5.6. Its slope is given by:

$$(A.12) \qquad d\lambda/dw = -[1/km(w)]v$$

Effects of a reduction of the budget deficit and from a change in the amount of debt service paid in local currency can be calculated from:

$$(A.13) \qquad \begin{bmatrix} (1-m)k & -v \\ mk & v \end{bmatrix} \begin{bmatrix} d\lambda \\ dw \end{bmatrix} = \begin{bmatrix} fda + (1-s)dt - dg \\ -fda \end{bmatrix}$$

Balancing the budget:

A budget improvement is defined as $dbu = (1-s)dt - dg$. We also observe that:

$$d\lambda = -(v/mk)dw$$

For flexible real wages, $dw = -(m/v)dbu$, and $d\lambda = (1/k)dbu$.
Real wage resistance implies $dw = 0$, and $d\lambda = 0$.

Recycling interest:

An increase in the amount of interest paid in domestic currency is defined as a reduction in a. From (A.13) we can calculate for flexible wages:

$$dw = -(f/v)da, \text{ and } d\lambda = 0.$$

Recycling interest and reducing the budget while keeping real wages unchanged yields:

$$d\lambda = (f/mk)(-da)$$

Table 5.1A

Macro Indicators: Argentina and Brazil (percentage)

	Real growth rates		Inflation rates		Investment/GDP	
	Argentina	Brazil	Argentina	Brazil	Argentina	Brazil
1970–75	3.3	10.0	90.7	22.9	21.2	22.8
1976–80	2.0	7.1	181.0	56.9	22.7	22.4
1981–85	–2.0	1.8	390.0	165.6	14.6	17.4
1986	5.4	8.2	81.9	142.3	11.6	18.1
1987[a]	1.6	2.9	174.9	415.8	13.3	17.1

Sources: FGV, *Conjuntura Económica*; Banco Central do Brasil; IBGE; FIEL; and Dornbusch and de Pablo (1988).
[a]Indicates preliminary estimate.

Table 5.2A

Balance of Payments Indicators: Argentina and Brazil
(percentage and indexes)

	Current account/ GDP		Terms of trade		Real exchange rate	
	Argentina	Brazil	Argentina	Brazil	Argentina	Brazil
1970–75	–0.7	–3.1	79	102	129	125
1976–80	0.0	–7.9	100	100	100	100
1981–85	–4.0	–7.0	82	67	99	89
1986	–4.3	–4.5	65	89	75	70
1987[a]	–6.1		62	95(?)	70	69

Sources: FGV, *Conjuntura Económica*; and FIEL, *Indicadores de Coyuntura*.
[a]Indicates preliminary estimate.

Notes

1. The second section draws on Cardoso and Dornbusch (1988) and the fourth relies on Cardoso and Fishlow (1988) as well as on Dornbusch and de Pablo (1988). An argument in favor of interest recycling is found in Dornbusch (1988) as well as in Cardoso and Dornbusch (1988). In a lecture in Brasilia in May 1988, Dragoslav Avramovic also advanced a proposition in favor of interest recycling in domestic currency.

2. The figure compares indexes for GDP in Brazil and Argentina at 1982 prices. We

Table 5.3A

Foreign Debt Indicators: Argentina and Brazil

	Total debt (billions of U.S. dollars)		External debt/GDP	
	Argentina	Brazil	Argentina	Brazil
1965	$2.7	$3.6	14%	16%
1970	3.9	5.3	17	21
1975	7.9	21.2	19	20
1980	27.2	64.6	37	27
1982	43.6	83.3	60	31
1986	51.4	110.6	65	39
1987	56.3	121.4	70	37

Sources: Banco Central do Brasil; and Dornbusch and de Pablo (1988).

avoid the comparison of GDPs measured in dollars because of the extreme oscillations of the Argentinian real exchange rate. We note though that in current dollars, GDP per capita, which was approximately 30 percent of Argentina's in the mid-1960s, was larger than 70 percent of it in the mid-1980s. Using Summers and Heston's (1984) PPP estimates, Brazilian GDP per capita was 79 percent of Argentinian GDP per capita in the early 1980s.

3. Economists disagree about exactly when stagnation in Argentina started. Bunge (1922) claims that stagnation originated in 1914 when railroad building came to an end. Díaz-Alejandro (1970) dates stagnation to 1930. By contrast, Rostow considered Argentina to have entered the takeoff to self-sustaining industrial growth during the 1930s. Di Tella and Zymelman (1967) first accepted Rostow's views but later pointed out that the acceleration of the 1940s was arrested by the 1952 crisis. Ferrer (1967) selects 1948 as the beginning of stagnation. Raul Prebisch and his ECLA team saw the period 1954–57 as the onset of decline, but Dornbusch and de Pablo (1988) only attribute stagnation and decline to the period since 1975.

4. Broad analyses of economic and political developments in Brazil and Argentina can be found in Bresser (1984), Cavallo (1986), Fishlow (1972), Goldsmith (1986), Mallon and Sourrouille (1975), Rock (1985), Símonsen (1988), Skidmore (1967) and (1988), Stepan (1973), and Wynia (1986).

5. See Kaufman (1987).

6. See O'Donnell (1973).

7. The Brazilian military remained in power for twenty years, while the military regime in Argentina was interrupted between 1973 and 1976 when the Peronists briefly returned to power.

8. Among studies of capital movements to Brazil and Argentina in the nineteenth century, one must mention Boucas (1950), Calogeras (1910), Campos (1946), Castro (1889), Edelstein (1982), Feis (1965), Fishlow (1988), Kindleberger (1985), Stone (1977), Taussig (1928), Wileman (1896), and Williams (1920).

9. H. M. Hyndman (1892).

10. *The Economist*, 10 January 1891.

11. *The Economist*, 10 January 1891.

12. See Williams (1920), Kindleberger (1985), and Fishlow (1988).

13. The 1930s debt crisis and its aftermath in Brazil and Argentina have been extensively studied. For different approaches and references see Cardoso (1987), Kindleberger (1984), Madison (1985), Felix (1987), and O'Connell (1984).

14. See Fernández (1985), Calvo (1983) and (1986), Corbo and de Melo (1985), Ramos (1986), and Rodríguez (1982).

15. See Cardoso and Fishlow (1988). The Brazilian debt strategy is also examined in Batista (1983) and (1988), Cardoso (1987a), Díaz-Alejandro (1983), and Símonsen (1985), among others.

16. For more detailed analyses of the programs used to stop inflation in Brazil and Argentina, see, for instance, Bruno et al. (1988), Cardoso (1986), Cardoso and Dornbus (1987), Dornbusch and Símonsen (1987), and Kaufman (1987).

17. This model is formalized in Cardoso (1988).

18. See Fishlow (1976) and Morley (1982).

19. The data is from World Bank (1988).

20. In the Appendix, we show formally the effects of a reduction of the budget deficit, as well as the effects of interest recycling.

21. Of course, there is the plausible alternative of a compulsory consolidation of the debt into long-term bonds. Yet another possibility is to give bondholders a forced conversion to equities in public enterprises.

References

Batista, Paulo Nogueira. *Mito e Realidade da Dívida Externa Brasileira*. Rio de Janeiro: Paz e Terra, 1983.

———, ed. *Novos Ensaios sobre o Setor Externo Brasileiro*. Rio de Janeiro: Fundação Getúlio Vargas, 1988.

Boucas, Valentím. *História da Dívida Externa*. Rio de Janeiro, 1950.

Bresser Pereira, Luis. *Development and Crisis in Brazil: 1930–1983*. Boulder: Westview Press, 1984.

Bruno, Michael et al., eds. *Stopping High Inflation*. Cambridge: MIT Press, 1988.

Bunge, Alejandro. *Las Industrias del Norte*. Buenos Aires: n.p. 1922.

Calogeras, J. Pandia. *La Politique Monétaire du Brésil*. Rio de Janeiro: Imprimerie Nationale, 1910.

Calvo, Guillermo. "Trying to Stabilize: Some Theoretical Reflections Based on the Case of Argentina." In *Financial Policies and the World Capital Market: The Problem of Latin American Countries*. Ed. Aspe, Dornbusch, and Obstfeld. Chicago: University of Chicago Press, 1983.

———. "Fractured Liberalism: Argentina under Martínez de Hoz" *Economic Development and Cultural Change*, April 1986.

Campos, Lemas de Souza. *Dívida Externa*. Rio de Janeiro: Impresa Nacional, 1946.

Cardoso, Eliana. "Exchange Rates in Nineteenth Century Brazil: An Econometric Model." *Journal of Development Studies* 19, no. 2 (January 1983): 170–78.

———. "What Policy Makers Can Learn From Brazil and Argentina" *Challenge*, September–October 1986.

———. *Inflation, Growth and the Real Exchange Rate: Brazil and Latin America, 1850–1983*. New York: Garland Publishing, New York, 1987.

———. "Latin American Debt: Which Way Now?" *Challenge*, May 1987a.

———. "Seigniorage and Repression: Monetary Rythms of Latin America," Fletcher School, Medford, Mass. mimeo, 1988.

Cardoso, Eliana, and Rudiger Dornbusch. "Brazil's Tropical Plan" *American Economic Review*, May 1987.

Cardoso, Eliana, and Rudiger Dornbush. "Brazilian Debt Crises: Past and Present," MIT, Cambridge, mimeo, 1988.

Cardoso, Eliana, and Albert Fishlow. "Macroeconomics of Brazilian External Debt," National Bureau of Economic Research, Cambridge, mimeo, 1988.

Castro Carreira, Liberato. *História Financeira e Orçamentária do Império do Brasil desde a sua Fundação*. Rio de Janeiro: Imprensa Nacional, 1889.

Cavallo, Domingo. "Long-Term Growth in the Light of External Balance Policies: The Case of Argentina." In *The Open Economy*, Dornbusch and Helmers, eds. Oxford: Oxford University Press, 1970.

Corbo, Vittorio, and de Melo, eds. "Liberalization With Stabilization in the Southern Cone of Latin America." Special issue of *World Development*, August 1985.

Díaz-Alejandro, Carlos. *Essays on the Economic History of Argentina*. New Haven: Yale University Press, 1970.

———. "Some Aspects of the 1982–1983 Brazilian Payments Crisis." *Brookings Papers in Economic Activity* 1, 1983, pp. 515–52.

Di Tella, Guido, and Manuel Zymelman. *Las Etapas del Desarollo Económico de la Argentina*. Buenos Aires: Editorial Universitaria de Buenos Aires, 1967.

Dornbusch, Rudiger. *Developing Country Debt: Anatomy and Solutions*. New York: Twentieth Century Fund, 1988.

Dornbusch, Rudiger, and de Pablo. "Debt and Macroeconomic Instability in Argentina," National Bureau of Economic Research, Cambridge, mimeo, 1988.

Dornbusch, Rudiger, and Mario Símonsen. *Inflation Stabilization with Incomes Policy Support*. New York: Group of Thirty, 1987.

Edelstein, Michael. *Overseas Investment in the Age of High Imperialism*. New York: Columbia University Press, 1982.

Feis, Herbert. *Europe The World's Banker, 1870–1914*. New York: Norton, 1965.

Felix, David. "Alternative Outcomes of the Latin American Debt Crisis: Lessons from the Past." *Latin American Research Review* 22, no. 2, 1987.

Fernández, R. B. "The Expectations Management Approach to Stabilization in Argentina 1976–82." *World Development* 13, no. 8 (August 1985): 871–892.

Ferrer, Aldo. *The Argentine Economy*. Berkeley: University of California Press, 1967.

Fishlow, Albert. "Some Reflections in post-1964 Economic Policy." In *Authoritarian Brazil*. Ed. Alfred Stepan. Yale University Press, New Haven, 1972.

———. "Brazilian Size Distribution of Income." In *Income Distribution in Latin America*. Ed. Foxley. Cambridge: Cambridge University Press, 1976.

———. "Lessons of the 1890s for the 1980s." In *Debt, Stabilization and Development*. Ed. R. Findlay, New York: Basil Blackwell, 1988.

Goldsmith, Raymond. *Desenvolvimento Financeiro Sob Um Século de Inflação*. São Paulo: Harper and Row do Brasil, 1986.

Hyndman, H. *Commercial Crisis of the Nineteenth Century*. Reprint. New York: Augustus Kelley, 1967.

Kaufman, Robert. "Politics and Inflation in Argentina and Brazil: The Austral and Cruzado Packages in Historical Perspective," Rutgers University, mimeo, 1987.

Kindleberger, Charles. "The 1929 World Depression in Latin America from Outside." In *Latin America in the 1930s*. Ed. R. Thorpe. London: Macmillan, 1984.

———. "Historical Perspective on Today's Third-World Debt Problem," ch. 12, pp. 190–211, and "International Propagation of Financial Crises," ch. 14, pp. 226–239, in *Keynesianism vs. Monetarism*, Boston: George Allen & Unwin, 1985.

Madison, Angus. *Two Crises: Latin America and Asia 1929–38 and 1973–83*. Paris: OECD, 1985.

Mallon, Richard, and Juan Sourrouille. *Economic Policy Making in a Conflict Society*. Cambridge, Mass.: Harvard University Press, 1975.

Morley, Samuel. *Labor Markets and Inequitable Growth: The Case of Inequitable Growth in Brazil*. Cambridge: Cambridge University Press, 1982.

O'Connell, Arturo. "Argentina in the Depression: Problems of an Open Economy." In *Latin America in the 1930s*. Ed. R. Thorpe. London: Macmillan, 1984.

O'Donnell, Guillermo. *Modernization and Bureaucratic-Authoritarianism: Studies in South American Politics*. Berkeley: University of California, 1973.

Peters, H. E. *The Foreign Debt of the Argentine Republic*. Baltimore: Johns Hopkins University Press, 1934.

Ramos, Joseph. *Neoconservative Economics in the Southern Cone of Latin America, 1973–83*. Baltimore: Johns Hopkins University Press, 1986.

Rippy, J. Fred. *British Investment in Latin America, 1822–1949*. New York: Arno Press, 1977.

Rock, David. *Argentina: 1516–1982*. Los Angeles: University of California Press, 1985.

Rodríguez, Carlos. "The Argentine Stabilization Plan of December 20th," *World Development*, no. 10, 1982.

Símonsen, Mario. "The Developing Country Debt Problem." In *International Debt and the Developing Countries*. Ed. G. Smith and J. Cuddington. World Bank, 1985.

―――. "Brazil." In *The Open Economy: Tools for Policy Makers in Developing Countries*. Ed. R. Dornbusch and L. Helmers. Oxford: Oxford University Press, 1988.

Skidmore, Thomas. *Politics in Brazil, 1930–1964: An Experiment in Democracy*. Oxford: Oxford University Press, 1967.

―――. *The Politics of Military Rule in Brazil: 1964–1985*. New York: Oxford University Press, 1988.

Stepan, Alfred, ed. *Authoritarian Brazil*. New Haven: Yale University Press, 1973.

Stone, Irving. "British Direct and Portfolio Investment in Latin America Before 1914." *Journal of Economic History* 37, no. 3 (September 1977): 690–722.

Street, James. "The Ayres-Kuznets Framework and Argentine Dependency." In *Latin America's Economic Development*. Ed. James Dietz and James Street. Boulder: Rienner, 1984.

Summers, R., and R. Heston. "Improved International Comparisons of Real Product and Its Composition: 1950–1980." *Review of Income and Wealth*, June 1984.

Taussig, F. W. *International Trade*. New York: Macmillan, 1928.

Wileman, J. P. *Brazilian Exchange: The Study of an Inconvertible Currency*. Buenos Aires: Galli Bros., 1896. Reprint. Westport, Conn.: Greenwood Press, 1969.

Williams, J. H. *Argentine International Trade under Inconvertible Paper Money 1880–1900*. 1920. Reprint. New York: AMS Press, 1971.

Wynia, Gary. *Argentina*. New York: Holmes & Meier, 1986.

World Bank. *Brazil, Public Spending in Social Programs, Issues and Options*. Washington, D.C., 1988.

COMMENTS

Miguel Molina

Eliana Cardoso's paper is an excellent summary of Brazil's and Argentina's economic and financial evolution during this century. She identifies the main differences between both countries and their uses and abuses of external debt. She shows that in the 1970s debt run-up, Argentina misused much of its external debt to finance capital flight, whereas Brazil made more productive use of its foreign loans. As a consequence, Brazil's real GDP per capita has risen from 70 percent of Argentina's in the 1960s to 80 percent in the 1980s.

There are many interesting insights deserving comment in Professor Cardoso's analysis, but I will concentrate on only one aspect: her proposal for interest recycling. The proposal is to pay part of the interest on foreign debt in domestic currency, with the creditors investing the proceeds in domestic assets. Combined with sound macroeconomic policies, interest recycling could break the vicious circle of debt, no growth, and deteriorating debt servicing capacity. The following remarks are of a complementary nature, placing the Cardoso proposal in a broader framework of a new debt strategy.

The Old Strategy

When the debt crisis arose six years ago, the strategy that was put together hinged on some key assumptions:

1. The debtor countries would adopt comprehensive market oriented macro-economic and structural policies.

2. There would be a recovery of world economic growth and international trade.

3. Real interest rates would return to their historically moderate levels of around 2 percent.

4. Commercial bank loans to indebted countries would resume to support the structural adjustment.

Miguel Molina is Chief of Staff, Sub-secretaría de Hacienda y Crédito Público, Mexico.

5. Finally, the IMF, World Bank, and IDB would support, promote, and finance effective structural adjustment.

Events have not evolved as premised. International trade grew at a third of its expected pace, real interest rates hovered at around 5 percent, and terms of trade for indebted countries deteriorated during the last six years.

Another key element of the strategy, the constant flow of new credits, did not materialize. Instead, the real net transfer of resources from indebted countries has been unprecedentedly high, while commercial banks reduced their Latin American exposure. Professor Cardoso observes that Brazil and Argentina transferred abroad at least 2 percent of their GDP per year between 1981 and 1986. In the Mexican case the net transfer was around 3.5 percent of GDP, and this year it is expected to be over 6 percent, an amount roughly equivalent to one year of agricultural production.

With such large net transfers to the industrial countries, growth is not possible. In Mexico gross national savings historically have averaged 20 percent of GDP, sufficient to finance a GDP growth of around 5 to 6 percent per year. Even with the sound macroeconomic strategy that it has pursued, with a 6 percent net negative resource transfer, the country cannot grow at more than 2 or 3 percent per year. This is grossly inadequate to provide jobs for a labor force that is growing at a faster rate and to respond to popular pressures to reverse the socio-economic deterioration of the past six years.

A New Strategy

These considerations require a new debt strategy that emphasizes the reversal of net transfers to allow adequate economic growth in indebted countries. Cardoso's proposal fits into the new debt strategy termed the "International Pact for Development," that my country has recently proposed at the Berlin meetings. The strategy assumes that macroeconomic and structural change in indebted countries is a *sine qua non* for restoring growth. The other elements include:

1. an explicit economic growth target for all macroeconomic and structural adjustment programs;

2. reversal of the net negative transfer of Latin America with the IMF, World Bank, and IDB;

3. a multi-year lending commitment by commercial banks that assures fresh money flows in a medium-term framework, so as to put macroeconomic policy planning on a firmer foundation;

4. debt reduction schemes to reduce the stock of debt to more manageable levels, reversing the rise of the debt/GDP ratio of the past six years;

5. modification of the legal and regulatory framework of industrial countries to encourage banks to engage in debt reduction operations;

6. debt guarantees by developed countries and/or multilateral institutions to further induce debt reduction.

To summarize, the current debt strategy has failed to accomplish a basic objective: to restore growth in Latin American countries. The new debt strategy that I have briefly sketched includes both reduction of the stock of old debt and a medium-term commitment of new commercial bank loans. The time to adopt this new strategy is running out. Growing social unrest in Latin America is an undeniable fact. The needed flows which allow growth cannot be obtained merely by debt reduction, unless banks and governments are prepared to entertain commercial debt reductions in the order of 60–70 billion U.S. dollars for Argentina, Brazil, and Mexico. Interest recycling or fresh commercial bank loans by themselves are not adequate. Interest recycling alone or new indebtedness alone would mean passing on the debt burden to future generations without reducing the debt/GDP ratio, thus making the debtor countries even less viable financially. A composite solution must be found, very soon.

6

Debt and Growth in Chile: Trends and Prospects

Ricardo Ffrench-Davis

This paper begins with a brief survey of the accumulation of foreign debt in Chile before the crisis in 1982. A rapidly rising debt produced a debt-led current account deficit: the liberalization of capital inflows generated the deficit rather than the opposite. The inflows principally financed increased consumer imports, capital flight was low, and there was no debt-led investment increase.

In 1982, the external shocks that struck Chile—the cutoff of bank loans, the rise of interest rates, and falling terms of trade—set off an ''automatic domestic adjustment process'' that included a 14 percent drop in real GDP, the largest drop among Latin American countries in that year. The Chilean economy then began to recover, though GDP per capita in 1988 was still one percent below its pre-crisis level.

The adjustment followed rather orthodox lines. Aggregate demand was curtailed sharply; most public policies were kept ''neutral''; tariffs and restrictions on imports remained low, but the real exchange rate was depreciated substantially; many public enterprises were privatized, and a harmonic relation was established with creditors. Private debt was ''nationalized,'' the public sector share rising from one-third in 1981 to 84 percent of total debt in 1988.

In 1987–88 Chile experienced three positive external changes—a sharp rise of the price of copper, an agreement with creditor banks to postpone half of the interest payments from 1988 to 1991–93, and other foreign exchange savings resulting from debt-swaps. As a result, the economy confronted relaxed external conditions. However, all this is transitory. Copper prices are expected to fall, the postponement of interest payments is temporary, and debt-equity swaps will result in higher profit remittances in the nineties. Moreover, the debt in 1988 of roughly 20 billion U.S. dollars is nearly as large as annual GDP.

Ricardo Ffrench-Davis is Vice-president, Center for Economic Research on Latin America (CIEPLAN), Chile.

Balance of payments and debt service projections show that in 1991–93 annual amortization commitments climb to 1.7 billion U.S. dollars, and interest and profit commitments to nearly $2 billion. It's unlikely that voluntary lending will supply the needed funding. In addition, output has been rising partly through the use of idle capacity. To grow at 5 or 6 percent when full capacity is reached, investment will have to increase beyond its 1987–88 ratio to GDP.

The data indicate that the debt problem has only been postponed and that, notwithstanding a significant increase in export capacity, actual growth of overall productive capacity has been and continues to be limited. That explains why GDP per capita is still below 1981 and about at the level of the early seventies.

A summary account of the causes, uses, and effects of foreign debt accumulation, both in the period of large positive net transfers in 1977–81 and of large negative net transfers in 1982–88, is presented first. This is followed by an analysis of the macroeconomic adjustments in 1982–88, including an assessment of the relative importance of external shocks and of demand-reducing and supply-demand-switching policies. The final section focuses on the debt service commitments in the next few years, offering estimates of the projected foreign gap and its main components.

Debt Trends during 1973–88

Fast Growth of Debt: 1977–81

Chile accumulated a large foreign debt in the 1977–81 period.[1] Borrowing was principally through foreign bank loans to private Chilean firms. The loans carried no guarantee from the Chilean government. Following a moderate rise of debt in 1973–77, total disbursed outstanding debt (DOD) rose from 5.8 billion U.S. dollars in 1977 to 15.7 billion in 1981, with the private debt share increasing from 22 percent to 64 percent (see Table 6.1). The public sector also borrowed moderately from private sources, the debt with foreign commercial banks rising to over 80 percent of DOD. Thus there was a major privatization of the sources and uses of debt.[2]

Until late 1981 the net capital flow into Chile exceeded the absorption capacity of the national economy, creating pressures for faster import liberalization and real exchange rate appreciation. Since the growth of imports outran exports, the deficit in the nonfinancial current account underwent persistent and substantial increases. Nevertheless, the pace of capital inflows to private debtors kept accelerating. The causal relation was not imports encouraged by exchange rate appreciation with loans flowing in to balance the foreign exchange market, but rather the loans setting in motion appreciation of the real exchange rate, increases of consumption, and of the current account deficit.

Therefore, the national economy became increasingly dependent on massive capital inflows. This was, however, of little concern in the country's official

Table 6.1

Foreign Debt of Chile, 1975–88 (millions of U.S. dollars)

Year	Total (1)	Public and publicly guaranteed		Private without guarantee		Capitalized debt (6)	Total including capitalized debt (7)
		Amount (2)	% (3)	Amount (4)	(%) (5)		
1975	5,453	4,667	85.6	786	14.4		5,453
1976	5,392	4,434	82.2	958	17.8		5,392
1977	5,763	4,479	77.7	1,284	22.3		5,763
1978	7,153	5,198	72.7	1,955	27.3		7,153
1979	8,790	5,369	61.1	3,421	38.9		8,790
1980	11,331	5,310	46.9	6,021	53.1		11,331
1981	15,700	5,623	35.8	10,077	64.2		15,700
1982	17,263	6,770	39.2	10,493	60.8		17,263
1983	18,133	10,497	57.9	7,636	42.1		18,133
1984	19,746	13,203	66.9	6,543	33.1		19,757
1985	20,490	15,251	74.4	5,239	25.6	85[a]	20,573
1986	20,785	17,160	82.6	3,625	17.4	355	21,123
1987	20,722	17,894	86.4	2,828	13.6	1,187	21,805
1988	19,033	16,057	84.4	2,976	15.6	2,112	20,917

Sources: Central Bank, *Chilean External Debt* for 1975–1986. *Boletín Mensual*, March 1989, for estimates for 1987 and 1988. Figures refer to end-of-year disbursed outstanding debt.

Notes: [a] Includes U.S. $10.8 million capitalized through the Statute for Foreign Investment (D.L. 600) before 1985.

(1) Total including IMF and debt payable in domestic currency, and excluding short-term trade credit to nonbank debtors; the latter amounted to U.S. $800 million in 1986.

(3) and (5) are percentages of (1).

(6) Face value of debt capitalized through D.L. 600 and debt-equity operations through Chapter 19 of the Foreign Exchange Law.

(7) Column (1) plus 100 percent of debt capitalized through D.L. 600 plus 93 percent of the debt capitalized through Chapter 19 until September 1987 and an average of 86 percent of that thereafter.

Table 6.2

Real Exchange Rate and Import Tariffs: Chile, 1970–88

	Exchange rate index deflated by		Average tariff[c] (%)
	CPI[a] (1974–78 = 100)	Wage index[b]	
1970	70.5	47.7	94.0[d]
1974	92.1	94.8	75.6
1975	126.2	135.4	49.3
1976	102.1	105.1	35.6
1977	85.2	80.6	24.3
1978	94.6	84.1	14.8
1979	92.4	75.9	12.1
1980	80.6	61.0	10.1
1981	68.5	47.6	10.1
1982	79.6	55.4	10.1
1983	95.5	74.4	17.9
1984	98.4	76.5	24.4
1985	122.7	99.8	25.8
1986	139.3	110.9	20.1
1987	142.9	114.0	20.0
1988	146.1	110.0	15.1

Sources: Banco Central de Chile; and CIEPLAN (1988).

[a] Nominal official exchange rate inflated by the external price index (an index of the international prices of Chilean traded goods) and deflated by the revised consumer price index.

[b] Nominal official exchange rate inflated by the external price index and deflated by the wage index.

[c] Unweighted annual average of tariffs. Excludes preferential treatment in free zones and in integration schemes.

[d] December 1973.

circles. There, the belief prevailed that a foreign exchange crisis was impossible because the debt was mainly private and thus would be efficiently used (Robichek 1981, 171–72), and because the fiscal budget was in surplus and reserves exceeded money supply.

The foreign currency from the loans was used largely to finance an "excess" of imports in the private sector. About three-fourths of the rise in the debt in 1977–82 was used to increase the import/GDP coefficient of the Chilean economy (Ffrench-Davis and De Gregorio 1987).[3] The data suggest that, in net macro terms, none of the loans financed the expansion of productive capacity; the rate of investment was lower during the monetarist era than in the 1960s.[4]

Table 6.3

GDP, GDP per Capita, and Investment: Chile, 1970–88

	GDP 1974 = 100	GDP per capita 1974 = 100	Investment rate
1970	91.8	98.4	20.4%
1971	99.2	104.4	18.3
1972	99.0	102.4	14.8
1973	94.8	96.4	14.7
1974	100.0	100.0	17.4
1975	83.4	82.0	15.4
1976	86.9	84.2	12.7
1977	94.2	90.0	13.3
1978	100.1	94.3	14.5
1979	107.9	100.1	15.6
1980	114.2	104.3	17.6
1981	120.0	107.9	19.5
1982	103.1	91.2	15.0
1983	102.4	89.0	12.9
1984	108.8	93.0	13.2
1985	111.5	93.7	14.8
1986	117.8	97.4	15.0
1987	124.5	101.2	16.5
1988	133.7	106.9	17.0
Average level			
1975–81	101.0	94.7	15.5%
1982–88	114.6	96.0	14.9
Annual growth rate			
1974–81	2.6%	1.1%	—
1981–88	1.6	–0.1	—

Sources: GDP data for 1970–81 are rates of change in Marcel and Meller (1986), and remaining years are calculated with the official (provisional) rates of change estimated by the Central Bank. The investment rate is gross fixed investment/GDP from official national accounts estimated by the Central Bank as of April 1989.

Excessive imports were a consequence of the trade and financial policies adopted. The across the board liberalization of imports that led to a uniform 10 percent tariff rate and the appreciating exchange rate (see Table 6.2) that a plentiful supply of bank loans encouraged allowed imports to increase beyond a level consistent with stable growth of the Chilean economy. By 1981, the real dollar/peso exchange rate was one-third below the average of 1974–78,[5] and average tariffs had been reduced to a uniform 10 percent. Excess imports crowded out domestic manufactures and trade related investment, while the growing current account deficit made a future downward adjustment inevitable.

The cutoff of foreign credit in 1982 coincided with higher real international interest rates and a sizeable fall in copper prices, which accounts for half of Chilean exports. Moreover, the Chilean economy had become particularly vulnerable to external shocks because the government had done away with regulatory mechanisms and instead relied on the automatism of the dollar standard, and because the private sector was overleveraged (Arellano 1983). The external shocks, therefore, had an unusually large multiplier effect on the domestic economy. GDP (excluding the effect of deteriorating terms of trade) fell by 14 percent in 1982, with manufacturing output falling by 21 percent. Expenditure-reduction dominated expenditure-switching policies, producing the sharp output declines recorded (see Tables 6.3 and 6.6).

Debt Trends in 1981–88

Since the 1982 external shock, there have been five rounds of negotiations with creditor banks,[6] framed by agreements with the IMF (in 1983 and 1985) and the World Bank (three SAL agreements). Liabilities with banks represented, as mentioned above, over four-fifths of total debt (with shorter maturities and higher interest rates) than debt with official creditors. The negotiations with banks have been geared to reschedule maturities, to maintain short-term trade credit, and to obtain new loans to finance part of the interest payments. The remaining interest payments were financed with a surplus in the nonfinancial current account. Net transfers to bank creditors implied a negative flow of roughly 1 billion U.S. dollars per year in 1985–88 (approximately 6 percent of GDP). On the other hand, official creditors have played a crucial role as net suppliers of funds. Multilateral institutions—IBRD, IDB, and IMF—have been the large lenders, the IBRD and IDB with positive net transfers of 300 million U.S. dollars per annum (Table 6.4). This was a relatively large transfer, as the net transfers from these two institutions to all Latin America averaged only 1 billion U.S. dollars annually in 1985–87, and turned negative in 1987 (see Feinberg,[7] in this volume).

Debt in current dollars kept growing until 1985. DOD rose by one-third between 1981 and 1985. It then remained approximately constant through 1987, at around 20 billion U.S. dollars, but with changes in the shares of the various creditors. A drop in bank debt due to debt-equity swaps was nearly offset by a rise in debt with multilateral institutions. Between 1981 and 1987, creditor banks' share decreased to 71 percent, but that of multilateral institutions rose from 3 to 19 percent. It was only in 1988 that large swaps produced a net drop of 8 percent in DOD.[8]

Chile has faithfully serviced its debt and has had rather harmonious relations with its creditors, but the claim that it was able both to service debt and to grow

Table 6.4

Net Transfers by Creditor, 1983–88
(millions of U.S. dollars)

	1983	1984	1985	1986	1987	1988
Direct foreign investment	−3	−46	−92	−111	−117	−186
Multilateral institutions	167	248	353	256	205	393
Bilateral official	−1	−8	−8	−71	−45	−52
Suppliers	−343	−41	−121	75	257	310
Banks medium- and long-term	−276	−732	−829	−1,114	−1,129	−900
Other medium- and long-term[a]	63	−267	−46	−98	−28	−36
Short-term[b]	−909	312	−24	383	51	−550
Total	−1,303	−533	−768	−681	−816	−1,020

Sources: Calculations based on data from Central Bank. Net transfers are disbursements minus amortizations of principal and interest payments in the case of loans, and net direct foreign investment (DFI) minus net profits remitted in the case of foreign investment. Debt swaps are not considered as DFI nor as debt amortization since there is no flow of funds.

[a] Includes interest payments, but excludes capital flows with the IMF.

[b] Includes bank trade credit, interest receipts, and unidentified flows.

cannot be supported.[9] It has taken six years for total GDP to overtake the 1981 level, while GDP per capita has yet to regain its 1981 level. Furthermore, income per capita is even lower than GDP per capita because of the negative external transfers.

By 1987, the outstanding debt was 109 percent of GDP (roughly double the ratio for Latin America as shown in Table 6.5),[10] with 87 percent publicly guaranteed, up from 36 percent in 1981 (Table 6.1). The "nationalization" of private debt took place in two forms: by increased borrowing of the Central Bank, in order to supply foreign currency to cover interest payments of both the public and private sectors, and by *ex post* public guarantees to the foreign debt of domestic banks.[11]

Debt Swaps

The leveling off of DOD since 1985 is related to debt-swap operations. Since mid-1985 there have been prepayment transactions leading to a reduction of the debt stock and some direct writedowns. (Ffrench-Davis 1987 and 1989; Fontaine 1988; Larraín 1987). The government initiated a two-tier system in May 1985 that allowed the prepayment of debt with creditor banks. The system is based on

Table 6.5

Debt Burden and Output Performance: 1987

	Chile	Latin America
Total GDP change (1987/1981)		
Total	3.8%	9.9%
Per capita	−6.2	−4.0
Debt burden (1987)		
Debt/GDP	108.7%	57.5%
Debt/exports	330.5	387.0
Interest/GDP	8.8	4.5
Interest/exports	26.7	30.5
Financial service/GDP	9.0	4.2
Financial service/exports	27.3	28.4

Sources: Estimates based on Central Bank of Chile and ECLAC.

Note: Debt includes that with the IMF; exports are goods and nonfinancial services; interests are gross payments; financial service is the sum of net interest payments and profits; GDP was converted into dollar equivalent with the 1987 exchange rate for Chile; for Latin America 1986 rates were used to estimate GDP in constant dollars, and then adjusted by the WPI of the United States.

the debt promissory notes (*pagarés de la deuda externa*) held by creditor banks who sell them at a discount in the international secondary market, and on the direct capitalization or conversion of external loans. The debt notes of Chile have been sold at discounts fluctuating between 30 and 50 percent of their face value.

Chapter XVIII of the Foreign Exchange Regulations of Chile is directed at repatriating capital flight and capturing foreign currency from the "parallel" exchange market. The Central Bank periodically auctions rights to purchase debt notes abroad to residents of Chile, using foreign currency from the sale of foreign assets or obtained in the "parallel" market.[12] The auctioning enabled the Bank to capture around 12 percent of the face value of the debt paper in 1985–88 (Ffrench-Davis 1987).[13] In international markets this is roughly 30 percent of the discount of the debt notes of Chile, the remaining 70 percent being captured by the other domestic agents.

Chapter XIX of the Foreign Exchange Regulations is intended to attract foreign investors. The Central Bank exchanges the dollar debt that is its direct liability for peso promissory notes; there is no monetary expansion, but a demand pressure results on the domestic capital market. The peso notes have been sold in the domestic secondary market at an average of 88 percent of their face value.[14] In the case of foreign debt of other debtors, the parties negotiate the terms of the transaction. They are influenced, however, by the terms granted by the Central Bank, which tend to provide a "floor" price. With the Chapter XIX mechanism, the Central Bank and other domestic debtors have captured between one-fifth and one-third of the discount of debt notes in international markets.[15]

In the first three and a half years, 4 billion U.S. dollars—19 percent of the debt stock—was converted via these two regulations. A sizeable share of the funds used to purchase promissory notes abroad under Chapter XVIII are from the domestic "parallel" foreign exchange market. An incentive to swappers using Chapter XVIII is a sort of capital laundering which, however, does not give them the right to make capital and profit remittances abroad. Swaps under Chapter XIX—amounting to 1.8 billion U.S. dollars—have been motivated by the discount in international markets and the availability of low-priced domestic assets.[16] There is a change in the form of the liabilities of Chile because of Chapter XIX from debt to risk capital, that will generate remittances of principal and profits after a required holding period.

In addition, there has been direct debt-equity conversion of loans that were originally associated with foreign investment under Decree 600. These have totaled 270 million U.S. dollars. Column 7 of Table 6.1 estimates the total liabilities including standard debt and equity swapped under Chapter XIX and Decree 600. Finally, there have also been writedowns or swaps of private non-guaranteed debt totaling 1.5 billion U.S. dollars according to the Central Bank.

The swaps reduce the debt stock and consequently interest payment commitments, but they also generate a series of other benefits and costs, the specifics depending on the particular forms of the swaps. In the case of debt-equity swaps, it is asserted that foreign buyers of domestic firms bring managerial and exporting capabilities, and that by increasing the knowledge abroad of investment opportunities in Chile they will encourage direct foreign investment in the future.

Criticism of the above mentioned debt-equity scheme relates mainly to five points.[17] One is the acceptance at nearly face value in Chile of notes that were priced in international markets at an average of 61 percent.[18] The fact that in Chile the investor received the peso equivalent of 88 dollars for each 61 dollars he had spent gives him, in effect, a subsidy or preferential exchange rate of 44 percent above the official rate. The second is the use of the peso funds to purchase "underpriced" Chilean firms. These purchases are, essentially, prepayments of debt that would otherwise presumably be rescheduled over and over into the future. Third, in the case of debt-equity swaps, interest payments are replaced by profits remittable in the future (after four years) whose mean expected value is greater than the interest payments. Consequently, while the reduction of debt under Chapter XVIII extinguishes the capital service, it tends to increase under Chapter XIX. Fourth, direct foreign investment previously intended to be made in cash is partially replaced by foreign investment funded with promissory notes.[19] Fifth, swaps do not provide cash but a debt note; in exchange, creditors have received established domestic firms. This is indicated by the coexistence of large debt-equity swaps with low investment ratios in 1987 and 1988 (Ffrench-Davis 1989).

Negotiations with Banks in 1987–88

In 1987, Chile agreed with creditor banks on a rescheduling of amortizations due in 1988–90. The terms improved on those prevailing since 1985 but were somewhat less favorable than the terms obtained by other Latin American countries (CEPAL 1987, Tables 19 and 20). The government agreed to pay a spread of 1 percent and to amortize the rescheduled debt over fifteen years.

Banks did not provide "new money," but accepted a retiming of interest payments. In the negotiations of 1985, these payments had already been rescheduled from quarterly to semi-annual. In the 1987 negotiations the timing was changed to one year beginning in 1988. As a consequence, interest payments in 1988 were reduced by 400 million U.S. dollars. The government also agreed, however, to return to a semi-annual term in 1991–93. Thus, the relaxation of the external gap in 1988 implies a larger restriction in 1991–93. As in the previous negotiations, the hope was expressed by the government and creditors that access to voluntary loans could be regained shortly. Finally, short-term trade credit was renewed until the end of 1989.

Meanwhile, the external conditions faced by Chile improved notably. The price of copper rose sharply as did other export prices. The improvement of the terms of trade may represent over 1.3 billion U.S. dollars in 1988 (CEPAL 1988).[20] Together with the postponement of capital services—because of the timing of interest payments and of the debt swaps—the foreign constraint appeared to be nonbinding in 1988.[21]

This encouraged renewed negotiations with the creditor banks. In August 1988 it was agreed to reduce the spreads to 0.81 percent, a markup similar to that applied to other debtors like Argentina and Mexico. The arrangement also was made more flexible, and within limits Chile could now deal with each bank separately. This is a potentially important advance for Chile over the *pari passu* or "most favored bank" clause, which had been the general rule in the rescheduling agreements with the LDC debtors.[22]

The main components of the greater flexibility for Chile include the following options:

a) to buy back up to 500 million U.S. dollars of debt notes at a discount; cash payments are to be made with reserves accruing from the improved price of copper;[23]

b) to prepay debt in Chilean pesos to creditors who agree to lend "new money" for investment projects. This has already been used to finance a small fraction of a foreign investment project in mining. The peso fraction of the financing was provided by the Central Bank;

c) to guarantee up to 500 million U.S. dollars of new loans that would be senior to old debt;

d) to swap directly up to 2 billion U.S. dollars of old debt for new debt at a discount.

The main implication of this flexibility is that the debtor country can bargain separately with each bank or group of banks within the boundaries listed above, thus breaking the bank cartel. Of course, each operation has to have the approval of the creditors whose assets are to be swapped.

The benefit/cost implications for Chile depend on the terms of each operation, and on the expected interest rates, discount of debt notes, and availability of financing in the future. For instance, if liquidity becomes a constraint in the near future, buybacks at the current market discounts could be unattractive.[24] It is also doubtful that buybacks will stimulate voluntary lending. Thus, given present discounts in international secondary markets, the buybacks with own cash could reduce the availability of funds to Chile in the short and medium term.

Recession and Recovery in the Eighties

The five renegotiation rounds notwithstanding, Chile experienced significant negative transfers after 1981. Together with deteriorated terms of trade, they led to a sharp drop in the expenditure capacity of the Chilean economy. Adjustment was unavoidable, no matter how well Chile might have managed relations with creditors after 1982. With creditor banks, the best possible outcome certainly would have been a zero net transfer. Even that would have implied a large fall in the net inflow of funds compared to 1977–81.

The fact is that Chile suffered three external shocks in the early eighties. The strongest related to gross capital flows. After climbing to 18 percent of GDP they fell to one-half of that figure in 1982 and to one-fourth in 1983 (see Table 6.6). Clearly the 18 percent figure recorded in 1981 reflected a gross policy mistake. Since 1977, the Chilean economy was adjusting to an unsustainable level of capital inflows. Even without an international debt crisis, a major readjustment would have been needed in the near future (Ffrench-Davis 1983b). A second shock was the rise of interest rates, although the resulting impact was not totally exogenous since it was affected by the negotiations held by the government with each creditor. The third external shock was the fall in the terms of trade, led by the drop of the price of copper.

Associated with the external shocks was the strong domestic recession of 1982. A policy of "automatic adjustment," set in motion by a contraction in the supply of foreign currency, exacerbated the fall in aggregate demand, and resulted in a 17.5 percent decline of GDP per capita in the period 1982–83. Since then, there has been a gradual recovery of economic activity and investment.

The ideal adjustment is one in which excess aggregate demand is eliminated without a drop in the level and rate of growth of aggregate output. In a perfectly

Table 6.6

Production, Consumption, Investment, and External Shocks per Capita: Chile 1980-87
(percent of GDP per capita in 1981)

	1980	1981	1982	1983	1984	1985	1986	1987	Average 1982-87
GDP	96.3	100.0	84.5	82.5	86.2	86.8	90.2	93.8	87.3
Domestic expenditure	102.7	112.9	84.3	79.1	84.3	81.3	84.2	88.9	83.7
Consumption	79.7	85.3	74.9	71.4	71.1	69.2	70.7	72.1	71.6
Fixed capital formation	17.0	19.5	12.7	10.6	11.4	12.8	13.5	15.4	12.7
Domestic savings	16.5	14.7	9.6	11.0	15.1	17.6	19.5	21.7	15.7
Nonfinancial current account	-6.5	-12.9	0.2	3.4	1.9	5.5	6.0	4.9	3.6
Goods[a]									
Exports	18.0	16.6	17.9	17.9	18.7	20.3	21.4	22.3[b]	19.7
Imports	-22.8	-26.8	-16.0	-13.4	-16.1	-14.6	-15.6	-17.6	-15.6
Services[a]	-1.7	-2.7	-1.7	-1.0	-0.7	-0.1	0.2	0.3	-0.5
Net transfer of funds	4.5	12.9	1.9	-2.3	0.8	-2.2	-3.1	-3.3	-1.3
Capital inflow[b]	7.9	17.9	8.6	4.2	8.1	5.0	4.1	2.7	5.5
Net payment of interests and profits	-3.4	-5.1	-6.7	-6.5	-7.3	-7.2	-7.2	-6.0	-6.8
Terms of trade effect	2.0	0.0	-2.1	-1.1	-2.7	-3.3	-2.9	-1.6	-2.3

Sources: Banco Central de Chile, *Boletín Mensual*, January and February 1988; INE-CELADE; and ECLAC.

[a] Estimated using data from ECLAC, *Balance of Payments Statistics*.

[b] Includes unilateral net transfers. Measures the effective use of foreign funds, including changes in reserves.

flexible economy, the drop in output should be negligible. In an economy with initial underutilization of capacity in the production of tradables, adjustment with an appropriate dose of switching policies could even cause an increase in output. But in an economy with price inflexibility and imperfect factor mobility, neutral demand-reducing policies can cause a significant drop in output, because the demand for both tradables and nontradables diminishes. In the real world, adjustment processes usually involve a drop in output, although selective policies that facilitate switches in the composition of output and expenditure can dampen the output reducing effects. A good combination of expenditure reducing and switching policies would tend to allow an outcome closer to a constant rate of utilization of potential GDP (see Ffrench-Davis and Marfán 1989).

Here follows a brief account of estimates of the external shocks and of the paths taken by Chilean output, aggregate demand, exports, and imports during 1980–87.[25] The particular purpose is to provide rough estimates of two components of the economic costs of adjustment: underutilization of installed capacity and slackened creation of new capacity.

All variables have fluctuated widely in this period, as shown in Table 6.6. Economic activity peaked in 1981. It was not associated with abnormally high output as compared to capacity. On the contrary, there was still some unused installed capacity in the production of agricultural and manufactured tradables, as a consequence of trade liberalization and exchange rate appreciation. Probably this underutilization was larger than the overutilization of capacity in the production of some nontradables. We take the actual GDP of 1981 as a conservative indicator of productive capacity as of that year.

In rough terms, the increase in installed capacity in subsequent years was approximately equal to the rise in population.[26] We thus assume that output capacity per capita was roughly constant in 1982–87. The differences between actual output in the 1982–87 adjustment period and 1981 GDP per capita is our measure of underutilization of productive capacity after 1981.

In Table 6.6, all figures are adjusted for the increase in population and are expressed as percentages of the GDP in 1981. Comparing any figure in a given line with its value in 1981 indicates the change with respect to a situation of constant GDP per capita and constant shares of all other variables in the table. For instance, the 1987 figure for fixed capital formation indicates a fall from 19.5 in 1981 to 15.4 in 1987, that is, 4.1 points from 1981 GDP, or 21 percent in relative terms. As a share of 1987 GDP, the decline was from 19.5 percent to 16.5 percent.

The large shortfall of output, averaging 13 percent of the 1981 GDP in 1982–87 (line 1), indicates strong output-reducing effects, weak switching policies (exchange rate, trade regulations, selective fiscal policy, etc.), and inflexibility in the composition of output and demand. The GDP outcome was a response to the three external shocks which are measured in lines 7 and 8. With a fixed exchange rate and passive monetary policy at the outset of the crisis, they gave rise to the reduction in domestic expenditure (line 2) on both consumption and investment. They were transmitted to the external sector (line 6), reducing imports and increasing exportable supply. To reduce the external gap, the indirect tool of an extremely large reduction in aggregate demand was used as the main policy variable.

The 13 percent drop in utilization of GDP capacity is the "static" output-reducing effect of the combination of external shocks and weak switching policies. Along a "dynamic" dimension, investment by 1983 had fallen 46 percent (line 4), reducing both potential GDP growth and the capacity to restructure the composition of supply and demand.

An "automatic adjustment" mechanism, as was used in 1982, relies heavily on the shock effects of demand-reducing policies. After a one-shot endogenous downward adjustment of domestic expenditure, some switching in demand and supply composition usually takes place; as time goes by, the reallocation of resources and demand tends to increase. That endogenous switch was assisted additionally by a series of sizeable exchange rate devaluations (Table 6.2).[27] The delayed switching allowed a gradual recovery of output and expenditure, as can be seen by comparing 1982–83 and 1987 with macro data for Chile. Yet GDP per capita by 1987 was still 6.2 percent below the level achieved in 1981, while investment per capita was 21 percent below.

In the external sector the adjustment was stronger, with imports more responsive than exports to the drop of domestic expenditure. Again, time allowed a change in the behavior of these two variables. Encouraged by large exchange rate depreciations (Table 6.2), exports grew faster in the latter part of the adjustment period. The quantum of exports of goods per capita was 24 percent above the peak level attained in 1980,[28] where, however, GDP per capita was lower. This is not precisely a case of export-led growth, but rather of an export drive led by a recessionary adjustment. Subsequently, however, the dynamic export expansion contributed to the recovery of economic activity.

The Foreign Gap: A Preliminary Forecast

After seven years of adjustment to the three sources of shocks, the external gap has relaxed in 1988. What are the prospects for subsequent years? The main components of the current and capital accounts are projected in this section.

Debt Service Commitments for 1989–95

Since 1983, the bulk of debt with banks has been rescheduled. With bank debt initially composing four-fifths of total DOD, the effective amortization paid has been low. In 1987, only 310 million U.S. dollars, or 1.5 percent of debt, were paid to all creditors. New reschedulings in 1987 leave amortization commitments

Table 6.7

Amortizations, 1987–93
(millions of U.S. dollars in annual averages)

	1987–88	1989–90	1991–93
Multilateral organizations	98	268	395
Foreign governments	40	81	150
Banks and financial institutions	171	211	632
Suppliers and others	171	254	482
Gross amortizations	480	814	1,659

Sources: Estimates based on Central Bank, *External Debt Document*, December 1987; and *Quarterly Economic and Financial Report of Chile*, March 1989.

Notes: Includes external debt reductions through debt equity swaps (Chapters 18 and 19). It also includes principal payments of post-1987 projected financing (see Table 6.9, row 5). It does not include amortizations of future loans required to finance post-1990 deficits.

with banks at a low level until 1990.[29.] However, the increased debt with multilateral creditors will require a moderate overall rise of yearly amortization to 650 million U.S. dollars in 1989–90 (see Table 6.7).[30]

The scene changes after 1990. In 1991 there will be an abrupt jump in commitments, with further rises in subsequent years. They climb to an annual average of 1.7 billion U.S. dollars in 1991–93. In all, one-half of the medium- and long-term debt is due in 1991–95.[31] This is an abnormally high concentration of debt service in a short period, especially for a country whose debt to GDP ratio is also very high.

The obvious implication is that a new rescheduling of amortization will be needed. The share of creditor banks covering nearly one-half of total amortization due in 1991–95 would be most affected. However, the government asserts that it is seeking a quick full recovery of access to international voluntary lending.[32] This assumes that such lending would be available by 1992 to refinance amortization. In the same period, at the interest rates projected in Table 6.8, financial servicing would amount to 2 billion U.S. dollars per year.

Thus, amortization and interest payments represent a sizeable burden for Chile. How might this be financed? By new reschedulings, "forced new loans" and debt reductions? By a large surplus in the nonfinancial current account and regained access to voluntary lending?

Trade Prospects and External Financing

It is risky to forecast balance of payments accounts, as shown by the sizeable errors in estimates of the international institutions and other forecasters. There are many alternative and differing assumptions about the crucial variables. Here we present a baseline scenario. The assumptions adopted for the main variables are given in Table 6.8. These include for 1991–93: a price of copper of 85 cents per pound, a common assumption by the experts in the area;[33] an increase of non-copper export volume of 7 percent per year; GDP growth of 5 percent; a growth of import volume of 7 percent per year, implying an income elasticity of 1.4; and a LIBOR rate of around 8 percent in 1991–93.

Table 6.9 summarizes the current account effects (lines 1 and 2) which combined with amortization (line 3) determine the gross financing need (line 4). This is followed in the table by calculations based on Central Bank estimates of available financing from different creditor sources (line 5), excluding medium- and long-term bank loans and rescheduling,[34] and an estimate of reschedulable bank loans (line 6). These represent the supposedly more easily obtainable funding. The balance determines the needed additional financing. The annual gap appears in line 7.

In 1988–89 there is a surplus, resulting from the high copper price and improved prices and volume of other exports. Since 1987, part of the increased export proceeds have been sequestered in a copper stabilization fund to be used when the price drops below the normal range. Along with other terms of trade improvements and postponed interest payments, partly offset by larger imports, the surplus would be sufficient to cover financial needs up to 1990.[35]

There are, however, two problems to be faced. First, it is not easy to lose reserves without negative effects on the expectations of creditors and on capital flight. Second, the price of copper, which is expected to remain high during part of 1989, may drop sharply thereafter as it has in past copper cycles. With a normal price range of 80–85 cents per pound, the residual gap in line 7 rises further, exposing the true structural balance of payments situation of Chile to the financial market rather suddenly. With the debt agreements in force and the baseline scenario, a large deficit in the current account appears. New additional financing or saving of capital services would then be needed to balance the external accounts.

It is extremely important to be clear that the current relaxed balance of payments situation is transitory. Under a "normal" scenario, such as that in Table 6.8 after 1989, there is a significant current account deficit. The path expected to be followed by crucial variables foretells the appearance of a deficit to coincide with the first year of the long expected return to democracy in Chile. The gap tends to be enlarged further by policies implemented by the government in 1988 and early 1989: exchange rate appreciation, reduction of the average import tariff, and cash buybacks of debt.

The opposition to the dictatorship has been making responsible economic proposals both before and after the plebiscite that was won by the democratic opposition on October 5, 1988. What is being offered are sound, efficient policies for handling the huge inherited debt, the uneven distribution of income, and

Table 6.8

Base Scenario, 1987–93
(annual average)

	1987	1988–90	1991–93
Copper price (U.S. cents/pound)	81.1	109.8	85.3
Volume growth copper exports	−0.1%	4.7%	8.9%
Nominal growth non-copper exports	22.4%	12.1%	10.8%
Volume growth non-copper exports	11.3%	9.0%	6.7%
Non-copper exports price index	100.0	108.3	116.8
Nominal growth in imports	28.9%	16.8%	10.3%
Volume growth in imports	17.2%	10.5%	6.0%
Imports price index	100.0	112.6	127.8
GDP growth	5.7%	5.8%	5.0%
Interest rate (LIBOR)	7.3%	9.1%	8.0%

Sources: Based on estimates and assumptions of Central Bank and of CIEPLAN.

Table 6.9

Foreign Gap and Financing, 1987–93
(millions of U.S. dollars)

	1987	1988–90	1991–93
Nonfinancial current account	892	1,047	205
Financial services	−1,700	−1,852	−2,516
Gross amortizations	−310	−760	−1,659
Gross financial gap	−1,118	−1,565	−3,970
Projected financing[a]	1,419	1,894	2,404
Reschedulable bank amortizations	0	0	569
Annual residual gap	301	329	−998

[a] Estimates based on financing projected by Central Bank from all creditors except medium- and long-term gross loans from banks. Includes net short-term capital and direct investment, but excludes changes in asset values and errors and omissions.

low investment. From 1991 on, the financing gap will require the rescheduling of amortization and new loans, barring favorable changes in the baseline scenario, such as swaps of old debt for new debt with a significant discount. The projections are very sensitive to changes in the parameters and to policy variables. With a high copper price, a more dynamic rise of exports, low interest rates, and lower income elasticity of imports, GDP growth could be sustained by domestic savings despite significant transfers to creditors and the debt servicing gap could disappear.[36] With more pessimistic assumptions than those of the base case, the gap can be made to widen awesomely. The assumptions of Tables 6.8 and 6.9 are within the likely range. The results they generate suggest that there is an unsolved debt problem and an external gap that must be bridged in the 1990s in order to achieve growth with stability.

Notes

The author appreciates the comments of J. P. Arellano, S. Edwards, D. Felix, M. Marfán, C. Massad, J. Vial, and the collaboration of J. M. Cruz and A. Gómez-Lobo. The responsibility for all opinions and errors are his.

1. For more detailed analyses of external borrowing and related domestic economic policies in Chile see Ffrench-Davis (1983b and 1988a), Arellano (1983), and Eyzaguirre (1988).

2. A comparative analysis of Latin American cases in the 1970s and early 1980s is presented in Ffrench-Davis (1983c). The eighties are examined in Bianchi, Devlin, and Ramos (1985), Feinberg and Ffrench-Davis (1988), and Griffith-Jones (1988).

3. The other important use of debt was to offset a negative shock in the terms of trade. The sum of these two uses varied over the period since other variables were at work, such as changes of the export volume.

4. The investment rate was 20.2 percent in the sixties, dropping to 15.5 percent in 1975–81 and to 14.7 percent in 1982–88 (see Table 6.3). This decline can be explained by the trade-policy-induced fall in the domestic real prices of imported consumer goods, and the general role played by the financial system in diverting income from savings to consumption. See Arellano (1983) on the latter issue. For a more detailed discussion of import behavior see De Gregorio (1984). Trade policies are analyzed in Ffrench-Davis (1986). The estimate of excess imports is made in Ffrench-Davis and De Gregorio (1987).

5. Estimated using the CPI as domestic deflator. The appreciation rises to 52 percent with the wage index as deflator. Calculations based on Table 6.2.

6. The first five rounds—those of 1983, 1984 and 1985, 1987, and 1988—are discussed in Ffrench-Davis (1988b).

7. The "favorable" treatment for Chile is discussed in the paper by Caskey and Felix in this volume and in Ffrench-Davis (1988a). In 1985–87 Chile received 30 percent of the net new loans of the IDB and the World Bank to Latin America, whereas Chile produced only 3 percent of the GDP of the region (at 1986 exchange rates).

8. In 1988 swap deals rose to 2.9 billion U.S. dollars or 14 percent of DOD. As in previous years there was an increase of debt with the multilateral institutions.

9. It has been asserted frequently by supporters of the government of Pinochet that Chile was able to pay and grow. The assertion is based on the recovery of economic activity since 1984, disregarding the drop in 1982–83.

10. Chile's debt/export ratio is relatively more favorable, since the Chilean economy is more trade intensive; but the debt/GDP ratio is a better indicator of the direct impact of debt on national welfare and on the financing of investment.

11. The public guarantee was granted free of charge to debt of domestic banks rescheduled in 1983. Since 1985, it has been granted to rescheduled debt on the request of creditor banks and provided they pay a small fee. Private debt with a public guarantee amounted to 3.3 billion U.S. dollars in 1987.

12. Most of the notes bought abroad under Chapter XVIII correspond to liabilities of domestic banks.

13. Transactions totaling 590 million U.S. dollars under Chapter XVIII were exempt from the auctioning. Excluding these increases the average share of the face value captured by the Central Bank from mid-1985 to December 1988 was 16 percent.

14. The discount on the peso notes in the domestic secondary market is determined partly by the interest rate paid by the Central Bank; the rate has been set by the Bank slightly below the average market rate. The average price of notes in the domestic capital market has fluctuated between 85 percent and 93 percent of par.

15. This represents an average of 7 of the 35 discount points in international capital markets in the period June 1985–December 1987. During 1988, the relation has been 14 out of 42 discount points.

16. The decline of the stock market and of the real exchange rate in constant dollars reduced the price of domestic equity by half between 1980 and 1987. See Ffrench-Davis (1987).

17. Features of Chapter XVIII are discussed in Larraín (1987). Here we concentrate on Chapter XIX. A theoretical analysis of benefits and costs for debtors and creditors can be found in Krugman (1988).

18. The price actually has been supported by the government guaranty and subsidies to domestic debtors, as well as by the large net transfers to creditor banks and the features of the swap scheme itself.

19. In the case of direct investment by creditor banks it is estimated that "additionality," i.e., additional foreign investment, is close to 100 percent, whereas in the case of other investors substitution is significant, with a negative effect on the inflow of capital as foreign exchange (see Bergsman and Edicis 1988). There has been some effort by the government to force "additionality." The standard concept of "additionality" is misleading; "100 percent additionality" does not mean that a given deal provides cash funds to the host country. It means that, in the short run, there are zero net capital flows resulting from the debt-equity swaps.

20. Starting in late 1987, a "copper stabilization fund" went into operation. It sterilizes part of the fluctuations in the price of copper.

21. It should be recalled that under debt-equity swaps of Chapter XIX, interest payments are replaced by profit remittances with a lag. In 1992 and beyond, remittable profits will show a sharp rise.

22. The recent dealings of Bolivia in buybacks and Mexico in old-for-new debt swaps are two other exceptions.

23. The Central Bank spent 170 million U.S. dollars in November 1988 to buy back debt from creditor banks, with a discount that was determined by auction. The average discount captured was 43 percent, similar to the market pricing at that time. The 299 million U.S. dollars buyback represented 1.6 percent of debt, and the 168 million U.S. dollars spent was 8 percent of the net international reserves of the Central Bank.

24. With a cash buyback, the debtor saves the interest payment on the face value of debt, while losing reserves and their earnings. If the discount is 90 percent, the debtor recovers the reserves spent on the buyback in one year. With a 44 percent discount and present interest rates, it would take close to one decade.

25. A more detailed analysis is presented in Ffrench-Davis (1988b).

26. Artiagoitia and Marfán (1988) estimate that gross capital formation in 1982–87 generated an increase of potential GDP slightly larger than the rise of population.

27. The exchange rate was depreciated in succesive steps only after the government gave up using a fixed rate as a price stabilization tool in 1982. Since early 1988, the

government has again been appreciating the real exchange rate in order to hold down inflation.

28. Notice that by 1981 the quantum of exports was decreasing because of exchange rate appreciation. Use of export capacity rapidly recovered in 1982–83 after devaluation.

29. Non-reschedulable bank loans include those associated with direct foreign investment made under D.L. 600.

30. All figures exclude amortization to the IMF.

31. Total debt refers to the disbursed outstanding stock in late 1988. Amortization includes an estimate of the payment schedule of "officially projected financing." These projections can be affected by additional new loans with amortization starting before 1995, by debt swaps, and by reschedulings.

32. Communiqués of the Central Bank of Chile, 20 September and 9 November 1988.

33. The price of copper in early December 1988 was 160 cents per pound, compared to an average of 81 cents in 1987 and 62 cents in 1986.

34. Includes multilateral bank loans, supplier credits, and short-term trade credit. The estimate is based on data from the Central Bank; trade-related credit flows were adjusted here, making them "endogeneous" to imports of capital goods and current trade flows.

35. The projected near-term financial gap is a strong argument against using the reserves to buy back debt that otherwise would be maturing during the next fifteen years.

36. The implicit assumption is common to two-gap balance of payments models, in which the removal of the current account gap suffices to produce the required GDP growth and financing of the required investment, without an explicit analysis of the domestic requisites for generating that investment.

References

Arellano, J. P. "De la liberalización a la intervención: el mercado de capitales en Chile, 1974–83." *Colección Estudios CIEPLAN* 11. Santiago, December 1983.

Arellano, J. P., and M. Marfán. "Ahorro-inversión y relaciones financieras en la actual crisis económica chilena." *Colección Estudios CIEPLAN* 20. Santiago, December 1986.

Artiagoitia, P., and M. Marfán. "Inversión productiva y crecimiento económico en Chile: 1960–87." CIEPLAN, Santiago. Mimeo. April 1988.

Banco Central. *External Debt of Chile*. Annual issues.

———. "Quarterly economic and financial report of Chile." Santiago, quarterly since 1985.

———. *Informe económico y financiero*. May and November 1986.

Bergsman, J., and W. Edicis. "Debt-Equity Swaps and Foreign Direct Investment in Latin America." Washington, D.C.: International Finance Corporation, August 1988.

Bianchi A., R. Devlin, and J. Ramos. *External Debt in Latin America*. Boulder: ECLAC/Lynne Rienner Publishers, 1985.

CEPAL. "Balance preliminar de la economía latinoamericana, 1987." Santiago, December 1987.

———. "Panorama económico de América Latina." Santiago, September 1988.

CIEPLAN. "Reconstrucción económica para la democracia." Santiago: CIEPLAN-Editorial Aconcagua, 1983.

———. "Set de Estadísticas Económicas." CIEPLAN, May–June 1989.

Cruz, J. M. "Revisión del modelo de proyección de mediano y largo plazo del Banco Mundial. Aplicación para el caso chileno." *Notas Técnicas* No. 115. Santiago: CIEPLAN, May 1988.

De Gregorio, J. "Comportamiento de las exportaciones e importaciones en Chile: un estudio econométrico." *Colección Estudios CIEPLAN* 13. Santiago, June 1984.

De la Cuadra, S., and J. Desormeaux. "La renegociación de la deuda externa y el programa económico de mediano plazo." Universidad Católica de Chile. Santiago. Mimeo. 1985.

Edwards, S. "The Order of Liberalization of the Current and Capital Accounts of the Balance of Payments." *Essays in International Finance* No. 156. Princeton, N.J.: Princeton University Press, 1989.

Edwards, S., and A. Edwards. *Monetarism and Liberalization: The Chilean Experiment.* Cambridge, Mass.: Ballinger Publishing Co., 1987.

Eyzaguirre, N. "La deuda interna chilena, 1975–85." In *Deuda interna y estabilidad financiera: estudios de casos.* C. Massad and R. Zahler, eds. Buenos Aires: Grupo Editorial Latinoamericano, 1988.

Feinberg, R. E., and R. Ffrench-Davis, eds. *Development and External Debt in Latin America: Basis for a New Consensus.* Southbend, Indiana: University of Notre Dame Press, and *Ediciones CIEPLAN,* Santiago and Grupo Editorial Latinoamericano (GEL), Buenos Aires, 1986.

Ffrench-Davis, R. "The Monetarist Experiment in Chile: A Critical Survey." *World Development,* November 1983(a) and *Colección Estudios CIEPLAN* 9. Santiago, December 1982.

———. "The External Debt, Financial Liberalization and Crisis in Chile." In *Politics and Economics of External Debt Crisis.* Ed. M. Wionczek. Boulder: Westview Press, 1985, and in *Coleccion Estudios CIEPLAN* 11. Santiago, December 1983(b).

———, ed. *Relaciones Financieras Externas y Desarrollo Nacional en América Latina,* Fondo de Cultura Económica, Mexico, 1983(c).

———. "Import Liberalization: The Chilean Experience, 1973–82." In *Military Rule in Chile.* J. S. and A. Valenzuela, eds. Baltimore and London: The Johns Hopkins University Press, 1986.

———. "Conversión de pagarés de la deuda externa en Chile." *Colección Estudios CIEPLAN* 22. Santiago, December, 1987.

———. "The Foreign Debt Crisis and Adjustment in Chile, 1976–86." In *Managing World Debt.* Ed. S. Griffith-Jones. Sussex: Wheatsheaf Books Ltd., New York: St. Martin's Press, 1988(a).

———. "Adjustment and Conditionality in Chile, 1982–88." Mimeo. October 1988(b).

———. "Debt-equity Swaps in Chile." *Cambridge Journal of Economics,* forthcoming.

Ffrench-Davis, R., and J. De Gregorio. "Orígenes y efectos del endeudamiento externo en Chile: antes y después de la crisis." *El Trimestre Económico* Nos. 213 and 214, Mexico, January–March 1987.

Ffrench-Davis, R., and M. Marfán. "Selective Policies Under a Structural Foreign Exchange Shortage." *Journal of Development Economics* Vol. 29, 1989.

Foxley, A. "Experimentos neoliberales en América Latina." *Colección Estudios CIEPLAN* 7. Special issue. Santiago, March 1982, and *Latin American Experiments in Neo-Conservative Economics.* California: University of California Press, California, 1983.

Krugman, P. "Market-based Debt-reduction Schemes." NBER Working Paper No. 2587. Cambridge, 1988.

Larraín, F. "Market-based Debt-reduction Schemes in Chile: A Macroeconomic Perspective." *CPD Discussion Paper* No. 1987–2. Washington, D.C.: February 1987.

McKinnon, R. "Foreign Exchange Policy and Economic Liberalization in LDC's." *Alternativas de Políticas Financieras en Economías Pequeñas y Abiertas al Exterior. Estudios Monetarios* VII. Santiago: Banco Central de Chile, 1981.

Massad, C., and R. Zahler, eds. *Deuda interna y estabilidad financiera: estudios de casos.* Buenos Aires: Grupo Editorial Latinoamericano, 1988.

Marcel, M., and P. Meller. "Empalme de las cuentas nacionales de Chile 1960–1985. Métodos alternativos y resultados." *Colección Estudios CIEPLAN* 20. Santiago, December 1986.

Meller, P. "Un enfoque analítico empírico de las causas del actual endeudamiento externo chileno." *Colección Estudios CIEPLAN* 20. Santiago, December 1986.

Robichek, W. "Some Reflections about External Public Debt Management." *Alternativas de Políticas Financieras en Economías Pequeñas y Abiertas al Exterior. Estudios Monetarios* VII. Santiago: Banco Central de Chile, 1981.

Valdes, S. "Orígenes de la crisis de la deuda: nos sobreendeudamos o nos prestaron en exceso?" *Centro de Estudios Públicos* No. 105. Santiago, August 1988.

COMMENTS

Sebastian Edwards

Ricardo Ffrench-Davis has provided an eminently sensible interpretation of the debt crisis in Chile. I have, in fact, little quarrel with his analysis of the process leading to the crisis. However, he does not analyze the recent Chilean experience with debt-conversion mechanisms in sufficient detail. In fact, I believe that his assessment is too negative and does not consider all important aspects of this problem. My comment, then, concentrates on evaluating the recent debt conversion schemes.

As of June 1988 the Chilean debt had been reduced by more than 4 billion in U.S. dollars—approximately 25 percent of Chile's long-term bank debt—through the use of diverse mechanisms based on the secondary market (see Table 6.10). In this comment I evaluate the two most important mechanisms—the debt conversion program and the debt equity-swaps program, Chapters 18 and 19, respectively of the *Compendium of Rules on International Exchange*.[1]

The Chapter 18 mechanism allows domestic debtors to (indirectly) buy their own foreign liabilities in the secondary market. The Central Bank does not provide foreign exchange at the official rate for these operations; those institutions that participate in this scheme have to obtain the required foreign exchange in the domestic parallel market. Due to a number of macroeconomic effects discussed below, the Chilean authorities have tightly controlled the access to this mechanism. Until September 1985, the Central Bank of Chile allocated a monthly quota to private banks. This allowed them to acquire up to that amount of its debt in the secondary market. Starting in October 1985, the Central Bank has auctioned quotas instead of allocating them. In March 1988 Chapter 18 operations were suspended. Although the Chilean authorities have called this a temporary measure, it is unclear if and when Chapter 18 conversions will be allowed to resume.

The actual mechanics of debt conversions are rather complicated. A typical Chapter 18 debt operation can be described as follows: A Chilean institution,

Sebastian Edwards is Professor of Economics, UCLA.

Table 6.10

Debt Conversion Mechanisms in Chile
(millions of U.S. dollars)

	1985	1986	1987	1988[a]	Total U.S.$	Total %
Chapter XVIII[b]	115.2	410.6	695.8	527.6	1,748.2	41.0
Chapter XIX	25.9	217.0	711.5	252.1	1,206.5	28.8
Capitalizations D.L. 600	53.0	56.3	124.6	0.0	233.9	5.6
Portfolio swaps	41.0	27.2	0.0	0.0	68.2	1.6
Other[c]	88.7	275.9	451.0	119.0	934.6	22.3
Total	323.8	987.0	1,982.9	898.7	4,192.4	100.0
Accumulated total	323.8	1,310.8	3,293.7	4,192.4	4,192.4	

Source: Larraín (1988).

[a] As of June 30.

[b] Includes Chapter 18 and Chapter 18 Annex 4.

[c] Includes direct operations and co-donations.

e.g., a private bank, decides to rescue some of its outstanding foreign liabilities. The first step is to buy a quota in the Central Bank auction. Next it locates, through an international broker, a holder of its debt that is willing to sell it. At that point the Chilean bank will have to obtain foreign exchange in the local parallel market. This will imply two steps: (1) Pesos have to be obtained to buy the foreign exchange; for this purpose the bank issues domestic debt which it sells in Chile. (2) It contacts an intermediary who buys the foreign exchange in the parallel market; once the foreign exchange is on hand, the debt is actually bought and the liability is extinguished.

The public sector, and most notably the Central Bank and the state-owned Banco del Estado, have also used Chapter 18 to reduce some of their debt. In this case, however, the payment is not made with foreign exchange. Instead, the public sector foreign liabilities are exchanged for long-term bonds denominated in domestic currency. The value of these peso bonds has fluctuated in the Chilean secondary market at around 88 percent of par value. A variant of the Chapter 18 program is the Annex 4 of Chapter 18. This scheme amounts to exchanging liabilities in foreign currency for newly issued stock shares in a Chilean corporation. These operations are directly monitored by the Central Bank and are not subject to the quota allocation. A key aspect of this scheme is that it has not been financed with reserves or other official funds but rather with reversed capital flight. This turns out to be very important in determining the benefits of the scheme.

An important aspect of Chapter 18 operations is that Chilean residents capture most of the secondary market discount. Three agents have shared the discount: (1) the Central Bank, (2) the suppliers of foreign exchange in the parallel market, and (3) the various intermediaries. Larraín (1988) has recently calculated that in 1987 the average discount on Chapter 18 operations amounted to 35.7 percent. Of these, the Central Bank got the lion's share, 20.5 points, the suppliers of foreign exchange in the parallel market got 3.3 percentage points, and the rest corresponded to various fees.[2]

Chapter 18 conversion schemes have several macroeconomic effects. First, there is pressure on the black market for foreign exchange. It is for this reason that the government established the quota system in 1986. It was expected that in this way the spread in this market would not become excessively high, and this was basically accomplished. In the first half of 1988, however, the parallel market premium started to increase, mainly for political reasons. To avoid additional pressures on this market, Chapter 18 operations have been temporarily suspended. An important question is whether the funds currently used to finance this scheme in the parallel market—funds corresponding to past capital flight—could have been lured to the country in a more efficient way. If the answer to this question is positive, the desirability of this program becomes more dubious.

The second macroeconomic effect is related to the scheme's effect on interest rates. The domestic counterpart of the rescue of foreign liabilities is the creation of internal debt. This, of course, puts pressure on the domestic capital market and as a result, domestic interest rates will tend to rise. It is important to notice, however, that contrary to some popular accounts, the Chapter 18 program has no short-run consequences on the creation of money by the Central Bank.

It is difficult to quantify exactly, or to summarize in a single number, the costs associated with these macroeconomic effects. There seems to be consensus, however, that they are relatively minor.[3] The desirability of the scheme, then, will basically depend on whether it is beneficial for the country to capture a discount that fluctuates around 32 percent. The answer to this depends partially on whether Chile expects to pay its debt in full, or if it expects to have a large proportion of its debt forgiven (or alternatively, if it expects to repudiate it). If, as the Chilean authorities have pointed out recently, the government expects to pay all its debt in full, then buying some of it at a discount is a good deal. If, however, it is expected that at the end of the road the country will not pay all of its debt and that a large fraction of it will be forgiven, it is not clearly beneficial to buy it in the secondary market, even if it carries a sizeable discount. This has been the view of prominent opposition economists who have openly called for putting an end to these programs once the Pinochet government is replaced by a new democratic administration.[4]

The Chapter 19 program corresponds to debt-equity swaps or a debt capitalization scheme. A typical operation can be described in the following way: A foreign investor buys Chilean private debt at a discount in the secondary market, and converts it into internal debt. This debt is then sold in the domestic secondary market and the proceeds are used to acquire domestic (productive) assets or to finance domestic investment projects. Participants in this scheme cannot repatriate profits for the first four years, and the principal can only be repatriated after ten years. Chapter 19 operations are not subject to quota allocation and are approved on a case-by-case basis by the Central Bank; it is expected that this approach will allow for screening of bona fide investors and avoid round-tripping operations. There is no Central Bank commission on these operations. Most participants in Chapter 19 schemes have invested in the mining and other natural resources sectors such as forestry.

Chapter 19 operations, contrary to Chapter 18, do not result in the extinction of a foreign liability. They constitute just a replacement of one type of liability for another. As noted above, to the extent that profit repatriation is delayed for four years there is a beneficial liquidity effect. While Chilean residents have captured most of the secondary market discount from the operations approved through Chapter 18, in the case of Chapter 19 most of the discount has been captured by the foreign investor. This, of course, is equivalent to providing a major subsidy to foreign investment. Larraín (1988) has recently estimated that this subsidy amounted to approximately 35 percent in 1987. It is unlikely that providing such a sizeable subsidy is the most efficient way to attract additional foreign investment.

As Ffrench-Davis argues in his paper, an important element in evaluating the Chapter 19 program refers to its crowding out or additionality effects on foreign investment. The question is whether those participants in the program would have invested in Chile anyway. If this is the case, the program has crowded out other investments. Alternatively, the program may have attracted new investors; in this case there would be additionality. It is not easy to quantify this issue, and the opinions appear to be divided. Previously, for example, Ffrench-Davis (1987) questions the existence of additionality, while Fontaine (1989) argues that there is a significant proportion of new funds. Larraín (1988) takes a somewhat intermediate position, arguing that since foreign banks have opted to participate, in spite of the fact that equity investment is not their main line of business, this is a sign that there is at least some additionality.[5]

The 1988 Chilean rescheduling proposal included the possibility of implementing a debt buyback scheme where the Central Bank would use its own reserves. This proposal allowed a qualified majority of the creditor banks to waive the sharing clauses and the negative pledge clauses. On the 27th of September the Central Bank announced that it was calling for bids for up to 200 million U.S. dollars of buybacks. It is unclear, however, how the recent results from the plebiscite will affect this program.

To sum up, Chile has been tremendously successful in using the secondary market to reduce its debt in at least one dimension. Approximately 25 percent of Chile's long-term debt to banks has been converted in the last few years. The two main mechanisms used for these purposes are fundamentally different.

Chapter 18 consists of debt conversions or debt rescue schemes where Chilean residents have captured most of the secondary market discount. After the access quota allocation system was implemented, moreover, it has been the Central Bank that has captured most of this discount. By and large, given the fact that it has been financed with reversed capital flight, Chapter 18 has been an innovative program that seems to have resulted in positive net benefits to the country. Chapter 19, on the other hand, is a debt capitalization program. It has provided an implicit subsidy to foreign investors of approximately 30 percent, and has resulted in very little, if any, additionality.

Notes

In preparing these comments, the author benefited greatly from discussions with Felipe Larraín.

1. These names stem from the fact that the regulations that govern these operations are contained in Chapters 18 and 19 of the *Compendium of Rules on International Exchange* of the Central Bank of Chile.

2. These computations refer to all operations that have used Chapter 18 and not merely to the private sector.

3. Larraín (1988).

4. See the Opposition manifesto, "El Consenso Político Económico es Posible," *La Época*, September 1988.

5. Obviously, in evaluating this program the usual considerations on the desirability of foreign investment should be taken into account.

References

Ffrench-Davis, R. "Debt Conversions in Chile." Mimeo. 1987.

Fontaine, J. A. "The Debt Crisis and the Chilean Economy." In *Debt, Adjustment and Recovery: The Latin American Crisis*. Ed. S. Edwards and F. Larraín. London: Blackwell, 1989.

Larraín, F. "Debt Reduction and the Management of the Chilean Debt." World Bank. Mimeo. 1988.

7

Mexico: The Transfer Problem, Profits, and Welfare

Clemente Ruiz Durán

During 1982–1988, Mexico transferred over 60 billion dollars abroad, equivalent to 7 percent of GDP. In absolute and relative terms, this was the highest negative transfer of any of the Latin American countries (see Appendix Table 7.1A). Historically, transfers of this magnitude have only occurred as war reparations, e.g., Germany after World War I or France after the Franco-Prussian War (see Devlin 1987; Reisen and Van Trotsenburg 1988). In Mexico's case the transfer, while unrelated to defeat in war, was exacted from a regime that also was under great political and economic pressure from foreign creditors.

This is an analysis of three interrelated problems: the transfer problem, the impact on accumulation, and the welfare effects. First the mechanics of the transfer process are explored, interrelating the effort realized in the external sector with the budgetary problem and its economic effects. Next, is an analysis of the impact of the transfer process on profit generation. Finally, the impact of the transfer process on the standard of living of the population is assessed. The paper concludes by suggesting an alternative path that Mexico may have to follow, given that the authoritarianism which has allowed the current transfer strategy to be imposed is weakening, and the political pressures to resume growth are intensifying.

The analyses are a preliminary attempt to reassess some basic ideas about Mexican growth and development. They are offered as an alternative to the equilibrium analysis and economic orthodoxy that have shaped Mexican policy making in the eighties, and whose technical failures and high welfare costs are now evident.

Clemente Ruiz Durán is Professor of Economics, National Autonomous University of Mexico and former advisor to the Central Bank of Mexico. He thanks, without implicating, David Felix and Rudiger Dornbusch for their comments, Manuel Herrera for help in processing some of the statistics, and Hector Chavez for some of the estimates.

The Transfer Decision: A Problem in Political Economy

In August 1982, the Mexican government announced a temporary suspension of debt service payments. After three months of international negotiation, the government opted for a cooperative rather than an adversarial approach to the debt crisis and decided to "restructure the economy" for resuming debt service payments in return for restructuring of the payment schedule by the creditors. A contractionary program (IMF style) was adopted to generate internal and external surpluses; first by cuts in government expenditure, second initially by contracting imports, and subsequently by expanding non-oil exports. The external and domestic aspects of the transfer process (Cohen 1987; Reisen and Van Trotsenburg 1988) can be expressed as:

$$NT_t \; = \; K_t - Pf_t = EA = DA \qquad\qquad (1)$$

where:

NT   is net transfer,
K   is capital account,
Pf   is payments abroad,
EA   is external adjustment, and
DA   is domestic adjustment.

To evaluate the Mexican government's strategy, one needs to start with pre-crisis policy making. During the sixties and the seventies, Mexico's economic growth had become tethered to the flow of external financing, which was influenced in turn by fluctuations of export receipts. The resulting credit cycle can be described as follows: "An expansion of credit and investment at first stimulates a genuine increase in income. Prices and interest rates rise. Then euphoria develops. Speculators no longer evaluate rationally the prospective return relative to risk. They engage in 'overtrading.' At length, another incident makes clear that the boom has gone too far. A 'revulsion' takes place against commodities and securities. Banks cease to lend, and everyone strives at once to increase liquidity" (Minsky 1972; Schuker 1988).

In the Mexican case, external financing did not compensate for export fluctuations, but reinforced their impact; i.e., a collapse in export earnings was followed by a reduction in external credit. Adjustment to the shortage of foreign exchange during the downward part of the cycle mainly involved reducing public expenditure and the rate of economic growth. The drop of domestic expenditures reduced the current account deficit, restoring creditor confidence, reviving voluntary lending, and allowing growth to be resumed (Ruiz Durán 1983).

Policy makers in 1982 believed that the economy was enmeshed in another such cycle. The orthodox adjustment strategy therefore was chosen in expectation that voluntary lending and economic growth would resume within one to two years. Thus the targets in the original IMF agreement, signed in November 1982, assumed that growth would resume with a 3 percent increase of real GDP in 1984, 6 percent in 1985, and that the current account deficit, 2.2 percent of GDP in 1983, would decline to 1.2 percent by 1985 (SHCP 1982). Such estimates based on equilibrium analysis did not, however, adequately anticipate the depressing effect of the transfer effort on the accumulation process. In general, excessive faith in self-adjusting markets tends to produce simplistic strategies which eschew state intervention and protectionism and rely instead on market forces to shape a more efficient economy. The Mexican restructuring program was of this genre. It focused on two main goals: maintaining debt servicing (negative transfer decision) and reducing state intervention and protectionism (structural change decision).

To attain these goals the strategy used:

(a) the reduction of domestic demand via cuts in government programs to depress internal purchasing power and generate surpluses in the external balance;

(b) increases in relative prices of key tradeable goods in order to shift demand from the domestic to the export sector;

(c) privatization of state enterprises and reduction of protectionism to induce higher and more efficient private investment.

In choosing its strategy, the government policy makers adopted IMF orthodoxy without really taking into account the size of the required transfer. With central bankers and conservative financial groups dominating the choice of policy and with little congressional opposition, as was the case in Mexico under de la Madrid, policy making becomes quite authoritarian. Fiscal budgeting thus was guided by financial programming (IMF 1984) rather than real economic and social needs. The chief aim of financial programming was to facilitate foreign debt servicing, i.e., to generate large domestic surpluses in order to carry out the external transfers. The consequences of this policy approach have been dramatic. Table 7.1 shows that the abrupt reversal of external transfers from inflows to outflows after 1982 was accompanied by a sustained decline of GDP per capita, an experience unknown to Mexico since the Great Depression.

The change of macroeconomic behavior was also dramatic. In the preceding credit cycles, current account deficits in the balance of payments were accompanied by large fiscal deficits that stabilized profits. With the abrupt shift after 1982 to surplus, the Mexican economy was no longer able to sustain profits and economic growth.

To analyze the "surplus generating process" we disaggregate equation (1) into:

$$EA_t = TB_t + NFS_t \pm (R + EO)_t \tag{2}$$

where:

TB	is the trade balance,
NFS	is nonfactor services balance,
R	is foreign reserves, and
EO	is errors and omissions.

Table 7.1

Mexico's External Transfers and GDP Growth
(millions of U.S. dollars)

	1960–1981	1982–1987
Balance of payments		
Current account balance	−49,632	6,881
Capital account	66,549	5,069
Factor payments abroad	33,702	60,635
Net transfer	32,847	−55,566
Annual GDP growth rate	6.9	−0.2
Annual GDP per capita growth rate	3.4	−2.4

Source: Banco de México, Dirección de Investigación Económica, *Indicadores Económicos*, various issues.

The trends in these components of the balance of payments during 1982–87 are given in Table 7.2. Accounting for the TB and NFS trends were the following:

· Annual exports in current dollars rose modestly during 1982–84, but have declined since. The chief cause was falling export prices, which affected mainly public sector exports (petroleum). Partly offsetting this, the share of private exports, assisted by the government's export promotion policies, rose from 16 percent of all exports in 1982 to 52 percent in 1987. This sufficed to keep the average annual value of total exports measured in nondeflated U.S. dollars at around the 1982 level.

· Imports fell drastically in 1983 (41 percent). Thereafter private sector imports revived; by 1987 they had risen above 1982 when measured in current dollars, whereas public sector imports remained 49 percent below 1982. In constant dollars, both remained well below 1982.

· The nonfactor services balance moved into surplus after 1982, primarily from the expansion of maquiladoras and tourism and from a decline of Mexican expenditure abroad.

To analyze the corresponding domestic adjustment effort, we adopt the simplifying assumption that all the external debt is public or publicly guaranteed so that debt payments are a "budgetary problem." (The fact that the Mexican government assumed *ex post* the exchange burden and risks of private foreign debt is brought in later.) That is, the fiscal budget must produce a surplus large enough to effect the transfer of national savings to foreign creditors. The external surplus equals the domestic surplus, which is the sum of the surplus of the government's primary budget and net private savings. The surplus on external

Table 7.2

Changes in Equation (2) Variables, 1982–87, Percent of GDP

	EA/GDP	TB/GDP	NFS/GDP	(R+EO)/GDP
1982	−2.3	4.0	0.5	−2.1
1983	−10.1	11.6	1.9	3.3
1984	−7.7	8.1	2.3	−2.7
1985	−8.1	5.5	2.4	0.2
1986	−6.0	3.7	2.5	−0.1
1987	−5.8	6.1	3.4	−4.7

Source: Same as Table 7.1.

account is also necessarily the counterpart of the government surplus and the increase of its domestic debt (Cohen 1987). It can be expressed as:

$$NT_t = DA_t = PBAL_t + [D_t - (1 + r_t) D_t{-}1] + S \qquad (3)$$

where:

PBAL   is the public sector primary balance,

D   is public sector domestic debt,

r   is the real interest rate on public sector domestic debt, and

S   is money creation.

When the simplifying assumption is dropped, the impact of the monetary and fiscal components of the domestic adjustment (DA) on profits, accumulation, and welfare can be shown more clearly. For this, equation (3) is restated as:

$$DA_t = BG_t + ACC_t + W_t \qquad (4)$$

where:

BG   is the budgetary problem,

ACC   is the accumulation problem, and

W   is the welfare effect.

Each of these problems is discussed in the following sections.

The Budgetary Problem or the Politics of Overkill

Adapting Mexico's economy, with its chronic fiscal deficits, to the production of large fiscal surpluses was a daunting task. At issue was not merely the choice of policy instruments and their uses, but perhaps more importantly, the impact of the choice on the government's relations with different power groups. Here, only the power relations involved in the first problem, the budgetary decision, are emphasized.

Table 7.3

Mexican Direct and Indirect Tax to GDP Ratios

	1970–1981	1982–1987
Direct taxes/GDP	0.0501	0.0442
Indirect taxes/GDP	0.0634	0.0914

Source: Banco de México, *Informes Anuales e Indicadores Económicos*, various issues.

As stated earlier, the budgetary objective was to generate surpluses in the primary balance of the public sector which, complemented with "forced savings" from other sectors, could be converted into external resource transfers sufficient to service the foreign debt. The primary surplus could have been obtained through increased revenues or via cuts in noninterest expenditures. The de la Madrid regime chose to rely mainly on expenditure cuts rather than tax increases and/or an aggressive incomes policy. The justification by the Ministry of Finance was that the enterprises had been hit too hard by the crisis to absorb tax increases (Gabinete Económico 1983).

Income taxes declined from 5 percent of GDP in 1982 to 3.9 percent in 1987. Offsetting this were increases in indirect taxes, mainly value added taxes and import duties, which sufficed to raise the real value of tax income above 1982 levels. The shift of tax incidence to indirect taxes is shown in Table 7.3.

The increase of indirect taxation was inflationary, and collection lags held back fiscal revenues, the average lag during 1982–87 was 0.82 percent of GDP (Banco de México 1988). The dynamics of the adjustment, it could be argued, reduced the flexibility of the fiscal system.

To compensate for this, government chose to raise the prices of public goods. The ratio of the prices of government goods and services (excluding petroleum) to the prices of private sector goods rose around 27 percent between 1982 and 1987. This depressed the demand for and production of public goods and services, and their share of GDP declined during 1982–87. With declining revenues, many public sector firms reduced capacity by cutting back on maintenance and replacement. The failure of the policy of "getting prices right" is patent in the case of government goods. Activities producing essential economic and social services were decapitalized, and the regressive incidence of the cutbacks helped worsen the already highly unequal income distribution, while their contribution to the fiscal surplus was negative.

To generate that surplus, the government relied on large cuts in programmable expenditures. It was politically easier for the government, lacking serious legislative opposition, to cut expenditures than to rely on a strong incomes policy that could worsen its relations with the powerful business interests that had traditionally opposed progressive fiscal reforms. The drop in programmable expenditure from 28 percent of GDP in 1982 to 20 percent of GDP in 1987 mainly affected public investment. It was a costly choice for the country: temporary benefits for the creditor banks at the expense of future productive capacity and growth.

More specifically, public expenditure was reduced through the following actions:

• Public enterprises were shut down or sold to the private sector under the program of *desincorporación de entidades paraestatales*. The number of public enterprises was reduced from 1,155 at the end of 1982 to 449 by mid-1988. However, although the extent of *desincorporación* was large, it augmented public sector savings only a modest 10 percent (Pichardo Pagaza 1988).

• Much more important was the reduction or elimination of programs related to industrial development, social welfare, infrastructure, and rural development. Programmable expenditure was reduced from 28.2 percent of GDP in 1982, to 20.4 percent in 1987, while nonsectoral expenditures (e.g., regional development expenditures) were reduced from 8.5 percent to 4.7 percent of GDP during 1982–87. Public sector savings generated through these actions totaled 11.6 percent of GDP in the period 1982–87.

The reductions turned the primary budget from deficit to surplus. Nevertheless, the primary surplus covered only 33 percent of the interest service on the external debt. The rest was financed by new foreign credits (Ponzi financing) and seigniorage. Since new foreign credit was difficult to obtain, the government had to try to extract much of the requisite domestic financing of foreign debt servicing through imposing high reserve requirements on the banks and through extensive money market operations. Figure 7.1 illustrates the main changes after 1982 from the pre-crisis pattern of financing the fiscal deficit.

More specifically, state-owned banks have become instruments of fiscal policy. The state now uses around 80 percent of bank credit to finance interest payments, an additional 10 percent goes to meet reserve requirements, leaving only 10 percent for new private credit. Casas de Bolsa (brokerage houses) have become brokers for the state. Before nationalization, Mexico had moved toward the concept of universal banking, but in 1984, the Congress passed legislation which separated brokering from banking. To place paper in the money market, it is now necessary to use the Casas de Bolsa circuit. This way of compensating the former owners of the nationalized banks who control the Casas de Bolsa is an ironic reversal from the 1950s when the state, in order to promote banks as the main source of deficit financing, undertook to support their profitability by paying high interest rates on bank reserves with the Central Bank. New fiscal debt was also financed through forced savings. Government bonds had paid negative real interest until 1985. Thereafter, the real rate has been positive. In all, investors increased their holdings of government securities from 1.9 percent of GDP in 1982 to 4.4 percent in 1988.

Figure 7.1. **Public Sector Deficit and Financial System Reordering**

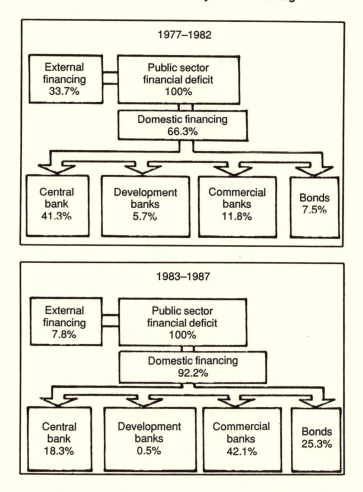

Equation (6) decomposes equation (4) (following Cohen 1987):

$$\sum_{t=1}^{T} \frac{EA\,(t)}{(1+i)}\,t = \sum_{t=1}^{T} \frac{S\,(t)}{(1+i)^t} + \sum_{t=1}^{T} \frac{PBAL\,(t)}{(1+i)^t} + B\,(0) - \sum_{t=1}^{T} \frac{B\,(t)}{(1+i)^t} \qquad (6)$$

where t = 1 corresponds to 1983:1, and t = T to 1988:3. The left side is the discounted sum of the external surpluses. The right side is the sum of government revenues generated by seigniorage, the primary surpluses, and the net increase of government domestic debt. With the left side as the scale factor, the decomposition is as follows: the seigniorage tax plus the primary surplus summed to 62 percent of the external surpluses, while the rest was financed by domestic debt increases.

The real interest rate on government securities turned positive in 1985:2 and has remained so as of 1988:3. High positive real rates have trapped the budget in a vicious circle, pushing up the domestic debt while constricting the financing of public investment.

To summarize, the budgetary problem has been handled mainly through three mechanisms: expenditure cuts, seigniorage, and increasing domestic debt. The latter two have forced the Central Bank to follow an accommodating monetary policy, not to assist the financing of economic and social needs but the financing of the resource transfer.

Accumulation, Profits, and the External Surplus

In late capitalism, profit generation through public deficits nurtures private investment. Mexico is no exception. The strength and stability of its accumulation process has largely depended on the multiplier effect of fiscal deficits on aggregate demand. Equation (7) is the Kalecki formulation of the relation between deficits and profits:

Gross Profits = Budget Deficit + Capitalists' Expenditure + Export Surplus   (7)

In the initial phases of Mexican development, the dynamics of domestic market demand was mainly governed by exports and fiscal deficits. In the 1940s the import substitution strategy adopted to foster industrialization increased the degree of monopoly of the industrial sector and reduced the profitability of exported-oriented activities. Until the 1960s, the more dynamic firms were those in the import substituting sector, but as import substitution lost momentum, business expansion became more dependent on direct state expenditure.

Thus when the transfer process of the 1980s transformed primary budget deficits into surpluses, the effect was to collapse accumulation. The gross investment coefficient dropped from 0.25 in 1981 to 0.15 in 1987, while net investment fell from 0.204 to 0.10 in the same period. The investment drop has, of course, reduced the potential growth of the Mexican economy.

Reducing deficits and import protection was seen by the government as essential for giving market forces a stronger role in the growth process. With government expenditure reduced, private investment, disciplined by intensified external competition, would be able to drive the economy more efficiently. But has this approach actually effected a permanent change in the fueling of the profit-generating mechanism from public deficit to exports? While there is no final answer as yet to this key question, the evidence suggests that the "transfer process'' thus far has depressed profit expectations and that mainly it was depressed imports that have accounted for the external surpluses.

The conclusion that the shift in the public sector's primary balance from deficit to surplus depressed aggregate demand and thus profit generation holds even when the adjusted operational deficit is used to measure the government's impact on aggregate demand (as suggested by Tanzi, Blejer, and Teijeiro 1987; CEPAL 1987; and Banco de México 1986). In addition, the drop in foreign credit availability for financing the current account deficit has forced the government to turn to deficit financing for its foreign exchange needs. From facilitating the flow of finance to the private sector during the pre-crisis era, the state has been crowding out private financing since 1982.

To offset the depressing effects, the government has resorted to the neoclassical remedy of adjusting relative prices, i.e., "getting prices right," hoping that deregulation would generate a more competitive economy and a more efficient accumulation process. For this purpose the following policies were adopted:

• Trade liberalization to force a reduction in the profit/output ratio. Protection had allowed higher markups and profit rates for business and higher costs for consumers. Opening the economy to more international competition was expected to lower these, stimulating real aggregate demand and output. Accordingly, in 1987, the government signed the General Agreement on Trade and Tariffs (Miguel de la Madrid 1987), committing itself to trade liberalization. The commitments are being met. Import licenses have been eliminated, and tariffs now average 10 percent, the lowest in Latin America.

• Undervaluing the real exchange rate in order to increase the profitability of investment in and production of tradeable goods. The undervaluation was greatest in the early years of the debt crisis, and is still above 10 percent.

• The replacement of subsidies to public sector enterprises, with higher prices on public sector services.

Reliance on a neoclassical "get prices right" strategy was, however, supplemented by resort to a more Keynesian type of stimulus to profits, namely, financial subsidies to the private sector. These show up as the "financial intermediation balance" between the private sector and the development banks and government funds. That balance rose from 0.5 percent of GDP in 1983 to a peak of 1.45 percent in 1984, diminishing afterwards to 1.2 percent during 1985–87. By contrast the average for 1965–81 was 0.85 percent of GDP.

In the initial crisis years, the authorities averted large-scale bankruptcy by allowing firms in financial distress to roll over their loans with the nationalized banks. This *revolvencia* has now become as a sort of quasi-permanent "entitlement." Firms were also given preferential exchange rates on their foreign currency liabilities with the nationalized banks (Ruiz Durán 1984; Tello 1984). For firms whose foreign exchange liabilities were to foreign banks, a joint renegotiation facility was created to reduce the impact of exchange rate depreciation (Banco de México 1983). The favorable effect of these measures in rescuing the

Table 7.4

Average Liability to Equity Ratios of
Enterprises Listed on the Mexican Stock Exchange

1981	90.4
1982	163.6
1983	126.5
1984	107.3
1985	91.6
1986	90.3
1987	89.3

Source: Bolsa Mexicana de Valores, *Anuario Estadístico*, various years.

large, financially strapped private sector firms (those listed on the Bolsa) is indicated in Table 7.4.

To further encourage exports, preferential credit lines were established at a time when new bank credit for other private operations was almost completely crowded out by deficit financing (Bancomex 1988). Exchange controls were greatly eased, and export firms were granted the right to spend their export proceeds freely on imports required for producing their exports. Finally, despite accelerating inflation, the official policy was to raise profit margins from the cost side by lagging and adjusting wages to past period inflation, thus disregarding wages as a major demand component.

This policy package was intended to promote an expanding nucleus of export firms that would become the new engine of growth. In reality, most of the nucleus has consisted of transnational corporations (with the automotive firms the most important), while national firms thus far have been minor contributors (see Appendix Table 7.2A).

Overall private sector exports of goods and services rose from 2 percent of GDP in 1982, to 7.55 percent in 1987. The increase reflected the factors which follow.

Excess Capacity. Some import substituting industries with depressed home markets, notably textiles, steel, and glass, diverted production facilities to exporting. Their export share, negligible in 1982, rose to 0.6 percent of GDP by 1987.

Reorganization of World Sourcing of Transnationals. The Mexican government's pro-export policies lowered the cost to transnational corporations of using Mexican plants to produce components and final products for the U.S. market. In addition, debt-equity swaps enabled them to obtain pesos at very favorable exchange rates (in the period 1986–87 the approved swaps were 2,945 million in U.S. dollars, of which 23 percent were in tourism and 17 percent in automotives). Figure 7.2 shows that transnational exports in current dollars increased

Figure 7.2. **Exports by Locally Owned Firms and by Firms with Foreign Ownership**

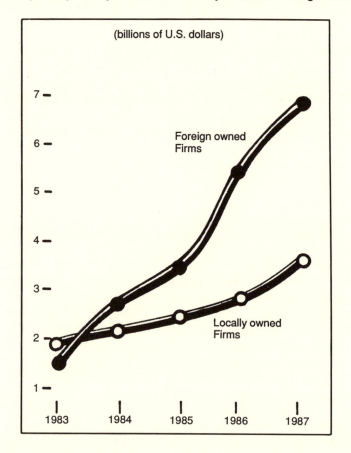

more than fivefold during 1982–87, accounting for 80 percent of the increase of private sector exports. Exports of the auto firms alone rose from 0.2 percent of GDP in 1982 to 2.2 percent in 1987.

The Expansion of Tourism. Reducing the real exchange rate made Mexico a tourist bargain, the annual number of foreign tourists increasing 43.5 percent between 1982 and 1987. Dollar expenditure per tourist rose, however, only 12.7 percent.

Although the exporting nucleus expanded, the expansion came mainly from idle rather than added capacity. Workers in this nucleus benefited from the exporting, however. Jobs were preserved and real wages fell less than the economy-wide average.

The nucleus transformed the private sector's balance of trade from its chronically large deficit to small surpluses in 1986–87. However, the sector's rising import coefficient—from 5.3 percent of GDP in 1982 to 6.8 percent in 1987—held the private sector's contribution to less than 10 percent of the total foreign exchange surplus mobilized in 1986–87 for debt servicing. The dominant contribution came from reduced public sector imports generated by the budgetary adjustments discussed earlier. Moreover, the percent of firms engaged in exporting is still very small. Most import substituting firms have not shown the flexibility to shift to exporting and remain dependent on the old profit-generating circuit. But fiscal deficits no longer stimulate the expansion of aggregate demand, while the export expansion remains too limited to sustain the demand expansion needed to raise GDP growth above the population increase.

The Welfare Effect: Impoverishment of the Society

The domestic adjustments have affected welfare through various channels. IMF type adjustment policies assume implicitly that labor markets clear at above subsistence wages. But this is not how the markets function in Mexico, where there is not merely unemployment in the formal sector but also fragmentation of labor markets between formal and informal. Workers in the latter lack recourse to institutionalized services that can provide a subsistence safety net, e.g., purchasing power to sustain nutritionally adequate food consumption. Unemployment and falling real wages in the formal sector and deteriorating conditions in the informal sector have increased not only the already very unequal income distribution but also the incidence of destitution.

Mexican social security institutions, broadly defined to include the provision of health care, have three notable features. The poor are not the principal beneficiaries of most of the policies. Except for retirement benefits, there are no significant financial transfers to beneficiaries. Except for housing, where home ownership rather than renting is promoted, Mexico's welfare system is built on the concepts of income and consumption, much like those of advanced welfare states. The standard assumption, hardly ever questioned, is that income determines the level of welfare. There is a great deal of discussion in the Mexican press and among Mexican social scientists about income and salary levels, but little analysis of delivery systems and other features of the institutional setting (Sherraden and Ruiz Durán 1989).

Given the highly unequal income distribution and weak welfare institutions, implementing the negative resource transfers has had disastrous welfare consequences. The implementation has been effected through cuts in public sector programs that lower the social consumption level; forced savings that have impacted most severely on the consumption of the wage earning poor; lagged indexing of wages to past inflation that has depressed real wages in general (Lustig and Ros 1987); and layoffs that have accelerated the movement of labor from the formal to the informal sector. These factors in combination have produced major alterations in the levels and distribution of real income in Mexico.

To analyze the effect of the transfer process on welfare, we have constructed the following simple welfare index:

$$WL = ER_t + ARW_t + PSENI_t$$

where:

WL   is welfare level, an unweighted average,
ER   is employment rate, the complement of the open and disguised unemployment rate,
ARW   is average real wage, and
PSENI is public sector expenditures excluding interest.

The preliminary calculations reported in Table 7.5 show that by 1987, WL had fallen to 68 percent of its 1980 level. This reflected a decrease in the employment index of 17 percent, a 57 percent decline of the average real wage, and a 23 percent decline in PSENI.

The deterioration of employment reflects an increase in the percentage of the economically active population (EAP) in the informal sector, including an increased share of unremunerated family workers as well as layoffs in the formal sector (Cordera and González 1987). Moreover, since the decline of the welfare index and each of its components far exceeded the decline of GDP per capita, it is apparent that the main burden of the transfer effort has fallen on wage earners and the poorer self-employed strata of Mexican society.

Paralleling these trends has been the deterioration of human capital, shown in Table 7.6, that is putting future productivity at risk. Nutrition levels have fallen, and health problems related to malnourishment are increasing (Carrasco and Provencio 1988). The increase of morbidity by more than 6 million between 1982 and 1987 is probably also related to the declining government expenditure on preventive medicine.

Educational outlays have focused primarily on basic education, yet adult illiteracy in 1988 is estimated still to be 2.5 million, around 5 percent of the population above fifteen years of age. Investment in human capital is 46 percent of gross nonresidential investment in physical capital; the U.S. ratio is one-third larger (U.S. *Economic Report of the President* 1988).

A nutritionally adequate food basket now costs 3.3 times the minimum wage, compared to 1.8 in 1978–82 (Carrasco and Provencio 1988). Inflation has significantly reduced the proportion of the population able to purchase the basket. Per capita consumption of grains has diminished and consumption per capita of beans and corn, the basic diet of the Mexican poor, is down 28 percent and 40 percent, respectively, from pre-crisis levels. Meat and milk consumption has also fallen. The deterioration of welfare is pushing against the subsistence floor.

* * *

Table 7.5

Mexico: Welfare Indicators (1980 = 100)

	Composite welfare	Employment rate	Real wage	Noninterest public outlay	GDP per capita
1981	107.4	100.0	108.7	113.6	105.5
1982	100.2	95.9	100.5	104.2	102.5
1983	85.7	91.4	74.1	91.7	94.9
1984	84.9	90.5	70.5	93.6	96.3
1985	81.6	88.3	70.3	86.1	96.9
1986	76.2	83.6	61.4	83.7	91.2
1987	68.0	83.7	43.0	77.4	91.0

Source: C. R. Cordera and T. E. González, *Crisis y Política Económica: Saldos Productivos y Sociales 1982–1987,* 1987, mimeo.

The Mexican electorate voiced its opposition to the government's strategy by almost voting the entrenched ruling party, the PRI, out of power in 1988. The unprecedented protest vote is seen as an imperative demand that economic growth resume.

As pointed out in this paper, the new nucleus of accumulation is inadequate to sustain a positive growth of GDP per capita. The impetus to profits and growth still has to come in large part from primary fiscal deficits. Reversing the public sector's primary balance from surplus to deficit requires, in turn, reversing the current account balance from surplus to deficit. The transfer effort has also shown that a noninterest fiscal outlay of only 20 percent of GDP is insufficient to generate profits to support the Mexican full capacity investment rate, which averages around 25 percent of GDP. Public sector outlays will have to be at least as large as that investment component of GDP, perhaps even higher since substantial welfare improvement is now also a political imperative.

A growth strategy that gives due attention to job creation and welfare improvement will require more than merely a reversal of transfers. Growth alone does not automatically better the lot of the poor; redistributive reforms are also essential. Mexico has to move toward an institutional setting where full employment can become a reality. The Mexican economy and its supporting institutions have been adapted to a level of activity below full employment, with labor and product markets segmented into formal and informal components. The challenge is to adapt the institutions of Mexican capitalism to a dynamic in which a larger role for market forces is made compatible with welfare enhancing reforms.

Table 7.6

Mexico: Human Capital Indicators

	Population				
	Total	Over 15	Housing[a]	Health morbidity	Education
	(thousands)			(thousands)	PSEED[b]
1980	69,655	38,845	5.8	13,591	3.6
1981	71,388	40,263	5.6	16,235	4.3
1982	73,069	41,732	5.5	8,785	4.4
1983	74,707	43,258	5.5	10,440	2.9
1984	76,325	44,849	5.4	12,055	3.0
1985	77,938	46,507	5.4	13,678	3.0
1986	79,542	48,200	5.4	12,780	2.6
1987	81,139	49,952	5.3	14,164	2.5
1988	82,721	51,738	5.2	n.a.	n.a.

	Food consumption per capita (Kg)						
	Rice	Beans	Corn	Wheat	Meat	Meat (pig)	Milk (liters)
1980	5.6	19.8	237.8	52.9	15.1	18.0	112.4
1981	7.3	25.5	245.2	60.5	15.8	18.3	111.9
1982	4.9	14.6	242.0	65.3	16.7	18.7	110.6
1983	3.7	16.6	236.8	51.6	13.8	19.2	107.4
1984	6.4	12.6	201.5	63.4	12.6	19.1	107.2
1985	9.0	13.5	203.1	70.9	12.1	16.6	113.1
1986	4.5	15.9	168.4	62.8	15.0	12.1	103.7
1987	5.0	13.1	186.7	59.1	14.6	11.3	101.2
1988	3.0	14.2	142.4	49.3	14.0	12.6	113.7

Source: Miguel de la Madrid Hurtado, *Sexto Informe de Gobierno 1988*, Anexo Estadístico.

[a] Population per house.

[b] Public sector expenditure on education per capita in thousands of 1980 pesos.

References

Banco de México. *Informe Anual*, 1983.
———. *Informe Anual*, 1986.
Bancomex. *Reunión Extraordinaria del Consejo Directivo del Banco Nacional de Comercio Exterior*, S.N.C. Mimeo. 1988.

Carrasco, R., and E. Provencio. "La política social 1983–88 y sus pricipales consecuencias." *Investigación Económica*, Revista de la Facultad de Economía de la UNAM No. 184, April–June 1988.

Cohen, D. "External and Domestic Debt Constraints of LDCs: A Theory with a Numerical Application to Brazil and Mexico." In *Global Macroeconomics*. Ed. Ralph C. Bryant and Richard Portes. London: Macmillan Press, 1987.

Comisión Nacional De Inversiones Extranjeras. *Informe 1983–1987*. Mexico, 1988.

Cordera, C. R., and T. E. González. *Crisis y Política Económica: Saldos Productivos y Sociales 1982–1987*. Mimeo. 1987.

De la Madrid, H. M. *Quinto Informe de Gobierno*. 1987. Mexico, D. F., Mexico.

———. *Sexto Informe de Gobierno*. 1988. Mexico, D. F., Mexico.

Devlin R. "América Latina: reestructuración económica ante el problema de la deuda externa y de las transferencias al exterior." *Revista de la CEPAL*, Santiago, Chile, Naciones Unidas, 32 (August 1987): 75–104.

Government of Mexico, Gabinete Económico. Internal document, 1983.

IMF. Instituto del FMI, *Programación Financiera Aplicada: El Caso de Colombia*; Institut du FMI, *Analyse et programmation financière: Application à la Côte d'Ivoire*, 1984.

Lustig, N., and J. Ros. *Mexico: Wider Stabilization and Adjustment Policies and Programmes*. Country Study 7. World Institute for Development Economics Research of the United Nations University, 1987.

Minsky, H. "Financial Instability Revisited: The Economics of Disaster." *Can It Happen Again?* Armonk, N.Y.: M. E. Sharpe, 1984.

———. *Stabilizing an Unstable Economy*. New Haven and London: Yale University Press, 1986.

Pichardo Pagaza, I. *El Proceso de Desincorporación de Entidades Paraestatales: El Caso de México*. Secretaría de la Contraloriá General de la Federación, Mexico, 1988.

Reisen, H., and A. Van Trotsenburg. *Developing Country Debt: The Budgetary and Transfer Problem*. Paris: Organization for Economic Cooperation and Development, 1988.

Ruiz Durán, C. "Crisis y Estado: Reflexiones sobre el Desarrollo Económico." *Economía Informa* No. 111. Facultad de Economía, UNAM, 1983.

———. *90 Días de Política Monetaria y Crediticia Independiente*. UAP/DEP, 1984.

SHCP (Secretaría de Hacienda y Crédito Público) *Technical Memorandum of Understanding*. Mexico, 1982.

Sherraden, M., and C. Ruiz Durán. "Social Welfare in the Context of Development: Toward Micro-asset Policies: the Case of Mexico." Mimeo. 1989.

Shucker, S. *American "Reparations" to Germany 1919–33: Implications for the Third World Debt Crisis*. Princeton Studies in International Finance No. 61, July 1988.

Tanzi, V., M. Blejer, and M. Teijeiro. "Inflation and the Measurement of Fiscal Deficits." IMF *Staff Papers* 34 no. 4 (December 1987).

Tello, C. *La Nacionalización de la Banca en México*. Mexico, D.F.: Editorial Siglo XXI, 1984.

Appendix Tables 7.1A–7.4A: Mexico

Table 7.1A

External Net Transfers, 1982–88
(millions of U.S. dollars)

Mexico	$–66,644
Brazil	–55,859
Venezuela	–27,527
Argentina	–21,091
Chile	–5,248
Colombia	–3,775
Ecuador	–2,959
Panama	–2,009
Uruguay	–1,528
Peru	–299
Dominican Republic	–91
Bolivia	87
Costa Rica	159
El Salvador	591
Honduras	701
Haiti	862
Guatemala	1,272
Paraguay	1,303
Nicaragua	2,536
Latin America	$–179,519

Source: CEPAL.
Note: Net transfer is defined as the capital account balance less factor payments.

Table 7.2A

Mexico: External Transfers as Percentages of GDP

	1982	1983	1984	1985	1986	1987	1982–87
Net transfer	-2.3	-10.1	-7.7	-8.1	-6.0	-5.8	-6.7
Interest payments	-7.1	-8.5	-7.4	-6.6	-6.7	-5.8	-7.0
Private	-1.5	-2.0	-1.5	-1.2	-1.3	-1.0	-1.4
Public	-5.6	-6.5	-5.9	-5.4	-5.4	-4.8	-5.6
Capital account	4.9	-1.5	-0.3	-1.4	0.7	0.1	0.4
Net investment	0.2	0.1	0.0	-0.1	0.5	1.6	0.4
Amortization	-0.5	-3.1	-1.2	-0.9	0.1	-1.8	-1.2
Loans	5.2	1.5	1.0	-0.4	0.1	0.4	1.3
Trade and service account							
Trade surplus	4.0	11.6	8.1	5.5	3.7	6.1	6.5
Private sector	-3.3	0.6	0.0	-1.9	0.2	0.8	-0.6
Public sector	7.2	11.0	8.2	7.5	3.5	5.3	7.1
Exports	12.4	18.8	15.2	14.2	12.9	14.8	14.7
Private sector	2.0	4.2	4.0	3.9	6.7	7.5	4.7
Automotive	0.2	0.8	0.9	0.9	1.7	2.2	1.1
Steel, glass, and textiles	0.0	0.4	0.3	0.3	0.4	0.6	0.4
Public sector	10.4	14.6	11.2	10.3	6.1	7.3	10.0
Oil exports	9.6	13.4	10.4	9.6	5.0	6.1	9.0
Imports	8.4	7.2	7.1	8.6	9.2	8.8	8.2
Private sector	5.3	3.6	4.1	5.8	6.5	6.8	5.3
Public sector	3.2	3.6	3.0	2.9	2.7	2.0	2.9
Nonfactor service	-0.5	0.5	0.6	0.4	0.8	1.4	0.5
Exports	2.9	4.1	3.7	3.9	4.7	4.9	4.0
Maquiladora	0.5	0.7	0.7	0.8	1.0	1.1	0.8
Imports	3.4	3.6	3.1	3.4	3.9	3.5	3.5
Errors and omissions	-4.0	-0.7	-0.6	-1.4	0.4	0.6	-1.0
Official reserves	-1.9	2.6	2.1	-1.6	0.5	4.3	1.0
Memorandum item: transnational exports	0.7	1.4	1.7	2.2	4.4	4.9	2.6

Source: Banco de México, Dirección de Investigación Económica, *Indicadores Económicos*, various issues.

Table 7.3A

Mexico: Public Sector Finance as Percent of GDP

	1982	1983	1984	1985	1986	1987
Total revenue	28.9	32.9	32.2	31.2	30.2	30.2
PEMEX	9.9	14.2	13.0	11.5	9.0	9.7
Non-PEMEX	19.1	18.7	19.1	19.7	21.2	20.5
Taxes	9.9	10.2	10.3	10.2	11.2	10.6
Public enterprises	6.9	6.2	7.2	7.7	8.1	7.8
Total expenditure	44.5	41.0	39.3	39.2	45.1	44.4
Programmable	28.2	24.3	23.5	23.0	24.3	21.9
Current	20.5	18.6	18.3	18.0	18.7	16.5
Capital	7.7	5.7	5.2	5.0	5.5	5.4
Non-programmable	15.3	16.2	15.3	15.6	19.5	22.4
Interest payments	8.2	12.4	11.9	11.5	16.4	19.5
Domestic	4.9	7.7	8.0	7.8	12.1	15.2
Foreign	3.3	4.6	3.9	3.7	4.3	4.3
Miscellaneous	1.4	0.5	1.4	1.6	1.1	1.6
Financial balance	-16.9	-8.6	-8.5	-9.6	-16.0	-15.8
Primary balance	-7.3	4.2	4.8	3.4	1.5	4.7
Deficit financing	14.1	6.1	7.6	9.7	15.1	15.0
Domestic						
Central bank	7.8	5.5	4.2	4.1	4.4	1.1
Other banks	4.2	0.0	2.3	4.5	8.2	8.5
Government securities	2.1	0.6	1.1	1.1	2.5	5.4
Other						0.9
External financing	3.7	2.9	1.3	-0.1	1.4	1.1

Sources: Banco de México, *Indicadores Económicos* and *Informes Anuales*, various years.

Table 7.4A

The Impact on the Mexican Economy of the Transfer Process
(percentage of GDP)

	1982	1983	1984	1985	1986	1987	1982–87
GDP	100.0	100.0	100.0	100.0	100.0	100.0	100.0
Domestic absorption	95.0	90.4	92.2	95.1	95.2	89.2	92.9
Private consumption	61.6	60.9	63.1	64.0	67.7	61.5	63.1
Government consumption	10.5	8.8	9.2	9.2	9.1	11.8	9.8
Investment	22.9	20.8	19.9	21.9	18.5	15.9	20.0
Private	11.7	8.8	9.2	10.1	10.0	10.1	10.0
Public	11.2	11.9	10.7	11.8	8.5	5.8	10.0
Trade Surplus	5.0	9.6	7.8	4.9	4.8	10.9	7.2
Exports	15.3	19.0	17.4	15.4	17.3	17.8	17.0
Imports	10.3	9.4	9.6	10.5	12.6	6.9	9.9
Primary balance	−7.1	4.5	5.0	3.7	2.2	4.7	2.2
Seignorage	5.1	3.8	3.8	3.7	3.9	3.7	4.0
Security financing	1.9	1.2	1.1	0.8	2.4	4.4	2.0

Sources: Secretaría de Programación y Presupuesto, *Sistema de Cuentas Nacionales*; Banco de México, *Informes Anuales*, various years.

COMMENTS

Sylvia Maxfield

Generating sufficient resources to service foreign debt requires squeezing "surplus" out of the domestic economy. Only a massive transfer of resources from society to the state makes foreign debt service possible. In other words, a domestic resource transfer undergirds the external transfer of money from debtor country to creditor bank. This is the main point of Ruiz's essay. Alone, it is not a new insight. In cases ranging from Mussolini's Italy to Pinochet's Chile, bankers, at least, have noted the virtues of doing business with authoritarian states which can easily extract economic resources from society. Nevertheless, the economic and political implications of viewing the debt issue as a domestic transfer problem are subtle and complex. Ruiz's essay pursues some of these implications; I will take up four of them here: first, the growth and welfare implications of the domestic transfer which neoclassical analysis fails to capture; second, the way political variables shape the pattern of domestic transfer; third, how the exigencies of engineering the domestic transfer influence the power of different government actors and modes of government decision making; and fourth, the relationship between the domestic transfer and possibilities for a successful transition to export led industrialization.

Growth, Welfare, and Neoclassical Analysis

Mexican growth, Ruiz argues, became increasingly tied to the flow of external financing during the 1960s and 1970s. But private foreign lending, the main source of external capital in the 1970s and 1980s, was highly countercyclical. When growth and exports declined, so did lending. If growth requires a net inflow of resources, then Secretary James Baker's idea of "paying to grow" cannot work. By taking a Keynesian demand-stimulated view of accumulation, Ruiz suggests that the external-cum-domestic transfer chokes growth.

Sylvia Maxfield is Assistant Professor of Political Science and International Management, Yale University.

Ruiz also indicates that an international extension of Minsky's financial instability theory might give us analytical power in evaluating the growth implications of debt repayment. Unfortunately, he doesn't pursue this promising suggestion. Dow, among the few who have tried to develop an international extension of Minsky's model, contrasts the "small" open economy monetarist model with a "small" open economy post-Keynesian model (1986). In the former, openness adds more power to the process of dampening cyclical instability evident in the monetarist's closed economy model. In the post Keynesian model, openness increases the destabilizing impact of financial markets. Rigorous analytical extensions of this "international financial instability thesis" *are* sorely needed because, as Ruiz notes, neoclassical general equilibrium analysis does not capture the negative impact of financial markets on the growth potential of open economies.

Ruiz does well to explain the mechanism whereby the domestic transfer (necessitated by countercyclical international financial flows) constrains growth. But he does not develop the theoretical assumptions or implications of his critique of general equilibrium theory. This leads to some confusion as, for example, in his discussion of the impact of rising domestic debt on accumulation rates. Although seemingly adopting some elements of post Keynesian analysis, Ruiz suggests that neoclassical crowding out occurs. Public sector borrowing forces interest rates up, restricting private borrowing and, therefore, investment. Here, Ruiz appears to assume that the cost and availability of external finance determines investment. In other words, savings constrains investment in classical monetarist fashion. Crowding out and the model of investment behavior assumed are at odds with Ruiz's otherwise seemingly post Keynesian assumptions.

Ruiz's suggestion of crowding out also presents empirical as well as theoretical problems. Crowding out only occurs to the extent that private investment is largely externally financed. Most evidence on private investment finance in Mexico, albeit somewhat outdated, finds limited external financing (Fitzgerald 1980; Brothers and Solís 1966; and La Cascia 1969). Fitzgerald's data indicates that private savings climbed significantly from 1971 to 1976, precisely at a time when public sector deficit spending was rising faster than it had since the 1940s (Fitzgerald 1980, 400).

Ruiz is on firmer ground in his welfare critique of general equilibrium analysis. Even when they deviate from the standard full employment assumption, neoclassical general equilibrium models rarely detail specific welfare implications. Ruiz argues that it takes an institutional approach to see how great the welfare impact of the domestic transfer is and will be. Mexico lacks all but the most minimal social welfare institutions and suffers from serious income inequality. Under these circumstances, the poor are disproportionately hurt by the domestic transfer.

The Politics of Domestic Adjustment

Ruiz's argument about the politics of economic adjustment in Mexico contrasts with that of Remmer in this volume. He suggests that debt repayment has been possible so far because Mexico is an authoritarian regime. Public sector expenditure in Mexico could be cut to partially finance debt service because there was no congressional opposition. The implication is that authoritarian regimes have political leeway for economic management that democratic regimes lack. Remmer argues cogently against this view.

Ruiz's contention that drastic public sector budget cutting is due to congressional weakness is also simplistic. The institutional strength of Congress in the United States certainly did little to prevent the dramatic Reagan-era rollback of government support for social welfare. As Piven and Cloward have spent decades showing, it takes social movements to push for and protect public expenditure on social welfare (1978). Even if the balance of power between the Mexican executive and legislative should shift in favor of the latter, public expenditure cuts might still disproportionately hurt the poor. This would be especially true if a PRI-PAN alliance dominated Congress. There is evidence to suggest that such an alliance is forming; coincidentally, one of PAN's political demands has been for a relative increase in legislative and judicial branch powers.

Another aspect of the politics of adjusting economic policy for maximum debt service, Ruiz points out, is the might of the private sector and its representatives within the government. In 1983, this precluded the option of raising government revenue through taxation as a way of increasing resources available for debt interest payments. Large-scale Mexican businessmen represented in the exclusive CMHN (Consejo Mexicano de Hombres de Negocio) have always exercised implicit veto power over economic decision making. Their leverage comes largely from the threat of capital flight which is especially powerful because of the Mexican government's commitment to free exchange convertibility. This threat has been emphasized often by ministers of finance and directors of the Central Bank as an argument against raising taxes or restricting domestic or international capital mobility. As far back as 1939, for example, Central Bank director Luis Montes de Oca convinced Cárdenas to repeal a tax on capital exports with the argument that fears of higher taxes encouraged capital flight. Ortiz Mena, Finance Minister during the 1950s (when a major tax reform proposal was proposed and dropped), argued that one of the primary goals of the tax structure should be to inspire business confidence. Central Bank director Fernández Hurtado, backed by private sector representatives, argued against a 1972 tax reform proposal which would have created a wealth tax, closed many tax loopholes, changed the tax treatment of profits and dividends, and prohibited anonymous ownership of stocks and bonds on the grounds that it would precipitate capital flight (Maxfield 1988, ch. 3).

The political problem in all these cases, including the one Ruiz notes, stems from the Mexican government's long-held commitment to free exchange convertibility and fixed exchange rates. As Lance Taylor (1984, 308) suggests, Mexico is "virtually the only developing country in which the economically powerful classes have the privilege of such an open capital market." This privilege makes their threat of capital flight a powerful political lever in debates over economic policy. As Ruiz must know from his experience working with Carlos Tello to implement the bank nationalization decreed in September 1982, restricting that privilege must be a first step in any economic reform effort. Removing this economic source of large-scale business's political power in Mexico is at least as important as strengthening the Congress in the effort to make the political environment hospitable to a debt repayment policy not based on squeezing the poor and/or limiting domestic growth.

Financiers and Authoritarian Decision Making

Almost as an aside, Ruiz notes that the exigencies of shaping a domestic policy which will allow for debt repayment heightened the decision-making power of central bankers and conservative financial groups in Mexico. In addition, the decision-making process has become increasingly authoritarian. Both trends, the growing power of financiers and the increasingly authoritarian nature of economic policy making, have been noted in a variety of Latin American countries. In recent comments, Ricardo Ffrench-Davis referred to the growing hegemony of financial rather than production-oriented entrepreneurs and government officials in Chile. O'Donnell notes (1986; Conaghan 1986, 36) the growing breach between entrepreneurs engaged in production (and often heavily dependent on the state) on the one hand, and "predatory" businessmen involved in speculative finance on the other. Conaghan's research on Bolivia, Ecuador, and Peru reveals that the exigencies of debt management foster and provide a justification for increasingly exclusionary patterns of economic decision making (Conaghan 1986, 37–50). Despite dramatic political openings, the pressures of the debt crisis led to a "relatively closed, top-down pattern of economic policy making in Argentina and Brazil during the 1980s" (Maxfield 1989).

These regionwide similarities between countries as different as Mexico, Argentina, and Peru suggest that the growing power of financiers and increasingly authoritarian patterns of economic decision making correspond to the causal weight of the similar international economic events all these countries face. Yet the relative explanatory power of international economic events compared to other variables such as regime type or historical patterns of state and social organization, often referred to as domestic structures, is open to considerable debate. The link between the growing role of financiers in business and government and the increasingly exclusionary nature of government decision making on the one hand and the foreign debt crisis of developing countries on the other is well worth exploring further.

Is a Transition to Private Sector Export-led Growth Possible?

Ruiz concludes his analysis by asking this question. His answer is largely negative. The growth in exports has come largely from assembly industries and tourism which generate few backward linkages to the rest of the Mexican economy. The recovery to date has come largely from depressing domestic demand, which is not feasible as a long-run strategy. Finally, private export growth has responded to government credits and subsidies; these merely aggravate the domestic debt problem.

These are severe limitations in current Mexican economic policy, as are the larger growth and welfare considerations Ruiz highlights earlier. It is frustrating that Ruiz offers no alternatives. Those hoping to move Latin American economic policy makers away from orthodox approaches must provide a theoretical critique sufficiently rigorous to appeal to and persuade the unconverted. They must also spell out the policy alternatives flowing from this critique *and* point to the political coalitions which would have to be organized to back such policies. This is a large agenda; Ruiz joins the many who are working on small parts of it.

References

Brothers, Dwight S., and Leopoldo M. Solís. *Mexican Financial Development.* Austin: University of Texas Press, 1966.

Conaghan, Catherine M. "Technocrats, Capitalists, and Politicians: Economic Policy-Making in Redemocratized States." Paper presented at the Latin American Studies Association XIII International Congress, Boston, Massachusetts, October 23–25, 1986.

Dow, Sheila C. 1986–87. "Post Keynesian Monetary Theory for an Open Economy." *Journal of Post Keynesian Economics* 9, no. 2 (Winter 1986–87).

Fitzgerald, E. V. K. "A Note on Capital Accumulation in Mexico: The Budget Deficit and Investment Finance." *Development and Change* 11, 1980.

La Cascia, Joseph S. *Capital Formation and Economic Development in Mexico.* New York: Praeger, 1969.

Maxfield, Sylvia. "International Finance, the State, and Capital Accumulation: Mexico in Comparative Perspective." Ph.D. dissertation, Government Department, Harvard University, 1988.

————. "National Business, Debt-Led Growth, and Political Transition in Latin America." In *Debt and Democracy in Latin America.* Ed. Stallings and Kaufman. Boulder, Colo.: Westview Press, 1989.

O'Donnell, Guillermo. "Líneas Temáticas del Proyecto 'Consolidación.' " Kellogg Institute, University of Notre Dame. Mimeo. 1986.

Piven, Frances F., and Richard Cloward. *Poor Peoples' Movements: Why They Succeed, How They Fail.* New York: Random House, 1978.

Taylor, Lance. "La Crisis y su Porvenir: Problemas y la Política Macroeconómica en México." *Investigación Económica* no. 170 (Oct./Dec. 1984).

PART IV

TRENDS IN THE SOURCES OF INTERNATIONAL FINANCE FOR LATIN AMERICA

8

The Debt Crisis: From Declining Hegemony to Multilateralism

Pier Carlo Padoan

Introduction

The Latin American debt crisis has developed in a period of declining U.S. hegemony. The mid-1980s recovery led by the United States has provided partial relief to the debt problem but has left the structural aspects substantially unresolved, to say the least. This episode clearly has brought to the surface the fact that the international system has entered a new and extremely problematic phase, characterized by the progressive drift away from the hegemonic system which was built at Bretton Woods, toward a multi-polar structure itself in rapid evolution. The relief provided to the indebted countries has been accompanied by the transformation of the former hegemon into the world's largest debtor and, symmetrically, by the emergence of new leading powers, the most prominent of which is the world's largest creditor, Japan.

This paper discusses aspects of the interconnection between the North-South debt crisis and the more recent North-North debt crisis. It takes a systemic and medium-term perspective, in the sense that it neglects all the relevant domestic aspects of the indebted countries as well as short-term developments. The systemic view, in addition, is limited to some of the aspects involved.

The theoretical framework is based on the financial instability hypothesis developed by Hyman Minsky and adapted to consider the international system. This theoretical view is then considered in the perspective of international regime theories developed by a number of political economists in recent years and partially taken up by some economists, e.g., Charles Kindleberger (1986).

The international financial instability hypothesis is described first and connections to the theory of international regimes are drawn. The next section summarizes relevant events of the last few years and describes the connection between

Pier Carlo Padoan is Professor of Economics, Università degli Studi di Urbino, Italy.

the North-South and the North-North debt crises. This is followed by an analysis of the connection in terms of overlapping and simultaneous games. Then, a simple conceptual framework is presented for assessing the implications of the emergence of a multi-polar financial system for the indebted countries.

International Financial Instability and International Regimes[1]

The actors involved in the mechanism of financial instability in a closed economy are: firms, which finance their activities through debt; financial institutions, which provide the funds; the government, which acts as the ultimate source of effective demand; and monetary authorities, who stabilize the system by providing, among other things, lender-of-last-resort intervention when the possibility of a financial crisis appears.[2] In an international economy, the actors are: national policy authorities of both North and South countries, private banks operating in international financial markets, and international institutions. National governments in the South implement expansionary policies; by so doing, they will run into balance of payments problems and, therefore, seek to obtain loans to meet payments commitments.

In an international economy, the ultimate source of finance is represented by exports. Net exports assume the role played by profits in the closed economy case. Insofar as the growth process produces negative net exports, international credit will be demanded by developing countries. A country will, in general, be willing to pursue an expansionary policy required by a development process if today's negative net exports are likely to be financed by positive net exports tomorrow. In this respect, a country will assume a hedge finance position if it expects to have positive net exports for each future period in order to service outstanding debt in each period ahead. However, in the first stages of the development process, the country is more likely to assume a speculative (or even Ponzi) position, in which the debt service is expected to be fully paid from net exports only in some future period.

If the development mechanism is successful and well monitored, loans will be channeled into activities (investments) that generate enough net exports to repay initial debts. In this case, we are faced with a speculative finance position (in Minsky's terminology). A Ponzi finance position may arise if current exports are so low that the country has to raise new loans just to meet payment of interest on outstanding debt, thus increasing its debt burden but not the net inflow of foreign resources.

Given the terms of trade, we may assume that exports depend on international demand and domestic capacity (and hence on domestic investment), while payment commitments depend on the level of the interest rate for a given outstanding debt. For these purposes, it is sufficient to consider that the level of the world demand for the system as a whole depends on the policies pursued in the North—i.e., we can assume away the hypothesis that the South can be the engine of growth for the system. In order to describe the buildup of financial fragility in the North-South system we will assume, for the moment, that the level of world demand is exogenously given.

For a given level of world demand and of the world interest rate, each country in the South will establish a rate of investment growth which will eventually lead to a balance of trade deficit.[3] For a given rate of world demand, the rate of growth of exports will increase with domestic accumulation, which relaxes supply constraints. If the country is successful in its export growth process, it will be easier for it to obtain international credit as its creditworthiness will increase. Credit availability will enhance the country's investment opportunities and export capacity, starting a virtuous circle.

This situation may change the attitude of countries and banks by increasing the euphoria of both. The success of the growth process will encourage countries to borrow more and banks to lend more.[4] In the expansionary phase, both borrowers and lenders will assume speculative (and possibly Ponzi) finance positions. Countries will borrow to finance trade deficits and interest payments, while banks will *de facto* finance medium- and long-term investment while having to face short-term deposit servicing on the liability side. An orderly development of such a process—i.e., a situation in which the system neither slips into recession leading to negative net exports and the deterioration of the indebted countries nor explodes into uncontrolled euphoria—rests on the fulfillment of two crucial conditions: the existence of a high and stable effective demand to provide outlets for the indebted countries and what may be called a source of "ultimate liquidity" to prevent the system from slipping into situations of financial distress.[5] In this respect these two macroeconomic conditions represent the public goods which are necessary for an orderly functioning of the system (Head 1962; Kindleberger 1981; Wallace 1983). And indeed, financial history suggests that whenever these two conditions were not fulfilled a financial crisis inevitably broke out (Kindleberger 1978). In a closed economy, these public goods are provided by the national government and monetary authorities. In an international system, where no supranational government exists, the production of these public goods depends on interaction of national policies, i.e., on the organization of international regimes.

International regimes have been defined as the set of norms, rules, and institutions which govern the behavior of an international system (Krasner 1983). Here, regimes are considered in a slightly different perspective, as the way in which the production of international public goods—such as international effective demand—is organized. We will speak of an international macroeconomic regime as the way in which and to what extent international effective demand is generated.[6] Two types of international regimes may be considered for these purposes: hegemonic regimes and multi-polar (or oligopolistic) regimes.[7]

In a hegemonic system, such as the one prevailing in the long decade after World War II, the necessary and sufficient condition for the provision of public goods is the existence of a hegemon, i.e., a country whose economic and political power is large enough to allow for the unilateral production of public goods in spite of free-riding policies pursued by other countries.[8] The hegemon will act as the "residual country" whose expansion ultimately determines the expansion of the system as a whole.[9]

In a situation of oligopoly, the conditions for the production of international public goods are much more complex and require an increase in international cooperation, i.e., an agreement among the larger countries in the system.[10] A hegemonic system will resist as long as the hegemon possesses enough economic power to exert international leadership. The definition of economic and financial power raises a complex and debatable issue which will not be considered here in any depth.[11] For these purposes, it is sufficient to establish some links among the international financial position of a country and its ability to generate international effective demand and to provide "ultimate liquidity." The provision of ultimate liquidity requires a series of conditions, such as the existence of an international banking system supported by efficient lender-of-last-resort facilities and international creditworthiness for the currency which dominates debt. To discuss this latter point again, we take into consideration some of Minsky's ideas.

A country is internationally creditworthy (Minsky 1979) as long as it generates profits in the international economy; that is, its trade balance is in surplus. This will assure international creditors that debt can be serviced. When a country is creditworthy, it is in a position to pursue expansionary policies financed by its own currency. In the Bretton Woods hegemonic system the U.S. was in the position to act as the international source of effective demand, to issue the world's currency, and to act successfully as the base of the international financial system, as long as its trade balance was in surplus (and it kept its creditor position vis-à-vis the rest of the world). When the system was officially buried in 1971, the U.S. trade balance had moved to deficit for the first time in the century. The hegemonic system, in addition, had witnessed the expansion of a largely U.S.-based private international banking system. The public good of financial stability for that system was the main responsibility of the U.S. monetary authorities.

From Declining Hegemony to Multilateralism

The Latin American debt crisis has emerged in a period of rapidly declining U.S. hegemony. The foreign debt of Latin American countries, as well as of many other southern economies, grew in an international environment which was favorable to debt accumulation along the lines discussed in the previous section. Unusually easy conditions prevailed in international financial markets, reflecting easy monetary conditions in the center economy. Banks were eager to push loans, lending to rapidly growing developing countries, which seemed to be an extremely favorable business.

More critical, however, were the conditions in which international effective demand was generated. The breakdown of the Bretton Woods system had shown that the U.S. was no longer in the position to provide unilaterally to the international system the public good of demand growth for reasonably long periods of time. In the absence of closer coordination between the major industrialized countries, U.S. expansionary policies would lead to a rapid deterioration of both its trade balance and of the international position of the dollar. These two facts, in turn, weakened the position of the U.S.-based international banking system. The generation of a *stable and sustained* rate of growth of demand required the existence of a new macroeconomic regime based on multilateralism.

At the Bonn summit held at the end of the seventies, the declining hegemon and the emerging German and Japanese powers seemed to have reached an agreement on managing the world economy (Putnam and Bayne 1984). This was an illusion. Agreement soon broke down, leading to drastic changes in U.S. monetary policy (the 1979 Volcker shock) and fiscal policy (Reaganomics). The consequences of this drastic change for the indebted countries were dramatic. The international environment became increasingly restrictive. Real interest rates soared to historic levels and, aided by the second oil shock, the world economy plunged into recession. The public good of effective demand was no longer there to sustain a process of indebted growth. The rise of interest rates had turned even the most conservative financial positions into *de facto* Ponzi ones. The provision of the public good of effective demand was interrupted also because the hegemonic regime had collapsed into a multilateral system which did not meet the conditions for cooperation.

The debt crisis thus exploded in 1982 from the workings of an international financial instability dynamic that lacked an international regime strong enough to contain it. The declining hegemon, however, made a final effort to provide the public goods necessary for the functioning of a financially complex system. After the outbreak of the crisis, U.S. monetary authorities intervened heavily to allay financial collapse by sustaining the U.S. banking system, which was in deep trouble due to its heavy Latin American exposure. The recovery of the U.S. economy, sustained by an expansionary fiscal policy, also provided some relief to the indebted countries. The global collapse which many had feared when the debt crisis broke, was avoided.

Of course the management of the debt crisis was, and is, much more complex than what has been indicated so far. The role of multilateral institutions such as the IMF in helping to manage the crisis and in mediating between indebted countries and the creditors must also be included (Padoan 1987). These and other aspects will be skipped, however, to keep to the main focus on the implications for the debt crisis of emerging multilateralism.

The solution to the debt crisis showed once again the importance of leadership in the production of international public goods. The novelty, which has drawn general attention only recently, is that the effort at hegemony represented by U.S. unilateral expansion in the mid-1980s has further eroded U.S. financial power, to the point of no return in the view of some.[12] The expansionary policies pursued by the U.S. administration have generated a trade deficit, which enhanced by the massive dollar revaluation has produced an unprecedented debt accumulation. The peculiarity of this event does not lie so much in the total amount of debt (or in the debt to income ratio) but in the fact that the world's former hegemon has turned into the world's largest debtor. The management of the North-South debt crisis has produced a new North-North debt crisis which is now closely linked to the former one. The position of the U.S. as a debtor reflects almost symmetrically Japan's position as a world creditor.[13] Consider this point in light of the importance of the public goods of demand growth and ultimate liquidity for the functioning of a complex financial system. In a period of declining hegemony these public goods have been provided, at an increasing cost, by the declining hegemon with little or no support on the part of the other large economies whose restrictive policies (leading to trade surpluses) have subtracted a share of world demand.

The production of public goods under declining hegemony has further eroded the financial power of the United States, accelerating the transition from hegemony to bilateral monopoly, i.e., to a situation in which the management of the international financial system rests on the cooperation among two nations, the U.S. and Japan. From the point of view of the production of public goods, the situation is now more complex. After the transition to multilateralism, the generation of demand and ultimate liquidity no longer lie with the same actor. While the U.S. still represents the most important source of effective demand for the world market, it can no longer supply the public good of ultimate liquidity. This role is rapidly being assumed by Japan.[14]

Validating this judgment requires extensive documentation beyond the scope of this essay, in which merely a few supporting arguments are offered. Thus the continuing U.S. leadership role in demand generation is evidenced in the temporary easing of the 1982 debt crisis that the expansion of the domestic U.S. market has provided. Similar relief could not have come from the Japanese economy for both policy and structural reasons. Until very recently Japan's economic policy stance could be neomercantilist, i.e, sustaining external competitiveness while restraining the expansion of the domestic market. This had been achieved (see Bergsten and Cline 1987, ch. 3). by tight fiscal policies and nontariff import protection.[15] Partly as a consequence of external pressures, mainly from the U.S., the policy stance is being liberalized. Fiscal policy has become more expansionary and commitments have been made to lower the explicit and less explicit barriers to domestic market penetration. For the purpose of this analysis, however, what matters is that the Japanese market for the exports of indebted Latin American countries is still minor.

The second element is more complex. As we have seen above, the supply of ultimate liquidity requires some conditions: the existence of a widespread financial system supported by lender-of-last-resort facilities and international creditworthiness of the currency, itself based on a sound balance of payments position as well as a sound asset position. The financial system involved in Latin American debt is still largely U.S.-based, and lender-of-last-resort responsibilities still lie with the U.S. monetary authorities. The Japanese banking system, however, has been expanding internationally quite rapidly in the recent past (Iwami 1988), and the Japanese financial system is undergoing an extremely fast expansion and opening up.[16] The Japanese banking system, on the other hand, is still only partially involved in direct debt financing and, more importantly, the dollar remains by far the leading international currency, denominating Latin American debt, U.S. debt, as well as most other international transactions. Yet the dollar is issued by a country whose international creditworthiness is being undermined both in flow terms (trade deficit) and in stock terms (the U.S. as an international debtor).

As long as the international financial system is dollar based—a state of affairs likely to prevail for at least several more years—ultimate liquidity must be provided in dollars. However the soundness of the system depends on the willingness of other countries, especially Japan, to provide credit to the U.S. The management of international debt today must, therefore, face a double problem. Latin American countries are tied as debtors to the U.S., while the latter is tied to other countries, notably to Japan, as a debtor.

Overlapping and Simultaneous Games
in the International Financial System

Game theory has become quite fashionable among economists, since it helps clarify interconnections between the actors. The problem under discussion here is certainly characterized by complex interdependencies. These will not be formalized here, but concepts derived from game theory will be used to try to clarify them.

Several authors have addressed the debt problem in game theoretic terms.[17] In its simplest form a game is set up between the borrower and the lender. Players have the option to defect or to cooperate. For our purposes, the lender is the country which provides both markets to debtors (exports) and ultimate liquidity. Defection means debt repudiation for the borrower, and cooperation means adjustment in the attempt to meet debt service commitments. For the lender, defection means refusal to provide further liquidity and/or expansionary policies (imports), while cooperation means the opposite.

The financial picture may be described in terms of overlapping games. Overlapping games arise (Alt and Eichengreen 1987) when the same game is played simultaneously by one player with two other players. In this case, the U.S. is simultaneously involved in a debt game with the indebted countries and with

Japan. The two games, in addition, are linked in the sense that the solution to one influences the solution to the other.

Let us consider the U.S.-Latin American debt game. If both countries defect by defaulting and not providing additional liquidity and larger markets, the situation collapses into a debt crisis. If both cooperate the debt game can continue, and the conditions for the sound performance of a financial system are met. In a sound hegemonic regime the system will function even in the absence of cooperation on the part of the debtor, as both effective demand and ultimate liquidity will be provided unilaterally by the lender-hegemon while the debtor may, and probably will, take a free ride. This solution, as has been seen, is partially possible in a situation of declining hegemony. In such a case, however, the exercise of hegemony will ultimately destroy the bases upon which the system rests by deteriorating further the international creditworthiness of the hegemon.

This brings in the game between the U.S. and Japan. The issue at stake here is the maintenance of the dollar-based financial system as a means of providing ultimate liquidity. The borrower (the U.S.) may choose to defect by not adjusting its fiscal (and hence its trade) deficit, or it may cooperate by trying to turn its external deficit into surplus in order to meet debt service commitments and thus sustain international confidence. The lender, in turn, may choose to defect by ceasing to finance the U.S. debt or to cooperate by continuing to do so.[18] Note that adjustment by the U.S. cannot mean an adjustment of the trade deficit through a substantive dollar depreciation, as this would undermine the value of the assets in the hands of the lender and could thus undermine the defense of the dollar-based financial system. Adjustment by the U.S. can only mean a generation of trade surpluses by means of a restrictive policy aimed at cutting the budget deficit. If both players cooperate, the dollar-based system survives; otherwise it collapses.

Note also that cooperation is needed, and a situation of Japanese hegemony has not been reached yet which would allow unilateral provision of the public good of financial stability. Were that the case, the Japanese economy would be able to absorb U.S. exports in an amount large enough to produce a U.S. trade surplus.

It is easy to see that the solutions to the two games interfere with each other. Cooperation in the second game requires a restrictive policy in the U.S. economy which means defection in the first game. If the U.S. wishes to maintain creditworthiness with its major creditor, it must pursue adjustment policies which dampen its domestic market for Latin American exports. This would be perceived by the indebted countries as defection in their game, to which they may retaliate by repudiating their debt. In such a case the international financial position of the U.S. would deteriorate further, making the solution in the second game even more difficult to achieve.

On the other hand, suppose that the U.S. continues to cooperate in the first game by keeping on an expansionary course. This might prevent defection by Latin American countries but could trigger retaliation by Japan as it would mean larger U.S. indebtedness. What are the solutions to this situation? Two general ways out may be envisaged. One is overall cooperation and the other is the introduction of simultaneous games in the picture.

Overall cooperation must be understood in different terms than those sketched thus far, where cooperation in one game triggers defection in the other. This is because implicitly we have been assuming one-period static game situations in which players have but one choice to make. A different perspective arises if one considers the suggestions arising from the theory of cooperation "under anarchy," i.e., cooperation without hegemony (Oye 1985; Axelrod and Keohane 1985). Conditions for cooperation without hegemony are the following: (a) players must sense a "long shadow of the future," i.e., they must be involved in repeated games as this will minimize the advantages from defection; (b) players must be prepared to alter their preference structures, which implies a change of the payoff matrices and hence the possibility of defining superior cooperative solutions; (c) the number of players must be small so as to minimize free-riding behavior; (d) the role of institutions as providers of information must be enhanced (Runge 1984; Langlois 1986).

If these conditions prevail in our two debt games, a cooperative solution could be found through a substantive change in the game structure. If actors recognize the simultaneous nature of the games they are involved in (Alt and Eichengreen 1987), i.e., if they take a global and long-term perspective, they will not try to defect. However this will not be enough if the terms of the games described above remain the same. In particular, adjustment must not be understood in simple macroeconomic terms—to expand or deflate, to lend or not lend—but in much deeper structural terms. It is not possible to give a full account of the structural transformation required, but a few obvious hints can be offered. Latin American countries must adjust their economies to decrease their dependence on external finance. The U.S. must increase its structural competitiveness to improve its trade performance without resorting to massive devaluation. Japan must smoothly and rapidly open its markets to foreign goods. If these conditions are met, a cooperative solution could gradually emerge that avoids the risk of triggering a worldwide recession and financial crisis. At the same time, it would be possible to design and develop a financial system in which the role of the dollar is gradually diminished without producing destabilizing shocks. This solution is probably the most desirable but also the most difficult to implement and is surely one that requires a very long time horizon (Cohen 1988).

Let us now turn to the other possible solution, related to the introduction of simultaneous games. Simultaneous games are played by the same two players over two (or more) different areas at the same time. The problem here is to discuss whether the existence of simultaneity increases the prospects for cooperation. As Alt and Eichengreen (1987) warn, this is not necessarily so. Players engaged in simultaneous games may have incentives to defect from all games rather than only one, since they know that defection from one game could trigger retaliation by the other player(s) in all of the other games. However, if they recognize that the solution to one game produces favorable spillovers to another game(s), they might be induced to increase cooperation in both games. In other words, whether or not simultaneity is more conducive to cooperation depends on the nature of the games involved. The U.S. and Japan are simultaneously involved in more than one game in the international system. In addition to the financial game there is a trade game and a security game, i.e., the problem of sharing defense expenses. For the sake of simplicity we will ignore the trade game and consider the simultaneous game played on the security field.[19] In the security game, cooperation implies the assumption by each country of a share of military expenses proportional to its relative economic weight, while defection implies a disproportionately low share. In a situation of hegemony, the hegemon would bear a more than proportionate share of the costs of producing the public good (Olson and Zeckhauser 1966). In hegemonic decline, the hegemon would be pushing the other cooperating players to increase their shares, as indeed the U.S. is doing now.

This fact has obvious spillovers to the financial game. If a cooperative solution to the security game is reached, i.e., Japan increases her share of defense expenditure,[20] the problem of financial adjustment by the U.S. is made less severe, since part of the defense outlay in the U.S. budget could be canceled. It follows that by increasing its share of defense expenditure, Japan would lower the risk of financial default by the U.S.; it would thereby preserve the value of its assets more effectively than by simply pressuring the U.S. to reduce its budget and trade deficits (as in the financial game taken in isolation). Conversely, were Japan to defect in the security game by refusing to increase military expenditure, the U.S. would have a greater incentive to defect in the financial game, for example by refusing to adjust the budget and by pursuing an aggressive dollar devaluation.

The recognition of spillovers between the two games may, therefore, increase cooperation in both games. Consider Japan's position once again. The recognition of the spillover and the assumed interest of Japan in both maintaining financial stability and providing the public good of defense should encourage cooperation in both games. This can be seen as a two stage process. In the first stage, i.e., in the short run, by sustaining the U.S. external debt position Japan allows the U.S. to continue to provide the public good of defense. In the medium run (second step) Japan significantly increases its military expenditure, thus alleviating the burden of U.S. debt. Concurrently, a cooperative Japanese strategy would foster a cooperative response by the U.S. in both fields: maintaining its share of military expenditure in the short run and adjusting its fiscal and hence financial position in the medium run. The simultaneous games approach suggests a solution to the U.S.-Japan financial game that does not require economic contraction by the U.S. and, thus, defection in the U.S.-Latin American debt game. Recognition of simultaneity could encourage both the U.S. and Japan to take a longer time horizon and to alter their preferences, especially in the military sphere. In other words, simultaneity allows some of the conditions for cooperation under anarchy to be fulfilled.

What are the implications for the debt game played by the U.S. and Latin America? The obvious implication is that the longer time span and the more gradual adjustment of the U.S. economy also would allow a smoother adjustment of the debt crisis. Financial support to the U.S. by Japan in exchange for security would allow the former to avoid an abrupt recession, thus keeping the debt game open and fostering cooperative behavior by the debtor countries.

This point can also be stated in terms of regime theory. The cooperative solution to the simultaneous games played by the U.S. and Japan improves the supply of the public goods of ultimate liquidity and ultimate demand to the world system. The hegemonic role assumed by the U.S. alone through the 1970s would be played jointly by the two countries in the 1990s. Bilateral monopoly will have taken the place of hegemony.

A Graphical Summation

In this part, a graphical summation of the interaction between the development of financial instability in the North-South debt relationship and the presence of simultaneous games in the U.S.-Japan relationship is presented.[21]

In Figure 8.1 the BB schedule is a transformation curve of credit (C) into exports (X). It represents the ability of the borrowing country to use funds obtained in the credit market to expand exports by increasing productive capacity. It represents, therefore, a long-term relationship between credit and exports (where a short-term relationship would assume exports and credit to be substitute sources of funds for the country in question). In other words, the BB schedule may be considered a production function in which credit is the input to the export producing sector.

The LL schedule represents a credit supply curve of the banking system. Credit awarded is a positive function of exports, since increasing exports mean increasing creditworthiness. If we assume that credit rationing conditions prevail, the amount of credit is supply determined, in the sense that the borrower accepts all the loans the banks decide to award.

It is easy to see that the equilibrium described in Figure 8.1 is unstable. If, starting from the equilibrium point "a" where $0C_1$ credit is awarded, banks decide to increase their advances to the borrowing country (e.g., because sovereign lending has become more attractive), they shift to point "b" and the new amount of credit is $0C_2$. This allows the borrower to move to point "c" on his BB schedule, thus increasing exports from $0X_1$ to $0X_2$. Higher exports induce

Figure 8.1. **Stability Conditions in International Lending**

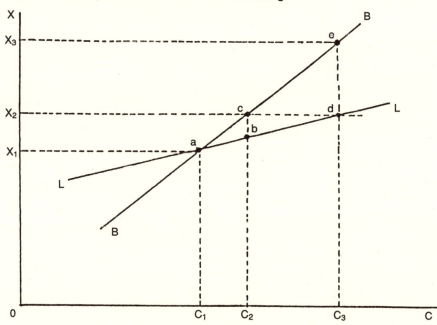

banks to award the higher amount of credit $0C_3$, corresponding to point "d" on their LL schedule, and so on.

This unstable movement away from point "a" clearly depends on the relative slopes of the schedules. Were the slopes of BB and LL inverted, the behavior of the two agents would have produced a stable motion toward point "a." The slopes in the figure reflect the behavioral assumption that the marginal propensity of banks to lend with respect to exports (the creditworthiness of the borrowers) is proportionally greater than the ability of borrowers to transform credit into exports. In other words, we assume that banks are affected by lending "euphoria" in sovereign lending. This behavioral assumption has received detailed treatment in recent works by Guttentag and Herring (1983, 1985) analyzing the behavior of banks in the Latin American debt crisis. They relate the propensity of banks to overlend to "disaster myopia," i.e., the tendency to neglect low probability risks that might produce heavy losses such as a major financial crisis. This also implies that financial instability results from an endogenous mechanism which is rooted in the behavior of the market. It does not reflect, in other words, a form of "speculative bubble."

This very simple representation can take into account the effects of the state of the international economic environment. We may assume that, *ceteris paribus*, the position of the BB schedule depends on the level of world demand. A higher

Figure 8.2. **Effects of a Decline of U.S. Demand on International Debt Deflation**

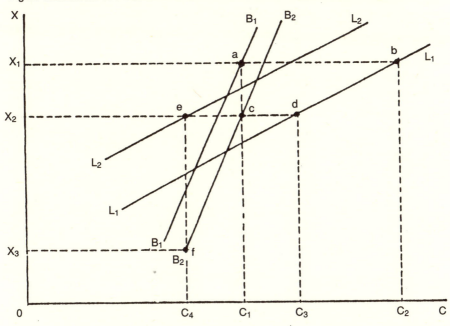

level of world demand shifts the schedule to the left and vice versa. The assumption is that exports depend on both productive capacity, which depends on credit (supply conditions), and external demand. For a given amount of credit (and hence capacity), exports will be higher, the higher world demand. If higher world demand is associated with easier monetary conditions in the international economy, banks will be willing to lend more for a given creditworthiness assessment of borrowers and the LL schedule will shift to the right. The opposite is the case when monetary conditions tighten.

Now suppose that as a result of the debt game between the U.S. and Japan, an adjustment takes place in the U.S. economy that leads to a decrease in the level of world demand. This situation is depicted in Figure 8.2. Starting from point "a," the initial credit allocation, $0C_1$, allows the borrower to export $0X_1$ for a given state of world demand (B_1B_1 schedule). If general conditions do not change, banks will react to $0X_1$ by granting $0C_2$ by moving to point "b" on their L_1L_1 schedule. Now suppose that a drop in U.S. (and hence world) demand takes place. The drop in world demand shifts the borrowers' export schedule to B_2B_2. The quantity of credit, $0C_1$, produces $0X_2$ exports. If banks are unaffected by the change in international conditions, they will react to $0X_2$ by granting $0C_3$ credit (point "d" on the L_1L_1 schedule). However, if we assume that the weaker international demand dampens bank euphoria, the credit supply schedule shifts,

Figure 8.3. **U.S.-Japan Cooperative Gaming to Avoid Debt Deflation**

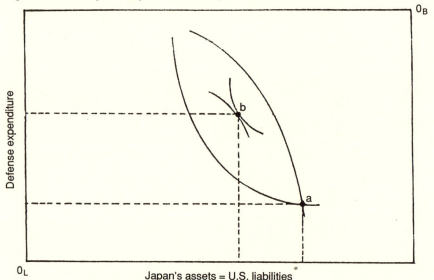

e.g., to L_2L_2. Consequently, for the volume of exports $0X_2$, banks, moving to point "e," are willing to lend only $0C_4$. This allows borrowers to export only $0X_3$ (point "f" on the B_2B_2 schedule). The interaction produces an explosive motion away from the initial equilibrium and to debt deflation.

Simultaneous games between the U.S. and Japan are now introduced, on the assumption that the level of world demand is dependent on the ability of the U.S. to decrease its debt to Japan. As discussed in the previous section, the U.S. and Japan are engaged in two simultaneous games, a debt game and a security game. This situation is described in Figure 8.3. The box diagram shows the indifference curves of the U.S. and Japan. The borrower's (U.S.) utility increases when its liabilities decrease, i.e., when the lender's (Japan) assets decrease. Financial assets are measured along the horizontal axis. The utility of the U.S. and Japan increases with the amount of defense expenditures. This configuration reflects the peculiar positions of the two countries in the international system. The U.S., as a declining hegemon, is interested in decreasing its financial dependence on Japan but is also interested in maintaining an adequate level of military expenditures so as to provide the public good of military alliance. Japan, as an emerging leader, is interested in strengthening its financial position as an international creditor and, at the same time, is interested in increasing its military buildup. It is irrelevant here to decide whether Japan's preferences are self-generated or induced by outside pressures.

Starting at "a," where Japan's assets (U.S. liabilities) are high and her military expenditure is low with respect to that of the U.S., a cooperative solution for the two games will shift the two countries to point "b" which is clearly superior

Figure 8.4. **U.S.-Japan Cooperative Gaming as Solution to the LDC Debt Crisis**

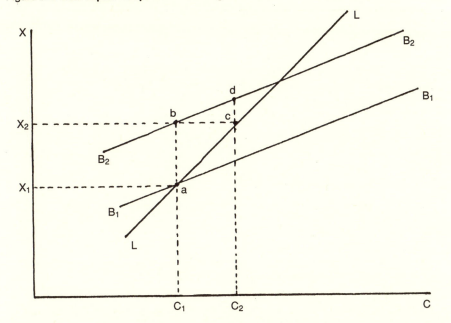

to point "a." In this situation, U.S. liabilities and defense expenditure are both lower. The two outcomes are connected; as discussed above, lower defense expenditures allow an improved external position.

This outcome feeds back onto the debt market, the sounder U.S. financial position generating a higher level of world demand. This prevents the BB and LL schedules in Figure 8.2 from shifting to B_2B_2 and L_2L_2, keeping the debt deflation process from developing.

This simple graphical representation suggests also that a stable solution to the debt crisis can be reached, if there are appropriate behavioral changes on the part of the banks and the borrowers. If banks decrease their lending euphoria and take a more conservative attitude toward sovereign lending, and borrowing countries find it more difficult to transform credit into exports, the relative slopes of the BB and LL schedules would reverse. In that case, the borrower-lender interaction would turn into a stable process. This also means, however, that the importance of world demand in validating more exports would increase considerably. This case is depicted in Figure 8.4. Starting from point "a" which is a stable equilibrium, exports increase only as a consequence of a higher world demand which shifts the BB schedule to B_2B_2. The movement is thus through points "b" and "c" to a new stable point, "d," and so on.

* * *

The analysis of a financial crisis must encompass both the interaction between creditors and debtors and the evolution of the environment within which the crisis develops and eventually breaks out. In an international financial crisis the environment is shaped largely by the interaction of the larger economies.

We have argued that the Latin American debt crisis may be interpreted in terms of Minsky's financial instability hypothesis extended to the international economy. According to this approach, the proper functioning of a complex financial system requires the fulfillment of two conditions: a high and stable rate of growth of demand and an adequate provision of ultimate liquidity to handle major financial distress. How these two public goods are provided is determined by the international environment or, to put it differently, by the organization of international regimes.

We are in a period when declining U.S. hegemony is being replaced by a multi-polar structure. More likely, it is a duopoly of the world's largest market, the U.S. and the world's largest creditor, Japan. This profound change in the structure of the international system has been accompanied by what has been called a North-North debt crisis, i.e., the transformation of the former hegemon into the world's largest debtor. The solution to the North-South debt crisis is tied closely to the solution of this new debt crisis. While some argue that the next century (if not the next decade) will witness Japanese hegemony in the world system, the present crisis requires some form of cooperation between the two leading economies to support the dollar denominated international financial system. Such cooperation may be facilitated if one recognizes that relations between the two economies involve more than one field. Apart from finance, the U.S. and Japan must cooperate in other critical fields such as trade and security.

An example has been given of how augmenting cooperation in fields other than finance and macroeconomic policy could improve the international economic environment so as to allow a cooperative solution of the Third World debt crisis. In particular, cooperation in the security field could increase cooperation in the financial field to the benefit of that crisis. This is merely one possibility. It is to be hoped that cooperation in the debt area could be improved by greater cooperation in specific areas such as trade, rather than through increases in military commitments. One point, however, should be stressed. A positive solution to the debt crisis requires the generation of a stable international environment which requires, in turn, an improvement in international cooperation. It is indeed surprising that some scholars and commentators are still arguing that the U.S. should adopt what may be defined a "new benign neglect" in its international economic policy.[22] With the decline of U.S. hegemony, this is no longer feasible.

Notes

1. This part draws on Padoan (1986), chapter 7.
2. Aivazan technical and effective bankruptcy. The latter develops when the lender decides to suspend further support to the borrower already in a situation of technical bankruptcy.

3. See Darity and Fitzgerald (1984) for a more formal treatment of a similar model.

4. See Guttentag and Herring (1985) for a formal analysis of a similar process.

5. See Guttentag and Herring (1985).

6. This aspect is discussed in Guerrieri and Padoan (1988).

7. The discussion of regime theory can be found in Krasner (1983), Keohane (1984), Oye (1985).

8. Free riding may take the form of neomercantilist macroeconomic policies, i.e., the pursuit of trade surpluses. See Padoan (1986), chapter 7.

9. This is not in the sense that U.S. demand directly determines world expansion, rather in the sense that U.S. policies determine the environment for growth.

10. A detailed analysis of this point can be found in Oye (1985).

11. An analysis of international economic power can be found in Keohane (1984). For a discussion of financial power, see Strange (1982).

12. See for instance Gilpin (1987). Susan Strange (1987) has recently reaffirmed that the U.S. is by far the most powerful country in the world if one takes into account economic size, technological and military capacity. We wish to stress that what matters in our discussion is ''macroeconomic power,'' i.e., the ability to implement unilateral sustained expansionary policies.

13. On Japan's changing international financial power see e.g. Frankel (1984); Haynes, Hutchison and Mikesell (1986); Matsukawa (1987).

14. We may disregard at this stage the role of Europe as an ''engine of growth.''

15. See Bergsten and Cline (1987), chapter 3.

16. On the expansion of the Japanese financial system see e.g. Frankel (1984); Sakakibara and Nagao (1985), Iwami (1988).

17. See e.g. Sachs (1984), Krugman (1985), Cohen (1988).

18. Given the degree of centralization and policy control over Japan's financial system, this may be considered a policy choice rather than a reaction of the market.

19. The linkage between security and finance is a fundamental characteristic of international relations. See Gilpin (1987).

20. See Defense Agency (1988).

21. For a model of North-South and North-North debt crises, see Taylor (1986).

22. See for instance Feldstein (1988).

References

Aivazian, V., and J. Callen. ''Reorganization in Bankruptcy and the Issue of Strategic Risk.'' *Journal of Banking and Finance* (March 1983): 119–33.

Alt, J., and B. Eichengreen. ''Overlapping and Simultaneous Games: Theory and Applications.'' Paper presented at the IAI, NBER conference on *The Political Economy of International Macroeconomic Policy Coordination*, Andover, Mass., November 6–7, 1987.

Axelrod, R., and R. Keohane. ''Achieving Cooperation under Anarchy: Strategies and Institutions.'' *World Politics* 38, no. 1, 1985.

Bergsten, C. F., and W. Cline. *The United States-Japan Economic Problem*. Policy Analyses in International Economics, no. 13. Institute for International Economics. Revised edition. 1987.

Cohen, B. J. ''Global Debt: Why Is Cooperation so Difficult?'' In *The Political Economy of International Cooperation*. Ed. P. Guerrieri and P. C. Padoan. London: Croom Helm, 1988.

Darity, W., and E. Fitzgerald. *A Keynes-Kalecki Model of World Trade, Finance and Economic Growth*. International Finance Discussion Paper, no. 238. 1984.

Defense Agency. *Outline of Japan's Defense Budget for Fiscal 1988*. Japan: Foreign Press Center, 1988.

Feldstein, M. "Distinguished Lecture on Economics." *Journal of Economic Perspectives*. (Spring 1988).

Frankel, J. *The Yen/Dollar Agreement: Liberalizing Japanese Capital Markets*. Policy Analyses in International Economics, no. 9. Institute for International Economies. 1984.

Gilpin, R. *The Political Economy of International Relations*. Princeton: Princeton University Press, 1987.

Guerrieri, P., and P. C. Padoan. "International Cooperation and the Role of Macroeconomic Regimes." In *The Political Economy of International Cooperation*. Ed. P. Guerrieri and P. C. Padoan. London: Croom Helm, 1988.

Guttentag, J., and R. Herring. "The Lender of Last Resort Function in an International Context." *Essays in International Finance* no. 151. Princeton: Princeton University Press, 1983.

———. "Commercial Bank Lending to Developing Countries: From Overlending to Underlending to Structural Reform." In *International Debt and the Developing Countries*. Ed. G. Smith and J. Cuddington. World Bank, 1985.

Haynes, S. M., Hutchison, and R. Mikesell. "Japanese Financial Policies and the US Trade Deficit." *Essays in International Finance* no. 162. Princeton: Princeton University Press, 1986.

Head, J. G. "Public Goods and Public Policy." *Public Finance* no. 3. 1962.

Iwami, T. *Internationalization of Japanese Banking: Factors Affecting its Rapid Growth*. Discussion Paper. Faculty of Economics. University of Tokyo, 1988.

Keohane, R. *After Hegemony*. Princeton: Princeton University Press, 1984.

Kindleberger, C. *Manias, Panics and Crashes*. New York: Basic Books, 1978.

———. "Dominance and Leadership in the International Economy: Exploitation, Public Goods and Free Rides." *International Studies Quarterly* no. 2 (1981): 242–654.

———. "International Public Goods without International Government." *American Economic Review* 76, no. 1 (March 1986).

Krasner, S., ed. *International Regimes*. Ithaca: Cornell University Press, 1983.

Krugman, P. "International Debt Strategies in an Uncertain World." In *International Debt and the Developing Countries*. Ed. G. Smith and J. Cuddington. World Bank, 1985.

Langlois, R., ed. *Economics as a Process*. Cambridge, Eng.: Cambridge University Press, 1986.

Matsukawa, M. *The Japanese Trade Surplus and Capital Outflow*. Occasional Paper no. 22. Washington, D.C.: Group of Thirty, 1987.

Olson, M., and M. Zeckhauser. "An Economic Theory of Alliances." *Review of Economics and Statistics*, 48:3, 266–279.

Oye, K. "Explaining Cooperation Under Anarchy." *World Politics* 38, no. 1. 1985.

Padoan, P. C. *The Political Economy of the International Financial Instability*. London: Croom Helm, 1986.

Putnam, R., and T. Bayne. *Hanging Together: The Seven Power Summits*. Cambridge: Harvard University Press, 1984.

Runge, C. F. "Institutions and the Free Rider: the Assurance Problem in Collective Action." *Journal of Politics* 46 no. 2. 1984.

Sachs, J. *Theoretical Issues in International Borrowing*. Princeton Studies in International Finance no. 54. Princeton: Princeton University Press, 1984.

Sakakibara, E., and Y. Nagao. *Study on the Tokyo Capital Markets*. JCIF Policy Study Series no. 2. March 1985.

Smith, G., and J. Cuddington, eds. *International Debt and the Developing Countries.* World Bank, 1985.

Strange, S. "Still an Extraordinary Power: America's Role in a Global Monetary System." In *Political Economy of International and Domestic Monetary Relations.* Ed. R. Lombra and W. Witte. Ames, Ia: Iowa State University Press, 1982.

———. "The Persistent Myth of Lost Hegemony." *International Organization,* vol. 41, Summer 1987.

Taylor, L. "Debt Crisis: North-South, North-North and in Between." In *World Debt Crisis.* Ed. M. Clandon: Cambridge: Ballinger Publishing Co., 1986.

Wallace, M. "Economic Stabilization as a Public Good: What Does It Mean?" *Journal of Post Keynesian Economics* (Winter 1983): 295–302.

COMMENTS

Gary Hufbauer

Pier Carlo Padoan's interesting and provocative analysis has two main parts: financial instability and international games. Let me start with financial instability; and, in the spirit of commentators, let me emphasize points of difference rather than points of agreement.

Padoan extends Hyman Minsky's financial instability hypothesis to the international arena. In this extension, a country's net exports become the analogue of a company's net profits. The national economy is viewed as an engine that trasnsforms international credit into net exports over the medium term. Meanwhile, the enthusiasm of private bankers for making international loans is a positive function of the country's net exports.

If the lending schedule (depicted in Figure 8.1 as LL) cuts the transformation schedule (depicted as BB) from above (an inverted relationship), rather than from below (a "normal" relationship), then financial instability will result. Under an inverted relationship, a transitory shock may, for example, cause lending to exceed the equilibrium. Net export prospects will improve so much that private bankers will fall over themselves to extend even more credit—and away the system goes, until it collapses.

The big question posed by the international financial instability hypothesis is whether the inverted relation between the BB and LL schedules depicted in Figure 8.1 is a rare occurence or merely an infrequent occurence. If the inverted relation is rare, then international financial instability can be viewed as an aberration inflicted by the private banking system, perhaps once in a generation. On the other hand, if the inverted relationship is merely infrequent, then financial instability will recur often enough to be characterized as a systemic disease. In that case, the *volume* of international lending will come to resemble the emotional *price* fluctuations witnessed on the stock market. It follows that a much stronger case can then be made for vigilant and detailed regulation of bank lending practices.

Gary Hufbauer is Wallenberg Professor of International Financial Diplomacy, Georgetown University.

Let me offer a few brief arguments why the inverted relation is likely to be rare, and the normal relationship is likely to prevail most of the time. First, the net export prospects of a country are a *weak* positive function of external credit availability and a *strong* positive function of internal policies. Indeed, external credit often erodes national resolve to pursue the disciplined fiscal and monetary policies that improve net exports: witness not only Mexico in the 1970s, but also the United States in the 1980s. Second, private bankers generally look at many factors in addition to net exports when extending credit to foreign countries. Political stability, investment climate, and inflation rates are among the other variables examined. This implies that private willingness to lend is likely to be rather inelastic to net export prospects, viewed in isolation.

Together these two arguments suggest that BB will be rather flat, and LL will be rather steep, so that international bank lending will exhibit stable behavior far more often than not. I am not asserting that loan defaults are rare; we know that they are common. Instead, I am asserting that most defaults on sovereign lending originate not in over-enthusiastic bank lending behavior and over-optimistic appraisals of net export prospects, but rather in exogenous shocks (falling commodity prices, world recessions, etc.).

I turn now to the game theory section of Padoan's paper. Here I have two comments, one methodological and one substantive.

The methodological comment is that game theory applied to international negotiations leaves me fascinated but unpersuaded. My skepticism originates with the implicit assumption of a single actor on each side of the table, and the explicit assumption that outcomes can be predicted (in part) by postulating multiple plays of the game. These assumptions have the "count" all wrong. In most international negotiations there are many actors and, therefore, *multiple* hands on the levers of power; most international negotiations are *single* events.

I find analysis that concentrates on the case-specific institutional setting more satisfying than game theory explanations. For example, the degree of default by LDC borrowers (measured by secondary market discounts) is, I think, better explained by "old fashioned" variables, such as internal political discipline and the magnitude of external shocks, than by game theory.

My substantive comment concerns Padoan's argument that a conflict exists between resolution of the North-North debt problem (the huge U.S. external deficit, matched by German and Japanese external surpluses) and the North-South debt problem (the LDC debt burden). Padoan's argument suggests that the resolution of the North-North problem depends on a U.S. recession, whereas resolution of the North-South problem depends on continued U.S. expansion. My own view is that this conflict wrongly excludes the possibility of a major change in dollar/yen and dollar/mark exchange rates. I would not regard a substantial devaluation of the dollar against those two currencies as a betrayal; in fact, such a devaluation offers a logical resolution of the two debt problems.

9

How to Reverse the Defunding of Latin America by the Multilateral Lending Agencies

Richard E. Feinberg

The international financial institutions (IFIs) must address two key issues as they confront the debt and development problems of Latin America. Both issues center on the crying need to reduce the approximately $20 billion in resources being transferred each year from Latin America to the international financial system.[1] First, can the IFIs reverse the disturbing trend whereby they have joined the commercial banks as net financial drains on the capital-short region? Second, what role should they play in reducing the persistent transfer of financial resources from Latin America to private lenders?

Both issues are central to the basic agenda of the International Monetary Fund (IMF), World Bank,[2] and Inter-American Development Bank (IDB). These institutions were established in part to transfer capital from North to South (for the IMF such transfers are temporary, until a balance of payments problem has been resolved) and to catalyze the movement of private capital to profitable investments in developing nations. The challenge that faces the IFIs in the 1990s is to fulfill these laudable missions in the face of new and difficult circumstances.

Trends in IFI Resource Transfers

The transfer of wealth from North to South makes sense on both economic and moral grounds. The rates of return should be higher in capital-poor nations. However, private investors may hesitate to commit their capital because of perceptions of high risk; therefore, public institutions with their longer, broader

Richard E. Feinberg is Vice-President, Overseas Development Council, Washington, D.C.

view must step in. At the same time, raising living standards in the Third World is a humanitarian act which generally serves the commercial and security interests of the United States, by widening markets for U.S. products, strengthening market mechanisms, and promoting political moderation. These statements are noncontroversial and explain why the IFIs have generally enjoyed bipartisan backing.

But the IFIs are no longer serving this basic purpose. In 1987, for the first time ever, all three IFIs drained more money out of Latin America than they put in. The combined net resource transfer (NRT)—disbursements minus principal and interest repayments—was a negative $2.5 billion (Table 9.1). The IMF received nearly $2 billion in net transfers, the World Bank $800 million, and the IDB just $100 million. Most important, this reverse capital transfer is not a momentary blip, but rather the result of underlying trends that, if not altered, will produce similar outcomes into the 1990s. Under current policies, and even assuming approval of capital injections and subsequent substantial increases in annual loan commitments by the World Bank and IDB, the negative net resource transfer will persist at least through 1991 (Table 9.1).

Last year was a turning point in financial relations between the IFIs and Latin America. From being a significant source of financial resources, the multilateral lending agencies became a net drain on the region's balance of payments. Earlier in the decade in the wake of the debt crisis and the halt in private lending, the IFIs sharply increased their disbursements, causing the combined NRT to jump from under $3 billion in 1982 to over $13 billion during 1983–84. All three institutions contributed to this effort to pump funds into the region. In 1986, however, the IMF began to show a negative NRT, driving down the combined effort to under $1 billion. In 1987, all three IFIs turned in a negative performance and are well on their way to doing so again in 1988.

The main cause of this negative trend is the same for all three institutions: amortization and interest charges on outstanding debt shot up from a combined $2 billion in 1980 to $10 billion in 1987 (Table 9.2). For example, as a result of loans made earlier in the decade to Latin America, annual repayments to the IMF jumped from around $200 million in 1982–84 to $1.9 billion in 1986, and to $3.3 billion in 1987 (Table 9.2). Charges (including interest and commitment fees), which were nominal in the early 1980s, reached $1 billion annually during 1985–87. (The IMF periodically adjusts its interest charges, which floated around 7 percent in 1986 but fell to around 6 percent by 1988.) These charges will decline as loans are amortized, but of course the amortization payments greatly exceed the interest savings.

World Bank principal repayments have been rising at an accelerating rate during the 1980s, from $398 million in 1980 to $2.3 billion in 1987 (Table 9.2). Under current Bank policy assumptions, repayment requirements will reach $3.8 billion by 1991. Interest payments have also increased, reflecting the Bank's decision to adjust its rates (fixed at 7.6 percent as of September 1988) to cover

Table 9.1

The IFIs' Net Resource Transfer to Latin America, 1980–91
(billions of U.S. dollars)

	1980	1981	1982	1983	1984	1985	1986	1987	1988[a]	1989[b]	1990[b]	1991[b]
IMF	-0.2	-0.3	1.7	6.4	3.0	0.4	-1.0	-2.0	-0.6	-0.6	—	—
IBRD	0.6	0.5	0.6	0.8	1.1	0.8	1.3	-0.5	-0.8	-1.0	-1.5	-2.0
IDB	0.6	0.6	0.7	0.7	1.2	0.9	0.5	-0.1	-0.5	-0.3	-0.2	0.2
Total[d]	0.9	0.8	2.9	7.9	5.3	2.1	0.8	-2.5	-1.9	-1.9	-1.7[c]	-1.8[c]

Sources: IMF: *World Economic Outlook,* April 1988 and September 1988, and *International Financial Statistics,* July 1988; World Bank: *World Debt Tables* (1987–88) and by communication; IDB: *Annual Report 1986* and by communication; and author's calculations.

Notes: World Bank estimates include the recent GCI. IDB estimates assume agreement on the seventh replenishment, commitment levels of $4 billion in 1989 and $6 billion in 1990 and 1991, and traditional disbursement schedules.

[a] Estimates.

[b] Projections.

[c] Excludes the IMF.

[d] Totals may not add due to rounding.

Table 9.2

The Rapid Rise in Latin American Debt Service to the IFIs
(billions of U.S. dollars)

	1980	1981	1982	1983	1984	1985	1986	1987
IMF								
Amortization	0.5	0.3	0.2	0.2	0.2	0.4	1.9	3.3
Interest	0.1	0.1	0.2	0.5	0.8	1.1	1.1	1.1
World Bank								
Amortization	0.4	0.5	0.7	0.8	1.1	1.2	1.8	2.3
Interest	0.6	0.7	0.7	0.8	1.0	1.1	1.7	2.0
IDB								
Amortization	0.3	0.3	0.3	0.3	0.4	0.4	0.6	0.7
Interest	0.3	0.4	0.4	0.5	0.6	0.7	1.0	1.1
Total	2.2	2.3	2.5	3.1	4.1	4.9	8.1	10.5

Sources: Same as Table 9.1.

its cost of funds and the growth of the region's outstanding disbursed debt from $7.7 billion in 1980 to $18.7 billion in 1986.

Similarly, IDB repayments have risen from $260 million in 1980 to $712 million in 1987 and are projected to hit $1.5 billion in 1991 (Table 9.2). Interest and other charges have risen from $330 million to $1.1 billion.

For all three agencies, disbursements have not kept pace with repayments. After the surge in lending in 1983–84, IMF disbursements have actually declined. Reflecting a stagnation in commitment levels, IDB disbursements are lower today than in 1984. In contrast, the World Bank more than doubled its disbursements from 1981–82 to 1986–87, but the increase was still insufficient to compensate for the rise in repayments and interest. Even with the general capital increase (GCI), the World Bank's NRT will remain negative if the Bank adheres to its stated intentions of increasing commitment levels by only 10 percent annually over the next five to six years—to about $20 billion in the early 1990s.

Theoretically, a net positive inflow could be a sign of success for the IFIs. For the IMF, it could signal that member states successfully had restored equilibrium to their balance of payments. For the development agencies, it could mean that borrowers had reached that stage of rapid, sustained growth where they are ready to graduate from dependency on official finance and are capable of relying on private capital markets for their external financial needs. Alas, neither is a true picture of Latin America today. The region's external accounts are under severe strain, and Latin America has lost access to private capital markets.

At some point in time, lenders inevitably experience net reflows. The inflection point arrives more quickly when interest rates are high, as they have been during the 1980s. But this emergence of a negative NRT vis-à-vis the IFIs comes at a most inopportune time for Latin America. Public capital is needed to offset the sudden and dramatic withdrawal of private lenders and investors.

A positive public inflow is particularly critical at a time when many Latin American nations are attempting ambitious adjustment programs that require high rates of investment. Monies are needed to construct the modern plant and equipment whose output will be competitive on world markets. The IFIs themselves are strong advocates of this investment-intensive adjustment strategy. However, the negative NRT undermines the very policies they advocate and threatens to frustrate the region's efforts at structural adjustment.

Improving IFI Performance

There are two basic ways to correct the IFIs financial performance: increasing the disbursement rate and altering the amortization schedule. It would not be advisable for the IFIs to significantly lower their interest charges unless their cost of funds falls; on the contrary, the IFIs need an income stream sufficient to compensate for the rising volume of loans on non-accrual status. Let us first consider the disbursement options open to each institution.

The International Monetary Fund

The IMF has the resources to lend much more to Latin America, as it is definitely not experiencing a liquidity crunch.[3] It holds over $40 billion in unused loanable hard currencies, about $40 billion in gold valued at current market prices, and lines of credit from several capital-surplus nations. In addition, the IMF could seek to activate the General Arrangements to Borrow (GAB), a pool of funds that industrial countries can make available to the IMF to support major debtor nations, among other functions. Alternatively, the IMF Board could decide to create more of its own money, or Special Drawing Rights (SDRs), as most members have advocated, and industrial countries could agree to provide a disproportionate share of the SDR issue to developing nations. While such generosity would be financially equivalent to a loan or grant, it could be engineered outside of normal national budgetary processes and, therefore, be politically less taxing for industrial country governments.

The IMF maintains that it does not have this kind of leeway, i.e., that it needs to husband its liquidity to cover potential borrowings by industrial countries. However, no industrial country has borrowed from the IMF for more than a decade. In reality, industrial nations in need of finance have alternatives to the IMF, including the greatly expanded private capital markets and swap arrangements among their own central banks.

IMF management wants a 100 percent increase in its basic resources, or quotas, equal to about SDR $90 billion. It wanted action in 1988, but the U.S. government preferred to wait until the World Bank's capital increase passed through the Congress. IMF management argues that the Fund needs this doubling of its resources to keep pace with the growth in international capital markets and in world trade and to be able to increase lending levels to developing nations. This case would be more persuasive if the IMF were making better use of its existing resources and capabilities.

The World Bank

The approval of a $75 billion GCI in 1988 gives the World Bank the means to sharply increase disbursements. The Bank also has a vehicle for quick disbursement: its structural adjustment loans (SALs), which provide balance of payments support for agreed upon reforms. SALs can include broad macroeconomic variables or can focus more narrowly on particular sectors. Sector loans, which have been more common in Latin America, typically pursue such reforms as trade liberalization, reorganization of state-owned enterprises, reform of financial markets, and agricultural taxation and pricing policies. Structural adjustment loans account for about one-quarter of Bank lending. The apparent ceiling of $500 million per loan is arbitrary and reflects political pressures coming from the Bank's executive directors more than a calculation of what is needed to make the program work economically. The Bank's ability to persuade countries to undertake politically risky reforms would also be enhanced if it could put more money on the table. There is no good reason why strong adjustment programs, which require massive investments and sustained political support, should not receive more substantial external assistance.

The Inter-American Development Bank

The IDB's search for new capital resources has been stalled by its conflict with the Reagan administration and by an inability to disburse all of its existing resources because recipient governments cannot provide the necessary counterpart funds. In the hope of attaining a $20–22 billion replenishment that would permit a near doubling of loan commitments, IDB management has already acceded to U.S. demands that 20–25 percent of resources be used for policy-based lending and that hand-picked U.S. personnel be placed in key policy positions. The major Latin American nations have drawn the line, however, at the U.S. insistence that it be given a virtual veto power over individual loans. The U.S. position reveals unwarranted insecurity and distrust—it already enjoys substantial power to block loans. Moreover, IDB management has acceded to the United States' main substantive demands, and many Latin American governments are now ready and willing to undertake structural reforms.

The IDB's other major financial problem stems from the inability of financially strapped recipient governments to provide the required counterpart funds. The result is $10 billion in committed but undisbursed project loans. These funds could be put to use through temporary relaxation of counterpart requirements and the initiation of policy-based loans, which would not be tied to specific investment projects and therefore require no counterpart funds.

Amortization Schedules

All three institutions have resisted participation in the Paris Club, where official bilateral debts are rescheduled, in order to protect their preferred creditor positions. This posture, however, does not rule out alternative approaches to grappling with the problem of rising repayments. For example, the IMF has lengthened the repayment period for the more ambitious standbys (extended fund facilities) from 5–7 years to 5–10 years. It could strengthen this reform initiative by introducing contingency clauses that would allow for slower repayments in the event of adverse shocks, just as current agreements call for accelerated repayments in the event of good fortune. Furthermore, the IMF could transform past standby arrangements retroactively into extended arrangements, thereby stretching out amortization schedules.[4]

Recognizing the mounting repayment problem, the World Bank temporarily extended the grace period on new loans to middle-income countries from three to five years and approved an annuity scheme for low-income borrowers (those with per capita incomes below $836 in 1986) that will reduce repayment burdens in the earlier years of a loan. The World Bank could go further by lengthening grace periods significantly on existing as well as new loans. Such retroactive terms adjustments would be justifiable on several grounds. First, borrowers' economic conditions have deteriorated sharply, creating circumstances not envisioned when loan agreements were originally structured. Second, the IFIs are finding that structural adjustment programs often take longer to yield results than was anticipated when the programs began. Third, the external payments crisis facing debtor nations warrants adjustment by all creditors. The simple doubling of the current five-year grace period by the World Bank would immediately affect repayment on the $8 billion in disbursements made to Latin America from 1980 to 1984 and eventually delay amortization on the $16 billion in disbursements made from 1985 to 1988. The result would be an annual savings for Latin America of about $700 million in 1990, rising to $1.7 billion by 1993. These reforms would, however, cause the Bank to reach the lending ceilings fixed by the recent GCI before 1998 as currently anticipated.

The fear at the Bank that such retroactive terms adjustment might injure the Bank's credit rating is unwarranted. If implemented as a unilateral, once-and-for-all action, it would not pull the Bank into the troublesome reschedulings that bilateral and private creditors are immeshed in. Moreover, the World Bank's credit rating on private markets is more a function of the guarantees of the major industrial country governments than of the quality of the Bank's portfolio.[5]

The New Vision

In sum, there are more than enough options available to enable the IFIs once again to become sources of resources for Latin America. Rather than the projected negative NRT of some $3 billion, the IFIs could manage a positive NRT of some $5–6 billion by around 1991 (Table 9.3). Most significantly, this transformation could be accomplished without additional resources beyond the proposed IDB replenishment, although a quota increase for the IMF would make it easier for the monetary authority to boost lending while maintaining large liquid reserves.

The IMF could achieve an increase in disbursements of about $2 billion by either permitting greater access to its existing resources or by issuing SDRs; it could raise this sum by another $2 billion through a quota increase. The World Bank could increase disbursements by $2 billion through doubling the size of

Table 9.3

Potential IFI Expansion to Latin America, circa 1991
(billions of U.S. dollars)

	Increase in Disbursements			Net Resource Transfer	
				(A) Current Policy	(B) Potential Flows
IMF	$2.0		(existing resources or SDRs)		
	2.0		(quota increase)		
Subtotal		$4.0		−1	3
World Bank	2.0		(doubling SAL size)		
	1.1		(retroactive terms adjustment)		
Subtotal		3.1		−2	1.1
IDB	1.2		(replenishment plus SALs)		
	0.5		(counterpart funds relaxation)		
Subtotal		1.7		0.2	1.9
Total		$8.8		−$2.8	$6.0

Sources: Same as Table 9.1 and author's estimates.

those structural adjustment loans likely to be signed under existing policies and by reducing repayments by $1.1 billion through the retroactive terms adjustment discussed above. The IDB could double its annual commitments to $6 billion and devote one-quarter to fast-disbursing policy-based loans through the contemplated seventh replenishment; within two years, this faster pay-out rate could increase disbursements by an estimated $1.2 billion. Faster utilization of the IBD's pipeline—jammed up by the counterpart funds requirement—could inject an additional $500 million. This $8–9 billion improvement in the IFIs' combined NRT would equal better than 40 percent of the average annual resource drain that Latin America experienced from 1985 to 1987.

Individual loans, of course, would still be made on a country-by-country basis and be conditioned upon the design and implementation of necessary stabilization and strong structural adjustment programs. The international agencies have both a moral and financial right to condition their loans on the adoption of policies that will improve the welfare—and the future payments capacity—of borrowing nations. Importantly, the offer of more resources would increase the IFIs' power to promote such reforms, as well as the ability of borrowers to sustain reform programs. The provision of more resources would also help to catalyze private capital flows to Latin America.[6]

Private Financial Markets

The heart of the resource transfer problem is the private credit markets. By lending heavily in the 1970s and early 1980s, and then closing the credit windows after 1982 when global interest rates rose and loans came due, the banks first provided strongly positive—and then demanded strongly negative—resource transfers. The volume of resources involved (in both positive and negative phases) far surpasses the activities of the IFIs. For Latin America, net disbursements alone to the private credit markets swung from an annual average of *positive* $42 billion in 1980–81 to *negative* $3 billion in 1986–87.[7]

The Bretton Woods agencies have always viewed themselves as catalysts of private capital flows. In the short term, Fund and Bank programs often seek to gather associated private flows to help finance stabilization programs and supplement development efforts. In the longer run, by promoting successful stabilization efforts and more vigorous growth, they strive to promote additional private investment.

The debt crisis and the closely related resource transfer problem have heightened IFI attention to the private credit markets. Although the IFIs have only recently begun to use explicitly the resource transfer terminology, as soon as the debt crisis struck in 1982 they began to seek ways to reduce effectively the NRT from the debtor nations to the commercial banks. In particular, the IMF pressed commercial banks to cover a portion of interest payments falling due by participating in new money packages. More recently, the IFIs have begun to entertain methods for slicing the negative NRT by reducing the stock of outstanding private debt and, therefore, debt service.

As the debt and development malaise has persisted, the IFIs' interest in stemming the NRT to the private markets has grown. They are alarmed at the economic decline of their clients, annoyed that their own capital is "round-tripping" to service the assets of other creditors, and fearful that their own rising exposures are increasingly in jeopardy. Particularly at the World Bank, many staff members express fatigue at playing handmaiden to dispirited private banks.

New Lending

The IFIs have tried hard to catalyze new commercial bank lending through a variety of mechanisms. The IMF has sometimes conditioned its standbys on modest amounts of new lending by the commercial banks. This "concerted lending" generated $32 billion in private commitments in 1983–84, accounting for the bulk of new private lending to the major debtor nations.[8] More recently, however, its persuasive powers have waned. Private bank commitments tied to

IMF programs declined to $2.2 billion in 1985, to negligible amounts in 1987 (exclusive of one big money package for Mexico), and to zero through the first three quarters of 1987 (exclusive of a $2 billion commitment for Argentina). While predictions of the death of new money packages have proven premature, as the $5.2 billion commercial bank commitment to Brazil in 1988 suggests, it is increasingly difficult for the IMF to convince banks to increase their exposure in heavily indebted nations.

The World Bank is now tentatively attempting to step into the breach. With the support of the U.S. Treasury, the Bank has used its guarantee authority very sparingly, based on two premises: first, that private banks should bear some of the risk; and second, the Bank might just as well make the loan itself since guarantees are billed 100 percent against Bank lending capacity. It is a matter of debate as to whether the Bank's Articles of Agreement would have to be amended for the Bank to adopt a system in which only a fraction of contingent liabilities are charged against total lending amounts.

The Bank's efforts to attract private capital through traditional co-financing arrangements have largely failed. The Bank is now trying to persuade private creditors to participate in financial packages tied to economic reform programs. It is arguing that the medium-term nature of its programs offers comfort to banks beyond that gained by association with 12–18 month IMF standbys. In 1985, the commercial banks agreed to co-finance policy-based loans to Colombia and Chile, and more recently have agreed to participate in joint IMF-World Bank concerted lending packages to Mexico and Brazil, with some commercial bank disbursements contingent upon compliance with World Bank sector agreements. Nevertheless, most World Bank sector loans continue to be unaccompanied by private financing. The World Bank has yet to establish the mechanisms and procedures for ensuring that the commercial banks make significant contributions to most reform programs backed by the Bank.

Debt Service Reduction

In light of the reluctance of commercial banks to increase their exposure, attention is increasingly turning to the option of reducing debt service. The World Bank is anxious to play a role in pioneering debt service reduction schemes as is IMF Managing Director Michel Camdessus, but the U.S. Treasury Department has been a decisive restraint. Understandably, both institutions would shy away from any grand debt conversion scheme which left them, directly or indirectly, holding $100 billion or more of Third World debt. As an alternative, the IFIs might participate in some of the following approaches.

Buybacks

The IMF has already facilitated the Bolivian buyback of about half of its commercial debts by administering funds provided by bilateral donors that were then used to purchase bank debts at 11 cents on the dollar. The IFIs might initiate their own such program whereby they provide a portion of the financing for deep-discount buybacks that would increase a member nation's development prospects. For smaller debtors whose liabilities are selling on secondary markets at a small fraction of their face value, buybacks could significantly reduce scheduled debt service.

Guarantees for asset swaps

The IFIs could provide partial or full guarantees for financial instruments issued by debtor nations that would buy back at a discount old debts owed commercial banks. The problem with this option is that guarantees of the full stream of interest payments would dip deeply into IFI resources, while simple guarantees of principal provide a weak inducement for the banks as indicated by the disappointing response in early 1988 to the Mexican bond offer.

Interest guarantees

Guarantees of interest could take two forms. The IFIs could guarantee interest payments on new instruments that the debtors swapped at a discount for old debts. Alternatively, without altering the stock of debt, the IFIs could guarantee renegotiated, below-market interest payments for either the entire maturity or for two to three years on a rolling basis. If two years of 4.5 percent interest payments were covered on $250 billion in commercial bank debts owed by the highly indebted developing nations, the guarantee ceiling would be $22.5 billion.

Any of these mechanisms to reduce debt service could be tied to IFI-approved reform programs that over the longer run should increase the value of the banks' remaining exposure. At the same time, as long as the mechanisms were to significantly reduce the immediate NRT to the commercial banks, they could be advanced as "burden sharing" rather than a "bank bailout."

Net Resource Transfer Reduction

As the central conceptual framework for a new attack on the debt problem, the IFIs could adopt a strategy of "net resource transfer reduction." The World Bank and IMF could set country targets for new lending and debt restructuring that leave enough capital in each developing country to permit adequate investment and growth. Reversing the current approach, debt strategy would be subordinate to growth objectives.

To implement this strategy, the IFIs would require the firm support of key member governments. But it is in the interest of the industrial countries to restore growth to Latin America, to reopen export markets, and to help stabilize the region's democratic institutions. While a NRT reduction strategy might cause short-term pain among some banks, it also promises to increase the value of the banks' remaining assets.

It could be argued that the proposed strategy simply postpones the problem by piling new debts on old ones. Of course, to the extent that the negative NRT is slashed through debt reduction, the stock of debt would diminish. But even where new loans are made, it is to be hoped that the combination of enhanced capital availability and policy reform will improve nations' debt service capital in the medium run. As a result of fiscal reform and export growth, Latin America could be in a stronger position to manage its debts and repay loans by the mid-1990s.

A NRT reduction strategy would require that debtors be treated on a genuine case-by-case approach. Some nations, such as Colombia and South Korea, have strong enough export performance and actual or prospective access to private capital markets to be able to fully meet interest obligations and reach growth targets. Other nations will require an alleviation of debt service. Correspondingly, for some nations the relief can be temporary, while for others more permanent debt reduction arrangements will be necessary.

Under this strategy, each creditor could choose for itself whether it wishes to provide new monies or receive less debt service, negotiating with each debtor the exact choice of financial instruments. A formula such as the present discounted value of each creditor's contribution could be used to measure rough equivalence. Whereas it is unreasonable to expect commercial banks to become a source of net capital in the foreseeable future, they would be called upon to reduce their receipt of net financial resources. At the same time, the IFIs would generally be expected to sustain positive transfers to nations undertaking reform programs, at least until they resume growth.

A variation on this approach would be to establish the politically attractive and simple objective of a zero NRT for Latin America. If the current negative NRT is about $20 billion, the IFIs and the commercial banks could roughly divide the burden. The IFIs would make their contribution of $8–10 billion by transforming the projected $3 billion drain into a positive $6 billion net flow. The banks would reduce their net intake by about $10–12 billion through country-by-country combinations of new lending and debt service reduction. The IFIs' contribution would in effect be recycled to cover payments to the commercial banks, but now in the context of a more equal burden sharing and a new strategy supportive of the international financial institutions' ultimate objective: the growth of developing nations within a stable and expanding international economic system.

Notes

1. U.N. Economic Commission for Latin America and the Caribbean, *Economic Survey of Latin America and the Caribbean, 1987: Advance Summary*, April 1988, table 16, p. 45.
2. The term World Bank is used here as synonymous with the International Bank for

Reconstruction and Development (IBRD), the hard-loan window of the World Bank Group, which is also composed of the soft-loan International Development Association (IDA) that does little business in Latin America, and the International Finance Corporation (IFC) that promotes private investment.

3. For a fuller discussion, see Richard E. Feinberg and Edmar Bacha, "When Supply and Demand Don't Intersect: Latin America and the Bretton Woods Institutions in the 1980s," *Development and Change*, forthcoming.

4. I am indebted to Jacques J. Polak for suggesting this idea.

5. This point is forcefully argued in Charles Blitzer, "Financing the World Bank," in *Between Two Worlds: The World Bank's Next Decade*, ed. Richard E. Feinberg (Washington, D.C.: Overseas Development Council and Transaction Books, 1986), pp. 135–160.

6. The important issues of policy reform and "conditionality" are addressed in Richard E. Feinberg, "The Changing Relationship between the World Bank and the International Monetary Fund," *International Organization* 42, no. 3: (Summer 1988).

7. IMF, *World Economic Outlook.* (Washington, D.C.: IMF, April 1988), table A41, p. 163.

8. IMF, *International Capital Markets: Developments and Prospects* (Washington D.C.: IMF, January 1988), table 24, p. 76.

COMMENTS

Francisco Báez Rodríguez

My comments are an extension of Richard Feinberg's excellent assessment of the current relationship between the international financial institutions and Latin America. They are intended to enlarge the picture.

The negative net resource transfer between Latin American countries and the multilateral lending agencies puts into question the policy-conditioned lending which these agencies have been promoting. The stabilization and structural adjustment programs sponsored by these institutions have been accepted by the indebted countries in expectation that there would be a positive flow of funds from the international organizations and commercial banks to facilitate implementation. Reverse capital transfer with even the international organizations makes it still more difficult for peoples and governments in Latin America to pursue restructuring programs that mean immediate hardship, whatever their long-run promise.

There are many "catch-22s" in the debtor-creditor relationship. Feinberg emphasizes that adjustment programs require high rates of investment, that there can be no real structural adjustment with a continuous negative net resource transfer, and that chronic recession is inconsistent with the reorganization of economies, which undermine the policies and the international institutions' credibility.

In creditor circles, however, the contrary view has prevailed, that "if there is easy availability of finance, it is also highly likely that this will reduce the discipline on countries to adopt better economic policies."[1] This alternative view, that the restructuring programs do not depend on the ability of borrowers to sustain them but on the capacity of the financial institutions to enforce them, assumes that societies and governments in Latin America do not feel the need for better economic policies. Left alone, they would continue their carefree spending and rampaging. For the debtors, the consequent credit rationing is increasingly

Francisco Báez Rodríguez is Professor of Economics, the National Autonomous University of Mexico (UNAM).

being viewed as a lever to enforce policies that have little to do with economic rationality but rather fatten the trade surpluses to satisfy creditors. They see the negative net resource transfer not merely as an unpleasant side effect, but as part of a perverse rationale that enhances the power of big private financial institutions.

I believe that the problem of the defunding of Latin America by the multilateral lending agencies (and, of course, by the commercial banks) is systemic and is intertwined with the adjustment policies advocated by the international financial organizations. Had the indebted nations not adjusted their economic policies so as to generate the requisite interest, the creditor banks would have needed extraordinary financial aid programs and subsidies from governments and international financial organizations to alleviate their distress. In return, the banks would have come under much greater public scrutiny and control, and would have lost power over the international allocation of capital.

Commercial banks were protected from all this, and the above scenario is no longer likely. This should permit a broader set of options for the multilateral lending agencies to reverse the current resource transfer trend. Dr. Feinberg shows us that there are indeed such options. But his paper also shows the many obstacles the international financial institutions have to overcome in order to reverse the trend. Some obstacles are internal; institutions that seek to diminish bureaucracy elsewhere also have to cope with their own. Others are external; the IMF, the World Bank, and the Inter-American Development Bank have had difficulty increasing their resources. Feinberg's paper shows us that some of these difficulties stem from the relationhip between the international financial institutions and the U.S. administration. Barring a change of attitude in the governments of highly industrialized nations (and within the international financial organizations' bureaucracy), major alterations of the disbursement flows and amortization schedules by the multilateral agencies are unlikely.

On the other hand, debt service reduction seems to be a favored alternative at least rhetorically, and participation by the international financial institutions seems likely, as debtor nations focus their attention on secondary markets and interest rates. Discounts and below-market payments are increasingly a condition for the financial survival—within the prevailing system—of capital-troubled nations, and such departures from orthodoxy may require international institutional guarantees. Even so, and even if institutions like the World Bank succeed in their efforts to increase the flow of private capital to indebted countries, the funds are not likely to suffice to restore sustainable growth in the 1990s for many of the debtor countries.

This leads to the last part of Feinberg's paper, which calls for the creditors to start viewing matters from the debtors' side. Debtor nations feel that they have carried a disproportionate burden in terms of investment, income distribution, inflation, unemployment, and real consumption, with the foreign creditors as the primary claimants and most domestic economic agents as the residual ones.

There is a desperate need in our countries to reverse the priorities. Foreign debt servicing must be subordinate to national economic goals, rather than domestic goals subordinate to servicing objectives, as has been the case.

This would, as Feinberg emphasizes, imply a genuine case-by-case approach and would require different choices of financial instruments by institutional and commercial creditors. Such a change in the conceptual framework of the debt issue would also help create a new economic order, in which the current "in depth" model of development would be modified to include the many nations that are now being left behind. It also implies a redefinition of the role of the multilateral lending agencies, which raises other questions. Are they to resume capital transfer from North to South and promote fairer terms of commercial and financial exchange between different types of nations? Are they going to tackle the stock adjustment process for the dollar liabilities of the Latin American region? Can the objectives of growth promotion and liquidity control coincide? Does the latter conflict with a genuine case-by-case approach? These questions are likely to have practical answers only after important, and probably lengthy, negotiations, tensions, and struggles. And the new framework is unlikely to come alive if too much stress is put on monitoring and conditionality.

Monitoring has been required by creditors in exchange for new financing, but it must be understood that without enough financing there can be no effective monitoring. Financing (or, to put it in another way, net resource transfer reduction) is necessary to keep the international financial system functioning. One may agree that "the offer of more resources would increase the IFIs' power to promote [stabilization and structural adjustment] reforms" (and, of course, the ability of borrowers to sustain reform programs), but tying disbursement, amortization, or debt service reduction to infeasible targets or overly specific economic policies will encounter growing resistance. The change of framework must restrain policy conditionality.

A new conceptual framework means accepting that in countries such as Mexico, major debt relief is needed for any growth and stabilization program to succeed; and that internally, profound economic crises can be overcome only with policies that do not rely on deceptive devices, imported or locally made.

Note

1. Eduardo Weisner, then director of the IMF's Western Hemisphere Department, as quoted in Edmar L. Bacha and Richard E. Feinberg, *The World Bank and Structural Adjustment in Latin America* (Rio de Janeiro: PUC, July 1985).

10

Recapitalizing the Nation: Efficient Commercial Financing for Latin America

Donald R. Lessard

The debt crisis has now entered a new phase. The emphasis has shifted from buying time to debt reduction, triggered by two major sets of events. The first consists of signals within major debtor countries that debt burdens, whether or not economically repayable, are politically intolerable. In Mexico, the government's policy of fully honoring its external obligations resulted in the near defeat of the ruling party. In Venezuela, economic adjustments required for compliance with the existing debt program have led to riots, threatening the new government, and forcing it to move strongly on the debt front. The second set of changes involves shifts in the policies of creditor governments and the international agencies. The most visible element of this shift is the Brady Plan, which commits the United States to a course of debt reduction, as yet undefined, involving the acceptance of losses by commercial banks coupled with new support from the International Monetary Fund and the World Bank.

This paper focuses on the efficient use of commercial finance, including commercial alternatives to general obligation finance such as direct foreign investment, portfolio investment, project lending, and various forms of mezzanine finance which combine features of debt and equity, in the inevitable restructuring of Latin American countries' obligations and, eventually, in the recapitalizing of their economies. The reasons for focusing on the structure of countries' financial obligations, and not just the aggregate amount of these obligations, is that modes of finance differ in several important dimensions including (expected) cost, the extent to which they provide *ex ante* risk sharing, and the extent to which they entail managerial participation in specific projects or enterprises. These differ-

Donald R. Lessard is Professor of International Management, Sloan School, Massachusetts Institute of Technology.

ences have important implications for the pattern of countries' obligations across circumstances and for the creation of incentives for efficient investment and management in these economies.

In this analysis, it is taken as given that the overriding goal of restructuring a country's obligations and recapitalizing its economy is to restore an acceptable level of growth in the short run and provide the basis for dynamic long-run development, involving domestic as well as foreign private interests. The primary reasons for changing not only the amount but also the structure of financing are to:

(a) reduce the "overhang" of senior obligations (official and commercial bank debt) that distort public and private economic incentives within the country, preclude the issuance of new, asset-linked claims (project financing, direct investment, local equity investment), and impose explicit and implicit costs on debtors as the result of current or potential future noncompliance;[1]

(b) more closely match countries' obligations with their ability to pay over time and across circumstances (e.g., commodity prices and interest rates), thereby simultaneously increasing the potential value of their obligations and reducing potential costs of noncompliance; and

(c) rearrange the allocation of risks, rewards, and responsibilities among agents in order to increase the benefits of diversification and participation.

This paper is organized in several sections. The first defines alternative commercial financing modes, shows how they differ in terms of the extent to which they involve risk sharing and managerial control, and illustrates why an efficient financing structure is likely to involve a mix of these modes. The second suggests why these alternatives have not played an important role in LDCs' financing to date, even prior to the onset of their debt crises, in order to identify the political and institutional preconditions for their implementation. The third section examines the efficient use of commercial finance for countries with a debt overhang, both as part of a debt reduction program and subsequent to such a program. The final section summarizes the discussion and identifies a series of steps that can and should be taken by countries, their external creditors, and the key international institutions to support the implementation of these alternative financing arrangements.

Commercial Financing Alternatives

Modes of Commercial Finance

There are a variety of modes of external commercial finance for developing countries. The most prevalent of these is noncontingent general obligation borrowing, which may entail either floating or fixed interest rates. The key element of this type of finance is that the obligation to repay is either entirely predetermined in nominal terms or, in the case of floating rate debt, determined by an external index of interest rates that bears little relationship (and possibly even a negative relationship) to countries' ability to pay. Further, since it is a general obligation, it is due without regard to the success or failure of the programs or projects that it financed.

Direct investment, the traditional alternative to sovereign borrowing, entitles the investor to a *pro rata* share of the distributed profits of a specific firm. It typically is motivated by the return the parent firm expects to be able to earn by making use of its existing knowledge in a local operation and/or by incorporating the local operation in its global production and marketing network. Thus, it responds to firm-specific, microeconomic factors as well as to macroeconomic prospects in the host country. In some cases, however, direct investment also serves to overcome limits to the enforceability of other cross-border claims posed by country risk or the absence of the necessary local institutions.

Portfolio investment in equities quoted on public stock markets, like direct investment, entitles the investor to a share in the profits of private enterprise. Unlike the direct investor, however, the equity investor typically is seeking only a share of profits and not the responsibilities of control. Indeed, many equity investors deliberately restrict their holdings to a small percentage of the total stock (less than 5 percent) in order to maintain liquidity and avoid being forced to take responsibility for saving the firm if they lose confidence in its management.

Portfolio equity investment can involve varying degrees of penetration of the domestic economy. The least penetrating mode, popular in many LDCs, is the offshore investment trust (closed end fund) that invests in a broadly diversified portfolio of domestic shares. Other more penetrating modes involve investments in individual shares, either through offshore listings of LDC firms or local purchases of locally listed shares. While portfolio investment is typically defined as involving little or no managerial control, this, too, can vary substantially. A national index fund may or may not participate in the governance of the firms in which it invests. If it does, though, the general practice is to separate the nationality of ownership and control by appointing a local investment management firm that represents shareholder interests on boards, etc.

Quasi-equity investments break open the package of risk sharing and managerial control that direct investment has typically constituted. These new forms of international investment include joint ventures, licensing agreements, franchising, management contracts, production sharing, and international subcontracting.[2] They permit the host country to select those functions for control by the foreign enterprise that cannot economically be obtained elsewhere without allowing total foreign control.

Nonrecourse project or stand-alone finance provides another way to shift risks and responsibility to foreign investors by linking borrowing to particular enterprises or projects without a general guarantee. In such cases, the lender is exposed to the downside risks of the undertakings being financed, but in contrast to equity or quasi-equity claims, does not share in the upside potential. From the perspective of the borrower, such financing can be thought of as borrowing at a rate that is independent of the project's success and purchasing insurance to service the debt in case the project fails. It may also involve the earmarking of project revenues for servicing the project borrowing. Clearly, therefore, the lender would require a higher promised interest rate on such loans than on general obligations.[3]

Just as equities or quasi equities linked to particular projects or firms transfer some or all of the risks of those undertakings to investors, contingent general obligations do the same for the country as a whole. A country that is heavily dependent on, say, oil or copper revenues could issue commodity-linked bonds. With such bonds, debt service would remain a sovereign obligation with the implied enforcement leverage, but the amount of the debt service under any set of circumstances would be determined by the price of the commodity.

Desired Dimensions of Alternative Financing Modes

Financing modes differ in several dimensions of prime importance to LDC borrowers. These are: (a) expected cost; (b) degree of risk sharing or hedging; and (c) the alignment of the incentives they create for macroeconomic and debt management on the part of the borrower, as well as for local and foreign private agents operating within their economies.

Other things equal, a borrower will desire the lowest possible expected cost but may be willing to accept a higher expected cost in return for greater risk sharing, improved performance incentives, or both. In this section, each dimension is discussed individually. In the following section efficient combinations of these dimensions are explored.

Expected Cost

Cost is not a single, simple dimension. Rather, each mode of finance entails a pattern of costs across circumstances and a (probability weighted) expectation of these costs. This expected cost may differ significantly from the promised or contractual cost of a particular instrument. Risky debt, for example, will carry a high promised interest rate to reflect the high probability of nonperformance. Its expected cost, however, will be an average of the promised rate across those circumstances where interest is paid, and zero or some partial amount across those periods where full interest is not paid. With equity there is no promised cost, simply the expectation of a particular return across circumstances.

The expected cost of a specific mode of finance has three components: the required expected return to investors, which is usually higher for riskier obligations; the deadweight cost or penalty in the case of nonperformance; and the monitoring and control costs associated with particular forms of finance. We assume that the required expected return to investors depends on the extent to which returns vary in line with risk factors that are unavoidable in the world economy, such as business cycles in major industrialized countries, world interest rates, and commodity prices.[4] Therefore, short-term floating-rate obligations, and price-level indexed obligations whose returns are largely independent of variations in aggregate world output, will command minimal investor risk premiums, while, for example, copper-linked bonds which have a significant positive covariance with aggregate output will require a substantial risk premium.[5] A broadly diversified portfolio of local equities though, will command only a slightly higher cost than floating rate debt, since empirical analyses show that returns on these assets bear little relation to external economic factors (see, e.g., Errunza 1989).

The enforceability of sovereign credit, in general, depends on the lenders' ability to impose penalties in the case of nonperformance (see, e.g., Eaton, Gersovitz, and Stiglitz 1986). These penalties generally result in deadweight costs, since their cost to borrowers is not offset by a corresponding gain to lenders. However, there is no generally accepted model of deadweight costs associated with nonperformance, nor are there any reliable estimates of its magnitude.[6] We assume that expected deadweight costs depend on two factors: the expected incidence of nonperformance and the ability of lenders to distinguish between bad luck and bad faith on the part of borrowers with respect to their meeting commitments on particular claims. Therefore, these deadweight costs are expected to be highest for noncontingent general obligations, especially floating-rate obligations that enhance the probability of default through adverse interest rate movements.

Monitoring costs depend on the amount and frequency of information and influence required for the enforcement of particular claims. At this stage, it is assumed that they are equal for all forms of general obligations and are higher for claims that penetrate the economy and hence may require information and influence at the level of firms or projects.

Risk Sharing and Hedging

Risk sharing refers to the extent to which the contractual obligation is linked explicitly to some aspect of the borrower's economic situation and, hence, shifts risks inherent in the domestic economy to other participants in the world economy. Equity investment, for example, entitles the investor to a *pro rata* share of the profits of a particular firm, while commodity-linked bonds or export participation notes perform the same role at the level of the economy as a whole. This attribute is most valuable to a borrower when the risks that are shifted contribute significantly to the variability of income or the availability of foreign exchange or both; in other words, they are risks that are systematic at a local level. The outstanding examples are countries whose exports are dominated by one or two primary products, such as Chile (copper), Malaysia (tin, palm oil), or Mexico, Nigeria, and Venezuela (oil).

All investment involves risk taking. When a developing country finances an investment project by incurring debt, it implicitly accepts virtually all of the risks of the activity being financed. Losses can be passed on to the lender only by default or the credible threat of default—a strategy that typically involves dead-weight costs. An oil producing country, for example, might consider financing its needs either with general obligation borrowing or with a share of its oil income. With general obligation borrowing, it would be committing itself to repay an amount of foreign exchange that is independent of the condition of the domestic economy. Thus, the same debt service will be due when foreign exchange is scarce as when it is not. If servicing obligations take the form of a share of net foreign exchange earnings, in contrast, repayments will be smallest when foreign exchange is scarcest, and vice versa. Clearly, finance giving rise to obligations keyed to a country's capacity to pay is less costly in terms of its well being, other things being equal, and hence it should be willing to pay a somewhat higher expected monetary cost for such financing.

Because borrowing countries and investors who participate in world capital markets differ in the risks to which they are exposed, they will possess comparative advantage in bearing particular risks. The economies of Mexico, Venezuela, and Ecuador, for example, are much more exposed to shifts in energy prices than the world economy as a whole. This comparative advantage will be reflected in the fact that the premium demanded by world investors for bearing oil price risks will be substantially lower than the premium such countries should be willing to pay to avoid them. Thus, these oil exporters can gain by laying off some of these risks through financing arrangements. In contrast, oil importers such as Brazil or Chile would benefit from financing arrangements that relate debt-service inversely to oil prices.

Hedging is accomplished when financing terms are selected to minimize the borrower's exposure to adverse fluctuations in the cost of finance resulting from shifts in external economic variables, such as interest rates and exchange rates. Because of domestic rigidities, developing countries face greater effective exposure to variations in real and nominal interest rates than industrial country borrowers or lenders.[7] This exposure will be reinforced to the extent that variations in world interest rates, or the exchange rates of currencies in which they borrow, accentuate the volatility of their foreign exchange earnings before debt service. As a result, developing countries will, other things being equal, benefit from financial terms that limit their exposure to such variations.

Once the question of cost is extended to one of how the costs are distributed across circumstances, selecting appropriate terms for borrowing becomes an issue of comparative advantage. Assuming that world financial markets work reasonably well and that a particular developing country is a price taker in those markets, it should finance itself on those terms that most closely align its exposures with those of the world economy on a whole. A country where a few commodities make up a significant fraction of GNP or exports—relative to the role of these commodities in the world economy—should seek to shift the risks of these commodities to world financial markets. A country that has a relatively high negative exposure to short-term interest rates, as a result of heavy borrowing, should seek forms of financing with fixed or capped interest rates, and so on.

Incentive Alignment

This dimension refers to the extent that the incentives that particular modes of finance create for macroeconomic and debt management of the borrower and for local and foreign private agents operating in the debtor economy are aligned so that the parties share a common interest. Most of the debt literature focuses on the incentive effects of external borrowing on the macroeconomic choices of the borrowing country. A large debt overhang, for example, makes the country less willing to forego current consumption to invest, since it will suffer the full current loss but will capture only a fraction of the potential future benefits. These effects can either be exacerbated or ameliorated by alternative modes of finance. Since they are most important when there is a large debt overhang, they are discussed in the section which focuses on existing debt overhang.

Incentive effects are also applicable to lenders, often without regard to whether there is a debt overhang. When financing takes the form of a general obligation, the lender has little stake in the success of the project financed and, hence, has little motivation for intervening in its design or management. In contrast, when debt service obligations are linked to the outcome of specific projects or undertakings, with limited recourse to a country's general credit, foreign lenders or investors have a stake in the success of the project. This linkage can improve performance and reduce risk when lenders or investors have some control over variables crucial to a project's success. For example, if all or part of the yield on an obligation is tied to the performance of the project financed, the lender (investor) has a greater interest in seeing that the project design is appropriate and its management is satisfactory. Similarly, if the obligations of a borrowing country are linked to its volume of manufactured exports, lenders have a greater interest in assuring that country's continued access to markets for its products. However, if the potential lenders do not have control over variables relevant to the project's success, the main incentive effect of linking debt service obligations to outcomes is an improvement in the credit analysis undertaken before the loan is made. Where the project is not seen to generate returns sufficient to service the debt under a wide range of circumstances, lenders may not provide any project finance and thus may kill the project.

The incentive effects on investors of any financial contract depend on its specificity. Since an equity share is specific to a particular firm, it gives investors an incentive to promote that firm's success. Because a production-share or risk-service contract (typically employed on oil and gas projects) links investor returns to a narrower measure of project success, it focuses incentives on managing those dimensions appropriately. General obligation borrowing, in contrast, is not linked to any particular project or risk dimension and hence provides lenders with a stake only in a country's overall foreign exchange situation.

In cases where a foreign investor can add significantly to the value of an undertaking through its knowledge base or access to markets, some form of stakeholding will be beneficial. But in cases where domestic policy choices are the primary determinant of project success or failure, such foreign participation will confront moral hazard. The risk of self-serving government policies will tend to confound the incentives facing the foreign investor and reduce the credibility of the contract. Since most activities involve both types of risks, it is beneficial to be able to separate them in contracting.

Efficient Commercial Finance

The positions along the three dimensions of expected cost, risk sharing, and incentive alignment for various modes of finance, including general obligation financing, direct foreign investment, portfolio equity investment (both in individual shares and in national funds), quasi-equity, and project lending are shown in Figure 10.1.

General obligation financing, the origin, provides the benchmark. On an *ex ante* basis, it offers the lowest cost, but involves no *ex ante* risk sharing or managerial involvement. Direct foreign investment typically has a higher expected cost, but combines risk sharing with managerial control of investments and, often, a substantial international integration of operations. Other alternatives typically are more focused in the dimensions that they provide. Commodity bonds, for example, provide risk sharing but no managerial involvement. In portfolio equity and quasi-equity investment, the lender's income depends in some well-defined way on the success of the project, but he has only a narrow claim to participate in ownership or control and shares risks and responsibilities over a narrower range of outcomes than under direct investment.

Given that most alternative modes of finance involve somewhat higher expected costs than floating-rate, general obligation borrowing, why should borrowers ever prefer them? The key reasons are that these alternatives have more attractive distributions of costs over time and across circumstances and incentive effects. In contrast to expected cost, which by definition is a zero-sum game between lenders and borrowers, these dimensions can give rise to positive-sum combinations, increasing the security of these claims.[8]

Apart from offering preferred combinations of expected cost, risk sharing, and performance incentives at the macro- and microeconomic levels, the alternatives

Figure 10.1. **Modes of Commercial Finance**

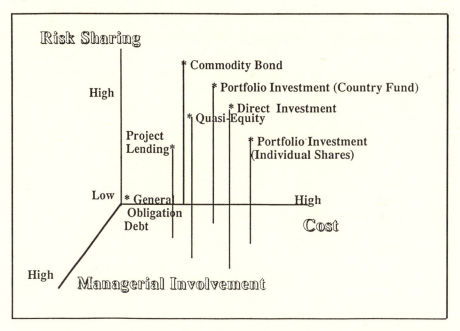

modes of finance may also promote local savings and deter capital flight through their interactions with local capital markets.

Impact on Domestic Savings and Capital Flight

International finance can never be more than a complement to domestic savings. It will be available on the best terms, and employed most usefully, when it is accompanied by healthy domestic capital formation. A major problem in many developing countries is insufficient capital formation. Indeed, capital flight has been a principal contributor to a number of countries' external financial crises. This poor record reflects unattractive climates for domestic savings including poor macroeconomic prospects, high taxes, and regulations limiting the scope of investment; discrimination against domestic savings such as repressed interest rates and the threat of changes in the level of inflation or other forms of default on implicit financial contracts; and macroeconomic policy distortions, especially in foreign exchange markets. It also reflects an underinvestment, in many cases, in the institutional infrastructure required for financial deepening.

International finance in the form of general obligation borrowing has allowed LDC governments to bypass local financial markets. As a result, many of the policy measures necessary to stimulate domestic capital formation have been neglected. Certain forms of international finance, in contrast, especially portfolio investment in corporate equities and bonds, make use of domestic markets and hence will be successful only to the extent that these markets flourish.

Obstacles to Alternative Modes of Finance

Even if the alternative modes of finance are preferable in terms of economic efficiency, they are not necessarily feasible. They are generally harder to enforce across national boundaries than general obligations and they require specific domestic legal and institutional infrastructure. An obligation to pay a share of foreign exchange earnings, for example, is ideal in terms of matching a country's payments with its capacity to pay. But because foreign exchange earnings are both hard to define and subject to the borrowing country's actions, this kind of contract presents moral hazard of a degree that makes it unlikely that finance would be available on this basis. Similarly, while portfolio equity shifts firm-level risks to investors, it is an open-ended contract that relies on a body of company and securities law which few LDCs possess in order to protect minority investors against conveyance by insiders. Further, to the extent that alternative modes of finance penetrate the national economy, they may result in an impairment of national sovereignty, a reduction in the role of the state, and, perhaps, a loss in rents to privileged domestic suppliers of capital. Thus they are likely to be opposed by various national constituencies.

Country Risk

Financial contracts across national boundaries face a hierarchy of risks. All contracts, with the exception of those involving a legal set-aside of specified foreign exchange earnings, are exposed to transfer risk, i.e., the risk that the country will not have or make available the foreign exchange to service the debt. Equity investments or loans to specific companies or projects are also subject to the commercial risks of the firm or project, as well as a series of country policy risks. These commercial risks include changes in market conditions, costs, and technology, as well as elements at least partly under managerial control. Policy exposures can be to measures the country may adopt in managing its economy or to policy measures of other countries. Examples of the former are the austerity measures adopted by developing countries in response to their debt crises, which have thrown many local firms into severe financial crises of their own. Examples of the latter are protectionist policies that threaten export markets. Thus, in many cases, there is no clear dividing line between country and commercial risks.

The greater exposure of the alternative modes of finance to various country risks results from at least four factors. First, since they are subject to a wider variety of policy impacts, nonperformance is significantly harder to define than with general obligations. Second, since they typically create divergent risk/return profiles among investors, they undermine the effectiveness of lender cartels on which the enforceability of cross-border contracts often depends. Third, due in part to the second factor, they usually are subordinated implicitly to general obligation claims, exacerbating the conflict among various classes of claimants. Fourth, because of this conflict, they face an increased likelihood of opportunism by the borrowing country.

Investors in alternative obligations will therefore seek measures that protect them against transfer risk or at least put them on a par with scheduled creditors. This can be achieved in some export oriented projects by putting the export proceeds in escrow. In some cases this might even enable a country to borrow on better terms for a stand-alone project than would be possible for general obligations, despite the fact that the lender would be accepting the commercial risk of the project. In general, though, this will be opposed by other creditors and violates the principle of not pledging specific assets or revenues to strengthen general obligations.

Market oriented projects that do not generate direct export revenues present a more complex problem. Even if financed on a limited recourse basis, they remain subject to transfer risk and, in many cases, to other risks emanating at least in part from domestic policy choices such as output pricing. These risks often inhibit financing from lenders who have the expertise to take on the commercial risks. Further, except in those cases where enforcement can be transferred to another jurisdiction through escrowing, there is a "catch-22"; the same factors that create these heightened exposures undermine the credibility of most steps that might be taken by the borrowing country to ameliorate them.

Most of these points apply to domestic as well as to foreign investors. If anything, domestic investors with their typically larger proportional exposures to the national economy are more subject to the spectrum of country risks than foreigners, which helps explain their shift to foreign assets, i.e., capital flight.

Institutional Preconditions

Most alternative modes of finance that penetrate the borrowing economy require institutional preconditions. First and foremost, the domestic legal system must provide effective enforcement of contractual terms, and private investors, especially foreign ones, must have access to that system and the sanctions it imposes. Portfolio equity investment, for example, depends on the existence of a body of corporate and securities laws and practices that provide arms-length minority shareholders with something close to a *pro rata* participation in the benefits of the firms in which they invest. These institutions, in turn, will only develop and function if the tax and regulatory environment does not discriminate against share ownership as opposed to direct investor control of enterprises. Further, in order to attract foreign investors, the country must be willing to allow foreign investors access to their market, and to allow them to withdraw their funds when they feel that opportunities are better elsewhere.

Direct investment, even in the form of cross-border joint ventures, typically does not rely to the same extent on local company law and is virtually unaffected by securities legislation because of the linkages it creates through technology and product transfers. However, it remains exposed to a variety of policy risks, including steps that limit the parent's discretion over local operations or constrain its ability to remit profits.

Quasi-equity contracts, since they are narrower and more explicit than equity contracts, may overcome some of these obstacles. Typically, they do not require the same sophisticated, capitalist, institutional infrastructure in the host country, and since they generally expose investors only to certain relatively well-defined risks, they may be credible even when the investor has little or no control over the activity in question.

With traditional direct or portfolio equity investment, the foreign investor faces the whole spectrum of these risks. This arrangement will be inefficient if such investors do not possess a comparative advantage vis-à-vis the host country in bearing some of them, whether because their exposure to such risks is greater or because the risks involve a substantial element of moral hazard, i.e., the possibility that the host government will influence outcomes to its benefit but to the detriment of the foreign investor. The degree of inefficiency, and hence the benefit of a more narrowly drawn risk contract, naturally depends on the specific circumstances of each investment. Again, these arguments apply to domestic as well as foreign investors.

Political Considerations

As in the case of equity investment, many of the obstacles to increased quasi-equity flows lie in the policies of the developing countries themselves. In many cases, alternatives have been spurned because of their perceived high cost. While this may be in part justified if the supply of alternatives is not competitive, many countries have underestimated the cost of the downside risks they have retained by financing projects with general obligation borrowing.

The fact that the alternatives typically bypass the state, and hence reduce its control over the internal allocation of resources, is another factor that has led borrower countries to prefer general obligation borrowing. As Frieden (1981) and others point out, the increased state control over resources provided by sovereign borrowing was a major factor favoring its use. The same elements appear today in the debate over who should control the allocation of local resources should any portion of interest payments on sovereign debt be made in local currency.

Finally, of course, certain local private interests may also benefit from restrictions on alternative finance. This is most likely where certain local groups have access to offshore general finance, while most firms are cut off from such flows.

Investor Country Obstacles

While most obstacles to alternative modes of finance lie in the policies and institutions of LDCs, significant obstacles also have been created through the policies and institutions of industrialized countries. Tax laws and foreign investment insurance schemes in investor countries, for example, tend to favor direct investment over more limited forms of contractual involvement. However, OPIC and several of the European insurance schemes cover contractual schemes that do not involve ownership. The World Bank confines itself exclusively to lending rather than taking risk positions, although it is now considering commodity-price linked financing and forms of co-financing that support quasi-equity investment. The International Finance Corporation has made quasi-equity investments in mining and forest products, but given its mandate to finance only private sector undertakings, these deals have typically been small.

Alternative Finance with an Existing Debt Overhang

So far, the focus has been on how a country should structure its external obligations if it were starting with a clean slate. In this section, we reexamine the desirability and feasibility of alternative modes of finance for countries with a debt overhang, where the current market value of their obligations is discounted from their face value, and access to new, voluntary financing is limited or nonexistent. The presence of this overhang clearly complicates the analysis. It raises the tantalizing possibility of "capturing" some of the discount, but at the same time, it exacerbates the conflicts between various classes of claimants and changes borrowers' incentives regarding the overall structure of their obligations. The key question is whether exchanges involving alternatives offer a viable third option—recontracting—to the existing options of financing or forgiving.

We address these issues in three different contexts: the conversion of general obligations into alternative obligations as part of a negotiated or concerted exchange, the voluntary conversion of general obligations into alternative modes of finance, and the contracting of separate new finance involving alternative modes of finance despite the existence of a debt overhang.

Concerted Recontracting

There is a very strong case that borrowers and creditors would benefit from concerted recontracting that incorporates efficient alternatives to floating-rate general obligations. Mexico's 1986 proposal that sought to link some fraction of payments to oil prices, for example, would have benefited both parties if it could have been incorporated at a price that yielded lenders the same *ex ante* market value as the package they actually obtained. Under current circumstances, it is more likely that Mexico can achieve its desired reduction of current debt service and of the face value of its obligations if it agrees to allow banks to "recapture" some of the concession if oil prices rise, and/or to recycle some of the interest they forego in the form of local currency to be invested or lent as they see fit.

Concerted exchanges are likely to be limited to recontracting of government obligations, such as indexing to a commodity price, rather than conversion of these claims into private claims such as debt-equity swaps. The reason is that conversions involving individual firms or projects cannot be readily packaged for across-the-board exchanges. Commitments to a program of such exchanges are not likely to be viable either, since the actual terms of the exchanges would have to be worked out over time and would have to be voluntary in nature.

The presence of a possible mutual gain, of course, does not mean that recontracting will be easy given the myriad conflicts and gaming possibilities present in the debt situation. In particular, creditors would have to grant the borrower some "breathing space" on debt service in exchange for the commitment to greater payments in more favorable circumstances.

Voluntary Recontracting

Voluntary recontracting involves the exchange of existing general obligations for new obligations that are more attractive to lenders. To be mutually beneficial, the exchange must also result in a more efficient mix of expected cost, risk sharing, and incentive effects for the borrower country.

Much of the apparent magic of debt-equity swaps, or exchanges involving any other alternative claim, disappears when they are broken down into their two component parts: a buyback of debt and a sale of equity (or other alternative asset) with at least part of the secondary market discount being retained by the private parties to the transaction. The benefits of marginal buybacks even at the secondary market price are the subject of considerable dispute, with the conclusion that they are limited at best.

Whether any discount should be offered on equity purchases depends primarily on whether they improve the aggregate investment base through encouraging new, beneficial investments that would have otherwise occurred, or improve the efficiency of existing assets. Equity investors with strategic stakes in local firms will have incentives to improve their performance, which could be significant if the investors also bring the relevant expertise or network linkages. The improvement is likely to be greatest when the conversion involves firms that had been controlled directly or indirectly by the local government. This benefit is not limited to takeovers by foreign firms. Domestic private investors might do as well, with the added benefit that they will augment the domestic political constituency for allowing a greater role for market forces.

Granting a discount is also desirable if the exchange alters the aggregate structure of obligations in the right direction, e.g., if it induces an investor to accept a subordinated claim that pays dividends only in good states of nature.

However, it should be recognized that many debt-equity swaps merely shuffle the ownership of assets between investors with no potentially beneficial aggregate effects. Moreover, they also often result in abuses such as "round-tripping." Nevertheless, debt-equity swaps could have indirect benefits by breaking the existing financial log-jam and augmenting the interest of financial markets in the country.

Many debt-equity swaps that have taken place to date appear to make little sense, even when arranged through open auctions that recapture as much of the discount as possible. Foreign purchases of public utilities, where there is no effective technology transfer by the new owners, little or no beneficial risk shifting, and the possibility of increased conflicts between investors and the consuming public, are probably unwarranted. Further, risk shifting and even incentive benefits do not always require the full sale of assets. Intermediate, quasi-equity forms of investment can both improve the structure of a country's obligations and bring in foreign expertise, while avoiding some of the inevitable conflicts of foreign ownership.

Separate New Financing

The key obstacle to new financing for badly overburdened countries is their inability to create new obligations that are senior to the existing obligations, which are already discounted by the market. The rights of the existing lenders, especially the negative pledge clauses that deny the borrowing country the right to pay any claimant at the expense of another, typically limit new lenders to a share of the general obligation pool. The value of their claim, therefore, immediately gets the average market discount, destroying the incentive to lend voluntarily. There are, however, at least two cases where linking a buyback with the issuance of a new security may be mutually beneficial and thus may overcome this obstacle. One is a buyback coupled with the issuance of new project-linked finance, the other a buyback coupled with the issuance of indexed exit bonds.

As regards project financing, consider a country whose creditworthiness is too weak to sustain new general obligation borrowing, but which has a highly promising, export oriented project whose development would be impossible without foreign finance. With stand-alone project financing (where project earnings are put in escrow to cover debt service), the project would go ahead without loss of free foreign exchange to the country and without affecting the position of existing creditors. But if the project was successful, it would add to the supply of free foreign exchange and benefit the existing creditors. Thus the general creditors might waive their overhanging senior claim to the project revenues in order to obtain the residual benefits.

The case with indexed debt is similar. Consider an issue of bonds with below market interest rates offset by commodity price-linked options. Such options could be sold successfully to nonbank third parties if the bonds were senior to general obligation debt. Because debt service on these bonds would fall in bad times, banks might grant such waivers, whereas they would not grant waivers to an equivalent new issue that did not involve a reduction in current debt service.

Conclusions: How to Get There from Here

Alternative modes of finance for LDCs including equity, quasi-equity, and indexed general obligations offer major advantages of risk sharing and managerial participation over floating-rate, general obligation borrowing. The limited role they currently play in these countries' external financing reflects a number of factors during the years of debt buildup, including a lack of awareness of these benefits, an assertion of state power, and a series of obstacles to their issuance including country risk and inadequate domestic institutional infrastructure. The debt crisis has underscored many of the benefits of alternatives, but little has been done to change LDCs' financial structures because of the resulting loss of access to voluntary finance, the preoccupation of banks and international institutions with maintaining the appearance of compliance with existing debt terms, the perverse borrower incentives created by the debt overhang, and the heightened conflicts between classes of existing and prospective claimants given this overhang.

After reviewing the benefits and obstacles to alternative finance for a country that is starting with a clean financial slate, the focus has been on some of the special problems and opportunities created by the debt overhang. The conclusions are that:

(1) concerted refinancing arrangements should include recontracting along more efficient lines;

(2) despite the difficulties of marginal, voluntary exchanges in the face of debt overhangs, carefully designed and managed programs can result in significant mutual benefits; and

(3) alternative modes of finance appear to provide the most interesting channel for new financing to those countries that will continue to face a debt overhang, even after recontracting.

In the case of concerted exchanges, the inclusion of alternative forms of finance that shift payments across circumstances can significantly close the gap between levels of current debt service that are politically feasible and allow revived economic growth, and those that the creditor banks demand. Voluntary exchanges should take the form not only of debt-equity swaps, but also the exchange of existing government obligations for new ones that are indexed to external variables such as commodity prices or to some formula of profitability of domestic assets, e.g., revenue bonds to finance fee-generating infrastructure.

Since obstacles to the alternatives already prevalent prior to the debt crisis have been exacerbated by it, recontracting will not take place without significant changes in the policies on the part of creditor country regulatory agencies, international financial institutions, and the LDCs themselves. A brief review of these steps concludes this analysis.

Regulatory Agencies

The current practice of restructuring through concerted new money packages is largely the result of an accounting and regulatory system for U.S. banks that allows them to operate with impaired capital resulting from economic losses on LDC loans as long as they do not realize these losses through sales or swaps. Thus, the U.S. government, through its deposit insurance and bank regulatory system, implicitly shares some of these banks' losses as long as they continue to hold the original obligations or their restructured equivalents. A key step toward more efficient recontracting would be to allow banks to obtain similar benefits if they exchanged their holdings for alternative instruments.

Creditor country governments also apply much of the leverage required to put financing packages together, contending with conflicts and free-ridership among banks, and opportunism on the part of borrowers. This leverage can and should be applied to support alternative approaches.

International Financial Institutions

International financial institutions (IFIs), especially the IMF and the World Bank, have tended to work in concert with holders of general obligations, often at the expense of foreign and domestic holders of alternative claims. A change in this role could be particularly useful in promoting quasi-equity investments and project lending. In the case of quasi-equity investments, for example, the World Bank might extend its co-financing program to cover such operations. Alternatively, the mandate of the IFC might be broadened to allow it to take quasi-equity positions in government-sponsored projects that could be structured on a commercial, stand-alone basis. In addition, the World Bank or regional IFI might assist risk unbundling by enhancing such claims against transfer risk, perhaps by assigning some fraction of its net transfers to a country to a credit enhancement facility for designated claims. This would shift the benefits of such future financing from existing creditors to the new obligations, creating a type of *de facto* seniority for these new claims without violating existing agreements. Thus, the absence of a true risk-bearing capacity for the IFIs does not preclude them from playing a role in supporting quasi-equity investments. Rather, the nature of the IFIs' strengths, and their preferred creditor position, make them ideal for bearing and mitigating transfer risk obstacles to such transactions.

In the case of domestically oriented projects that provide no direct foreign exchange and which entail political performance risks, IFIs and investment guarantee authorities could do much to relieve this problem. An IFI, for example, could include the features and performance requirements as project convenants that lenders need. Similarly, an IFI or a guarantee authority such as OPIC or MIGA could guarantee against transfer risks. Such guarantees could be much narrower than those extended by the World Bank under its current co-financing programs, and thus would allow greater specialization in risk taking.

Borrower Governments

The first step for borrower governments is to actively seek to obtain relief through rescheduling, interest rate reductions, or outright forgiveness. This could present them with a conflict since moving to a more efficient structure of liabilities will actually reduce their bargaining power for relief. Thus, they probably will not be the first to propose such recontracting, but they should be ready to make it a key element in their subsequent negotiations.

Notes

This paper draws substantially on Lessard and Williamson (1985) and Lessard (1988) as well as on presentations to various groups over the last three years. I have benefited from conversations on these topics with many commercial and investment bankers, government officials, policy analysts, and fellow academics who are too numerous to name here.

1. For a discussion of the potential impact of a debt overhang on a country's incentives for appropriate macroeconomic management see Krugman (1988). For a discussion of how such an overhang may crowd out local private savings and investment, see Eaton (1987) and Lessard and Williamson (1985).

2. For a description of these instruments, see Lessard and Williamson (1985) and Oman (1984).

3. The exception would be a case where the lender is shielded from transfer risk by escrow arrangements that provide for debt service payments of export proceeds before they are remitted to the host country.

4. In more technical terms, we are assuming that expected returns correspond to a stylized international capital asset pricing model in which the risk premium is an increasing function of the covariance of return with aggregate world consumption, i.e., a world consumption beta, such as that developed by Stulz (1981).

5. Risk premia are defined here (as in the financial economics literature) as increments in the expected return on an asset relative to the expected return on a zero-beta asset, not as adjustments in promised rate to reflect anticipated defaults (as in common in the LDC debt literature).

6. There is a great deal of uncertainty over what penalties a country will face when it does not meet obligations. Most formal models assume that it will be relegated to financial and commercial autarchy for at least some period. Many observers, though, argue that these penalties are much smaller; see, e.g., Kaletsky (1985).

7. This is the equivalent to assuming that the country has a greater degree of risk aversion than the representative capital market agent if the country were being modeled as a unitary actor.

8. The exception would be the case where a reduction in current interest rates, by reducing the probability of default, would increase the present value of lenders' claims.

References

Bulow, Jeremy, and Kenneth Rogoff. "The Buyback Boondoggle." Paper presented at the Fall Conference of the Brookings Panel on Economic Activity. 1988.

Diwan, Ishac. "An End to the Debt Crisis: General Principles." In *Dealing with the Debt Crisis*. Ed. Ishrat Husein and Ishac Diwan. Washington, D.C.: World Bank, Forthcoming.

Dooley, Michael. "Analysis of Self-Financed Buy-Backs and Asset Exchanges." IMF Working Paper 88/39. May 1988.

Dornbusch, Rudiger. "Our LDC Debts." In *The United States and the World Economy.* Ed. Martin Feldstein. Chicago: University of Chicago and NBER. 1988.

Eaton, Jonathan. "Public Debt Guarantees and Private Capital Flight." *World Bank Economic Review* 1, no. 3. 1987.

Errunza, Vihang, and Prasad Podmanabhan. "Further Evidence on the Benefits of Portfolio Investment in Emerging Markets." *Financial Analysts Journal* (July–August 1988), 76–78.

Errunza, Vihang, Prasad Podmanabhan, Mark Gersovitz, and Joseph Stiglitz. "The Pure Theory of Country Risk." *European Economic Review* 30. 1986.

Frieden, Jeff. "Third World Indebted Industrialization: International Finance and State Capitalism in Mexico, Brazil, Algeria, and South Korea." *International Organization* 35, no. 3. 1981.

Froot, Kenneth. "Buybacks, Exit Bonds, and the Optimality of Debt and Liquidity Relief." Working Paper No. 2675, National Bureau for Economic Research. August 1988. (Forthcoming in *International Economic Review*).

Ganitsky, Joseph, and Gerardo Lema. "Foreign Investment Through Debt-Equity Swaps." *Sloan Management Review* 29, no. 2. 1988.

Helpman, Elhanon. "The Simple Analytics of Debt-Equity Swaps and Debt Relief." MIT. Mimeo. 1988.

Institute for International Finance. *The Way Forward for Middle Income Countries.* Washington, D.C., January 1989.

Kaletsky, Anatole. *The Costs of Default.* New York: Twentieth Century Fund, 1985.

Kitchen, Richard. *Finance for The Developing Countries.* Chichester: John Wiley, 1986.

Krugman, Paul. "Market-Based Debt Reduction Schemes." NBER Working Paper No. 2587. May 1988.

——————. "Market-Based Approaches to Debt Reduction." Paper presented at American Enterprise Institute Conference on Alternative Solutions to Developing Country Debt Problems. April 1989.

——————. "Financing versus Forgiving a Debt: Some Analytical Notes." *Journal of Development Economics.* Forthcoming.

Lessard, Donald. "Country Risk and the Structure of International Financial Intermediation." In *Financial Risk: Theory, Evidence and Implications.* Ed. Courtenay Stone. Boston: Kluwer Academic Publishers, 1988.

Lessard, Donald, and John Williamson. *Financial Intermediation Beyond the Debt Crisis.* Washington: Institute for International Economics, 1985.

——————. *Capital Flight: The Problem and Policy Response.* Washington: Institute for International Economics, 1987.

Oman, Charles. *New Forms of International Investment for Developing Countries.* Paris: OECD, 1984.

Regling, Klaus. "New Financing Approaches in the Debt Strategy." *Finance and Development* (March 1988).

Sachs, Jeffrey. "Efficient Debt Reduction." In *Dealing with the Debt Crisis.* Ed. Ishrat Husein and Ishac Diwan. Washington, D.C.: The World Bank, forthcoming.

Stulz, Rene. "A Model of International Asset Pricing." *Journal of Financial Economics* 9:4 (1981): 383–406.

Williamson, John. *Voluntary Approaches to Debt Relief.* Washington, D.C.: Institute for International Economics, 1988.

COMMENTS

Claudio A. Pardo

Professor Lessard gives an excellent description of the alternative modes of foreign financing available to a country. From that perspective, the work is a useful reference piece in designing the financial structure of *new* investment projects. But Professor Lessard's paper also tries to examine ways out of the current debt crisis. He argues, and I think correctly, that the solution of Latin America's debt problem must include some recontracting of prevailing senior sovereign external debt for more commercially oriented modes of financing, such as direct and portfolio foreign investment, quasi equity, suppliers credit, etc. The main thesis can be summarized as follows: a developing country—in fact any country—will have less trouble adhering to contractual financial terms if it uses a wide range of financial instruments to better align the servicing of its international obligations with its ability to pay over time and across circumstances.

While one cannot dispute the need to restructure and recontract part of the external debt of the region—indeed practically all of the countries already are doing it in varying degrees—one must not lose sight of the fact that the basic problem being faced by Latin America today is excessive debt. To be sure, most of the debt corresponds to senior obligations, but the basic difficulty in servicing them derives most surely from their amount, not from their intrinsic characteristics. Recontracting of the debt following commercial terms would help, but much more than that would have to happen in order to really solve the debt crisis. That crisis has evolved to a point where no one any longer questions that the solution will have to contain some debt and/or debt service reduction along with a restoration of solid growth in the heavily indebted nations.

Latin America is going through one of its most severe economic crises ever. The solution will have to contain a complex mix of ingredients that includes debt recontracting. How *much* is the question. Contracting external debt on a commercial basis when the country is starting with a clean financial slate is much

Claudio Pardo, a former World Bank Associate Director, is the Chilean Central Bank representative, the World Bank.

easier than when the country is severely overindebted. Professor Lessard recognizes that in most countries burdened with a severe debt overhang, the benefits of debt recontracting are more problematic since recontracting competes with debt forgiveness, whose prospects are increasing. Obtaining a more efficient structure of liabilities through debt recontracting would reduce a country's bargaining power for debt relief. Thus, given the extremely depressed secondary market price on Bolivian debt, that country is better advised to seek grants to buy back its own paper and to avoid debt recontracting that could raise the market value of its obligations. As for debtor countries with smaller market discounts on their paper, the strategy question is how to exploit both recontracting and debt relief to the best advantage.

One of the shortcomings of Lessard's paper is that the approach he takes to explain ways to solve the debt crisis is too exclusively micro. Probing the feasibility of solutions also requires testing them in the relevant setting. Addressing specific micro issues is important for carrying out successful structural change in Latin America, but the fact remains that the main task ahead is to work on reducing sovereign risk, and to do that, it is essential to have a clear macro approach to the problem. Without this, judging the extent of the benefits to be derived from specific micro solutions is not really possible. This is illustrated by Chile's experience, which shows that a sound macroeconomic framework, complementing a series of measures at the firm level, can greatly improve the ability of a country to service its foreign debt over time and across circumstances.

For countries like Chile that are working hard to regain their former access to international financial markets, improving the structure of their external debt is an imperative. But so is a sound macroeconomic policy mix that brings about significant improvements in the balance of payments picture and which holds the expansion of the external debt to a more serviceable rate. If overindebted countries are to avoid unacceptable levels of net resource transfers abroad, the improvement in their external accounts has to be accompanied by steady economic growth so as to dilute the debt burden without untenable social hardship. Chile has tried to get rid of its debt problem by a combination of policies that have changed the structure and reduced the size of the debt while promoting vigorous export led growth. The results have been impressive: real GDP has expanded steadily since 1984 (a 30.7 percent gain through 1988), while the medium- and long-term external debt has declined from $17.8 billion at end of 1986 to $15.4 billion (U.S. dollars) at the end of 1988. Financial indicators have improved accordingly, notably the interest/export ratio, which fell from 47.9 percent in 1984 to 21.7 percent in 1988.

The structure of Chile's external debt is quite different today from that of a few years back when the country was struggling to get its debt problem under control. A primary factor behind this change has been Chile's comprehensive program to reduce debts with foreign commercial banks. This has not only helped achieve a reduction of the country's overall external debt, but also has improved its composition. Since the debt conversion program started in mid-1985, the pool of rescheduled debt and "new money" loans with foreign commercial banks declined, to an anticipated $6.75 billion U.S. dollars by June 1989, from a peak of $14.3 billion U.S. dollars when the program began. Of the reduction of $7.55 billion in foreign commercial bank debt, $2.6 billion has come from the conversion of general obligations into equity and quasi equity in Chilean private companies. The remainder, $4.6 billion, has been the result of straightforward cancellation of these international liabilities, taking advantage of the large discount on Chilean paper in the secondary market. There is only limited statistical information about the sources of cash used by Chileans to buy back the discounted paper. Nonetheless, the lesson is clear: if the debt price is low enough and the overall economic environment of a given country is right, locals will find the foreign exchange to take advantage of a well-formulated debt reduction program.[1]

A discussion follows of three specific options presented by Professor Lessard for countries with debt overhangs.

Voluntary Recontracting

Most characteristic of this type of recontracting are debt-equity swaps. Lessard's conclusion is on the negative side: "Many debt-equity conversions that have taken place to date appear to make little sense, even when through open auctions which recapture as much of the discount as possible." My comment is that in the case of Chile, the experience has been rather positive. There has been clear additionality in the direct foreign investment brought about by debt-equity conversions. Even old-fashioned types of direct foreign investment have gone up substantially in unison with conversions. In most cases, the debt-equity swaps (which are approved on a case-by-case basis) have been accompanied by fresh money inflows in the form of equity, quasi equity, and/or loans.

Equity conversions also have had a favorable impact on the prices of local assets which were severely depressed after the onset of the 1982 crisis. This has been an important factor behind the subsequent economic recovery. In addition, debt-equity swaps have eased considerably Chile's debt service outflow, since profits related to the new investments cannot be remitted abroad before the fifth year and the principal until the eleventh year. Another nice feature of equity conversions is that the income they generate is expressed in local currency and varies with the country's business conjuncture, while dollar repatriations become a function of the exchange rate. Moreover, the tax rules, including those affecting profit remittances, are variables under government control. All in all, these new equity investments are more attuned to the country's capacity to service its external obligations. It is important that these new liabilities, as Professor Lessard emphasizes, ". . . offer major advantages of risk sharing and managerial participation over floating-rate, general obligation borrowing."

A note of caution is necessary, however, about voluntary debt-equity swaps.

Most Latin American economies do not have appropriate macroeconomic conditions to enable them to sterilize the inflationary pressures that can be generated by debt-equity conversions. This is particularly true in countries with large fiscal deficits and poorly developed capital markets, conditions that make it very difficult to handle further increases in overall liquidity.

New Financing

I place a great deal of importance on new sources of external funding for heavily indebted countries. Recent experience shows that financing along commercial lines is generally available when it is for well-defined, economically sound projects. The problem is not so much in the financing as in finding the right projects amidst widespread economic depression and business failures. It is somewhat misleading to claim that the key obstacle to new financing is the inability to create new obligations senior to old obligations. Suppliers credit (funded normally by foreign commercial banks and backed by official guarantees), lending by or under the umbrella of multilateral organizations (IFC, World Bank, IDB, and IMF) and short-term trade-related bank financing are all available. In addition to direct and portfolio foreign investment, those sources of funding have been sufficient for countries like Chile to show sound sustained growth and increases in its rate of investment to an historical high. This gives confidence that the current expansion will be maintained in the future.[2]

Concerted Recontracting

I agree with Professor Lessard that concerted recontracting that offers efficient alternatives to the floating-rate general obligations could be beneficial. He cites the 1986 Mexican proposal that sought to link debt service payments to oil prices. Chile could try tying its debt service payments to copper prices. Options like these have their appeal. The question is, are they feasible on a grand scale? They have been very difficult to implement, in fact, partly because lenders demand much higher interest rate spreads to compensate for the additional risk that commodity price fluctuations incorporate in the new instruments.

This requires alternative ways of dealing with risks related to changing conditions in world markets. The Chilean approach has been to reduce the cost of the insurance premium by hedging operations in futures markets abroad. For example, the Central Bank and major state enterprises have developed their own international liability management programs. Such programs are designed primarily to insure debt service payments against unexpected increases caused by jumps in the LIBOR rate.

Similarly, a program can be designed for managing international reserves to reduce the foreign exchange risks associated with debt service payments. This might require matching the currency composition of the international reserves with that of the debt service outflows. Single commodity exporters might also secure a specific price for their export by selling contracts in the Chicago commodity futures market. Chile has opted for establishing a Copper Stabilization Fund, which is basically a dollar savings account where higher than expected copper revenues are deposited to be drawn down during lean years. The point is that there are new ways by which perceived risks are beginning to be neutralized by heavily indebted countries. The basic tools for this kind of financial engineering already exist, and technical assistance is becoming more easily available. The task now is to find the most economical ways to insure against the risks associated with external debt servicing.

Notes

1. The amount of money necessary to acquire Chilean commercial debt in the secondary market has not been negligible. Considering the discount of between 35 and 50 percent for this type of debt prevailing in the past couple of years, sums on the order of 2.5 to 3.0 billion dollars were required to retire the debt not covered by the debt-equity formulas in Chile's debt reduction program. Among the sources of funds probably are the under-invoicing of private exports, the over-invoicing of imports, the nonreporting of tourism revenues, and other leakages of foreign exchange in the current and capital accounts of the balance of payments. Also mentioned as a source is old capital flight, although in the Chilean case this does not seem to be a very large source of funds. Well documented, on the other hand, is last year's auction by the Central Bank, which resulted in the purchase of debt with a face value of 299 million for 168 million U.S. dollars in cash from the Copper Stabilization Fund. Interbank swaps of Chilean debt held by banks of other developing countries for debt of those countries in the portfolio of Chilean banks has also contributed to the debt reduction effort (161 million U.S. dollars so far). Finally, it should be noted that the foreign exchange available for these debt reductions, by and large, is out of the reach of the Central Bank for use in general balance of payments financing. From the point of view of the national accounts, it means that national savings, and very likely investment, go under-reported.

2. Most new investment projects are private, with practically all sectors of production represented. The nine largest projects currently being carried out in Chile add up to more than 5 billion U.S. dollars in new investment, a rate of about 4 percent of GDP per annum; sectors favored are mining, pulp and paper, power generation, and telecommunications.

PART V

VIEWS FROM WASHINGTON, WALL STREET, LONDON

11

The Empire in Decline?

Daniel Patrick Moynihan

As I recently wrote in *The New York Times Magazine*:[1]

> An irony of the Reagan era is that having at mid-point reached a crescendo of triumphalism—morning in America—it is closing amid talk of decline.

The concern has spread to Wall Street. Consider what Henry Kaufman has just written:[2]

> Come the day after Inauguration next January, whoever is sworn in as the 41st President will have to deal with economic problems more complex and more potentially treacherous than any seen since the time of Franklin D. Roosevelt.

The next president will confront at least one circumstance not confronted by FDR. He will be leading a United States that is the world's largest debtor.[3]

How about this scenario from *Time* magazine: The year is 1992. A local conflict has closed the Strait of Malacca, blocking Japanese tankers laden with Persian Gulf oil from entering the South China Sea. The Japanese Prime Minister places a call to the White House.

> "Good evening, Mr. President," he says. "Would you consider sending the U.S. Navy to escort my ships through the Strait?" Pause. The President is well aware that the request is coming from America's biggest creditor. "Why, yes, of course," he replies. The Prime Minister thanks him, adding, "I am certain that your help will reassure our private investors enough so that they will buy their usual share of Treasury bills at next Tuesday's auction."

Perhaps it was intentional irony that this article was printed in the July 4 issue. Is this "morning in America?" What has happened to lead Henry Kaufman and *Time* magazine to such scenarios? The answer is, I suggest, not that complex.

Daniel Patrick Moynihan is senior U.S. Senator from New York State.

Let's recall. The central thesis of the Reagan drive for power was that the nation had been in decline for some time, and that a restoration of military and economic energy was critical. The 1980 Republican platform was a fearsome account of imminent collapse. A famous memorandum handed to the president-elect was titled "Avoiding a G.O.P. Economic Dunkirk." What happened then?

The Reagan administration's response was to deliberately slash federal revenues. The vehicle was the 1981 tax cuts which denied the Treasury $750 billion. Taxes were cut in a magnitude out of all proportion to the expenditure cuts that the president sought. Quite simply, Reagan's plan for reducing the size of the federal government was to create a fiscal crisis. "There were always those who told us that taxes couldn't be cut until spending was reduced," the president said in his first month in office. "Well, you know, we can lecture our children about extravagance until we run out of breath. Or we can cure their extravagance by simply reducing their allowance."

Did the president never consider that the children could be plunged into debt? As I told the New York State Business Council in September 1981, the cut had been too large, and we needed a mid-course correction. I asked:[4]

Do we really want a decade in which the issue of public discourse, over and over, will be how big must the budget cuts be in order to prevent the deficit from being even bigger?

I also warned in that speech: "Our defense budget, which finally was getting on a steady course, will now be torn apart once more. . . ." All of which came to pass. The deficit absorbed our political energies. And the National Economic Commission is one of the offspring. Our defense buildup halted after fiscal year 1985, when our spending turned down in real terms (see Table 11.1). On August 9, 1988, Defense Secretary Carlucci acknowledged this on the MacNeil-Lehrer Newshour: ". . . the Soviet [military] budget . . . continues to go up at a rate of about three percent a year in real terms. Ours is in its fourth year of decline."

What I did not foresee was how devastating the deficit would become: a trebling of our government debt and our interest payments; debt service that now exceeds the entire federal deficit; and high interest rates, an overvalued dollar, and huge merchandise and current account deficits.

The press has caught on. The fact that debt service exceeds the federal deficit rated a front page story in *The New York Times*. "Interest on U.S. Debt to Top Budget's $150 Billion Deficit," is the headline introducing an article by Peter Kilborn. The Congressional Budget Office projects a deficit of $148 billion in FY 1989, and net interest payments of $163 billion.[5] Kilborn noted that part of this interest—about 15 percent, or over $20 billion—is now flowing abroad. He also noted that interest is now the third largest item of the budget, after defense and social security, taking 14 percent of expenditures. One devastating statistic that he failed to note is that interest payments on the Reagan debt (the debt

Table 11.1

Annual Percent Change in the Defense Department Fiscal Year Budget
(constant dollars)

1980	1.9
1981	13.2
1982	11.6
1983	9.9
1984	4.8
1985	7.1
1986	−4.2
1987	−3.3
1988	−2.9
1989	−0.7

Source: Office of Management and Budget, *Budget of the United States Government*.

accumulated during the eight years of Reagan deficits alone) now absorb one-quarter of all personal income tax payments.

Seven years have passed since I identified the problems of the 1981 tax cuts, and five since I wrote that the huge budget deficits so created were intentional on the part of the administration.[6] More than two years have passed since David Stockman published the record of this deliberate mismanagement in *The Triumph of Politics*. Neither of us has been believed. Even though Stockman wrote that the Reagan plan was a "willful act of ignorance and grotesque mismanagement . . . ," the general public did not believe it. Worse still, the business community did not believe it. By and large, they still don't.

Instead, we confront scholarly interpretations of America as a declining power. Paul Kennedy's *The Rise and Fall of the Great Powers*, with its themes of "imperial overstretch" and "relative decline," is the most noted. And while Kennedy recognizes the twin budget and trade deficits, and the transformation of the United States from a creditor to a debtor nation, nowhere does he ascribe these developments to willful acts of the administration.

In my article in *The New York Times Magazine* of June 19, 1988, I challenged Kennedy's conclusions. I wrote that if we could undo in the 1990s what had been done in the 1980s, there was nothing irreversible about our decline. We were not inexorably the next Great Britain. If the policies can be remedied, the decline can be averted, if not, it becomes inevitable. That is our choice. I am growing increasingly pessimistic. Although there is alarm about our economic situation, no recognition of its political genesis exists. Therefore, no political response can emerge. The 1990s may be lost.

Before I speculate further on what may come, let me establish some reference points. What do we mean by a net debtor? The broadest measure, and the one

Table 11.2

International Investment Position of the United States, 1960–87
(billions of dollars)

1960	44.7
1970	69.2
1980	106.3
1981	141.1
1982	137.0
1983	89.6
1984	3.6
1985	−111.9
1986	−263.6
1987	−403.0

Sources: U.S. Department of Commerce, Bureau of Economic Analysis, *Economic Report of the President*, 1988, Table B-106; U.S. Department of Commerce, Bureau of the Census, *Historical Statistics of the United States*, Series U 26–39.

that appears to be most often cited, is the U.S. net international investment position. The Bureau of Economic Analysis of the Commerce Department defines this to be the difference between U.S. assets abroad and foreign assets in the United States. At the end of 1987, this number was minus $403 billion dollars—that is, the amount that foreign claims on the United States exceeded U.S. claims on foreigners (see Table 11.2). These figures include both government and private claims—reserves, loans, securities, and direct investment.

In contrast, in 1981, the U.S. net international investment position was plus $141 billion, having grown slowly from a level of $69 billion in 1970. Thus, the 1982 to 1987 experience is a truly astounding reversal given the experience of the prior decade. Indeed, the last time the United States was in a net deficit position was before World War I.[7]

Equally disturbing is the negative trend in the U.S. current account balance—the broadest measure of U.S. international transactions, including merchandise trade, investment income, services trade, travel receipts, military transfers, and some other unilateral transfers. The United States current account has deteriorated from plus $7 billion in 1981 to minus $154 billion in 1987 (see Table 11.3). This translates into U.S. borrowing from abroad of the same magnitude. In fact, the current account was in deficit in only eight years between 1946 and 1982. The total current account deficit for those eight years was $42.5 billion. The cumulative surplus for those other years was just over $100 billion. By contrast, from 1982 to 1987 the current account deficits equaled $570 billion. We are financing our current level of consumption by foreign borrowing—to the level of 4 percent of GNP in 1987.

Table 11.3

U.S. International Balance on Current Account, 1946–87
(billions of dollars)

1946	4.9	1960	2.8	1974	2.0
1947	9.0	1961	3.8	1975	18.1
1948	2.4	1962	3.4	1976	4.2
1949	0.9	1963	4.4	1977	−14.5
1950	−1.8	1964	6.8	1978	−15.4
1951	0.9	1965	5.4	1979	−1.0
1952	0.6	1966	3.0	1980	1.9
1953	−1.3	1967	2.6	1981	6.9
1954	0.2	1968	0.6	1982	8.7
1955	0.4	1969	0.4	1983	−46.2
1956	2.7	1970	2.3	1984	−107.0
1957	4.8	1971	−1.4	1985	−115.1
1958	0.8	1972	−5.8	1986	−138.9
1959	1.3	1973	7.1	1987	−154.0

Sources: U.S. Department of Commerce, Bureau of Economic Analysis, *Economic Report of the President, 1988*, Table B–102; U.S. Council of Economic Advisers, *Economic Indicators*, 1988.

And we cannot ignore the relationship between the current macroeconomic distortions and the federal extravaganza of the Reagan administration. The huge budget deficits of the 1980s gave us the overvalued dollar and the high consumption relative to our major trading partners, which largely precipitated the current account deficits.

We have grown to depend upon these foreign imports and foreign lending to a dangerous extent. Consider Kaufman again. "To sustain the current U.S. expansion would, among other things, require extraordinary cooperation from foreign creditors, particularly the Japanese, making us politically and economically more dependent on those nations. This is a serious issue." *Politically and economically more dependent.* This from a well-respected figure on Wall Street.

Dependence. Of course, we all know that we are living in the age of international integration. Interdependence. Capital flows and trade flows are acknowledged to create interdependence and dependence. Who's position is preferable, the creditor or the borrower?

Senator Dan Quayle would have us believe, as he stated in his debate with Senator Lloyd Bentsen on October 5, 1988, that the current flood of direct investment in the United States means we are "the envy of the world." But do we really envy the situation of those who are confronted with huge debts? Do we envy Brazil, Mexico, and Argentina their foreign borrowings? Consider that in 1950 the U.S. net *credit* position was almost 13 percent of GNP.[8] In 1987, our net *debt* position was about 9 percent of GNP.[9] Was our global economic position stronger in 1950 or 1987?

Despite this data, the economic seriousness of our debt situation remains hotly debated. We have the Quayle "envy" view. Somehow he would have us believe that because foreign lenders see us as a good risk and want to lend us money, that it is healthy for us. Didn't banks lend Brazil all sorts of funds because it was seen as a good credit risk in the 1970s?

A second view holds that the debt situation is a growing problem, but one that is not a serious threat to the economy of the United States, yet. We can service the current debt without a great strain on our resources. This view also generally acknowledges that the trend in the debt position is disturbing, and action should be taken to stop its growth. This will require the reduction of our current account deficit. I will call this the "economist's view" of the debt position.[10] I fully recognize that this may be an oxymoron, since a single view among economists on any issue is probably unknown.

However, most economists recognize that the U.S. debt position is not a positive development. Our debt has been used for consumption and not investment. For example, James Tobin, the Yale Nobel Laureate, has provided some numbers on investment for the National Economic Commission as follows. In the 1950s, 1960s, and 1970s, the United States had a net investment rate—investment minus depreciation—of about 9 percent of net national product. In the 1980s, this rate fell to 6 percent. And since we have been running a current account deficit of up to 4 percent—borrowed from Japan, Germany, and Taiwan, among others—real domestically owned investment has declined to only 2 percent of net national product. Clearly, we have not used our borrowing wisely.

The shades of difference between economists seem to revolve around just how large our debt will become given the current rate of debt accumulation—it will exceed $500 billion by the end of 1988. Current projections seem to suggest that we will ultimately hit the $1 trillion level. One forecast by Data Resources shows a net debt position of almost $2 trillion by 1995, or 24 percent of GNP, assuming the continuation of current macroeconomic factors.[11] How likely is it that the markets would permit our debt to reach such a level?

Again, some shades of difference emerge over how great a burden it will be to service this debt once we stabilize its level. But most economists acknowledge that the current recipe is one of economic decline for the United States. Consider the situation of Great Britain. The October 8, 1988 issue of *The Economist* highlights, despite the recent successes of "Thatcherism," how difficult it is to catch up once an economy enters a period of decline:

> Starting in 1983, Britain's gross domestic product has grown faster every year than France's; but in the previous 28 years, France has grown faster in all but two. There is a lot of ground to make up. If every country's GDP per person were to keep growing as fast as it has done since 1982, it would take Britain 16

Table 11.4

Per Capita GDP of the Principal Industrial Countries, 1963–87
(dollars at 1975 purchasing power parity exchange rates)

	1963	1973	1980	1985	1986	1987
Japan	2,206	5,025	5,996	7,026	7,124	7,302
France	3,616	5,777	6,678	6,919	7,030	7,107
Germany	3,999	5,914	6,967	7,481	7,668	7,783
Italy	2,749	3,971	4,661	4,792	4,912	5,037
United Kingdom	3,589	4,709	4,990	5,459	5,623	5,817
United States	5,589	7,480	8,121	8,721	8,854	9,009

Source: Bela Balassa and Marcus Noland, *Japan in the World Economy* (Washington, DC: Institute of International Economics, 1988), Table 1.1.

years to catch up with the French, 59 years with West Germans. Crude measures of course, but they do not change much if you use fancier methods of calculating the purchasing power of average incomes.

As Table 11.4 shows, Great Britain's per capita GDP in 1963 was almost identical to France's and only 10 percent less than Germany's. By 1987 the gap is much greater. Why? One thing is clear. Great Britain's rate of economic growth was consistently lower between 1963 and 1980.

A third view tends to focus on the political implications of our dependence on foreign lending to sustain our economy. Make no mistake. Our standing in the world is changing. We are on the threshold of being transformed—at least in perception—from an economic superpower into just one more bankrupt American republic. To borrow from a current movie, I will call this the "United States as Parador" view. Perhaps the red tide that we had to fear from Latin America was not one of communism, but of ink.

We are losing face in the world. We recently felt compelled to pay our back dues to the United Nations.[12] Not because we had suddenly rediscovered our faith in its purpose. But because the rumor was widely circulating that we were broke. We were the only OECD country with contributions outstanding, and we had joined the ranks of Burkina Faso, Cuba, Democratic Kampuchea, Iran, Libya, Panama, Syria, Vietnam, and such. Consider the political indignities we are now forced to face. It is not so nice to be treated as a debtor. Ask Mexico. Ask Brazil.

Like other debtor nations, the United States has begun to receive advice from the IMF. The basic message is to reduce international borrowing. As one respected American journal reported the message: "To The U.S. From The IMF: Shape Up!"[13] Will we face the need to tap IMF resources as Great Britain did in the 1970s? At least an IMF team sent to give advice to our government will not face large travel expenses.

Table 11.5

GDP Growth Rates

	1929–50	1950–60	1960–69	1966–73	1973–80	1980–85	1986–87
U.S.	2.9	3.9	4.5	3.6	2.5	1.9	2.9
Japan	0.6	9.7	11.1	10.1	4.3	3.8	3.3
Germany	1.9	6.8	4.7	4.3	2.6	1.4	2.1
U.K.	1.6	2.7	2.8	3.0	1.7	1.3	3.9
France	n.a.	5.3	5.8	5.8	2.9	1.1	2.0
Italy	1.0	5.6	5.6	5.1	3.5	1.8	3.0

Sources: *Historical Statistics of the United States*, Series F 10–16; Balassa and Noland, *op. cit.*, Table 1.2.

Indeed, the problems in our national finances are affecting the strength of our banks and securities companies. Our financial services industry is being overwhelmed by stronger Japanese and European institutions.[14] I predict that soon they will be seeking the help of Congress much the way the steel industry of the 1970s and the automotive industry of the 1980s did. Will the 1990s bring us the decade of "voluntary restraint agreements" on the accumulation of U.S. assets by foreign institutions or more calls for a "level playing field"?

Internationally, we need to reverse the current trend or risk losing our leadership role. The lender calls the shots. That means the Japanese and the Germans. Treasury Secretary Brady recently criticized proposals to increase the resources of the IMF and World Bank and attacked the Japanese for proposing a debt relief plan not in accord with the Baker Plan. Specifically, Secretary Brady complained:[15] "At a time of competing demands and budget constraints, the case for additional quota resources must be compelling." The United States just cannot, in Secretary Brady's view, afford to do more to relieve the debt situation in developing countries. We need to relieve our own.

The political perception of a weakened United States has spread around the globe, at exactly the time when communism has emerged as a spent and failed ideology. Consequently, I am deeply concerned that the wrong lessons will be drawn from the current state of American finances. Serious as our current debt situation is, our failure to understand how it happened and what can be done about it could be even more damaging.

Debt was not something endemic to the future of America in 1980. It was uncharacteristic of our experience in this century. Our debt problem is the direct result of deliberate policies pursued by the current administration. As I recently told a gathering of The Business Council of New York State, we are once again at a point where the management of public finance is central to the well-being of our nation. The last such time was when Alexander Hamilton had to get the "political arithmetic" right to assure the survival of our republic.

However, the question for Hamilton was whether we would pay our debts. He insisted we should, and we did, in full. Since our debt is denominated in dollars, the question today is not so much whether we will be able to pay our debts. Rather, as Professor Alan Blinder of Princeton states, the question today is "(a) how much longer foreigners will be willing to lend us $150 billion or so annually without insisting on much higher interest rates and (b) whether we might wind up inflating our way out of the debt."

The proposition is not purely hypothetical. I am a member of the National Economic Commission. Our government and national debts are now that large and the debt service that edgy. Should we ever slip over the line where our foreign creditors decide we are no longer worth the risk, we could swirl into instability. This is the "serious issue" of Henry Kaufman. In remarks at a hearing of the Joint Executive Committee, Alan Greenspan also recognized the existence of a "serious issue."

> Representative Scheuer: Can you see the possibility that at some time we may be perceived as not such a safe haven . . . but that we might be a very risky haven if foreign countries simply believe we're incapable of getting our act together and that they might just withdraw their markers. They might say, "We want to cash in our chips."

> Mr. Greenspan: Well, I think you're raising the fundamental question, Congressman. I think if there's one issue that should concern us over the long run, it is precisely that.

". . . cash in their chips." Clearly, the purchase of U.S. real estate and manufacturing companies—the rapid rise in foreign takeovers—is one way of cashing in U.S. dollars for real assets. Foreign bets are already being hedged, and our wealth is being transferred.

Where do we go from here? Right now it looks like the decline theorists are right. Henry Kaufman is right. *Time* is right. The American century didn't last. This seemed impossible only eight years ago.

One possibility remains. But it looks increasingly like we will not have the political leadership to succeed. It was a political act that created our debt. Only the same can restore our situation.

A *potential* solution exists. Let me go back to 1983. With the image of David Stockman's "$200 billion deficits as far as the eye can see" in our minds,[16] a group of us got together in January 1983 and in twelve days agreed to put in place a massive revenue stream. The principals were James A. Baker III, then-Chief of Staff, Bob Dole, then-Chairman of Finance, Barber Conable, then-ranking Republican member of Ways and Means, myself, Robert Ball, former head of the Social Security Administration, and Alan Greenspan, then-chairman of the deadlocked Social Security Commission. Our nominal task was to stabilize the finances of the Social Security System. Stockman's talk about impending "bankruptcy" made this seem more difficult than it was.[17]

For almost fifty years social security operated on a pay-as-you-go basis. Payroll taxes were kept at about the level that was needed to bring in what was to be paid out each year, with a small cushion for an occasional recession. But what we put in place in 1983 fundamentally changed the financing of social security to a partially funded system. This was a way to save for the retirement of the baby-boom generation. We needed to accumulate large reserves and increase investment over the next generation. As a result of the 1983 changes, we established a revenue stream over the next thirty years which will bring into the Treasury $3 trillion above and beyond outlays by 2018. (Larger sums, about $12 trillion in surplus by 2032, will ultimately be credited to the social security trust funds—but this larger number represents interest earned by the basic $3 trillion.)

In order to begin to save the surpluses, we need to restore an operating balance in the budget. The current administration has happily accepted spending the first few years of surpluses as a way to take credit for closing the federal deficit. Before he resigned as Secretary of the Treasury, James Baker told George Will on "This Week With David Brinkley," June 19, 1988, the following:

> I think it is quite appropriate to continue to do what Lyndon Johnson suggested that we do, and that is, treat the Social Security trust fund as a part of the unified budget. After all, every dollar that we take from the American taxpayer to pay into the Social Security trust fund hurts him just as much as every dollar that he pays in income taxes. And we need a process whereby we look at our government expenditures as a financial condition of the United States government as a whole. So people who suggest that we ought to take the Social Security trust fund off budget I think are to some extent politically motivated.

What Secretary Baker was really saying was that the fact that we moved to a partially funded social security system in 1983 to anticipate the demands of the baby-boom generation meant nothing to him. That there is no need to save the surpluses.

In fiscal year 1989, the Congressional Budget Office's forecast of a deficit of $148 billion includes a social security surplus of $52 billion. Thus, our deficits are still close to Stockman's "$200 billion as far as the eye can see." We are still spending the social security surpluses, and we are financing our deficits from abroad. Our current account deficit in 1989 will be far in excess of $100 billion. In fact, Congress has removed the social security trust funds from the rest of the budget. This was accomplished as part of the recommendations of the 1983 Social Security Commission. The current problem is that social security is still counted as part of the deficit for Gramm-Rudman-Hollings purposes. Since

Table 11.6

Projected Increase of U.S. Social Security Trust Funds
(billions of dollars)

	Annual net increase			Cumulative increase		
	Total	Interest	Principal	Total	Interest	Principal
1988	40	8	32	40	8	32
1989	45	12	34	86	20	66
1990	57	16	41	143	36	107
1991	65	21	44	208	57	151
1992	75	27	48	283	84	199
1993	86	33	54	369	117	253
1994	98	38	59	467	155	312
1995	110	45	65	577	200	377
1996	123	52	71	700	252	448
1997	137	59	78	836	310	526
1998	152	67	85	988	377	611
1999	168	75	93	1,156	452	704
2000	185	84	101	1,341	536	805
2001	202	92	110	1,543	628	915
2002	220	101	119	1,763	730	1,034
2003	243	115	128	2,006	844	1,162
2004	267	130	137	2,273	974	1,298
2005	291	146	145	2,564	1,121	1,443
2006	317	164	152	2,880	1,285	1,595
2007	342	184	159	3,223	1,469	1,754
2008	367	205	162	3,589	1,673	1,916
2009	390	227	163	3,980	1,900	2,080
2010	412	250	162	4,392	2,151	2,241
2011	432	275	156	4,823	2,426	2,398
2012	449	301	147	5,272	2,727	2,545
2013	464	328	136	5,736	3,055	2,681
2014	475	356	120	6,212	3,411	2,801
2015	483	384	99	6,694	3,794	2,900
2016	485	412	73	7,179	4,207	2,973
2017	483	441	42	7,662	4,647	3,015
2018	477	469	8	8,139	5,116	3,023

Source: Office of the Actuary, Social Security Administration, *Trustees Report*, August 1988.

Note: Projected net increase in the Combined Old Age and Survivors' Insurance (OASI) and Disability Insurance (DI) Trust Funds, based on alternative II-B, the less optimistic of the two "intermediate assumptions" used by the Trustees Report for its projections.

this is the number that would give rise to a sequester, it is the one that gets most of the attention. It is also the amount that the federal government must borrow from the capital markets.

But it does not reflect the real magnitude of the deficit problem. Spending the surpluses now foregoes the economic growth that will be necessary to provide for the baby boomers in the next century. And that is why I support legislation to remove social security from the calculation of the deficit under the Gramm-Rudman-Hollings legislation. If we continue to spend these surpluses, we will squander the best option to restore our financial position. If we can reach a situation in which the surpluses exceed the deficit in the current operating accounts, the federal government becomes a net saver. Our debt will be reduced, interest rates will decline, our debt service will fall, and our current account balance will improve and even move back to surplus.

The latter developments would benefit Latin America. The costs of their loans would decline, and we would be leaving more capital for investment in their economies. As Alan Greenspan also told the Joint Economic Committee ". . . there are limits to how long a country can depend upon savings from abroad, and at some point we will have to revert to financing our future from our own resources."

If we continue to borrow more and more overseas, even as we invest less and less, the payoff on the investment we do make will flow back to the foreign investors. This is the "political arithmetic" of a nation heading for debtor's prison. And so the question for the 41st president is whether he can take us to a balanced budget in time to save the social security surpluses. Such surpluses will increase savings and investment. If this happens, we will have a strong enough economy to pay full social security benefits to the baby boomers after the year 2018, when the net cash flow ceases and the money must come from some new combination of taxes and government borrowing.

George Bush seems to have answered this question. He is firmly pledged not to remedy the current deficit problem. He will spend the surpluses on current spending and debt service. And Parador is not far off. This administration could conclusively mark the end of the American century. All that might remain to be written is the postscript, a revised edition of Paul Kennedy's work. Instead, we are confronting the age of American calamity. We are on the verge of losing the last opportunity to restore order to our public finance. There is nothing more elemental to a nation's destiny than competence in such.

We have not had it. The American public has accepted the deliberate mismanagement of our economy and appears willing to affirm the architects of our decline. This despite the concerns top corporate leaders expressed at the Fall 1988 meeting of the Business Council.[18] They just do not want to believe that George Bush will be irresponsible. But the record of the preceding eight years is quite clear, and he promises to do nothing about it.

They don't believe me when I say the deficit was deliberately created. They don't believe David Stockman.

A final irony may yet emerge. We on the Senate Finance Committee may hold George Bush to his word. We can keep his promise for him, and thereby destroy his presidency.

Notes

1. "Debunking the Myth of Decline," 19 June 1988.

2. Henry Kaufman, "Memo To The Next President," *The New York Magazine,* 9 October 1988.

3. Between the years 1931 and 1945, the United States maintained a net international credit position of about $20 billion. *Historical Statistics of the United States,* Series U 26–39, pp. 868–869.

4. "Address to the Business Council of New York State," in *Came the Revolution: Argument in the Reagan Era* (New York: Harcourt, Brace, Jovanovich, 1988).

5. Congressional Budget Office, *Economic and Budget Outlook: An Update, 1988,* (Washington, D.C.: Government Printing Office, 1988).

6. "Reagan's Bankrupt Budget," *The New Republic,* 31 December 1988.

7. *Historical Statistics of the United States,* Series U 26–39.

8. GNP was $288.3 billion and our net surplus position was $36.8 billion.

9. GNP was $4526.7 billion and our net debt position was $403 billion.

10. Cf. Shafiqul Islam "America's Foreign Debt: Is the Debt Crisis Moving North?" *Stanford Journal of International Law* 23, no. 1 (1987): 99–129.

11. Statement of Nigel Gault, Senior Economist, Data Resources, before the Joint Economic Committee, 13 September 1988.

12. *New York Times,* 15 September 1988.

13. *Fortune,* 23 May 1988, p. 77, citing the IMF, *World Economic Outlook.*

14. In 1987, the only U.S. bank in the top twenty-five in the world by assets was Citicorp, ranked number eight. Seventeen of the top twenty-five are Japanese, four are French, two British, and one German. Only eleven of the top one hundred banks are American.

15. *New York Times,* 27 September 1988.

16. David A. Stockman, *The Triumph of Politics* (New York: Harper & Row Publishers, 1986).

17. Stockman, in testimony before the House Committee on Ways and Means Subcommittee on Social Security, on May 28, 1981, testified that unless something was done to shore up the insolvent Trust Funds, "the most devastating bankruptcy in history will occur on or about November 3, 1982." In fact, large surpluses were coming in the 1990s no matter what anybody did, having been put in place in 1977.

18. *Wall Street Journal,* 11 October 1988.

12

Beyond Baker: The Future of Developing Country Debt

Hans H. Angermueller

The IMF meetings in Berlin marked the sixth anniversary of the debt crisis and the third anniversary of the Baker Plan for dealing with that crisis. Much of this year's meetings centered on whether a new approach to the debt crisis was needed and what that approach should be. The following is an assessment of that debate.

These remarks do not cover all of the developing countries that are having trouble servicing their external debts. They specifically exclude the sub-Saharan African countries, whose debts are primarily intergovernmental, and whose economies have been devastated by drought and famine. The discussion will focus on the fifteen so-called Baker Plan countries. These are the fifteen larger middle-income developing countries, such as Mexico, Brazil, and Argentina, whose external debts primarily, though not exclusively, are due to commercial banks in the industrialized world.

The Baker Plan

Three principles guided the Baker Plan. The first was growth. Each country was to *grow* its way out of the debt problem rather than attempt to shrink its way out. The second principle was that there is no such thing as *the* developing country debt problem. There were as many debt problems as there were troubled debtor developing countries, and each country would have to solve its debt problem on its own, consistent with its internal social, political, and economic principles. The solution to the debt problems would be case-by-case; there would be no global solution. The third principle was public-private cooperation. Solutions would be negotiated between debtors and creditors, both public and private; but solutions would not be mandated by creditor country governments.

To implement these principles, each of the four major participants in the debt

Hans H. Angermueller is Vice-Chairman, CITICORP/CITIBANK.

problems of developing countries would take on a specific task. First, each troubled debtor country government was to adopt market oriented economic policies, including structural reforms that would open up protected domestic industries to greater competition. That was a prerequisite for everything else. Second, the multilateral financial institutions, such as the IMF and the World Bank, were to encourage countries to adopt such market oriented policies, both by conditioning new loans on countries adopting such policies and by increasing the volume of their lending to troubled debtor countries. Third, the private commercial banks were to lend new money to finance growth in the developing countries, provided the country had in fact adopted market oriented economic policies. Fourth, the creditor country governments would adopt economic policies that would sustain their real growth rates, keep their inflation and interest rates low, and keep their markets for developing country exports open.

The question now is, should we continue to adhere to these principles? On one principle there seems to be a consensus. Growth should continue to be the guiding objective in dealing with the debt problems of developing countries. All recognize that countries cannot shrink their way out of the debt problem. Countries must grow their way out, and to grow, countries must adopt market oriented economic policies.

Everyone also seems to realize that the industrial countries must continue to create a favorable economic climate. They must maintain their real economic growth, keep their inflation low and their interest rates steady, and grant continued access to their markets for the developing countries' exports.

Opinions differ, however, on the other two principles—the case-by-case approach and the reliance on negotiation. Some say these market-based techniques should be continued. Others say they should be jettisoned in favor of a global solution imposed by creditor country governments on private creditors that would grant significant debt relief to troubled debtor countries.

Which approach makes more sense for the troubled debtor countries? Both approaches envision that the debtor countries would adopt growth oriented, market-based economic policies. In this sense, conditionality would remain. Hence, from the debtor country's point of view, the question would seem to be which approach will more effectively promote the country's growth and development.

The current approach has not, as some would have us believe, been a failure. To the contrary, it has created a good record.

Countries wishing to obtain new money have in fact adopted market-based, growth oriented economic policies. Creditors have responded by rescheduling $150 billion in existing maturing loans, by raising over $13 billion in *new* money, and recently got commitments for an additional $5 billion for Brazil. The amount of new money in every case equaled the amount that the country and its creditors had agreed would be sufficient to finance the country's economic program. On the other hand, banks stood firm in refusing to lend new money to countries that made no attempt to service their debt or refused to adopt market-based economic policies. Rather than lend to such countries, banks significantly increased the level of their loan loss reserves.

During the past three years, the rescheduling process has become much more flexible and hence much more efficient. In particular, the introduction of fees for early commitments and the development of a market-based menu of options have shortened the interval between conclusion of the preliminary agreement with the country's principal creditor banks and the date on which the agreement is signed and the funds are actually disbursed to the troubled debtor country.

More importantly, these agreements have led to substantial reductions in the countries' debt service requirements. Spreads have been reduced, and repayment schedules have been stretched out. Some options, such as debt-equity swaps and conversions into local currency debt, have created an opportunity for countries to reduce their external debt significantly. Chile has already made extensive use of this option, cutting its external bank debt by $4.2 billion to $13 billion. Other countries are starting to do so as well.

During the first three years of the Baker Plan (1986–88) real GDP in the fifteen Baker countries will have grown by 8 percent. That is four times the rate of growth achieved during the prior three years, 1983–85. In ten of the fifteen countries covered by the Baker Plan, the ratio of interest to exports of goods and services fell. In some cases, notably Chile, Uruguay, and Yugoslavia, the fall in the ratio was dramatic, amounting to 25 percent or more of the initial year-end 1985 ratio.

Further progress can be anticipated. The Menu Approach is in its infancy— about three years old. With each deal, new innovations are added—innovations that permit banks greater flexibility in managing their exposure and allow countries to reduce their debt service requirements. In a sense, this is market-based debt reduction.

Is Mandated Debt Forgiveness Preferable?

Would mandated debt forgiveness be better? Proponents of a global compulsory solution to the debt problem think so. Under the global solution, private commercial banks would be "encouraged" (with what degree of governmental pressure is not clear) to sell to an international institution their existing loans to troubled debtor countries at a discount from par. Some or all of this discount would be passed along to the countries in the form of debt forgiveness. This debt forgiveness would, in turn, give countries the breathing room necessary to adopt growth oriented economic policies and such policies would in turn induce new voluntary flows of private capital to the troubled debtor country. The new result, the global plan proponents contend, would be faster economic growth in the troubled debtor nation than possible under the existing process.

The case for the comprehensive, compulsory debt forgiveness approach seems to rest on four factors: (1) the duration of the debt crisis, (2) the absence of a net resource transfer to developing countries having trouble servicing their external debt, (3) the alleged adverse effect of the debt crisis on the development of democracy in the troubled developing countries, and (4) the assumption that comprehensive, mandated debt forgiveness, the contrast to the market oriented approach of the Baker Plan, will induce the troubled developing countries to undertake policy reforms and attract new capital from abroad, and thereby re-ignite economic growth. Let me comment on each of these factors in turn.

As to the *duration* of the debt crisis, it should be noted that six years is a relatively short time. Historical studies have shown that previous exercises in debt rescheduling have extended over decades, not years. Six years appears long, but it is only a tenth of the time needed for Mexico to reschedule its debt in the nineteenth century, and only a fourth of the time needed for the developing countries to return to the markets after the defaults of the 1930s. Hence, time alone is no reason for abandoning the current market oriented approach. Indeed, if history is to be a guide for adopting solutions to the current debt problem, then history points in the direction of the market oriented, debt reduction options that are an increasingly prominent feature of the current rescheduling exercises. It should be emphasized that there is no historical precedent at all for a comprehensive, mandated program of debt forgiveness.

A second reason for comprehensive, compulsory debt forgiveness is said to be the absence of a net resource transfer to the troubled developing countries. Although this concept is frequently bandied about, I find that it lacks logic. To my mind, a net resource transfer occurs when one side conveys resources to the other either as a gift or at less than market price. Foreign aid is a net resource transfer. A loan contracted at market rates is not. The bank extends credit to the borrower in return for the borrower's promise to pay interest and principal in the future. There is a transfer of funds from the lender to the borrower at the outset, and there is a transfer of funds from the borrower to the lender over the course of the loan. But, if the loan is made at market rates, there is no net transfer of resources. In present value terms, the amount of credit extended equals the amount of repayments expected over the life of the loan. Simple calculations that interest and amortization on old loans exceed the amount of new loans do not imply, in my lexicon, that any net resource transfer is taking place.

The more proper concern is that developing countries should be able to supplement their own savings by attracting savings from abroad. They should, if they choose, be able to run a current account deficit. But this is primarily a function of how attractive the developing countries make their economies to the owners of foreign savings, and what type of investments foreign savers will be permitted to undertake. Attractiveness implies market oriented trade, exchange rate, fiscal, and monetary policies, and an openness to equity as well as debt as channels of investment for foreign savers. The fact that some developing countries are having trouble running a current account deficit, therefore, suggests that these countries are not making their economies attractive enough to foreign savers.

Concern for democracy is a third reason advanced by proponents of comprehensive mandatory debt forgiveness. The economic burden posed by external debt service is said to be hindering the development of democracy in the troubled, developing countries. However, the record does not bear out these allegations. Indeed, it was precisely during the debt crisis that Argentina and Brazil turned from military to civilian rule, that the Philippines deposed the Marcos dictatorship, that the Chilean dictatorship subjected itself to and lost a plebiscite, and that Mexico opened up its one-party system. Certainly, this amounts to a record of progress toward democracy in the years of the debt crisis. The adverse impact of the debt crisis on democracy seems to me, at best, a hypothesis not proven. It is hardly a reason for adopting compulsory comprehensive debt forgiveness.

The final reason for compulsory, comprehensive debt forgiveness is said to be greater efficiency. Simply put, advocates of such a plan contend that debt forgiveness will lead to faster and more sustainable economic growth than would be possible under the current process.

How realistic are such claims? The Baker Plan has posted a solid record of achievement. Growth has been faster; debt-service ratios are lower; and countries have received significant amounts of new money. Can mandated debt relief improve this record substantially?

Ignore for the moment the fact that there would, of course, be a considerable delay in setting up such a global scheme for mandated debt relief due to the differences in national laws, tax regimes, and regulatory systems that govern the thousand or so private commercial banks that are involved. Implementing a plan for comprehensive, compulsory debt forgiveness easily could take as long as the debt crisis itself has lasted. (It took five years to achieve unified capital guidelines for international banks.) During this period of delay, it is inevitable that the financing of the troubled debtor nations would be very much in doubt.

Yet, putting aside the effect of such a delay, will the global solution be as effective as the current process in inducing countries to adopt growth oriented economic policies? The record clearly says no. Countries that have unilaterally reduced their own debt payments have not, in fact, used the breathing space to adopt market-based, growth oriented policies. Indeed, Peru and Brazil did exactly the opposite. Both reduced their debt service by 100 percent! You can't gain more breathing room than that. Yet, Brazil voluntarily reversed course when it learned that its moratorium of payment of interest on old loans produced a complete moratorium on new lending. Peru has continued to maintain its moratorium, but its economy is sliding into an abyss.

Will comprehensive, compulsory debt forgiveness induce private firms to lend *new* money to the troubled debtor country? That is the real issue. Having been forced to forgive, will banks forget and fund the country anew, knowing that they may risk a new round of debt forgiveness down the road? I doubt it, and implicitly at least, so do those proponents of debt forgiveness who acknowledge that if such a solution were adopted, governments might have to "induce" private creditors to lend anew.

Thus, if comprehensive, compulsory debt forgiveness were adopted, in all likelihood it would push the troubled debtor countries into permanent dependence on aid from industrial country governments. Those governments would have to provide the aid either by taxing their population or by, in effect, confiscating the wealth of existing loans, and/or forced extensions of new credit.

Nothing suggests that dependence on aid from industrial countries is a solid base for development finance. In fact, the World Bank reduced the volume of its net new lending in 1987 to the fifteen countries covered by the Baker Plan, while the IMF actually took back $1.2 billion in net repayments. Nor has direct foreign aid increased significantly. Since 1970, industrial countries have allocated only 0.1 percent of their GNP to foreign aid, and the Baker Plan countries have received only one-tenth of that meager amount of aid.

In sum, troubled debtor countries face a choice. They can continue to work with their creditors along the current principles of case-by-case negotiation. This will ultimately bring the countries back toward the market, although not as fast as the countries would like, or as fast as the banks had originally expected. Conversely, troubled debtor countries can gamble that industrial country governments will mandate a global solution that will funnel unprecedented amounts of foreign aid to them. In other words, troubled debtor countries can take a bird in the hand or two in the bush.

The age-old proverb suggests, to me at least, that the former is the prudent choice for developing countries to make.

13

Latin American Debt

Harold Lord Lever

Discussions on international debt often lack historical perspective or search for clear principles. It should be remembered that the heavy private bank involvement in Latin America largely replaced the bond buying by smaller private investors usual earlier in the century. The collective experience of these investors left them with the common sense judgment that even government-guaranteed lending at compound interest to Latin America was not a commercial proposition.

In the 1970s the private banks, loaded with oil money and encouraged by their governments and central bankers, undertook the recycling of a great part of the oil funds. The delusion, shared by everybody concerned, was that just as advanced countries were able to borrow unlimited amounts in their domestic currencies, these countries borrowing in foreign currencies would be able to refinance their obligations for an indefinite period ahead. But foreign currency loans require an export surplus if they are to be serviced in real terms. There was no attempt by the private banks, the central banks, or the governments of creditor or debtor countries to seriously estimate when, if ever, the borrowings could be serviced in real terms. The whole operation was based on the delusion that continuous refinancing would be available.

The false equation between the domestic borrowing of rich countries in their own currencies and of the borrowing of poorer developing countries in foreign currencies held for a while. It produced private and government bank debt which ballooned continuously and with a built-in dynamic of mounting incredibility until it reached a crisis point in the early 1980s.

Commendable as the crisis efforts have been to deal with the consequences of these misguided actions, as yet there has been no acceptance by the governments of the advanced countries or their central banks of the principles which will have to be applied if we are to achieve the best outcome from these difficulties. My own views of these basic principles are:

Baron Lever of Manchester, a member of Parliament from 1947 to 1979, is coauthor with Christopher Hulne of *Debt and Danger: The World Financial Crisis*.

1. The advanced countries, governments, and peoples (yes, including taxpayers) have important economic and political interests in the economic and political progress of the Latin American debtor countries. They have a limited ability to influence this favorably, for the main responsibility for their economic and political achievements always will lie with the countries themselves.

2. A net flow of resources to the Latin American debtor countries (in aggregate) for a considerable period ahead will be a contribution to advancing our interests and theirs, and a premature outflow of their resources (in aggregate) will be prejudicial to these interests.

3. The ability of most of the Latin American debtor countries to service debts in real terms to the extent and within the time scale required by a purely commercial operation is wholly unpredictable.

4. If it is judged that substantial new credits to these countries are appropriate and relevant to our interests, it is dangerously speculative to expect that these can be served by a purely commercial operation. The object of the new lending would be to bring to an end at the earliest date the premature export surpluses of the debtors which are against the interests of debtors and creditors and of world trade.

5. Although private bank lending will be required, it follows that it must be controlled in its extent and terms: it must be supported and disciplined by the institutions of the advanced countries. The debtors, for their part, would submit economic policies designed to achieve the long-term strengthening of their economies, not, as at present, to create an export surplus to the prejudice of their economies. If debtors agreed to such policies an international agency, e.g. the IMF, either would provide or guarantee a flow of genuine new loans from the market sufficient to meet that part of the interest which now is being met by export surpluses. The lending would, by no means, be purely for use of governments. Indeed, the terms of the lending would ensure that private industry participated strongly in the new funding.

6. The lending on the scale required cannot be achieved in the years immediately ahead without government backing. Further, the private banks are not by themselves in a position to control either the total amounts of borrowing or the economic policies of the debtor countries.

7. Past lending was undertaken under a delusion shared by governments, regulators, and private banks. Important global interests, in fact, were served during this period but in a profligate and unsustainable manner. The result is a greatly exposed banking system and virtually bankrupt debtor governments. Although insufficient to cover the interest on the old debts, the necessary emergency actions included enforcing a premature export surplus from debtors. Hence the debt continues to increase, and the economies and politics of the debtor countries are injured as well as world trade.

To effectively deal with past debt, the objectives must be:

(a) To bring to an end all anomalous mistimed transfers of resources from the debtors as early as possible. They are damaging to important interests of both creditor and debtor countries and are likely to prove unsustainable.

(b) Ultimately, to achieve a positive flow of new resources to many of the debtor countries for a period ahead.

(c) To achieve these objectives while protecting the fundamental interests of the private banking system.

The Baker Plan implicitly accepted these objectives, but neither thought through nor willed the means to bring them about. I give below a suggestion (an outline) of one of the ways in which this could be achieved.

The G7, its institutions, or export credit agencies must ensure new funding to the debtors to the extent necessary to remove the negative transfers without further prejudicing the banks. In return, the banks would accept the obligation to continue to write down the existing stock of debt over the coming years to the extent that profits permit. The banks would have to accept the obligation to transfer the debts to an international agency when required at the appropriate book value. The governments' willingness to ensure the interest service would justify entirely the book value at any time and the obligation to dispose of it would not call that into question in any way. The agency would take over the debts at the book value at the appropriate time in the future and finance their purchase by the debtors at that value. Thus the debtors would be adding to their dollar debt by new borrowing to replace their export surplus, but with arrangements which ensured that the total debt would be vastly reduced over a period by ultimately acquiring the old debt at fractional cost. The creation of a sound basis for the resumption of new voluntary lending requires many years of improved policies and growth in the debtor countries. The present arrangements result in a steadily mounting dollar debt of increasing incredibility which makes the creation of such a basis almost impossible to conceive.

Governments still have not recognized that you cannot support financially important global economic and political interests in this area without taking some collective responsibility for the risks and losses involved. Conventional wisdom has great difficulty accepting that commercial agencies can be used to achieve social purposes, but on a basis which requires the intervention of public authorities to both discipline and support the operation. Yet, this principle has been taken for granted in many other areas such as export credits, financing of small businesses, etc.

In a somewhat incoherent way, it has also been recognized that some addition to purely commercial finance is required for international imbalances, especially in relation to developing countries. The World Bank, the IMF, and soft loans by governments are collective examples of this attempt to strengthen the financial and political hygiene of an increasingly liberal world economy. But the thinking behind this is too vague and unsystematized; there has been very little advancement since 1945. We need conscious appraisals and analysis of the areas where government intervention is desirable in handling imbalances in an advancing liberal world economy. We need to study in detail the extent and the manner of such intervention. Timely and coherent action will maximize its effectiveness and will also keep it to the minimum. Far from reducing intervention, failure to take timely action maximizes it when governments find themselves compelled to greater yet less effective intervention inevitable under the pressure of crisis.

14

Panel Discussion

Rudiger Dornbusch

Senator Moynihan told us we face the end of the empire; Mr. Angermueller said we were seeing genuine progress in Latin America, and Gene Rotberg told us the administration fell short of excellence in the management of the debt. With whom do I agree? I think Mr. Rotberg came closest to showing our problems.[1]

The Baker Plan was invented to keep the debt problem from becoming acute and from becoming an American financial industry problem. But the Baker Plan was found dead in the basement of the Treasury, and Senator Bradley has said let's do the decent thing and bury it. Unfortunately, we don't have anything else to put in its place. For the time being, as the Brazilian Agreement, the coming Argentina Agreement, and all the others show, we need some mechanism by which banks can be made to put up a major part of a new money package so that the country can be said to be performing on its external debt. A counterpart of that is an IMF Agreement which would be growth oriented.

Everybody recognizes, I think, that to say we see genuine progress after six years is close to *chutzpah*. We are having not the first, but the second round of extreme inflation in only a few years in Latin America. Brazil's monthly inflation rate was 28 percent recently; Argentina has very low inflation one month, and a really high rate the next. Hyperinflation is a real risk. Anyone who looks back to the 1920s remembers that hyperinflation was the door though which fascism ultimately came to Europe. Surely, nobody can say we are seeing progress. We do see in Mexico, I will say, a real potential for progress. But the Mexican case is extraordinarily special, and I'll return to it as the best basis for doing something constructive. No illusions at the outset: things are really bad, and the only question is whether we should take an interest in it or whether we should turn away politely as whatever must happen plays itself out. The conservative opinion on that, Milton Friedman's and Allen Meltzer's, is that we should pull out the U.S. government and with it the IMF and the World Bank, and let

---

Rudiger Dornbusch is Ford International Professor of Economics, Massachusetts Institute of Technology.

things fall into place in private negotiations between the banks and their debtors in the way that it has historically happened.[2]

Historically, the answer to debt problems has been a long, extended moratorium until a country comes into sufficient position in terms of debt servicing capacity to make an offer for reduced settlement. Today this option appears unattractive because the financial consequences of an open-ended debt confrontation certainly are difficult, knowing that two New York banks cannot afford a standstill on Latin American debt service for even one quarter. There is a real issue here. I agree with most observers that something should be done, and that it is undesirable to let the thing to the entire free market as a shoot-out between banks and debtor countries. But what to do about it?

We have heard two proposals. One is that we should create more private market opportunities for banks to get out. The other is that we should find gentler ways and better ways for banks to be kept in. Mr. Angermueller, in emphasizing new ways for private capital to participate, is really referring to the fact that more and more banks find it possible to get out by debt-equity swaps. In Brazil, informal debt conversions were a major way out; in these operations, banks receive domestic money that is taken out through the black market. Is that the way to go? For me, there is no doubt that the large inflation in Brazil today is associated with the government's printing of money at an extraordinary rate to pay off debt; that is not a good idea.

When a government can't pay interest, you have to ask how can they possibly pay the principal? In Brazil, that is not possible, and the hyperinflation the country is experiencing is the direct counterpart of the anticipated retirement of debt financed not by tax revenues, not by cutting expenditures, but by printing money or by issuing domestic debt, a very serious threat in the Brazilian economy today.

I do not believe there are effective private market ways of accelerating debt reduction. The budget situation in virtually all Latin American countries does not sustain that possibility. In Chile it was possible but, as we heard, it came at the cost of a major deterioration in social indicators in the home economy. Even for Chile, one has to ask whether the long-run political and economic stability of the country is better served by debt reduction than by targeted expenditures of the government in maintaining growth with social stability. The doubts about the economic viability of a democratic government in Chile surely have as their root the fact that so much has been spent on debt reduction rather than on social peace. Accordingly, I very much disagree with Mr. Angermueller's belief that the private market approaches to debt reduction let loose on Latin America are the answer to the debt problem. I would agree with him in every other respect that more private market orientation and more serious financial and legal institutions would certainly be a major vehicle for progress.

The alternative to bank exit is to make sure banks are locked in, and Gene Rotberg has made an extraordinary case for that. If he were in charge as our benevolent debt administrator I would stop here. But he won't be in charge, and we have to be concerned. Those in charge will, it seems, be the same people who were in charge the last six years and gave us all those wonderful hyperinflations. They will have to work with weak and weakening Latin American governments; they will continue to be mostly ill-informed; they will, perhaps, think that accelerated debt-equity swap programs are a good idea. In the end, we will experience another six years of growing economic distress and disintegration. But after another six years of this, who believes debtors or banks will be anywhere ahead?

Banks are concerned to get out; they definitely do not want to get involved even deeper in LDC debts. Their preoccupation is to get seniority on the new money they put in. But even if they put up new funds to cover some of the interest due, that doesn't change the fact that on the receiving side governments have to make external transfers that are large, perhaps half the interest bill, perhaps a third, but much too large for their current budget situation. And I emphasize current; perhaps in five years they can do it. Imagine that real wage cuts in Mexico were enough so that in the face of an oil price decline, half the interest can be paid next year. Many people will agree that this a poor idea for Mexico and even for the U.S.; political instability in Mexico serves neither us nor them, nor the banks. I am concerned that the emphasis on making it easier for banks to do the same thing they have been doing for the last six years will give us the next six years like the last, and therefore a major setback.

The choice today is to say let things play themselves out or else to say we really should take a very active hand in it. What does activism mean? Should there be a solution with active government intervention, case-by-case, involving debt forgiveness? I think the case-by-case approach is entirely appropriate. It would be a big mistake to do the same for Brazil, where the government refuses to balance the budget, and for Mexico, where major adjustments have been made and where in any event our political interests are very different from those in Brazil. Debt forgiveness, I think, is inappropriate in many if not most cases. If oil went to $28 a barrel, Mexico could cheerfully pay every penny, and it would therefore be a serious mistake to have forgiven all the debt prematurely. There is no justification to punish our banks by unnecessary "haircuts." We certainly must distinguish between *current* financing and the question of a debt overhang, and the debt overhang question really does not need to be resolved now.

But because banks want to get out rather than in, banks should be locked in. My preferred option is interest recycling. How does one effectively lock in banks without, in fact, locking in their equity? An effective program can be articulated for the case of Mexico. Imagine that having now achieved substantial balance in the budget at an oil price perhaps somewhat higher than yesterday's, the Mexican government started servicing its debt in local currency and allowed creditor banks to use that money for investment in Mexico in any area except oil, with only one restriction, they can't take it out. It is clear that Mexico's problems would be solved. The risk of an external debt crisis would be completely gone. Because in the external balance there would be enough room to finance a boom in imports that is happening as a result of liberalization, there would be no threat that the government has to devalue the currency tomorrow. Why? Because on the foreign exchange side, major relief has taken place. If there is no risk on the external side, then for the first time we would have a real opportunity for the return of private capital. So much private capital could come back, that banks could even be paid in dollars.

We face in Mexico today, quite realistically, the problem of a bank run. If everybody runs and wants their money (and commercial banks want current interest payments), then the bank is bust and you have to close it. If nobody touches it for a couple of years, called recycling investment in Mexico, then the bank is in perfect shape, and ultimately, even myopic bank shareholders will recognize that fact. The sooner banks get their hands off Mexico, the sooner they can get their hands back into Mexico's pockets. What is needed is merely three or four years of a stop on the external transfer plus full payment for investment in Mexico, to produce an investment boom without the risk of an external crash.

Imagine what would happen in Mexico under an interest recycling policy. We would have one case where debt strategy has worked, translating into financial stability and hence into sustainable growth. With that case in hand you can go even to the Brazilian government and say look, you could have a much more reasonable economy, no hyperinflation, and growth. Why don't you do the same? Balance your budget and we do a Mexican style deal. Is it likely that happens? Well, if oil falls low enough, Mexico will have to do it in a self-administered way. Much better if our administration recognizes that, rather than pushing restructuring and six years of the same, we should change the course, not by ruining the banks, but rather by looking at a program that makes economic sense. Balanced budgets, market oriented programs, and a moratorium on external debt service for a few years should be long enough to get financial stability back. There is just no gimmick that will achieve it, not even Mr. Rotberg's facility.

Notes

1. The Rotberg proposal is briefly summarized in the Introduction to this volume.

2. I report on this position in the background paper for the task force report of the Twentieth Century Fund on LDC debt. See *The Road to Recovery*, New York: Twentieth Century Fund, 1989.

15

Panel Discussion

Carlos Tello

I was asked to make some brief remarks on Latin America's foreign debt problems. I have doubts about the prospects for Latin American economic growth in the next decade, but my ideas are not as clear as I would like them to be. Nevertheless, I will share them, hoping that they will throw some light on the subject.

What can be said after six years of debt crisis? The pessimistic predictions of an imminent collapse of the world financial system did not come true. Neither did the optimistic view that the debt problem would be over in two or three years. What has happened is that the debtor countries have been enduring very rough weather with no safe haven in sight. We are no closer to solving the crisis than six years ago.

It is true that practically everyone now recognizes that both creditors and debtors will somehow have to share the costs of solving the crisis. But for the last six years, only the poor and indebted countries have carried the burden.

What has happened to both debtors and creditors since 1982? After first going through a process of demand adjustment and then through the so-called process of structural adjustment—both "negotiated" with the International Monetary Fund and the banks—the balance sheet of the Latin American debtors shows that in relation to 1980:

(a) real income per capita has declined,

(b) real wages have fallen,

(c) unemployment has risen,

(d) public expenditure on social welfare programs has substantially decreased,

(e) personal income, already badly distributed, has become even more concentrated,

(f) human resources—in terms of nutrition and education—have been negatively affected,

(g) plant and capital equipment have deteriorated,

Carlos Tello, former president of the Central Bank of Mexico, is President of the Advisory Council of the Program of National Social Solidarity.

(h) the investment rate has fallen,

(i) year after year, substantial amounts of capital resources have been transferred to the creditor countries (we are even transfering resources—in net terms—to the World Bank, the IMF, and the Interamerican Bank), and

(j) outstanding external debt has increased.

In contrast, the industrial world has been enjoying solid prosperity. Commercial banks have virtually ceased voluntary lending, have had part of their assets converted into long-term credits, have been receiving most of the interest on their loans, and are better equipped than they were in 1982 to deal with debt default. The governments of the creditor nations have adhered to orthodox pieties, although they are now recognizing that the debt crisis has serious political implications.

So where do we go from here?

There is increasing awareness that things have not worked the way they were supposed to have worked, and that a different approach is called for. To continue doing essentially the same things that we have done in the past six years means that we shall have more of the same results—but with one major difference. The passage of time will no longer work in favor of the banks. On the contrary, if things do not change, we shall witness, sooner rather than later, a series of country defaults (Mexico, Argentina, Venezuela, Brazil, . . .) which will come about in a disorderly, messy way. No one will benefit from this scenario.

We could persist with the Baker Plan: rich countries could keep up the flow of financing while the indebted countries undertake economic reforms to regain economic growth in order to pay the external debt. But we have learned that in order to have economic growth, the Latin American countries must *reduce* substantially—and in some cases even eliminate—the servicing of the external debt. Economic growth and full debt servicing are mutually exclusive objectives for Latin America.

There is a third scenario: a *new* process of negotiation between creditors and debtors. New means there would be two important innovations: a) whereas previous negotiations aimed at reaching a formula for servicing of the external debt, the new approach would aim at obtaining that reduction of the external debt burden that would allow for the renewal of economic growth; and b) in order to avoid endless negotiations, a time limit would be set—say six months—for reaching agreement.

This last scenario implies that: a) banks would have to accept sharing the cost of the solution; b) indebted countries must be willing to really negotiate by giving something in return; c) a country-by-country approach should continue; and d) a mixture of solutions (e.g., reduction of the rate of interest, reduction in the capital outstanding, payments in local currency, etc.) would have to be worked out. This scenario would—in the short and long run—benefit both creditors and debtors. It would avoid confrontation and the messy process of cascading country-by-country defaults. The resources liberated from debt servicing would, in part, return to the creditor countries through revived trade.

There is, of course, one last option—one which should only be adopted if the six months of negotiations lead nowhere. The debtor countries should simply stop payments and end the drain of resources which already has been going on for too long. A unilateral moratorium has its risks for the debtor countries. Ideally, they should act together. That would be convenient, but not essential. This last option implies that the rich countries, the creditors, would finally have to assume the cost and responsibilities of being rich.

Question and Answer Session on Part V

Senator Moynihan was asked to comment on what the political response by the U.S. would be, should a Latin American country, say Mexico, declare that it could no longer meet the required interest and/or principal payments on its foreign borrowing. Would the U.S. Senate support an imposition of some control and/or punishment for Mexico? The Senate, Moynihan replied, would not respond directly; the banks would be rushing down asking for help which they would probably get. Our obvious response would be to print more money and give it to the banks, just as we do to pay our own overseas trade debt. And the real question is how much more money we would print. This American problem would not be dissimilar to the Brazilian problem, the Argentine problem, or the Mexican debt problem. We would also need to look to the international institutions, the IMF and the World Bank, for handling the matter as it would affect them, even though both institutions have been American-directed for the most part.

Responding to Professor Dornbusch's commentary on the Rotberg and Angermueller proposals, Rotberg suggested that the most important ingredient for a solution to the debt crisis is to start a dialogue going, to do something which politically each side does not reject out of hand. It is much easier to do this in finance than in politics. Once the financial initiative, whatever it is, addresses the concerns of each side, political or otherwise, a workable framework can be established within which a solution can have a chance. Rotberg also agreed that the essential focus is new money, regardless of the risk that it may be used unwisely and unproductively. However, given the right incentives and motivations, one can be optimistic about the outcome.

Angermueller, agreeing with Rotberg, suggested that new money necessary for growth would not come from the World Bank, but most likely from commercial banks which have access to capital markets, assuming credit-worthiness is maintained. The issue, then, is what will induce banks to participate in extending new credit to countries already in default. Angermueller reiterated the need for a Menu Approach that could include the Rotberg proposal.

Summarized by Dr. Dimitri Papadimitriou, Executive Director, Jerome Levy Economics Institute. The panel of respondents included also Paul Volcker, former Chairman of the Board of Governors of the U.S. Federal Reserve System, and Eugene Rotberg, Vice-Chairman of Merrill-Lynch, Inc. The Rotberg proposal for resolving the debt crisis is summarized in Note 1 of the Introduction to this volume.

Dornbusch also agreed that an across-the-board solution was impossible. He was, however, strongly opposed to a free market–based solution, citing the case of Mexico which, having solved its budget deficit problem, is still faced with a capital flight problem. A solution for Mexico, one reckons, lies in making investment safe there. That can be engineered by paying the banks whatever they are owed but requiring that the same funds must be reinvested there. Removing all restrictions on direct foreign investment and selling off state enterprises is perhaps the ultimate market solution rather than the financial cover-up the Rotberg plan envisions.

Following Volcker's remarks, the question was asked whether the refinancing of Latin America should involve the writedown of principal, and, if so, how the banking industry would meet the erosion of capital. Volcker responded that even though he was not advocating such an approach, his view was that such a policy might be manageable, especially for most banks operating outside the U.S. in countries with appreciated currencies vis-à-vis the dollar and thus increased capital. Their exposure relative to capital, a critical measure, is therefore much reduced, though there are some exceptions, e.g., in the U.K., where the currency has not appreciated so as to reduce exposure. On a follow-up question of whether it would be in the interest of some Latin American countries to default on their debt, Volcker suggested that the evidence points in the other direction. Latin American countries, he maintained, unlike those of Africa, recognize that they are tied for their ultimate prosperity to foreign economies in general, and to the financial markets in particular. By and large, they have seen that it is not in their interests to stop paying. To another question of whether a potential conflict could arise between American, European, and Japanese banks in handling the debt problem, Volcker indicated that getting a number of banks, say a hundred, to adopt a unified position would be very difficult, since their exposure as it relates to their individual currencies vis-à-vis the dollar value of their loans implies different concerns, but he expressed some hope that the Japanese banks would cooperate.

Lever was asked whether he thought that German and Japanese banks would step in to fill the gap by extending new loans, since the U.S. and British banks might not be willing because of internal economic problems. His sense was that banks, irrespective of their nationality, would require some sort of government guarantee given the present state of the debt crisis. A follow-up question asked whether bypassing the banks and resorting to direct intergovernment loans might not be preferable, given that the banks would in all events require government guarantees. Lever insisted on the involvement of commercial banks, "a back-to-back relationship between the lending and borrowing banks," to insure the detailed and productive deployment of borrowed funds to private enterprises in the debtor countries.

Lever emphasized how important it was for the debtor governments to become "skillful wealth creators" with a more reliable administrative apparatus supporting their economic systems. They also need to adopt appropriate mechanisms to control inflation, advance technical education, and develop export service, so that the new money infusions could result in their economic advancement. The question was asked whether what Lever was advocating wasn't essentially a replay of the uncoordinated lending that occurred between 1974 and 1981, and whether a new program under the aegis of international organizations with no government interference would not be preferable. Lever suggested that this would be the very best solution, but expressed doubt about the prospect of establishing a genuine "Central Bank of Central Bankers."

Tello was asked whether his position that the payment of existing and new debt should not be in hard currency but in the debtor's currency would also allow the debtor the option of devaluing the currency, and if so, what safeguards and discipline can be established so that the debtor's financial obligations do not become meaningless. Tello suggested that creditors must assume that loans would be used wisely, and perhaps some safeguards could be established since all parties realize that past practices cannot be the business of the present. He reiterated that the solution of the debt problem can only be a negotiated solution that reflects the particular circumstances of the debtor country, otherwise there may be no solution at all. To the question of whether Mexico could absorb the additional investment resulting from debt repayment in pesos, Tello agreed that capacity might have to be increased progressively, but also cautioned that foreign ownership of corporations with broad discretionary authority could also become a troublesome matter that would have to be addressed as well.

Index

David Felix is Professor of Economics Emeritus at Washington University, St. Louis. He earned his B.A., M.A., and Ph.D. degrees from the University of California, Berkeley and has written and lectured widely on economic history, development, and international trade and finance in this country, Europe, and Latin America. Professor Felix has served on the editorial boards of the *Latin American Research Review* and the *Journal of Economic History*.